RESEARCH IN THE HISTORY OF ECONOMIC THOUGHT AND METHODOLOGY

Volume 10 • 1992

RESEARCH IN
THE HISTORY OF
ECONOMIC THOUGHT
AND METHODOLOGY

Editors: WARREN J. SAMUELS
              Department of Economics
              Michigan State University

              JEFF BIDDLE
              Department of Economics
              Michigan State University

VOLUME 10 • 1992

 JAI PRESS INC.

Greenwich, Connecticut   *London, England*

CONTENTS

REVIEW ESSAYS

LIST OF CONTRIBUTORS

Marina Bianchi

Department of Economic Science
Faculty of Economics
University of Rome
Rome, Italy

Bruce J. Caldwell

Department of Economics
University of North Carolina
Greensboro, North Carolina

Jerry Evensky

Department of Economics
Syracuse University
Syracuse, New York

Evelyn L. Forget

Department of Economics
University of Manitoba
Winnipeg, Canada

J. Daniel Hammond

Department of Economics
Wake Forest University
Winston-Salem, North Carolina

Robert F. Hebert

Department of Economics
Auburn University
Auburn, Alabama

Geoffrey M. Hodgson

The Judge Institute of
    Management Studies
University of Cambridge
Cambridge, England

Terence W. Hutchison

75 Oakfield Road
Selly Park, Birmingham, England

Tony Lawson

Faculty of Economics and Politics
University of Cambridge
Cambridge, England

S. Todd Lowry   Department of Economics
                                        Washington and Lee University
                                        Lexington, Virginia

Uskali Mäki   Department of Economics
                                        University of Helsinki
                                        Helsinki, Finland

D.E. Moggridge   Department of Economics
                                        University of Toronto
                                        Toronto, Canada

Michael Perelman   Department of Economics
                                        Chico State University
                                        Chico, California

Yaffa Machnes Reif   Department of Economics
                                        Bar-Ilan University
                                        Ramat Gan, Israel

Margaret Schabas   Department of Philosophy
                                        York University
                                        North York, Ontario, Canada

Nina Shapiro   Department of Economics
                                        Drexel University
                                        Philadelphia, Pennsylvania

Noel Thompson   Department of History
                                        University College Swansea
                                        Swansea, Wales

ix

ACKNOWLEDGMENTS

The editors wish to express their gratitude for assistance in the review process and other consultation to the members of the editorial board and to the following persons;

Peter Boettke	Philip Mirowski
Kenneth Boyer	Edward Puro
Hans Brems	Salim Rashid
John Davis	Malcolm Rutherford
Sheila Dow	Nina Shapiro
Kevin Hoover	Howard Sherman
Rajani Kanth	Karen Vaughn
Benoit Mandelbrot	James R. Wible

Editor's Note: T.W. Hutchinson's paper on "Hayek and 'Modern Austrian' Methodology: Comment on a non-refuting Refutation" and Bruce Caldwell's paper on "Hayek the Falsificationist?" were accepted for publication in 1986. Because of a misfiling and other factors, their publication has been, unfortunately, delayed. The paper which Caldwell has elsewhere cited as 1988, because he believed that it would be here in that year, is in fact the paper published in this volume.

HAYEK THE FALSIFICATIONIST?
A REFUTATION

Bruce J. Caldwell

I. INTRODUCTION

In *The Politics and Philosophy of Economics,* Terence Hutchison (1981) dissects the contributions of various heterodox movements in economics. Two chapters are devoted to the development of Austrian methodological thought. The writings of Friedrich A. von Hayek receive extended attention. Though Hutchison discovers "much constancy of view" in Hayek's work, he also finds that "on some quite fundamental and very important points of methodology and philosophy, vital and critical changes in Hayek's views can be discerned.... which have not received the attention and appreciation which they deserve" (p. 211). The magnitude of these changes leads Hutchison to claim that, in matters methodological, there exists a Hayek I and a Hayek II.

Hayek I's views are inferred from his work in the 1920s and 1930s on the trade cycle and the socialist calculation debate. The early Hayek is influenced by both Wieser and Mises, particularly in his claims about the indisputability of the general laws of economic science. Hayek I also advocates the use of

Research in the History of Economic Thought and Methodology
Volume 10, pages 1-15.
Copyright © 1992 by JAI Press Inc.
All rights of reproduction in any form reserved.
ISBN: 0-55938-501-4

equilibrium models in theorizing. Finally, the early Hayek parts company with certain other Austrians by making "some strong claims for prediction and forecasting" (pp. 210-14).

Hayek II emerges in the mid-1930s. This later Hayek is more circumspect about the use of equilibrium models. Such models should only be used if it can be shown that a tendency toward equilibrium exists. Though the existence of such a tendency is an empirical question, Hayek II notes that economists often simply assume the problem away. Hayek II also recognizes that the use of an equilibrium model necessitates some further analysis of the process of knowledge acquisition. But the most significant change in the development of the Austrian's thought is the "marked Popperian influence" revealed in his later writings. The later Hayek praises prediction, recommends testing "at every step," and emphasizes the importance of constructing economic theories that are falsifiable (pp. 214-19).

Although Hutchison is careful to support his argument with numerous citations, I believe that in certain areas he has misunderstood the exact nature of Hayek's methodological contributions. The goal of this paper is to critically evaluate Hutchison's interpretation of the development of Hayek's methodological thought.[1]

In section II, the methodological aspects of Hayek's *Monetary Theory and the Trade Cycle* (1932), a book chosen by Hutchison as representative of the Austrian's early thought, are examined. Hutchison's claim that the early Hayek advocated equilibrium theorizing stands undisputed, but I argue that Hayek's views on prediction and empirical work are more complicated than Hutchison indicates. Next, Hayek's 1937 "turning point" is examined. While agreeing that the publication of "Economics and Knowledge" (1948b) constituted an important turning point for Hayek, I challenge Hutchison's claim that Hayek's later work is best characterized as a move towards falsificationism. An alternative interpretation of Hayek's "new direction" is then briefly presented. In section IV, I note an anomaly in Hutchison's review of Hayek's methodology, his failure to examine the Austrian's famous 1944 essay, "Scientism and the Study of Society" (1952). A cursory examination of that methodological work suggests that Popper's influence on Hayek had yet to occur in the early 1940s. In the following section, I critically examine the major piece of evidence for the thesis that Popper greatly influenced Hayek's approach to methodology—five quotations, taken from Hayek's later methodological work and cited by Hutchison, which suggest a strong falsificationist strand in the Austrian's methodology. I argue that the quotations are taken out of context. When they are read in context, they support a very different picture from that found in Hutchison's text regarding Hayek's attitude toward the prospects for falsification in economics. The paper concludes with a suggested answer to the question; How could Hutchison have gotten Hayek so wrong?

II. MONETARY THEORY AND THE TRADE CYCLE

In *Monetary Theory and the Trade Cycle* (1932), Hayek argues that the origin of the trade cycle is monetary. In addition to defending a Mises-Wicksell approach to the origins of the cycle, Hayek criticizes a number of alternative theories. Among those found wanting are various nonmonetary theories (all of which, Hayek claims, must 'violate the assumptions of the standard equilibrium model to generate a cause of the business cycle) and the quantity theory of money (which errs in focusing on changes in the aggregate price level to the neglect of changes in relative prices) (Hayek, 1932, pp. 51- 135). Hayek also criticizes those who would replace theoretical explanations of the cycle with empirical descriptions of series of data; it is in this context that he discusses "empirical studies."

Citing a footnote from the book, Hutchison claims that Hayek makes some "strong claims" for the importance of prediction and forecasting in economics (Hutchinson, 1981, p. 211). Let us examine more carefully what the Austrian had to say on this topic.

Hayek begins Chapter One by noting the limitations of empirical studies in economics. Such studies cannot provide a new theoretical structure since that structure is already given by the self-adjusting equilibrium model (pp. 27-32). Nor are empirical studies very helpful for the verification of theories, except "in a negative sense."

> Either statistics can demonstrate that there are phenomena which the theory does not sufficiently explain, or it is unable to discover such phenomena. It cannot be expected to confirm the theory in a positive sense....There is no reason to be surprised, therefore, that although nearly all modern trade cycle theories use statistical material as corroboration, it is only where a given theory fails to explain all the observed phenomena that this statistical evidence can be used to judge its merits (Hayek, 1932, pp. 34-35).

Only after arguing against measurement without theory and for a weak "negative" view of testing does Hayek acknowledge a positive role for empirical studies: the pragmatic task of providing forecasts (pp. 35-36). It is curious that Hutchison chooses only this last point, which is relegated to a footnote by Hayek, as representative of the Austrian's thought. It is clear that Hayek's early methodological views did not include any inordinately "strong" claims for the importance of prediction in economics. His emphasis throughout *Monetary Theory and the Trade Cycle* is on the secondary position of empirical studies in relation to theoretical work. To acknowledge in a footnote that forecasting may play an important pragmatic role in assisting policymakers in no way alters Hayek's major point that empirical work is subsidiary to theoretical analysis in economics.

III. HAYEK'S TURNING POINT

If Hayek simply presumed in his earlier book that any adequate economic analysis must begin from an equilibrium framework he scrutinized the concept of equilibrium in a series of articles published in the mid-1930s. Like many economists at the time,[2] Hayek recognized that the idea of an equilibrium is inextricably linked to whatever assumptions are being made about the state of knowledge. His most direct statement of this relationship is found in his 1937 article, "Economics and Knowledge."

Hayek begins by contrasting the concept of equilibrium as applied to an individual with the concept as applied to a competitive economic system. The meaning of the latter concept has not always been clear. Hayek defines it in terms of a compatibility of plans: "For a society, then, we *can* speak of a state of equilibrium at a point in time—but it means only that the different plans which the individuals composing it have made for action in time are mutually compatible" (1948b, p. 41). But if plans are to be compatible, correct foresight is necessary:

> Correct foresight is then not, as it has sometimes been understood, a precondition which must exist in order that equilibrium may be arrived at. It is rather the defining characteristic of a state of equilibrium. Nor need foresight for this purpose be perfect in the sense that it need extend into the indefinite future or that everybody must foresee everything correctly. We should rather say that equilibrium will last so long as the anticipations prove correct and that they need to be correct only on these points which are relevant for the decisions of the individuals (1948b, p. 42).[3]

Hayek asks next why economists have concerned themselves with the notion of equilibrium, a concept which obviously refers to a "fictitious state" (1948b, pp. 44-45). Concern with equilibrium can only be justified if a "tendency toward equilibrium" exists. The existence of such a tendency is an empirical question that economists should explore: What conditions might bring it about, and by what process? To answer these questions, more must be known about the process by which knowledge is acquired, the kinds of knowledge that decisionmakers consider relevant, and the importance of the dispersion of knowledge. The fundamental problem confronting economists is posed by Hayek in the following way: "How can the combination of fragments of knowledge existing in different minds bring about results which, if they were to be brought about deliberately, would require a knowledge on the part of the directing mind which no single person can possess?" (1948b, p. 54).

Hutchison states that the publication of "Economics and Knowledge" in 1937 "marks a vital turning-point, or even a U-turn, in Hayek's methodological ideas, *and ought to be, but has not been, recognized as marking a fundamental shift in Austrian ideas"* (Hutchison, 1981, p. 215, original emphasis). The key question, of course, is whether it was a turning point towards Popperian thought.

Three pieces of evidence for such an interpretation exist. The article contains Hayek's first reference to Popper, a footnote citation of the concept of falsification. Next, Hayek's view that the existence of equilibrium is an "empirical question" suggests that he may believe that empirical studies of the process of knowledge acquisition are warranted. If this were true, it would constitute a reversal of Hayek's earlier views on the limited role of empirical work in economics, and such a reversal might be attributable to Popper's influence. Finally, Hayek states in an article written in 1964 that "Economics and Knowledge" initiated a change in the direction of his research, a change that led him away from "technical economics" and toward "questions usually regarded as philosophical" (1967c, p. 91). Was it Popper who led Hayek to turn his back on economics and embrace the study of philosophical questions?

Though it might be tempting to conclude that Popper's influence on Hayek's methodology reaches as far back as the 1930s, the evidence against such an interpretation seems compelling. Consider first the question of Hayek's footnote reference to Popper. As Hutchison notes, even though the footnote is found on the first page of the article, "the influence of Popper is not obvious in the subsequent pages" (Hutchison, 1981, p. 215). And there is good reason for this. Though both Hayek and Popper lived in Vienna in the 1920s, they did not know each other there. They first met in the 1935-1936 academic year, when Popper read an early draft of "The Poverty of Historicism" in Hayek's London School of Economics seminar (Popper, 1974, pp. 86; 169, n. 163). "Economics and Knowledge" was first presented in November 1936, and it is unlikely that Popper could have influenced Hayek's ideas in such a short time. But even more to the point, in private correspondence with the author Hayek remarks that, as he remembers, the footnote citation of Popper was inserted in the galley proofs of the article (letter, Hayek to Caldwell, of September 29, 1984). If this is true, the ideas expressed in Hayek's article cannot be attributed to Popper.

We may inquire next whether the fact that Hayek believed that the existence of a tendency towards equilibrium was an "empirical question" meant that the Austrian embraced an empirical approach to the study of equilibrium. Again the question must be answered in the negative. Indeed, in the last section of "Economics and Knowledge," Hayek directly addresses this question; his response is clear and explicit:

> [I]n stressing the nature of the empirical propositions of which we must make use if the formal apparatus of equilibrium analysis is to serve for an explanation of the real world, or in emphasizing that the propositions of how people will learn, which are relevant in this connection, are of a fundamentally different nature from those of formal analysis, I do not mean to suggest that there opens here and now a wide field for empirical research. I very much doubt whether such investigation would teach us anything new (Hayek, 1948b, p. 55).[4]

What about Hayek's later reminiscences concerning the importance of "Economics and Knowledge"? If we examine the relevant quotation in its entirety, it is clear that the "philosophical" questions that Hayek chose to address in his later career were not Popperian questions.

> ....though at one time a very pure and narrow economic theorist, I was led from technical economics into all kinds of questions usually regarded as philosophical. When I look back, it seems to have all begun, nearly thirty years ago, with an essay on "Economics and Knowledge" in which I examined what seemed to me some of the central difficulties of pure economic theory. Its main conclusion was that the task of economic theory was to explain how an overall order of economic activity was achieved which utilized a large amount of knowledge which was not concentrated in any one mind but existed only as the separate knowledge of thousands or millions of different individuals. But it was still a long way from this to an adequate insight into the relations between the abstract overall order which is formed as a result of his responding, within the limits imposed upon him by those abstract rules, to the concrete particular circumstances which he encounters. It was only through a re-examination of the age-old concept of freedom under the law, the basic conception of traditional liberalism, and of the problems of the philosophy of the law which this raises, that I have reached what now seems to me a tolerably clear picture of the nature of the spontaneous order of which liberal economists have so long been talking (Hayek, 1967c, pp. 91-92).

The U-turn in Hayek's thought initiated by the publication of "Economics and Knowledge" was not a movement toward Popperian thought. But the question remains: What was the exact nature of Hayek's transformation? I have dealt with this subject at greater length in a separate article (Caldwell, 1988), and will only briefly summarize my findings here.[5]

In the mid-1930s Hayek became a major player in the socialist calculation debate. By that time, the socialists were on the offensive. In a provacative article originally published in 1920 (Mises, 1935), an early article, Ludwig von Mises had advanced the claim that rational calculation (e.g., solving the allocation problem) was "impossible" under a socialist regime. The socialists replied that, at least formally, the standard equilibrium model that had been developed to describe the workings of a competitive economy could just as easily be used to describe a socialist economy. For example, if competition led to the long-run equilibrium condition that product prices equal marginal costs of production, the same result could be obtained in a socialist economy in which managers are instructed to set prices at marginal costs. This point was used to defeat von Mises' claim that calculation under socialism was impossible.

The Austrian counterattack involved questioning the ability of the standard equilibrium model to capture the dynamic properties of a competitive market system. Recall that in his earlier work, Hayek had insisted that any legitimate economic explanation of the trade cycle had to presume the validity of "equilibrium economics." But in "Economics and Knowledge," he questioned for the first time the efficacy of the equilibrium concept for describing a system in which knowledge is dispersed and subjectively-held. This questioning was to continue in later articles (e.g., Hayek 1948c, 1948d). Ultimately, Hayek was to reject the use of the concept of equilibrium and to recommend that it be replaced with the notion of a market process in which the information-coordination aspects of markets receive prominent attention. Given his earlier claim that the use of the equilibrium construct was a necessary condition for providing an *economic* explanation, it is not surprising that his rejection of the construct led him away from the study of "technical economics" and toward questions "usually regarded as philosophical."

To be fair to Hutchison, the meticulous reader can find elements of the above interpretation, though never explicitly rendered, hinted at in Hutchison's account of Hayek's U-turn. For example, after citing Hayek's reminiscences about the importance of "Economics and Knowledge," Hutchison remarks in a footnote that "Hayek's approach to fundamental problems of policy broadened out from what might be described as a narrowly 'Ricardian' to a comprehensively 'Smithian' approach" (Hutchison, 1981, p. 228, n. 17). In the text, Hutchison chooses to emphasize other ways in which Hayek's views changed, and even mentions the role of equilibrium and assumptions about knowledge among these (pp. 215-16). But looking at the chapter as a whole, there is an unmistakable stress on the influence that Popper allegedly had on Hayek's methodological work. The unwary reader would not be unjustified in concluding that the major difference between Hayek I and Hayek II was that the latter had become a falsificationist.

For some final evidence that Popper had little influence on Hayek's early methodological views, we turn next to an examination of "Scientism and the Study of Society" (1952).

IV. THE NEGLECTED SCIENTISM ESSAY

I begin by noting some oddities in Hutchison's treatment of Hayek's methodology. First, it is peculiar that Hutchison begins his appraisal by examining two nonmethodological writings by Hayek, his book *Monetary Theory and the Trade Cycle* and his discussion of the socialist planning debates. Next, it is strange that Hutchison chooses an article written by Hayek in 1937 as marking a methodological turning point when the next methodological article by Hayek he cites was not published until 1955. It is easy to agree with Hutchison that U-turns are seldom "clean breaks" (1981, p. 215), but how many turning-points take eighteen years to transpire? Finally, it is curious that in a treatment of Hayek's methodology Hutchison all but ignores (he gives it only a footnote citation) what is arguably Hayek's most famous and complete statement of methodological principles, "Scientism and the Study of Society."

A brief sketch of Hayek's lengthy and provocative "Scientism" essay shows that it is an important link in the chain of development of his methodological thought. In the essay Hayek contrasts Scientism, the "slavish imitation" of the methods and languages of the natural sciences, with the spirit of disinterested inquiry that characterizes true scientific study (Hayek, 1952, p. 24). He decries the objectivism, collectivism, and historicism of the scientistic approach to the investigation of social phenomena. The purpose of the social sciences is "to explain the unintended or undesigned results of the actions of many men" (1952, p. 41). Because of the complexity of social phenomena, the appropriate method to follow is individualistic and compositive: social phenomena are "built up," or composed, from the actions of the individual agents. Most important, those agents' actions are based on their subjective perceptions of particular situations. As such, the perceptions and purposes, the knowledge and expectations of individual agents are fundamental data in the social sciences. In Hayek's words, "it is probably no exaggeration to say that every important advance in economic theory in the last hundred years was a further step in the consistent application of subjectivism" (1952, p. 52). A few pages later, he links this concern with subjectivism with those problems he discussed in his earlier article, "Economics and Knowledge," namely, the dispersion of knowledge and the compatibility of expectations (1952, p. 57).

To summarize, Hayek rejects scientism, objectivism, collectivism, and historicism in his essay. He emphasizes that social phenomena are built up from the actions of many individuals, individuals whose knowledge is based on their subjective perceptions of data. And he reiterates his earlier theme that subjectively held knowledge is dispersed among many agents. These ideas are compatible with Hayek's later work in the theory of complex phenomena and, indeed, may be viewed as the bridge between his 1937 article and his later writings.

Why in a treatment of Hayek's methodology did Hutchison neglect Hayek's "Scientism" piece? There is no good answer. It may be pointed out, however, that the "Scientism" essay provides further evidence that Hayek's 1937 U-turn was not a movement toward Popperian thought. Though Hayek did not know Popper in the mid-1930s, he *was* familiar with his work by the time "Scientism" was published. Indeed, as editor of *Economica* during the war years, Hayek was responsible for publishing Popper's "The Poverty of Historicism" (1957) in that journal. Yet "Scientism and the Study of Society" contains not a single reference to Popper's work! (In contrast Popper's "Historicism" contains no less than sixteen citations of Hayek's writings.) If one wishes to maintain the strong thesis that "Economics and Knowledge" initiated Hayek's turning towards *Popperian* methodological thought, then his first explicitly methodological essay, published after Hayek had come to know of Popper's work, must be regarded as a troublesome anomaly that is perhaps best left unmentioned.

V. HAYEK'S LATER METHODOLOGICAL WORK AS REVEALED IN HUTCHISON'S FIVE QUOTATIONS

If it is now clear that Popper had little influence on Hayek's earlier methodological writings, it is equally evident that, in his later methodological work, Hayek refers approvingly and often to Popper's ideas. To support his thesis that Hayek ultimately embraced falsificationism, Hutchison selects quotations from three of the Austrian's methodological papers, one published in the 1950s, one in the 1960s, and one in the 1970s. While his choice of articles is exemplary, I argue that Hutchison's selection of quotations does not accurately represent Hayek's methodological position. This task is best accomplished by examining the five quotations in detail.

1.   Hutchison begins by asserting that all three papers show "a marked Popperian influence," which he buttresses with a quotation from Hayek on prediction and explanation. The text in Hutchison reads,

> This influence is apparent in Hayek's renewed emphasis on prediction: 'Prediction and explanation are merely two aspects of the same process' [1967a, p. 9]; so that to the extent that human action is unpredictable it is inexplicable (Hutchison, 1981, p. 217).

The full quotation from Hayek is "I assume that the prejudice of certain earlier positivists against the work 'explanation' is now a thing of the past and that it may be taken for granted that prediction and explanation are merely two aspects of the same process" (Hayek, 1967a, p. 9). The passage is taken from a footnote of Hayek's; its sole purpose is to point out a terminological distinction which was quite well-accepted in the philosophy of science of the mid-1950s. Furthermore, Hayek does not make this distinction in order to say that unpredictable human action is inexplicable. Rather, it is to point out that, because different "degrees of explanation" exist in science, an implication is that different "degrees of prediction " also exist in science.

More important, Hutchison focuses on a rather minor footnote while neglecting the important discussion of explanation and prediction found in the text. In that discussion, Hayek notes that prediction is usually defined as the process by which a person moves from a small group of known antecedent conditions to a conclusion. This view of how prediction takes place in science poses no problem for certain disciplines like physics. But Hayek goes on to say that "[t]he situation is different, however, where the number of significantly interdependent variables is very large and only some of them can in practice be individually observed" (1967a, p. 8). This latter case is characteristic of the social sciences, in which "complex phenomena" are examined. Hayek asserts that the standards applied to physics are often inapplicable in the study of complex phenomena, but that this need not lead us "to despair." What is required is "a kind of reversal of what has been described as the standard procedure of physics" (1967a, p. 9). That reversal, a reasoning from that which is known (about individual atomic agents) to that which is unknown (about the behavior of social aggregates) is characteristic of the individualistic and compositive methods espoused by Hayek in his earlier article on "Scientism."

2. Hutchison argues that Hayek favors falsifiability. The representative passage that Hutchison selects to support his claim is, "It is certainly desirable to make our theories as falsifiable as possible." The full quotation from Hayek actually reads,

> The advance of science will thus have to proceed in two different directions: while it is certainly desirable to make our theories as falsifiable as possible, we must also push forward into fields where, as we advance, the degree of falsifiability necessarily decreases. This is the price we have to pay for an advance into the field of complex phenomena (Hayek, 1967b, p. 29).

Hayek is arguing that, in the study of complex phenomena, certain general patterns are often all that can be predicted. Such "pattern predictions" possess small empirical content and as a result, "the range of phenomena compatible with it will be wide and the possibility of falsifying it correspondingly small" (1967b, p. 29). Nonetheless, this is often the best we can do, and we should not belittle such "pattern predictions" as less than scientific. It is only in the investigation of "simple phenomena" (as in certain areas of physics) that more can be hoped for.

Hutchison's quotation completely changes the meaning of the passage. By omitting the "while" from the sentence, Hutchison has made it appear that Hayek thinks we should *always* try to make our theories more falsifiable. Hayek actually says that we should push forward in fields where progress is accompanied by decreased falsifiability.

3. Hutchison's next sentence reads, "Testing '*at every step*' is also recommended [1967, p. 6]" (Hutchison, 1981, p. 217). The full quotation from Hayek actually reads:

> It is, no doubt, desirable that in working out such deductive systems the conclusions would be tested against the facts at every step. We can never exclude the possibility that even the best accredited law may cease to hold under certain conditions for which it has not yet been tested. But while this possibility always exists, its likelihood in the case of a well-confirmed hypothesis is so small that we often disregard it in practice. The conclusions which we can draw from a combination of well-established hypotheses will therefore be valuable though we may not be in a position to test them (Hayek, 1967a, p. 6).

Once again, Hutchison has taken a portion of a sentence from Hayek's work and, by ignoring the context in which it is found, has changed its meaning. But even more important, in this passage Hayek is talking about the physical sciences! His point is that, *even* in the physical sciences, scientific procedure does not always consist of testing natural laws. Rather, even in these sciences, scientists often simply assume such laws are true, and then apply them in new areas.

4.　Hutchison turns next to Hayek's Nobel Lecture, "The Pretence of Knowledge" (1978). He quotes from a sentence intended to show Hayek's affinity for prediction and falsifiability: "Nevertheless Hayek, surely justifiably, goes on: 'Yet as I am anxious to repeat, we will still achieve predictions which can be falsified and which therefore are of empirical significance'" (Hutchison, 1981, p. 218).

At least, this time Hutchison acknowledges that the quotation he has selected is from a qualifying remark of Hayek's. The sentence quoted follows a paragraph in which Hayek posits a ball game played by athletes of approximately equal skill. Part of the passage is reproduced here; it provides a graphic example of the sort of "pattern prediction" that Hayek thinks is possible in the social sciences.

> If we know a few particular facts in addition to our general knowledge of the ability of the individual players, such as their states of attention, their perceptions and the state of the game, we could probably predict the outcome....But we shall of course not be able to ascertain those facts and in consequence the result of the game will be outside the range of the scientifically predictable, however well we may know what effects particular events would have on the results of the game. This does not mean that we can make no predictions at all about the course of such a game. If we know the rules of the different games we shall, watching one, very soon know which game is being played and what kinds of actions we can expect and what kinds not....
>
> This corresponds to what I have called earlier the mere pattern predictions to which we are increasingly confined as we penetrate from the realm in which relatively simple laws prevail into the range of phenomena where organized complexity rules (Hayek, 1978, pp. 32-33).

Thus Hayek does indeed praise prediction. But it is a very different sort of prediction from that which prevails in sciences whose subject matter consists of simple phenomena. Hayek's whole point is to distinguish between the two types of prediction. Hutchison's exposition does little to illuminate the issue.

5.　Hutchison's final citation of Hayek is contained in the sentence, "He reiterates, in the most emphatic general terms, the demarcation principle of Popper: 'We cannot be grateful enough to such modern philosophers of science as Sir Karl Popper for giving us a test by which we can distinguish between what we may accept as scientific and what not'" (Hutchison, 1981, p. 218).

To show that Hutchison once again has misperceived Hayek's position, we need go no further than the next sentence of Hayek's article.

> There are some special problems, however, in connection with those essentially complex phenomena of which social structures are so important an instance, which makes me wish

to restate in conclusion in more general terms the reasons why in these fields not only are there absolute obstacles to the prediction of specific events, but why to act as if we possessed scientific knowledge enabling us to transcend them may itself become a serious obstacle to the advance of the human intellect (Hayek, 1978, p. 32).

VI. CONCLUSION

The purpose of this article is to challenge T.W. Hutchison's interpretation of Hayek's methodology. This is a negative exercise, an attempt at refutation. I have not attempted here the more positive and important task of systematically explicating Hayek's contributions to methodology, which is a subject that manifestly warrants attention.

But a puzzle remains. In a long and distinguished career as an historian of economic thought, Terence Hutchison has always been a careful, even judicious, scholar. But he was not very careful in his treatment of the development of Hayek's methodological thought. How might we account for this fact? Some background on the protagonists may help us to answer this question.

Those familiar with the writings of Professor Hutchison know that he has had what might well be described as a love-hate relationship with the Austrians for decades. On the positive side, Hutchison agrees with many of the Austrian criticisms of standard equilibrium theory. In particular, since 1938 Hutchison has argued that any adequate theory of choice must incorporate in a fundamental way an analysis of the role of expectations in the decision-making process. More recently, he has decried the economic profession's movement toward ever more sophisticated mathematical models, models which he feels have little relation to real-world policy problems. His views on the "crisis of abstraction" in economics would surely receive a sympathetic hearing in the Austrian camp (Hutchison, 1938, ch. 4, 1977, ch. 4).

On other matters, however, Hutchison has locked horns with the Austrians. In the course of nearly fifty years of methodological writing, Hutchison has been a consistent proponent of falsificationism. His latest writings indicate a more circumspect attitude toward the prospects for falsificationism in economics: if the Lakatosian labels were applied, one might say that Hutchison has evolved from a "naive" to a "sophisticated" methodological falsificationist. But one element of his thought has not changed: Hutchison from the outset has been a persistent critic of all forms of a priorism in economics. His (1938) *The Significance and Basic Postulates of Economic Theory* is a sustained attack on the methodological views of Lionel Robbins, and Hutchison has repeatedly criticized the a priorist "science of human action," or praxeology, developed by the Austrian Ludwig von Mises.[6] These two approaches to methodology, the a priorism favored by Mises and the falsificationism favored by Hutchison, are diametrically and irreconcilably opposed.

It is my contention that Hutchison misread Hayek on methodology. And I think that it is easy to understand why it happened. Given Hutchison's lifelong campaign against a priorism, and given the natural opposition of the falsificationist and a priorist approaches to methodology, it is understandable that Hutchison would choose for particular emphasis the falsificationist elements in Hayek's methodology. If he could but show that Hayek endorsed, and has long endorsed, Popperian falsificationism, Hutchison might be able to convince other Austrians to abandon their commitment to praxeology.

Though Hutchison's misreading of Hayek may be understandable, his interpretation cannot be allowed to stand unchallenged. In attempting to undercut a priorism, Hutchison distorted the true nature of Hayek's contribution. Though there are traces of falsificationism to be found in Hayek's methodological writings, they are far less important than Hutchison would have us imagine for explaining the Austrian's overall methodological vision.

ACKNOWLEDGMENTS

I greatly benefited from comments on earlier drafts of the paper from Friedrich von Hayek, T.W Hutchison, Wade Hands, Mark Blaug, Bill Butos, Bill Guthrie, Abe Hirsch, Neil de Marchi, John Pheby, and Dan Reavis. The present paper has been greatly modified from some of the earlier drafts. As such, the usual caveat exempting previous readers from any remaining errors must be stated with more than usual emphasis.

NOTES

1. Hutchison's text could be used to support either a weak claim or a strong claim regarding Popper's influence on Hayek. The weak thesis, that Hayek frequently makes reference to some of Popper's ideas in his later methdological writings, is both true and uncontroversial. The strong thesis is that Hayek's methodological thought underwent a "U-turn," beginning sometime in the 1930s, and that Popper's influence was decisive both in the U-turn and in the subsequent development of Hayekian methodology. It is not always clear from the text whether Hutchison supports the weak thesis, the strong thesis, or some intermediary position. In any case, it is the strong thesis that I hope to refute here.

2. One of the other economists was T.W. Hutchison. In 1938, Professor Hutchison published his treatise on methology, *The Significance and Basic Postulates of Economic Theory*. In chapter four, "The Basic Postulates of Pure Theory: Expectations, Rational Conduct, and Equilibrium,' Hutchison argues that the whole notion of rational maximizing behavior, and with it the notion of equilibrium, depend crucially on the further, and empirically false, assumption of "perfect expectation." That choice actually takes place under conditions of uncertainty forms the core of his methodological critique of standard theory.

Thus Hutchison and Hayek characterized the "problem of equilibrium" in nearly the same terms in the late 1930s. Hutchison's solution to the problem, one that has advocated in varying forms for nearly half a century, is for economics to become a more empirical science. Though Hayek began with the same problem, we will see that his solution differs from that embraced by Hutchison.

3. Hayek notes that this is a "special sense" of the term, correct foresight. It is interesting to compare Hutchison's treatment of these topics (1938, pp. 100-104). Note also Hutchison's disdain for the idea of a "tendency toward equilibrium" (pp. 104-109), and that Hayek's article is quoted there.

4. On the same page, Hayek says that empirical studies can be useful for the "verification" of the "applicability" of models. This is contrasted with the mathematical exercises that constitute the "Pure Logic of Choice." This role for empirical studies differs significantly from the view that theories can be confirmed or disconfirmed by testing. Compare Hutchison (1938, pp. 113-114), where such empirical investigations are embraced as the best way forward.

5. Though my 1988 paper preceded the present one in terms of date of publication, it follows it in terms of execution. It is also logically the successor: the present paper criticizes Hutchison's interpretation of Hayek's transformation, while the other offers an alternative interpretation of the episode.

6. See Caldwell (1982, ch. 6) for the argument that Hutchison's book may be read as a point-by-point refutation of Robbins' (1935) *An Essay on the Nature and Significance of Economic Science*. Though Robbins was not a priorist, he thought that the generalizations of economics were self-evident truths, a position that is anathema to a falsificationist like Hutchison. For examples of Hutchison's distaste for a priorism, see Hutchison (1956, pp. 482-483, 1981, pp. 218-19, 223, 230, note 26). For a critique of praxeology that does not involve falsificationism, see Caldwell (1984).

REFERENCES

Caldwell, Bruce J. 1982. *Beyond Positivism: Economic Methodology in the Twentieth Century*. London: Allen and Unwin.

_____. 1984. "Praxeology and Its Critics: An Appraisal." *History of Political Economy*, Vol. 16, pp. 363-79.

_____. 1988. "Hayek's Transformation." *History of Political Economy*, Vol. 20, pp. 513-41.

Hayek, Friedrich A. 1932. *Monetary Theory and the Trade Cycle*. Translated from German by N. Kaldor and H.M. Croome. New York: Harcourt Brace.

_____. 1948a. *Individualism and Economic Order*. Chicago: University of Chicago Press.

_____. 1948b. "Economics and Knowledge." Pp. 33-56 in Hayek, *Individualism and Economic Order*. Chicago: University of Chicago Press.

_____. 1948c. "Socialist Calculation III: The Competitive 'Solution.'" Pp. 181-208 in Hayek, *Individualism and Economic Order*. Chicago: University of Chicago Press.

_____. 1948d. "The Meaning of Competition." Pp. 92-106 in Hayek, *Individualism and Economic Order*. Chicago: University of Chicago Press.

_____. 1952. "Scientism and the Study of Society." In Hayek, *The Counter-Revolution of Science*. Glencoe, IL.: The Free Press.

_____. 1967a "Degree of Explanation." Pp. 3-21 in Hayek, *Studies in Philosophy, Politics and Economics*. Chicago: University of Chicago Press.

_____. 1967b. "The Theory of Complex Phenomena." Pp. 22-42 in Hayek, *Studies in Philosophy, Politics, and Economics*. Chicago: University of Chicago Press.

_____. 1967c. "Kinds of Rationalism." Pp. 82-95 in Hayek, *Studies in Philosophy, Politics and Economics*. Chicago: University of Chicago Press.

_____. 1967d. *Studies in Philosophy, Politics and Economics*. Chicago: University of Chicago Press.

_____. 1978. "The Pretence of Knowledge." Pp. 23-24 in Hayek, *New Studies in Philosophy, Politics, Economics and the History of Ideas*. Chicago: University of Chicago Press.

Hutchison, Terence W. 1938. *The Significance and Basic Postulates of Economic Theory*. London: Macmillan.

———. 1956. "Professor Machlup on Verification in Economics." *Southern Economic Journal* 20, pp. 476-483.

———. 1977. *Knowledge and Ignorance in Economics*. Chicago: University of Chicago Press.

———. 1981. *The Politics and Philosophy of Economics: Marxians, Keynesians and Austrians*. Oxford: Basil Blackwell.

Popper, Karl. R. 1957. *The Poverty of Historicism*. Boston: The Beacon Press, 1957.

———. 1974. "Autobiography of Karl Popper." In Paul Schilpp, ed. *The Philosophy of Karl Popper*, Vol. 1. La Salle, IL: Open Court.

Robbins, Lionel. 1935. *An Essay on the Nature and Significance of Economic Science*. 2nd. Rev. ed. London: Macmillan.

HAYEK AND "MODERN AUSTRIAN" METHODOLOGY

COMMENT ON A NON-REFUTING REFUTATION

T. W. Hutchison

I have before me, under various titles, and in one "greatly modified" version after another, successive editions of Professor Caldwell's "Working Paper" dated 1983, 1984, 1985, and 1986. I have been invited to comment on the version dated 1986—(though this same piece has been dated by Caldwell as "1988" in various of his other recent publications about Hayek, notably one, which has happened to reach me, listed below as 1988a). In this Comment on Caldwell's "Refutation," I shall also need to refer to others of his various recent writings, such as his 1982, 1984, 1988a and 1988b.

The trouble starts with Caldwell's choice of a deliberately confrontational, "macho" title, which involves him at once in serious ambiguity and exaggeration. The term "falsificationist" does not occur anywhere in what I wrote about Hayek. The only word beginning "fals-" which I used, and that once only, was "falsifiability," which also occurs in a quotation from Norman Barry; while "falsifiable" and "falsified" occur once each in quotations from

Research in the History of Economic Thought and Methodology
Volume 10, pages 17-32.
Copyright © 1992 by JAI Press Inc.
All rights of reproduction in any form reserved.
ISBN: 0-55938-501-4

Hayek. Like many words ending in "-ist" and "-ism", "falsificationist" is much too ambiguous a term on which to try to base a reasonably precise "refutation." In fact, in his 1988a piece, Caldwell states that Hayek borrowed from Popper "the idea that a theory must be in a certain sense falsifiable to be scientific" (pp. 82-83), while also admitting, somewhat grudgingly, that Hayek "is at best a minimalist falsificationist"—(whatever, precisely "a minimalist falsificationist" amounts to). It seems, therefore, that Caldwell may have refuted his own "Refutation" before, even, he has got it republished—perhaps some kind of record. Alternatively, Caldwell is bending and stretching the highly ambiguous term "falsificationist" on the basis of which he has chosen to launch this attack (or "Refutation"). It is, of course, one of the oldest ploys in the controversial business to bend or exaggerate some argument or statement, which one feels an urge to attack, in order to make it vulnerable. Meanwhile, whatever Caldwell's "Refutation" may or may not refute (if anything nontrivial) it certainly does not refute any proposition which I have ever stated or believed. It seems, in fact, that Caldwell may not perceive the distinction between a refutation and an assertion to the contrary.

At this point, I would simply call attention to one kind of ambiguity lurking in the package term "falsificationist." I am not referring to the rather imprecise distinction between a "naive" and a "sophisticated" falsificationist, but to the importance of distinguishing (as Caldwell fails to do) between (a) recommending, *in the interests of clarity,* that theories be formulated in falsifiable terms; and (b) recommending that serious critical efforts be made, as far as possible, to falsify theories. Under (b) alone, there may be quite a range of possible, or reasonable attitudes,[1]

Meanwhile, might I counter one of Caldwell's strenuous attempts to make mountains out of molehills, when he refers to my "chapter as a whole" (Caldwell, 1986, p. 11), suggesting that I had written an entire chapter on Hayek. My chapter as a whole dealt with "Austrians on Philosophy and Method since Menger"; that is, from Böhm-Bawerk and Wieser to Rothbard and Kirzner. I wrote eight and a half pages (plus notes) on Hayek, while Caldwell spends about 50 percent more than that on his nonrefuting "Refutation."

I would still venture to refer any interested reader to what I actually wrote on Hayek in my book of 1981 (pp. 210-219), and especially, also, to the following section entitled "Dilemmas of Modern Austrians." There is only one point where I wish to make an alteration, though there is quite a lot I would like to add here (as far as restrictions on space allow) while perhaps offering a fuller account in some future work.

II

Of the new primary material and information which have emerged in the decade since I was writing, one might mention first the announcement that an entire volume of Hayek's *Collected Works* is to be devoted to his correspondence with Popper, which began in 1937. This information will come, of course, as a fascinating surprise to most of those interested in our subject. But one cannot help wondering what has been made of this recent revelation of the length and scale of the intellectual relationship between Hayek and Popper by those "*many* modern Austrians*" who, according to Professor Richard Langlois, have been regarding Sir Karl as "a rabid empiricist noteworthy primarily for the bad influence he exerted on Hayek" (1982, p. 77, emphasis added). The news that Hayek has so long been exposing himself to the "bad influence" of such "rabid" empiricism must surely have been somewhat disconcerting to those "Modern Austrians" who have proclaimed, or assumed, that "praxeology" is the methodology of "Modern Austrian" economics.

The second new item which emphatically calls for mention is the very remarkable reminiscence of Hayek himself, which apparently dates from 1977 but was first published in 1982. This intensely intriguing account describes the two stages of Hayek's conversion to Popper's refutability (or falsifiability) principle. (Caldwell does not mention this reminiscence in this "Refutation' (1986), but he quotes it, at some length, in his 1988a paper, *while stopping exactly short of the most emphatic and precise sentence*. Regarding the criticisms of Popper by Kuhn, Lakatos, and Feyerabend, Hayek rejects those of Kuhn, while conceding some "reservations" about those of the other two. Hayek insists, however, that "basically I am still a Popperian," and goes on to state that he was a Popperian in the twenties, before the appearance of Popper's work. He explains that his own reaction to the pretentious claims of Marxians and Freudians, that their theories were in their nature irrefutable, had been similar to that of Popper, who had been led to "the conclusion that a theory that cannot be refuted is, by definition, not scientific. When Popper stated that in detail, I just embraced his views as a statement of what I was feeling. *And that is why ever since his Logik der Forschung first came out in 1934, I have been a complete adherent to his general theory of methodology*" (Weimer and Palermo, 1982, p. 323, emphasis added).

Caldwell apparently just could not face quoting this last definitive sentence of Hayek's reminiscence, which is so precise regarding dates. (Perhaps Caldwell wanted to protest about Hayek having "gotten Hayek so wrong" (1986, p. 31). Anyhow, very intriguing problems certainly arise as to the precise interpretation of these Hayekian recollections regarding his views in the 1920s. More recent statements in letters from Hayek certainly do not reduce these problems. Actually, however, Caldwell himself is to be congratulated on having, quite unintentionally of course, provided us with a strikingly

appropriate phrase, applicable to Hayek's account of his position at this earlier
period, to the effect that Hayek was "something akin to a closet Popperian."
(Needless to say, Caldwell never intended that this somewhat bizarre phrase
should be applied to Hayek. He concocted the phrase "closet Popperian" so
as to apply it to *my views about Hayek*, in order to ridicule them in a hit-
and-run footnote, inserted for the furthering of his "flirtation"—as Professor
Eugene Rotwein (1986) has so appositely described it—with his "praxeological"
readers).[2]

As regards Hayek in the twenties, there are, however, two points to be
emphasized. *First*, there seems to be not the faintest jot or trace, *in Hayek's
writings before 1937*, of any methodological ideas, remotely approximating to
those of Popper's *Logik der Forschung* (1934), on the subject of refutability
or related questions. *Second*, from the start of his studies of economics, and
of his career as an economist, Hayek at once came under very powerful
methodological influences almost diametrically contradictory of Popper's ideas
regarding refutability.

III

Whenever and however Hayek's phase as a "closet Popperian" may have
unfolded, when, in 1921, he chose economics as his subject rather than
psychology ("perhaps wrongly," as he puts it), he had as his most authoritative
teacher, Friedrich Wieser (Weimer and Palermo eds., 1982, p. 288). Later in
the 1920s, Hayek was to edit Wieser's collected essays, contributing a most
respectful introductory tribute to his "revered teacher." The first of these essays
represented Wieser's most striking methodological statement, his denunciation
of the youthful Schumpeter's "positivism." The importance of this essay of
Wieser has not been sufficiently recognized by 'Modern Austrians' (possibly
because it has not been translated into English, and possibly because of Wieser's
sympathy with socialism and social reform).[3] Anyhow, Wieser was the
predecessor whom Mises most closely followed with regard to the "necessity"
and certainty of the results of introspection, which at times Mises also stressed
with the same extreme pretentiousness.[4] In fact, Misesian methodology is
largely that of Wieser, *plus* an infusion of pseudo-Kantian dogmatism which
would probably cause Kant to turn in his grave.

Hayek has also described how, for the most formative decade of his career
as an economist, "the chief guide in the development of my ideas was Ludwig
von Mises" (Hayek, 1984, 1). Stephan Böhm, moreover, has referred to "the
intense methodological discussions in Mises 'private' seminar" (1989a, p. 204)—
which presumably left a mark. Indeed, that Mises's ten-year guidance of
Hayek's intellectual development somehow stopped just short of the hazy and
flexible frontier of methodology, though conceivable, seems highly improbable

(though, of course, Hayek's methodological views never became totally, 100 percent identical with those of Mises).

Mises did not publish any full version of his methodological doctrines until 1933, with the first, previously unpublished essay of his *Grundprobleme*. The complete Misesian conceptual framework, however, was not to appear until later. In 1933, though Mises insisted on the "apodictic certainty" and a priori nature of the truths on which the science of human action rested, he did not employ the term *"praxeologie."*[5] Anyhow, soon after the appearance of the *Grundprobleme*, Hayek published the following concise but comprehensive summary of his methodological tenets at this time:

> The essential basic facts which we need for the explanation of social phenomena are part of our common experience, part of the stuff of our thinking. *In the social sciences it is the elements of the complex phenomena which are known beyond the possibility of dispute. In the natural sciences they can be at best surmised.* The existence of these elements is so much more certain than any regularities in the complex phenomena to which they give rise that it is they which constitute the truly empirical factor in the social sciences (1935, p. 11; quoted in Hutchison, 1981, pp. 213-214, emphasis added).

Professional philosophers may, of course, argue interminably about the differences between the a priori apodictic certainties of Mises, and what is "known beyond the possibility of dispute"—according to Hayek. For economists, on the other hand, insistence on significant differences in epistemological status between various claims to certainty or indisputability, whether or not "a priori," (anyway, a highly ambiguous term), may justifiably be dismissed as a largely irrelevant philosophical quibble. The extreme closeness of Hayek (1935) to Wieser and Mises (without, of course, total 100 percent identity of views) is surely obvious regarding the two fundamental points of (a) the infallibilist irrefutability of "the essential basic facts of economics"; and (b) the fundamental contrast and difference in nature between the methods and basic postulates of the social sciences and those of the natural sciences—a contrast drawn with about equally preposterous pretentiousness by Wieser, Mises, and Hayek in favour of economics as a social science. Both these basic principles set out by Hayek (1935) flatly contradict, of course, the main doctrines of Popper, including, in particular, his refutability principle. In spite of having earlier agreed with Popper in firmly rejecting Marxian and Freudian claims for the irrefutability of their doctrines, after ten years of guidance from Mises, Hayek was, in 1935, quite prepared to claim "indisputability" for his version of the basic propositions— *which extraordinary propositions, however, like Mises, he never permitted critics to appraise for their possibly trivial, vacuous, or even tautological nature, because he never gave a coherent list, or indication of what they included in relation to human knowledge.*

It has been necessary to outline some main features of Hayek's intellectual biography down to 1935 in order to demonstrate the extreme sharpness of his

methodological transformation, or U-turn, from 1935 to 1937. Regarding
Hayek's methodological views in this period, where stands Caldwell? The
answer is on a heap of impenetrable ambiguities, which may be outright
contradictory, but which *just might* be reconcilable: (1) In 1982, while
recognizing differences regarding a priorism, Caldwell assured us of "a striking
similarity between the writings of, say, Ludwig von Mises or Friedrich von
Hayek and the positions espoused by Robbins . . . *all agreed that the
fundamental axioms of economics are obvious and self-evident facts of
immediate experience"* (1982, pp. 103-104, emphasis added). These statements
are, of course, substantially correct *regarding 1935*, though they are deprived
of most of their value by Caldwell's failure to mention either (a) any citations
or dates regarding Hayek, or (b) any subsequent changes in Hayek's published
methodological views—a seriously misleading omission in view of the profound
transformation occurring barely two years later. (2) In 1988a, however,
Caldwell states his belief that "in the field of methodology Hayek is not a
disciple of Mises *and never has been*" (p. 76, emphasis added). Again, it may
be complained that "discipleship" is a characteristically ambiguous concept.
It would seem rather a pity if Caldwell's inclination toward validity of 1982,
regarding the similarity between the methodological views of Hayek and Mises
(in 1935), has now been overridden by this ambiguous proposition of 1988.
When Hayek stated that for ten years of his early career as an economist, Mises
was his "chief guide," he did not exempt methodology. Anyhow, "disciple" or
no "disciple", Hayek in 1935 published methodological views which had "a
striking similarity" with those of Mises (without, of course, being totally 100
percent identical).

IV

The most serious omission from my eight-and-a-half page discussion of a
decade ago was that of fuller comment on Hayek's "Economics and
Knowledge" of 1937 (henceforward "EK"). Moreover, I very much regret the
remark that "the influence of Popper is not obvious" in this article—though
it cannot, of course, be obvious to those who have not read, *and understood*,
Popper's *Logik der Forschung* (henceforward *LF*) in its original, slim, powerful
form. It would be a profound mistake if my remark were assumed to lend any
countenance to Caldwell's thoroughly misleading statement that the "text of
this article does not show any Popperian imprint" (1988a, p. 82).

It was quite unnecessarily speculative on my part to have introduced the
often problematically biographical question of "influence." It would have been,
and is, quite sufficient to assert that, as between his Wieserian-Misesian
pronouncement of 1935, and his "EK" article of 1937, Hayek's methodological
views show a significant, and indeed decisive move in the direction of those

of Popper, whatever "influences" (from *LF* or anywhere else) may, or may not, have been at work. For Hayek has stated that "EK" was written "before I knew anything about Popper," (letter to this author, May 15, 1983), in spite of the apparent emphatic assertion in his earlier reminiscence that 'ever since his *Logik der Forschung* first came out in 1934" he had been "a complete adherent to his general theory of methodology."[6]

Hayek has also remarked that the "main intention" of "EK" was "to explain gently to Mises why I could not accept his a priorism" (personal letter, May 15, 1983). (Unfortunately, the message to Mises was imparted so "gently" that 40 to 50 years later, it had still not got through to some "Modern Austrians"). "EK," however, possesses the almost unique significance in Hayek's writings of containing a rejection—however gentle—of an idea of Mises. Certainly, this rejection of a priorism stamps 'EK" as centrally and fundamentally methodological—in contradiction to the opposite, quite untenable, suggestion of Caldwell (in his 1988b, p. 514). This break with Mises, and also with the claims about indisputability in his own 1935 article, mark an essential first step in Hayek's move toward Popper's views, perhaps promoted by a revival of his "closet Popperian" inclinations of the 1920s in favor of rejecting Marxian, Freudian (and then Misesian) claims to irrefutability.

Let us turn next to the vital footnote reference to Popper at the start of "EK," with which Hayek introduced the term "falsification" as a correction of "verification" in the text above. Hayek has explained that this footnote was added at the proof stage, from which Caldwell, with a mixture of ambiguity and non-sequitur, concludes that therefore "the ideas expressed in Hayek's article cannot be attributed to Popper" (1986, p. 7). Obviously, this follows with regard to a Popperian *influence*, if Hayek knew nothing about Popper in 1936—though Caldwell (1988a, p. 81) has stated that Hayek read *LF* in 1935. But, in an obvious sense, Caldwell's remark is the opposite of the truth. *Why on earth cannot ideas "be attributed to Popper" if Popper had been the first fully and powerfully to develop and publish these ideas? Caldwell must try to face the question as to why Hayek inserted this footnote.* Is it suggested that Hayek was merely concerned to display erudition, or to show that he was up-to-date with the literature? Or was this footnote based simply on guesswork, unsupported by a thorough grasp of the main thesis of *LF*? Hayek, presumably, inserted the footnote, in accordance with the practice of conscientious scholars, so as to indicate, at the start of his article, that some of the arguments he was putting forward ran, at important points, closely parallel with some of the principal ideas of Popper's *LF*. These ideas centered around the relationships between falsifiability, tautologies, and empirical content. Moreover, the replacement of "verification" by "falsification" was crucial for Hayek's argument, because tautologies, which he was criticizing for lack of empirical content, are, of course, verifiable, but not falsifiable.[7]

In the mid-1930s, there had been among economists considerable discussion of the nature and role of tautologies in economic theorizing. I might mention, incidentally, that my own first two publications were mainly concerned with this question (1935 and 1937a). I was, therefore, bound to be specially interested, when reading "EK" towards the middle of 1937 (having read *LF* in 1936) in the vital distinction, which Hayek drew right at the start of his article, between "the tautologies," of which formal analysis consists, and, on the other hand, "propositions which tell us anything about causation in the real world," that is, "the empirical element in economic theory—the only part which is concerned not merely with implications but with causes and effects, and which leads therefore to conclusions which, at any rate in principle, are capable, of verification,"—or, rather, "falsification."[8] This footnote might, indeed, quite reasonably be regarded as Hayek's announcement that he had become "a falsificationist " (*if* one can imagine that he would ever have been ready to employ such an ambiguous word).

It is also important to realize that, for several years before 1937, much discussion had been taking place among economists not only of the distinction between tautologies and explanatory statements, but also of the other main theme of "EK," that of the concept of equilibrium and the assumption of equilibrating tendencies.[9] Hayek's ideas on these subjects ran on similar lines to those of Johan Åkerman, who complained of some writers that: "They find the ideal of abstract description in the perfect logical circle. . . . The setting is thus *a priori* tautologous' it arrives at results which are exactly identical with the elements of thought which have been put into the argument" (1936, p. 118, quoted by Hutchison, 1937a, pp. 87).

Whenever, precisely, Hayek read *LF* between 1934 and 1937, by the time he reached page 13, he would have met with the challenging statement: "Ein empirisch—wissenschaftliches System muss an der Erfahrung scheitern können" ("It must be possible for an empirical-scientific system to be refuted by experience"). Hayek might, perhaps, have recalled that the Marxian and Freudian systems were claimed to be not thus refutable. In fact, he compared the analysis of Mises with "the pure logic of choice" (which actually is a misnomer for the logic of *omniscient or automatic choice*—which is not what most human choice resembles). Anyhow, resolved to break with Misesian claims to a priori, apodictic certainties, Hayek came out with the decisive summons: "To economics as an empirical science we must now turn" ("EK", p. 44).

Popper's falsifiability criterion, the emphasis on the empirical emptiness and unfalsifiability of tautologies, and his summons to the study of economics as an empirical science, were quite new themes in Hayek's writings, as was the methodological break with Mises and his vacuous "apodictic" certainties. It would certainly be difficult to conceive of a sharper methodological transformation, or U-turn, than that involved in moving from the Wieserian-

Misesian claim to indisputability of 1935, to the appeal to the Popperian falsifiability principle in 1937.

V

Professor Caldwell seems to entertain very simplistic notions as to how the ideas have developed of a thinker both prodigiously erudite and profoundly original, over an almost unprecedently long career, who has been engaged on an exceptionally wide range of different intellectual fronts. Caldwell seems to imply (1986, pp. 11-13) that Hayek's moves in the direction of Popper's ideas cannot have added up significantly because they took place over too long a period and have been interspersed with too many interruptions and moves in other directions. We would venture to suggest here, by way of contrast, that the kind of intellectual pilgrimage, of which Hayek's is a, or the, outstanding example, may not be comprehensible in terms of simple, rapid, continuous, unilinear progression.

In the early 1940s, Hayek turned from questions of the postulates, concepts, and criteria of economic theory toward broader comparisons of the methods of the natural and social sciences, in "The Facts of the Social Sciences" (1943) and in the mainly historical essays on "The Counter-Revolution of Science" (1961) and "Scientism and the Study of Society" (1942/1943/1944) dating from the early 1940s. Although Hayek still maintained a dualist position in comparing the methods and criteria of the natural and social sciences, *it is important to recognize that these papers contained no signs of the preposterous Wieserian-Misesian "pretences of knowledge," which had been reproduced by Hayek in 1935*, regarding (1) the certainty, or "knowledge beyond the possibility of dispute," on which economics and the social sciences are supposed to be based; or (2) regarding the distinct superiority, or greater reliability, of the basic propositions of economics, as compared with those of the natural sciences. These Wieserian-Misesian claims disappeared from Hayek's writings after 1935, as he moved further in the direction of Popper's views. (Surely, incidentally, on this much controverted issue of the similarities or differences in methods and criteria as between the natural and the social sciences, the only sensible position is somewhere in the middle, away from the extreme "pretences of knowledge").

Professor Caldwell indulges in quite misconceived complaints about my "neglect" of the essays on "The Counter-Revolution of Science." The reason for my brief treatment was the fact that *very soon, over the following decade, Hayek moved decisively away from the dualist emphasis in these essays (which therefore became obsolete as an expression of his methodological views) in a direction which brought him markedly closer to Popper (without, of course, total, 100 percent identity of views being reached)*. Hayek has explained that

"Popper's influence on me was great on the question of the methods of the natural sciences" (letter of May 15, 1983), and he had, indeed, proceeded to reformulate his ideas in terms of the differences between more complex and less complex sciences, or studies, making this difference one of gradual degree, and abandoning the idea of a fundamental distinction in kind. The two very important papers which marked this further fundamental break with Wieserian-Misesian ideas were "Degrees of Explanation" (1955)—which Hayek describes as "little more than an elaboration of some of Popper's ideas" (1967, p. 4n)—and 'The Theory of Complex Phenomena" (1964).

Professor Stephan Böhm has recently observed that "all Austrian subjectivists are staunch exponents of methodological dualism" adding, however, "with the notable exception of Hayek." "Notable exception," indeed! Böhm confirms that Hayek "in his sadly neglected (among economists) later methodological work appears to narrow down the radical differentiation between the problems of the natural and social sciences to one of degrees" (1989b, pp. 65, 91). This "sad neglect," it should be noted, has, of course, been most serious on the part of the "Modern Austrians." Indeed, Professor Caldwell seems to have succeeded in completely blinding himself to this further fundamental departure by Hayek from Misesian doctrines.

A number of other, mainly non-Austrian writers have, however, succeeded in discerning these important later Hayekian developments. I first called attention in 1978 to "the transition, which seems to be detectable over the decades in Hayek's methodological views, in a direction away from Mises and towards Popper"(1978, p. 841(. Norman Barry (1979) also noted the Popperian component in Hayek's methodological ideas. Since my brief treatment in 1981, a number of other writers have emphasized Hayek's turn in the directions of Popperian views on both (a) falsifiability, and (b) differences between the natural and social sciences—for example, Böhm(1982), Butler (1983), Klant (1984), Gray (1988), and, in her very thorough and profound study, Loy (1988).[10]

Caldwell obviously has lots more "Refutations" to concoct. He has recently come up, however, with the assertion that Hayek had nothing important to add on methodology after the early 1940s: "'Scientism and the Study of Society' is Hayek's most important methodological work . . . all the subsequent writings of Hayek on methodology virtually only deepen the themes which one finds in this essay; nothing truly important has been added in the meantime" (1988a, p. 79). Thus, because his "flirtation" with praxeology impels him to such desperate attempts to keep Hayek in line with the "dualism" of Mises, Caldwell is unable to recognize the obvious significance of Hayek's very important later methodological writings as a move in Popper's direction (as recently agreed by the various distinguished authorities cited above).[11]

VI

Professor Caldwell concludes his "Refutation" with an attempt at explaining my motives (which are, of course, strictly irrelevant in assessing the validity of my eight and a half pages). According, however, to Caldwell, if I "could show that Hayek endorsed, and has long endorsed, Popperian falsificationism" (together, perhaps, with Popperian "rabid" empiricism) then I might have been able "to convince *other Austrians* to abandon their commitment to praxeology" (1986, p. 20, emphasis added). My motives, in fact, were considerably broader. I have provided a clue to them by italicizing Caldwell's gratuitous introduction of that much misused term "Austrian." (There was no need for the word "Austrian" at this point. Caldwell could simply have asserted that I had been trying to convince those with a commitment to "praxeology" to abandon that commitment).

My chapter as a whole was concerned to demonstrate the widely contrasting methodological views held by Austrians, as, for example, by the brothers-in-law Böhm-Bawerk and Wieser, and also, more specifically, by Mises and Hayek. Much of my motivation, provocation, or even inspiration, was provided (as I indicated in 1981, pp. 219-221) by two leading "Modern Austrians," (or "MA's"), Professors Murray Rothbard and Israel Kirzner. In an earlier manifesto of the "MA" movement, published shortly before I was writing my chapter (Dolan, 1976) one finds the title of the opening essay by Rothbard (1976) proclaiming "Praxeology" as "the Methodology of Austrian Economics." This Austrian methodology is then defined by quoting precisely the very Wieserian-Misesian statement of Hayek (1935) which I discussed in section III, as though Hayek had there produced the authoritative, official statement of "MA" methodological, *and praxeological*, principles. The most fatal flaw in Rothbard's thesis was simply, of course, his assumption that no fundamental transformation in Hayek's methodological views took place after 1935 (in this respect, Caldwell seems to have followed Rothbard). Immediately after Rothbard's proclamation came an essay by Kirzner, "On the Method of Austrian Economics" (1976), which opened with the following astounding claim: "One of the areas in which disagreement among Austrians may seem to be non-existent is that of methodology" (cf. Hutchison, 1981, p. 220). Kirzner could hardly have set down such an extreme claim if he had not believed that it was then widely supported by his fellow "MAs" (e.g., Rothbard). Kirzner himself, however, went on to express profound doubts—all too well-founded— regarding "Austrian" methodological harmony, and proceeded to expose a fundamental "dilemma" regarding the empirical nature of the necessary assumptions of equilibrium theory and regarding the predictability of human preferences. The point here is that Kirzner identified the base of this crucial Austrian "dilemma" *precisely in the arguments first put forward by Hayek in "EK" (1937), when he was breaking with Mises.* Kirzner offered a long,

supporting quotation from "EK" (1976, p. 48).[13] My thesis of a U-turn by
Hayek between 1935 and 1937 was, I must therefore confess, largely, though
unintentionally, anticipated by Rothbard and Kirzner in 1976 and confirmed
by the contrasting quotations they provided from Hayek (1935, 1937).
Moreover, that is where Kirzner's fundamental Austrian "dilemma" started.
Forty years later, Kirzner (1976) was warning that "the future progress of the
Austrian school" required some resolution of this crucial dilemma—which has
never been faced, let alone resolved (1976, p. 50).[13]

Caldwell's record on this question of the extent of methodological agreement
among Austrians has proceeded from one baffling ambiguity to another. In
1982, though admitting that "many" "MAs" were "lukewarm" toward
praxeology, he put forward the extraordinary expository explanation that "for
ease of exposition, the terms "praxeology" and "Austrian methodology" will
be used interchangeably," while warning that this usage "should not be taken
to imply that all Austrians adhere to the praxeological position" (p. 119). Just
what, might one ask, *should* this terminological hijack "be taken to imply,"
especially regarding Hayek? What undoubtedly follows is that Austrians who
are not "praxeologists" are to be referred to as "praxeologists" for the sake
of an "ease of exposition," which surely only Caldwell can discern. What,
however, this peculiar expository device *does* serve is an attempt to paper over
the gaping cracks of fundamental methodological disagreement between Hayek
and Mises since 1937. Following Caldwell's recent switch to the view that
Hayek never was methodologically a disciple of Mises, it is not clear whether
"for ease of exposition" Hayek is still being called a "praxeologist"—or not.
Anyhow, our conclusion is that Hayek, though in a most valid sense an
Austrian (that is, by birth, education, and first language) is certainly neither
a "praxeologist", nor, methodologically, a "Modern Austrian," either regarding
(1) his advocacy of the falsifiability principle; or (2) his abandonment of
methodological dualism as between the natural and social sciences, or (3) his
views on prediction (in spite of Caldwell's desperate attempts to keep him in
line with "MA" doctrines).[14]

May I put two concluding points? First, I would venture to offer the simple,
personal suggestion to Professor Caldwell that he give this "Modern Austrian"
concept a very long rest, and that, "for ease of exposition" (so to speak) he
tried cutting out the word "Austrian" altogether for a year or two. Abandoning
this word will surely assist him in avoiding any number of ambiguous and
tendentious interpretations and questionable generalizations. Secondly and
finally, I would, nevertheless, like to express, in conclusion, my considerable
gratitude for having my interest reawakened in a fascinating subject which I
had felt strongly inclined to let drop.

NOTES

1. See the discussion by Lawrence Boland (1989, pp. 10-11).
2. Caldwell's footnote is as follows:

Hutchison's claim that Hayek in his later methodological writings is something akin to a closet Popperian seems to me completely unfounded, providing further evidence that falsificationist eyeglasses need not improve one's vision (1984, p. 373n.).

3. On Wieser's methodological views, see Hutchison (1981, pp. 205-207, 213). Wieser is not mentioned in the index of Caldwell, (1982). Too late to discuss here, I have learnt that Stephan Böhm has written about Wieser's methodological views.
4. For Mises's Wieserian claims for introspection, see Hutchison p. 210. The treatment of Menger by Mises is especially noteworthy. Though Mises refers to Menger's "path-breaking" *Untersuchungen* he alleges that they suffer seriously from the empiricism and "psychologism" of J.S. Mill. Moreover, Mises makes the extraordinary allegation that Menger's *Untersuchungen* "do not start from modern formulations of subjectivist economics, but from the system, methodology, and logic of classical political economy" (1933, pp. 20n, 67n).
5. It is quite misleading of Caldwell to state, regarding the term "praxeological," that it "can be found in Mises's 1933 work" (1982, p. 104). The term "praxeological,' or "praxeology," only occurs in a citation of a work by Slutsky, of which Mises expressed disapproval, though it may have provided him with the source of this term, adopted by himself later on. In the English translation of the *Grundprobleme* (1960) the term is introduced four items to render—though hardly to translate—such German terms as "soziologie," "praktik," and "gesellschaftslehre."
6. According to Popper, Hayek told him that it was Gottfried Haberler who called his (Hayek's) attention to *LF*. Incidentally, my most valuable encouragement and advice at that time (1937), with regard to criticizing Mises, came from Haberler—to whom I was, and am, deeply grateful.
7. See the very illuminating discussion by Boland of "Falsifiability versus Verifiability," and "Tautology versus Testability" (1989, pp. 47-48, 131-132).
8. Hayek clearly observed that tautologies cannot be falsified empirically because they do not "forbid" anything (except, of course, contradictions in terms). As Popper put it: "Not for nothing do we call the laws of nature 'laws': the more they prohibit the more they say" (*LF*, 1935, p. 73). This statement was quoted in my 1937b, (p. 651). I am delighted to find Dr. Claudia Loy (1988, p. 202) reaffirming, after half a century, the importance of Popper's aperçu. According to Popper, this may have been the first time he was quoted in English.
9. See Hicks (1933) and Myrdal (1933). Hayek himself in "EK" was following up some of his earlier contributions on intertemporal equilibrium and business fluctuations.
10. Professor Böhm (1982, p. 50) has stated: "It is important to note that Hayek's views on methodology have changed drastically since the late thirties and early forties . . . crudely put, in a direction away from Mises and towards Popper." Butler (1983, p. 137) notes that Hayek's views on the social sciences:

underwent a significant change in the early 1940s . . . He was originally of the view that the methods of the social and natural sciences were completely different. . . . However, in the meantime, Sir Karl produced a convincing explanation of the essential unity of all scientific method which forced Hayek to reconsider.

Professor J. J. Klant has observed of Hayek, how, "influenced by Popper, he shows himself to be clearly aware of the importance of the criterion of falsifiability" (1984, p. 79). Mr. John Gray has described how Hayek:

came to adopt Popper's proposal that falsifiabiity be treated as a demarcation criterion of science from non-science. Again Hayek followed Popper in qualifying his earlier Austrian conviction that there is a radical dualism of method as between natural and social science. (1986, pp. 19-20).

(Incidentally, it is rather disappointing to find Mr. Gray maintaining that I have not correctly identified "Hayek's real debts to Popper," when his sole quotation from Hayek in support of his own account—very sound, as far as it goes—is identical to one of my quotations, except for his addition of an erroneous and ungrammatical ("s").

Dr. Claudia Loy (1988, pp. 15-16) gives a very precise account of how, "under the influence of Popper, Hayek, towards the end of the thirties, gradually modified his methodological views." Incidentally, Dr. Loy also remarks in a footnote on the reverse influence of Hayek on Popper, which must almost certainly have occurred, to some extent, in such a lengthy exchange. Presumably, most of Popper's rather slight acquaintance with economics and political economy came from Hayek. The question is whether the results of the influence of Hayek on Popper (apart from helping Popper's move from New Zealand to the L.S.E.) were ever of nearly the same interest and importance, considering the minor role which economics and political economy have played in Popper's interests and achievements. Certainly the evidence seems very speculative and uninteresting for Caldwell's view that "Popper has had little influence on Hayek, but Hayek has greatly influenced Popper" (1988a, p. 81).

11. In section V (1986), Caldwell picks out five of the 25 to 30 quotations in my eight-and-a-half pages on Hayek and complains that I have seriously misrepresented him. Of course, the meaning of a quotation can always be altered, however slightly, by lengthening it. Caldwell proceeds to lengthen considerably my quotations and then to complain indignantly that their meaning has been altered. The question is, of course, whether the alteration in meaning is significant and nontrivial, which Caldwell invariable fails to show. By claiming three times (pp.s 14, 15, and 16) that he is replacing my quotations by "the full quoation," Caldwell might perhaps be taken to be implying that I have omitted words or sentences in my quotations without indicating the omission. If so, this is quite untrue. Caldwell's quotations are no more *the full* quotations than are mine. They are simply longer, and I could, of course, always, relevantly or—like Caldwell—quite irrelevantly, overtrump his longer quotations by still longer ones.

It must be noted that all five of Caldwell's complaints arise regarding the interpretation of Hayek's three later articles of 1955, 1964, and 1974. Like a number of writers quoted above, I certainly hold that these later articles are of the highest importance, and introduce modifications of fundamental significance in Hayek's views, which bring them significantly closer to those of Popper (though I renounce any speculations regarding influence). Caldwell objects to my quotations because they support this foregoing interpretation and are opposed to his view that 'nothing truly important' was added by Hayek in these later essays. Some of Caldwell's charges are obviously false (e.g., that a quotation of mine "completely" changes Hayek's meaning (p. 16), and again when Caldwell asserts to be Hayek's "whole point" what is clearly only a part of his point (p. 18). In particular, Caldwell has shown himself to be hardly qualified to pass judgment on other people's quotations by perpetrating such a seriously misleading truncation of Hayek's reminiscence as to how he became a "complete adherent" of Popper's methodology on the publication of *Logik der Forschung*.

12. In the very lengthy passage from "EK", quoted by Kirzner, Hayek stated that his "significant point" was that it is the "assumptions that people do learn from experience, and about how they acquire knowledge, which constitute the empirical content of our propositions about what happens in the real world." From which Kirzner straightway and inevitably concluded: "If we are able to say anything about the process of equilibration . . . we shall have to rely upon the particular empirical proposition that men learn from market experience in a systematic manner. This is inconsistent with the second tenet underlying Austrian economics that there is an inherent

indeterminacy in the way by which human knowledge changes" (1976, pp. 48-9; Hayek, 1937, p. 46).

13.   Dr. Claudia Loy (1988, pp. 188-90) comments very cogently on the "extreme polarities" and outright contradictions at the heart of "Modern Austrian" doctrines about expectations, equilibrium, and predictability. She describes it very politely as "astonishing" that such contradictions have not led to any reforms of Misesian claims to certainty. This condition of long-persisting contradictions between rival "apodictic certainties," without any accepted means of resolving such dilemmas, seems to point to a state of methodological bankruptcy—which certainly Caldwell's "pluralism" is incapable of relieving.

14.   For a detailed and discerning analysis of Hayek's views on prediction, see Graf (1978), who also suggests that, at some points, Hayek moved significantly toward Popper's views.

REFERENCES

Åckerman, J. 1936. "Annual Survey of Economic Theory." *Econometrica* 4:97.

Barry, N.P. 1979. *Hayek's Social and Economic Philosophy.* London: Macmillan.

Böhm, S. 1982. "The Ambiguous Notion of Subjectivism." In *Method, Process, and Suibjectivism,* edited by I. Kirzner, Lexington, MA: DC Heath.

————. 1989a. Hayek on Knowledge, Equilibrium and Prices." *Wirtschaftspolitische Blätter* 36:201.

————. 1989b. "Subjectivism and Post-Keynesianism." In *New Directions in Post-Keynesian Economics,* edited by J. Pheby.

Boland, L.A. 1989. *The Methodology of Economic Model Building.* London: Routledge and Kegan Paul.

Butler, E. 1983. *Hayek.* London: Temple Smioth.

Caldwell, B. 1982. *Beyond Positivism.* London: Allen & Unwin.

————. 1984. "Praxeology and Its Critics." *History of Political Economy* (16, 3): 363.

————. 1986. *Hayek the Falsificationist? A Refutation.*

————. 1988a. "La Methodologie de Hayek". In *Hayek,* edited by G. Dostaler and E. Ethler.

————. 1988b. "Hayek's Transformation." *History of Political Economy* 20(4):513.

Graf, H.-G. 1978. *"Muster-Voraussagern" und "Erklärungen des Prinzips" bel F.A. von Hayek.* Freiburg: Walter Eucken Institut.

Gray, J. 1988. *Hayek on Liberty.* 2nd ed. Oxford: Blackwell.

Hayek, F.A. 1935. *Collectivist Economic Planning.* London: Routledge and Kegan Paul.

————. 1937. "Economics and Knowledge." *Economica* 4:33.

————. 1941. "The Counter-Revolution of Science." 3 parts. *Economica* 8, 9, 119, 281.

————. 1942/1943/1944. "Scientism and the Study of Society." 3 parts. *Economica* 9:267, 10:234, 11:241.

————. 1943. "The Facts of the Social Sciences." *Ethics* 54(1).

————. 1955. "Degrees of Explanation." *British Journal for the Philosophy of Science* 6(23):209.

————. 1964. "The Theory of Complex Phenomena." In *The Critical Approach to Science and Philosophy: Essays in Honor of Karl Popper,* edited by M. Bunge.

————. 1967. *Studies in Philosophy, Politics and Economics.* London: Routledge and Kegan Paul.

————. 1974. "The Pretence of Knowledge." Nobel Lecture.

————. 1978. *New Studies in Philosophy, Politics, Economics and the History of Ideas.* London: Routledge and Kegan Paul.

————. 1984. *Money, Capital and Fluctuations.* Edited by R. Mcloughrey. London: Routledge and Kegan Paul.

Hicks, J.R. 1933. "Gleichgewicht und Konjunktur." *Zeitschrift für Nationalökonomie* 4(441).

Hutchison, T.W. "A Note on Tautologies and the Nature of Economic Theory." *Review of Economic Studies* 2(159).

———. 1937. Theoretische Ökonomie als Sprachsystem." *Zeitschrift fü Nationalökonomie* 8(636).

———. 1977. *Knowledge and Ignorance in Economics.* Oxford: Basil Blackwell.

———. 1978. Review of books by L.M. Lachmann, G.P. O'Driscoll, M. Rothbard, and J. Jewkes. *Economic Journal* 88(840).

———. 1979. Review of Hayek, 1978. *Economic Journal* 89(179).

Kirzner, I. 1976. 'On the Method of Austrian Economics." In *The Foundations of Modern Austrian Economics,* edited by E.G. Dolan. Kansas: Sheed and Ward.

Klant, J.J. 1984. *The Rules of the Game.* Cambridge: Cambridge University Press.

Langlois, R.N. 1982. "Austrian Economics as Affirmative Science." In *Method, Process and Austrian Economics,* edited by I. Kirzner.

Loy, C. 1988. *Marktsystem und Gleichgewichtstendenz.* Freiburg: Walter Eucken Institut.

Mises, L. von. 1933. *Grundprobleme der Nationlöćkonomie.* Jena: G. Fischer.

———. 1960. *Epistemological Problems in Economics.* Trans. by G. Reisman. Princeton: Van Nostrand.

———. 1962. *The Ultimate Foundations of Economic Science.* Princeton: Van Nostrand.

Myrdal, G. 1933. "Der Gleichgewichtsbegriff als Instrument der geldtheoretlschen Analyse." In *Beiträge zur Geldtheorie,* edited by F.A. Hayek. Vienna: J. Springer.

Popper, K.R. 1934. *Logik der Forschung.* Vienna: J. Springer.

Rothbard, M. 1970. *Power and Markets.* Kansas City: Sheed Andrews and McMead.

———. 1976. "Praxeology and the Methodology of Austrian Economics." In *The Foundations of Modern Austrian Economics,* edited by E.G. Dolan. Kansas: Sheed and Ward.

Rotwein, E. 1986. "Flirting with A Priorism: Caldwell on Mises." *History of Political Economy* 18(669).

Weimer, W.B., and Palermo, D.S. 1982. *Cognition and the Symbolic Process,* Vol. 2. Hillsdale, NJ: Erlbaum Associates.

Wieser, F., 1929. *Gesammelte Abhandlungen,* edited by F.A. Hayek. Tübingen: J.C.B. Mohr.

REPLY TO HUTCHISON

Bruce J. Caldwell

I

Professor Hutchison's comment contains a lengthy explication of his views on the relationship between the ideas of Hayek and Popper. In addition, he raises numerous questions about the consistency and coherence of some of my published work. In my reply, I will first try to answer his broadsides concerning my scholarship. I will then identify as best I can the differences in interpretation which still separate us.

II

Five of my publications are mentioned by Hutchison. Hutchison jumps around quite a bit in citing them, so that it may be difficult for the reader to keep straight what Caldwell was supposed to have said when. A brief description of the works which Hutchison cites may help to clarify matters.

Caldwell (1982) is my book, *Beyond Positivism*. The final draft of the book was completed during the 1981-1982 academic year, which I spent at New York University (NYU) on a postdoctoral grant to learn about Austrian economics.

Research in the History of Economic Thought and Methodology
Volume 10, pages 33-42.
Copyright © 1992 by JAI Press Inc.
All rights of reproduction in any form reserved.
ISBN: 0-55938-501-4

I mention this because the year at NYU led me to add some new material to the manuscript. For example, the chapter on the methodological positions of Robbins and Hutchison in the 1930s includes a discussion of the Robbins-Austrian connection.

Significantly, however, my focus in this section was not on Hayek but on Ludwig von Mises. Specifically, I undertook an extended analysis of Mises' a priorist defense of praxeology, the so-called "science of human action." I compared praxeology with Robbins' views, noting, for example, that though both he and Mises believed that the postulates of economics were somehow self-evident, only the latter characterized them as a priori true. There is no similar extended treatment of Hayek in *Beyond Positivism*. His name is mentioned in five places, always in passing. Ironically, my interest in Hayek was not awakened until late in the academic year, when Jerry O'Driscoll handed me a copy of Professor Hutchison's 1981 book, the one which contains his claims about Hayek's U-turn. By that time, *Beyond Positivism* had been sent off to the publisher.

Given its paucity of references to Hayek, why is Caldwell (1982) mentioned at all by Hutchison? It would appear that most of his citations are designed to cast doubt on either the quality of my scholarship or the consistency of my views. Thus, Hutchison (in note 3) chides Caldwell (1982) for failing to mention Hayek's teacher Wieser. This was hardly a sin, given that there was so little attention paid in the book to Hayek! In note 5, Hutchison complains about my statement that praxeology was first mentioned by Mises in a work published in 1933. I had read the English translation, where the word praxeology *was* used four times, but apparently in the German edition it was mentioned only once. Hutchison finds this "quite misleading," which it might have been had I discussed Mises' book in any detail. But there is no discussion of the book at all; the reference again was a passing one. When I examined praxeology, my references were to two other books by Mises, *Human Action* (1949) and *The Ultimate Foundations of Economic Science* (1962), or to the later secondary literature.

While these potshots are niggling irritations, Hutchison's next reference to my book is substantive. It also provides a vivid illustration of one of my complaints, that Hutchison at times misrepresents what others have said to suit his own interpretive purposes. At the end of his section III, Hutchison's text includes the following "quotation" from Caldwell (1982): "a striking similarity between the views of, say, Ludwig von Mises or Friedrich von Hayek and the positions espoused by Robbins.... *all agreed that the fundamental axioms of economics are obvious and self-evident facts of immediate experience"* (1982, pp. 103-104, italics added). The quote implies that in 1982, I saw little difference among the views of Hayek, Mises, and Robbins. Hutchison uses this quote to suggest that Caldwell (1982) is inconsistent with the another quote from a later paper of mine, "in the field of methodology

Hayek is not a disciple of Mises *and never has been*" (1988a, p. 76, italics added). It is bad enough that Hutchison had to add italics twice to help produce the desired interpretive effect. But worse, his "quotation" from pp. 103-104 is constructed from two different sentences which are separated by over a full page of text! Worst of all, the point I was making in my book is in fact the exact opposite of the one that Hutchison attributes to me. My point was that, although there are many similarities in the views of Robbins, Hayek, and Robbins, *none adhered to Mises' a priorist defense of the basic axioms of economics.* This can be seen from my next sentence, which Hutchison ignores: "But all did not agree with Mises' particular (and perhaps peculiar) vision that economic science is praxeological, that the basic postulates of the discipline are necessary and unquestionable truths about the human condition; that the status of the fundamental axioms is that of synthetic statements that are a priori true" (1982, pp. 104-5). Thus, in Caldwell (1982) I *denied* that Hayek (or, for that matter, Robbins or Frank Knight, who were also mentioned) accepted Mises' a priorism.

The second quotation is also taken out of context. It is the last sentence of a paragraph which deals exclusively with the question of whether Hayek ever accepted Mises' specific variant of a priorism. In that context, my meaning is very clear. When I said that Hayek is not a disciple of Mises in terms of method, I did not mean to imply that Mises had no influence on Hayek. I was simply reiterating the point that Hayek did not accept Mises' a priorism. Hutchison obviously disagrees with this view, which is his right. But rather than developing counterarguments to it, he chose to invent a new position for me, then claim to have caught me in an inconsistency.

Let us move to Caldwell (1984), "Praxeology and Its Critics: An Appraisal." This paper extends the analysis of Mises' views undertaken in *Beyond Positivism.* The paper contains two substantive claims. The first is that the usual attacks against praxeology in the methodological literature, attacks which are based on either logical empiricist or Popperian versions of the philosophy of science, are problematical. One reason that they are problematical is that Mises expressly opposed these philosophies. But more important, my understanding of the current philosophy of science was that it successfully challenged the logical empiricist and Popperian visions. My second substantive claim was that alternative routes to the criticism of praxeology exist. In the last section of the paper, I sketched such an alternative, an internal criticism of Mises' position.

Again the question arises: Why does Hutchison even bother to mention this article? What does it have to do with Hayek and Popper? Actually, Hutchison explicitly cites it only once (in his note 2). In the accompanying text he suggests that Eugene Rotwein's (1986) characterization of the article as a "flirtation with praxeology" is an accurate rendering. Later in his comment, in his discussion of what might have motivated my position, my flirtation with praxeology comes up again. Hutchison suggests that my hope was to "paper over the gaping cracks of fundamental methodological disagreement between Hayek and Mises since 1937," and further mentions "Caldwell's desperate attempts" to keep Hayek in line with the doctrines of the "Modern Austrians," the term he uses for Israel Kirzner and Murray Rothbard.

Hutchison thus represents me as someone who is trying to portray the Austrians as having closed ranks behind praxeology. In fact, this is the opposite of the position which I took, not only in *Beyond Positivism*, (p. 137, note 45, which begins "The claim that many contemporary Austrians do not embrace the tenets of praxeology is based on conversations I had with a number of Austrian economists ...") but also in the 1984 article, whose opening reads:

> The Austrian approach to methodology has never been monolithic. Two recent studies show that since Menger's time Austrians have differed, at times dramatically, in their views on methodology (White, 1977; Hutchison 1981 [!]). This diversity continues to be evidenced in the writings of modern day Austrians (1984, p. 363).

Should any questions remain about my motivation, perhaps the following statement will clear them up. For what it is worth, I think that Mises' a priorist defense of praxeology was a double mistake. My gut feeling is that the doctrine is mistaken epistemologically (though thus far there have been precious few demonstrations, as opposed to assertions, of this in the methodological literature in economics). I also think it was a mistake for so many American Austrians to have spent so much time trying to defend it. When I wrote the 1984 article, I was trying to convince some of the Austrians I had met at NYU to give up their attachment to a priorism. However, my understanding of developments within the philosophy of science led me to believe that the old arguments against a priorism were no longer effective. Taking these problems in philosophy seriously, I attempted to construct an alternative critique of Mises' position.

We may now move to my two principle works on Hayek, Caldwell (1992): "Hayek the Falsificationist?: A Refutation," and Caldwell (1988b): "Hayek's Transformation." These two began as one paper, but its length grew in subsequent drafts (all of these were sent to Professor Hutchison, hence his opening complaint); I finally decided to split it into two articles. The first is published here for the first time: though accepted for publication in 1986, with 1988 given as the anticipated year of publication, problems encountered by the editor prevented it from being published on time.

The two articles are clearly related. In the first, I dispute Hutchison's characterization of Hayek's "U-turn" in the 1930s and of Popper's subsequent influence on him. In the second, I offer my own version of Hayek's transformation. Very briefly, I argue there that Hayek changed from an economist who insisted that economics make use of equilibrium theory, to a broader social theorist who denied that equilibrium theorizing sheds any light on the central problem of the social sciences, that of social coordination. The ideas contained in these two papers form the core of my arguments against Hutchison. I expected that in his comment Hutchison would try to answer the objections I had raised against his version and to attack the accuracy of my alternative account.

Hutchison does, of course, respond to my criticisms of his version in his comment. But remarkably, he refers to my (1988b) paper only once, in section IV, where he leaves the impression that I deny that Hayek's 1937 "Economics and Knowledge" article contains any criticism of Mises. (Recall Hutchison's desire to picture me as an apologist for Mises.)

Again, this is a direct misreading. I spend three paragraphs in the middle of the article explicitly discussing how "Economics and Knowledge" marks Hayek's break with Mises. The first of these paragraphs begins as follows:

> Hayek states that the equilibrium of the individual follows a priori from the Pure Logic of Choice. Does this mean that the Hayek of "Economics and Knowledge" was a Misesian? Paradoxically, though Hayek unselfconsciously utilizes the Misesian Pure Logic of Choice in the paper, the case can be made that this article marks Hayek's first real *break* with his mentor (1988b, p. 528, italics in the original).

Contrary to Hutchison's incorrect portrayal of my views, I do believe that Hayek expresses disagreement with Mises in "Economics and Knowledge." Where I differ from Hutchison is over the *grounds* of the disagreement. Briefly put, I believe that even though Hayek repeatedly uses the term "a priori" (even in papers published in the 1940s, I might now add) in characterizing the axioms of economic theory, he never uses the phrase in the way that Mises does. This is hinted at in Hayek's article when he asserts that it is wrong to try to draw conclusions about social coordination from the axioms, something which Mises felt was permissible. In any case, instead of discussing these legitimate and interesting differences in our interpretations of Hayek's break with Mises, Hutchison ignores my position and focuses on an unrelated footnote.

The last article cited by Hutchison is Caldwell (1988a), "La Méthodologie de Hayek: Description, Evaluation et Interrogations." This was a conference piece, written for a colloquium on Hayek's work held in Montreal in January, 1988. In this paper, a number of episodes in the development of Hayek's methodological thought are quickly summarized. After each, I offer an evaluation of his position, then note a number of questions which remain in the literature. The stated purpose of the paper is to offer a broad survey of Hayek's methodological thought and to stimulate interest in Hayekian scholarship. I do *not* provide any extensive justification or defense of the claims I make. Indeed, I twice tell the reader that I am providing an intentionally provocative reading in order to stimulate discussion. None of this comes across in Hutchison's account. Hutchison latches onto two of my assertions: that little of importance was added to Hayek's methodology after the publication of his "Scientism" (1952) essay, and that at least as much evidence exists for the claim that Popper is a Hayekian as for the claim that Hayek is a Popperian.

Now though these claims are provocative, they are not outrageous: there is evidence for each of them. Much of Hayek's later methodological work concerned the theory of complex phenomena and the use of the compositive method, both of which were anticipated in "Scientism and the Study of Society" (1952). Also, in his social science writings (which Hutchison ignores), Popper advocates the method of situational analysis, which he describes in his autobiography as "an attempt *to generalize the method of economic theory [marginal utility theory] so as to become applicable to the other theoretical social sciences* (Popper, 1974, p. 93, italics in the original). If I am right that Hayek is a minimalist falsificationist, and if Popper modeled his philosophy of social science on economics, then the claim that Popper is a Hayekian rather than vice versa is at least plausible. Nonetheless, at this point these two assertions are best viewed as bold conjectures, hypotheses to be tested as work in the Hayek and Popper archives proceeds.

I finally must respond to Hutchison's complaint that I somehow misled readers of my (1988a) paper by leaving out a sentence from one of Hayek's reminiscences. Hayek's missing sentence reads, "And that is why ever since his *Logik der Forschung* first came out in 1934, I have been a complete adherent to his [Popper's] general theory of methodology" (Weimer and Palermo, 1982, p. 323). As Hutchison recognizes, the reminisence is problematical concerning the dates. But surely it is clear from the quotation that Hayek considers himself a Popperian.

In my paper, I list a number of problems which my account of the Hayek-Popper relationship faces. That Hayek claims to be a Popperian is mentioned explicitly in the list, as follows, "Not least of all, Hayek self-reports that he is a Popperian (e.g., Weimer, 1982, p. 323)." I then go on to argue that, *despite* Hayek's claim, his methodological views differ quite dramatically on a number of key issues from those of Popper. These differences are evident in work published by Hayek in the 1940s (even Hutchison admits that the "Scientism" essay of 1942-1944 show a "dualist emphasis"), and I argue that even in his later work, Hayek's views often depart from those of. Popper, and that his endorsements of Popper's positions are typically heavily qualified (Hutchison disagrees here).

Why, then, does Hayek represent himself as a Popperian? I use his quote to suggest that Hayek and Popper shared the same enemies (i.e., Marxists and Freudians), so that Hayek simply "embraced his [Popper's] views as a statement of what I was feeling" (Weimer and Palermo, 1982, p. 323). I certainly was not trying to *hide* the fact that Hayek reports himself to be a Popperian. Just the opposite, I was trying to *explain* it, since it poses a problem for my position.

Hutchisons italicizing of the sentence and his remark that "Caldwell apparently just couldn't face quoting this last definitive sentence of Hayek's reminiscence, which is so precise regarding dates" implies, of course, that I was trying to engage in a cover up.

I apologize to the reader for engaging in the tedious exercise of responding at such length to Hutchison's claims concerning the consistency of my views. I felt compelled to do so to protest Hutchison's dissembling account of my position. Legitimate differences in opinion separate us, and I have tried to be clear in my published work as to what those differences are. I wish that Hutchison had focused more of his attention on these differences, and on the arguments which underlie them. Instead, he sought to portray my position as full of ambiguities and inconsistencies, a portrayal which seems to me to border on willful and systematic distortion.

A final point: at the end of his section V, Hutchison lists a number of scholars, all of whom he claims agree with his views. All of them acknowledge that Popper had some general influence on Hayek, and I do, too. But not all of them agree with Hutchison's specific interpretation. Indeed, Gray (1986) spends two pages (pp. 18-19) explicitly criticizing Hutchison's (1981) account. And Boehm (1989), a paper listed in Hutchison's bibliography, includes the following footnote discussion of Hutchison's views of Hayek's "Economics and Knowledge" (1948b).

> Hutchison attributes to it the catalytic role of a "U-Turn" in Hayek's evolution of thought, away from an a priorist conception of economics grounded in apodictic certainty that he was supposed to have taken over from his mentor, Mises, to a hypothetico-deductive method based on conjectures and refutations in the Popperian spirit. Briefly, there seems to be little warrant for a periodization of Hayek's career in those terms. First, since among the Austrians Mises was the sole advocate of praxeology, there was nothing for Hayek to escape from in that respect; and secondly, in his philosophy of social science Popper is arguably more indebted to Hayek than vice versa (Boehm, 1989, p. 204).

In this brief paragraph, Boehm takes issue with three of Hutchison's claims: on the nature of Hayek's "U-turn," on Hayek's acceptance of Mises' views, and on who gained more in the Popper-Hayek exchange of ideas. It is simply incredible that Hutchison lists Boehm and Gray as among those who agree with him.

III

The reader can certainly be forgiven for losing track by now of who believes what concerning the Hayek-Popper relationship. To clarify matters, here is a brief summary of the points of accord and of diagreement between Hutchison and Caldwell, as I understand them.

1.   Both of us agree that Hayek reports to be a Popperian. Both presumably also agree that Hayek's refusal to publicly criticize the views of his friends (these include both Mises and Popper, whose positions are diametrically opposed) makes it quite difficult to discern his true position.

2.   Both agree that Hayek's 1937 "Economics and Knowledge" (1948b) contains a veiled rebuke of Mises' ideas.

3.   We disagree about the nature of the rebuke. Hutchison claims it was a denial of the two "Wieser-Mises theses": that the axioms of economics are a priori true or irrefutable, and that the natural and social sciences follow different methods. Caldwell claims that Hayek rejected the Misesian belief that the movement from statements concerning individual equilibrium (where a priorist reasoning was applicable) to statements concerning social equilibrium (where questions of expectations became important) was unproblematical.

It should be added that both interpretations face the same difficulty: How are they to make sense of Hayek's apparent adherence to the two "Wieser-Mises theses" into the 1940s, not just in the "Scientism" essay, but also in such pieces as his 1943 paper, "The Facts of the Social Sciences" (1948c)? Hutchison tries to finesse the issue by claiming that no breaks are ever clean breaks (though this, of course, undermines his claim in section III that Hayek experienced a methodological transformation of "extreme sharpness" between 1935 and 1937). Caldwell, who argues that Hayek never followed the Misesian line concerning the a priori status of the axioms, tries to dodge it by claiming that Hayek's usage of such terms as "a priori" is different from that of Mises.

4.   Hutchison asserts and Caldwell denies that Hayek's 1937 article marks a methodological "U-Turn" *away* from Mises and *toward* Popper. Caldwell offers an alternative account of the change in Hayek's research direction in the paper "Hayek's Transformation" (1988b). Hutchison has not commented on this alternative.

5.   Hutchison asserts that there is evidence of an early (meaning post-1937 but prior to the 1950s) Popperian influence on Hayek's methodological writings. Caldwell asserts that no such influence is discernable, and that in fact much of Hayek's early work is incompatible with Popperian principles concerning the unity of science, the importance of empirical work, and so on.

6.   Both agree that there was a later Popperian influence. But we disagree about the extent of the influence. For Hutchison, the later Hayek came to accept Popperian principles pretty fully; in any case, nowhere does he identify any differences of opinion separating the two. My position is as follows:

I acknowledge that Hayek accepts two of Popper's ideas: that science follows a hypothetico-deductive method, and that falsifiability provides a demarcation criterion between science and nonscience. This implies that Hayek accepts that the differences between the natural and the social sciences are differences of degree, which is one of Hutchison's key claims. However, if one reads Hayek's writings on complex phenomena, it is clear that he believes the "differences in degree" to be serious ones, and crucially, that they *concern the ability of the social sciences to produce falsifiable theories.* Thus, though economics *is* a science (it meets Popper's demarcation criterion), it is also a field for which progress comes at the cost of producing theories which are less falsifiable.

So, is the later Hayek a Popperian, or something else? I focused on Hayek's qualifications and, as a result, I interpreted him as only a minimalist falsificationist. Other interpretations are clearly possible. But I thought it was strange for Hutchison to simply *ignore* the qualifications in his (1981) portrayal of "Hayek II," so I called him on it in section V of "Hayek the Falsificationist?." This exchange has given me no reason to change any of the views expressed in that paper.

ACKNOWLEDGMENT

I gratefully acknowledge that the research for this project was funded by a summer grant from the John William Pope Foundation.

REFERENCES

Boehm, Stephan. 1989. "Hayek on Knowledge, Equilibrium and Prices: Context and Impact." *Wirtschaftspolitische Blätter* 36: 201-213.
Caldwell, Bruce J. 1982. *Beyond Positivism: Economic Methodology in the Twentieth Century.* London: Allen and Unwin.
_____. 1984. "Praxeology and Its Critics: An Appraisal." *History of Political Economy* 16: 363-379.
_____. 1988a. "La Méthodologie de Hayek: Description, Evaluation et Interrogations." *Politique et Economie* 9: 71-85.
_____. 1988b. "Hayek's Transformation." *History of Political Economy* 20: 513-541.
_____. 1992. "Hayek the Falsificationist? A Refutation." Pp. 1-15 in *Research in the History of Economic Thought and Methodology*, edited by Warren Samuels. Greenwich, CT: JAI Press.
Gray, John. 1986. *Hayek on Liberty.* 2nd. ed. Oxford: Basil Blackwell.
Hayek, Friedrich A. 1948a. *Individualism and Economic Order.* Chicago: University of Chicago Press.
_____. 1948b. "Economics and Knowledge." In *Individualism and Economic Order,* pp. 33-56. Chicago: University of Chicago Press.
_____. 1948c. "The Facts of the Social Sciences." In *Individualism and Economic Order,* pp. 57-76. Chicago: University of Chicago Press.
_____. 1952. "Scientism and the Study of Society." In *The Counter-Revolution of Science.* Glencoe, IL: Free Press.
Hutchison, T.W. 1981. *The Politics and Philosophy of Economics: Marxians, Keynesians and Austrians.* Oxford: Basil Blackwell.
Mises, Ludwig von. 1962. *The Ultimate Foundations of Economic Science.* 2nd. ed. Kansas City: Sheed, Andrews, and McMeel.
_____. 1963. *Human Action: A Treatise on Economics.* 3rd. rev. ed. Chicago: Henry Regnery.

Popper, Karl. 1974. "Autobiography of Karl Popper." In *The Philosophy of Karl Popper,* Vol. 1, edited by P. Schilpp. La Salle, IL: Open Court.

Rotwein, Eugene. 1986. "Flirting with Apriorism: Caldwell on Mises." *History of Political Economy* 18: 669-73.

Weimer, W. and D. Palermo (eds.). 1982. *Cognition and the Symbolic Processes,* Vol. 2. Hillsdale, NJ: Erlbaum Associates.

White, Lawrence. 1977. "Methodology of the Austrian School." *Occasional Paper Series,* No. 1. New York: Center for Libertarian Studies.

KNOWLEDGE AS EXPECTED SURPRISE

A FRAMEWORK FOR INTRODUCING LEARNING IN ECONOMIC CHOICE

Marina Bianchi

INTRODUCTION

A major innovation in recent economic analysis has been the introduction of themes involving expectations, learning, information and knowledge. These themes single out a new range of problems that it is often difficult to handle and to incorporate coherently in traditional choice theory.

In endogenizing the role played by expectations, economic theory has to cope with many analytical difficulties. There is, for example, the complexity of modeling choice when, in the presence of uncertainty, the demands on an individual's computational abilities become unmanageably high (a problem particularly stressed by H. Simon, 1982). There is also the difficulty of defining a unique equilibrium path when, for example, the problem of expectations

Research in the History of Economic Thought and Methodology
Volume 10, pages 43-58.
Copyright © 1992 by JAI Press Inc.
All rights of reproduction in any form reserved.
ISBN: 0-55938-501-4

about others' expectations arises (see Townsend, 1978; Bray, 1983). These and other difficulties are well known.

What I want to stress in this paper is that economic theory encounters not just modeling difficulties but fundamental logical difficulties, too, in analyzing expectations and learning. In particular, while the introduction of expectations requires the specification of the process of learning underlying their formation, the assumptions about knowledge in the models typically used logically excludes an analysis of the process of learning. In other words, the analytical tools offered by our models are not of the sort needed to solve the basic problem which the theory itself suggests that we must handle.

If this view is correct, the necessary next step is to specify the missing process of learning that underlies decision processes. The approach taken here is that errors, competing theories, and discoveries play a crucial role in the process of acquiring knowledge and, more specifically, in modifying the given alternatives of choice.

What the economic consequences of this approach to learning are, and what different choice settings we may expect, are still matters to be considered. Some suggestions and reflections are offered here without pretending to be exhaustive. It is immediately evident that a choice process which involves learning will be very difficult to model. In fact, when a process of learning and revising errors is introduced into the choice process, we may expect that the choice set implies not only the given and known alternatives, but also the alternatives which are still undiscovered and must be searched for. The choice set seems therefore so enlarged as to render choice indeterminate.

This difficulty will be addressed, but it must be stressed that I do not intend to suggest here an alternative general theory of choice to replace the old one, but simply a different analytical framework in which specific cases of choice may be analyzed and receive a theoretical status they cannot have in the traditional framework. In this alternative view, choice analysis ends up enriched because we can specify the conditions under which alternative solutions may be adopted.

The second section of this paper analyzes the logical difficulties connected with the traditional way of representing learning. In the third section, I try to disentangle the structure of the learning process. This section is somewhat abstract. That penalty, however, seems to be necessary in order to exploit the logical potential of a different sequence-of-learning approach. In the fourth section, an attempt is made to trace the possible economic consequences of adopting this alternative approach to learning.

II

A. The Exclusion of the Learning Problem in Standard Models

The way in which economic theory treats the problem of knowledge and learning by economic agents has become clearer and more explicit with the elaboration of the Rational Expectations Hypothesis (REH). When the role of expectations in economic models is endogenized, there is implied also some learning process which underlies expectations formation (Cyert and De Groot, 1974). But this underlying process is introduced in a very special way.

In a recent article, Lucas (1987, p. 218) says: "Economics has tended to focus on situations in which the agent can be expected to 'know' or to have learned the consequences of different actions so that his observed choices reveal stable features of his underlying preferences." Thus the knowledge embedded in choice decisions is seen as the stable result of some already completed process of learning, a kind of stationary point of a dynamic, adaptive process.[1] In fact, if the same environment exhibits only stochastic, random shocks no systematic errors are rationally conceivable.

The result of this particular reconstruction of the process of knowledge acquisition and choice is, therefore, that as long as the environment remains unchanged, the decision rules underlying choice need not change either. Consequently, knowledge can be taken as a datum, a result that remains correct and stable ("true") until the appearance of an unexpected shock. Thus, while it is admitted that expectations are the result of some process of learning and of adaptation by individuals, the process itself may be safely left unspecified in the theory.[2]

B. A Logical Difficulty

The conclusion we have just reached is worth stressing, for, even if we do not know an individual's learning process, we know its result—that correct knowledge can be achieved—and this suffices as a basis for discussing choice. But in formulating the matter in this way, the problem is simply shifted to explaining why we may assume that people do reach "true" conclusions or select the best actions. The hidden answer is that the process, even if unanalyzed, can be described as involving a knowledge that grows with positive confirmations until the final correct result is reached. In Lucas' version, given a stable environment, this is where an agent reacts through an improving process of adaptation until the best choice is made. The consequence of this process of acquiring knowledge is that as long as we may suppose that people can accumulate enough information and experience to be able to model truly the pattern of the economy, how they learn—just how they formulate their hypotheses, discover problems and errors, and attempt new hypotheses and solutions—is no longer important.[3]

Being no longer concerned with how people acquire the (true) model, the problem has thus shifted to the truth-justification of the model (see, for example, Attfield, Demery, and Duck, 1985; Sargent, 1986). This has often meant simply showing that the model works well enough to enable people to act with it, to make "good" predictions, to perform in a coordinated way (Lucas and Prescott, 1971), but again, without attending to how the model is obtained. The question thus becomes: Do we have good reasons for saying that knowledge positively grows until the best result, the best performing model, is realized?

Economic theory gives an implicit "yes" in answer to this question, but no justification is offered to support it. If we look outside economic theory for an answer, as the same modelers of rational expectations suggest we ought, the cumulative-knowledge assumption turns out to be dubious. There are two grounds for challenging it.

First, it may be said that the process involved in this view of knowledge is empirically indefensible. Agents cannot be seen only as reacting passively to their environment, but must also be viewed as creating their choice sets. Learning means not only an accumulation of information, but implies also a selecting activity, an active attempt to circumscribe and solve problems. (This response can be found in the works of Shackle and of neo-Austrian economists in the economic field, and of cognitive theorists in the psychology of learning).[4]

The second response is that the implied process of acquiring knowledge is logically untenable: no logical justification exists for calling the prevailing model the best performing or true one. As is well known, given Hume's critique of induction and given that the positivist theory of knowledge has been discredited (or is held suspect—see Suppe, 1977, p. 4), knowledge cannot be seen as truth growing by the application of correspondence rules. Experience never validates a hypothesis. Knowledge can be seen only as proceeding by hypothetical truths and tentative solutions (as has been argued, for example, by Popper, 1972, and Agassi, 1975; see also Unwin, 1987); knowledge is a self-changing activity so long as experience can invalidate a hypothesis (for the economic implications of this critique, see Rutherford, 1984; Boland, 1986).

This second response deserves more attention, and I will take it up in a limited way again later. But for our purposes now, it is sufficient to stress that knowledge can be endogenously transformed by experience through our responses to errors and our selection of new alternative hypotheses. Further, if our knowledge is subject to change, then how this process proceeds, what kind of rules are followed, and what kind of change takes place, become the new questions to answer.[5]

To summarize. If it is assumed, as in the REH extension of traditional economic theory, that knowledge once acquired can be presumed to be certain and stable, the only problems we face are those associated with validating this knowledge. The way it is *acquired* simply becomes redundant and the procedures of learning by economic agents may safely be left unexplored. But if we abandon this hypothesis, as seems necessary once we acknowledge that there is no logical justification for the implied steady progress towards truth, then learning becomes relevant. Once we admit that knowledge proceeds through tentative, fallible solutions to problems, then such matters as how this knowledge is acquired and what rules are followed become important and must be analyzed. But if this understanding of the traditional view is correct, we are also left without any tools for analyzing learning on the basis of the traditional model of choice. We must search outside traditional economic theory for answers to questions about learning.

III

A. The Learning Process

When we shift theoretical interest from the result to the procedures of learning and acquiring knowledge, the first question to address is: What is the starting point of the process? When does a problem of knowledge arise for an agent? So formulated, the question no longer concerns the given initial "stock" of knowledge that we suppose agents to possess; rather, it is about the definition of the "problem-solving" situation agents have to face.

How can we define a problem-solving situation? The range of possible answers is very large. Answers emanate from the psychology of learning and the philosophy of knowledge. Many complexities and differences arise in these disciplines and they are therefore difficult to analyze succinctly. On the other hand, many of these difficulties can be circumvented simply by starting with a negative definition of the problem situation, a definition which will prove useful.

Following Popper (1972) and the reconstruction of learning attempted by Berkson and Wettersten (1984), we may define a problem situation simply as the experience of something contrary to our set of expectations, as the recognition of a limit to our knowledge. The problem situation is connected to a new event which the model(s) we possess cannot handle.

Consequently, a second stage of the process focuses on attempts to cope with this novelty.[6] In this step, a procedure of trial and error is begun in order to confront the available answers, to advance new hypotheses, and to select alternative solutions.

A third stage consists of the choice of a new solution. Here, we have the discovery of the alternative hypotheses that replace the old, inadequate ones. However, no new solution can be considered a definitive solution. It is fallible, hypothetical, and tentative, just another way of defining the limits of applicability and the range of answers our theory is able to handle.

The result of this process is, therefore, twofold. First, it alters the initial set of expectations and theories we hold. As a result of trial and error, a new range of alternative hypotheses may be found in this set, a range previously absent and unknown. Second, and more important, because of the conjectural character of this new solution, the learning process does not stop at this point. The discovery of the new tentative solution means at the same time that a new problem-solving situation is produced, a new error-revising activity is performed, a new range of hypothetical answers is created, and so on.

Learning is characterized here as a sequential, procedural structure, in which the resulting solution itself is the starting point of a new process of learning (Laudan, 1977). The process thus undergoes endogenous modification because of changes in the initial hypothesis produced by novelty and by the revision of error (Bateson, 1971). Once learning is represented in this way, we discover that many terms like problem, error, and change play quite specific new roles.

B. The Role of Problem and Change

How should we characterize a problem ? That is the key issue in any theory that regards learning as the result of an active attempt by individuals to solve problems by trial and error rather than a passive reception of information. This is a common thread among otherwise diverse approaches to learning. For example, it links cognitive theory and its translation into artificial intelligence (cf. the approach in Newell and Simon, 1972), Piaget's theory and Gestalt theory.[7]

In early attempts to criticize the stimulus-response theory of learning (for example, the efforts of Selz—see Berkson and Wettersten, 1984, pp. 108 ff.) a problem was defined essentially as a gap in our knowledge. The trial and error procedure was therefore an attempt to fill the gap correctly. Learning became a cumulative process towards the filling out of a structure.[8]

Theories such as Selz's positively stress the importance of problems and problem-solving activities. But what is lost in their way of representing learning by accumulation is the role of change. In fact, these same problem-solving procedures imply either no change in the previous knowledge or a change which is left unexplained. Learning is a completing-of-knowledge activity, and new knowledge is an extension of the old. How it changes by virtue of learning remains quite unspecified.

However, change begins to play a completely different role if we define the problem situation as a limitation of or a failure in the theory. This redefinition makes change the endogenous result of the activity of revising errors. The method of modifying the disconfirmed hypothesis becomes the very aim of the trial and error procedures.

Of course, this change activated by learning may happen at different levels and in different degrees. If, for example, we refer to the theory of individual economic choice, change may simply mean, given the choice set, a change in the parameters of choice (for example a *shift* from preferring one good to preferring another). Or, more deeply, it may mean a change in the choice set (when, for example, *new* preferences appear). Or, finally, it may mean a change in the way individuals structure their choice set (changing their habits and models of choices). All these examples refer to the phenomenon of consumers' hysteresis (Georgescu-Roegen, 1971, p. 126). However we characterize it, the fact that change occurs indicates that learning has taken place.

Therefore, the answer to the question: how do we learn from experience, is simply that we learn by discovering errors. The underlying view of knowledge in this conception is that of acquisition proceeding by disproof rather than by proof, by successful criticism, rather than by confirmation (on this point, see also Agassi, 1975).

The economic counterpart of this approach—as shown later—is that choice decisions can now incorporate the active search for new, unexplored solutions. Rather than seeing agents as passively adapting to exogenous changes in supposedly known conditions, these new solutions become part of an active search process.

C. The Role of Error

In this different way of representing learning, the role played by error is also different. In the view of knowledge as an accumulation of validated hypotheses, there is no role for errors; "even if the validated hypothesis turns out to be not so good, at the time it was the best validated it was rational to choose it" (Agassi, 1975, p. 68). Therefore, error means persistence in using an invalid hypothesis, a refusal to use the most validated available one.[9]

In the opposite view suggested here, error simply means a contrast between previous knowledge and a new observed fact. Error in principle might be expected on the basis of one's own limited, fallible knowledge.

So, while from a negative point of view, error can be seen as a failure, a disappointment of previous expectations, from a positive and active point of view, error amounts to the identification and discovery of a new, unexplored fact. Rather than reflecting irrational behavior, the identification of errors becomes a positive, creative phase of the process of knowledge acquisition. Errors in fact are informative, they are an "opportunity to learn" (Rutherford, 1988, p. 41). They delimit the explicative power of a theory as well as identifying the possible range of its further developments, applications, and discoveries.

The alternative solutions that result from the process of learning are new but they may not be completely unexpected. They are new, in the sense that they are contrary to previous knowledge. But they can be predicted, either from previous theories, as new tentative solutions to their failures, or from new theories, as their new conjectural content (à la Popper).[10]

New solutions and discoveries, therefore, are not thought of as completely exogenous events, and hence inexplicable and unpredictable. Rather, even though surprising, they may be expected and predicted as an endogenous result of knowledge which changes by virtue of specific error-eliminating activities. Popper (1972, pp. 239-240) has properly stressed that this is an evolutionary process. As he views it, new theories are like new tools, new standards of selection, new functions of language. Through them we solve our problems and acquire new means of control. But this control is a *plastic* control which works by trial and error, by critical assessment of competing theories.[11]

To sum up, the introduction of a new problem-solving situation has at times been described, far too simply and narrowly, as the introduction of new pieces of information into an already well-defined and structured corpus of knowledge. Absorbing information, knowledge is assumed to grow linearly and thus expand its domain. In this view, no role can be left for the potential change that the discovery of a new problem can activate in a determinate state of knowledge. Change is exogenous and unpredictable, and can therefore be left unexplained. However, if we can by contrast conceive of problems and novelties negatively as disconfirmed aspects of a tentative theory, change may be thought of positively as the endogenous result of the activity of revising error. The directions of change are neither random nor strictly deterministic, but are located in the specific problem situation of which they represent the possible developments and solutions.

D.   Error as Treated in Standard Economic Theory

We have seen that learning has no role in traditional economic theory. What about error as such? Is there any trace of our new approach in traditional theory?

We can distinguish three ways in which error appears in the traditional theory of choice. First, on the hypothesis of a stable, deterministic environment and certain knowledge, error simply does not occur. Committing errors, or persisting in errors, is irrational behavior. Under the hypothesis of rationality, this behavior can be excluded from economic analysis.

Second, however, we may regard error as a "rational" behavior. In an unstable environment with stochastically uncertain knowledge, errors do occur. But, so long as they are the result of random and exogenous shocks, they are inevitable. Errors are the only rational response to erratic, unexpected novelty. In the same situation, people do "correctly" err, and in the same manner. If error is random, people can not learn from it; but by the same token, if it is truly random, error again can be excluded from economic analysis.

Third, error can be conceived as a step toward rationality. It plays a role in the adaptive process which is supposed to lead to rationality. When Bayesian procedures are introduced to explain "how to learn to be rational," individuals do change their behavior as a result of the feedback yielded by error. But this exploratory activity and learning process starts only because individuals are supposed not to have utilized all their available information; hence, they are not rational. So, error is originated only by the presence of an initial irrational behavior: through time, and by correcting errors, individuals will learn the "right" and stable behavior, in which no more errors occur. Error, therefore, is only a temporary step to the correct results adhering to rationality.

If errors play no substantial role, as is shown in these three cases, neither does change. Again, as long as we may regard knowledge as certain, this knowledge does not change until the next exogenous shock. When change occurs, it simply represents the correction of a temporarily erroneous behavior; as such, it can be overlooked and subsumed in the end result.[12]

The same can be said for the role played by novelties. In rational-expectations models, novelties, like erratic policy changes, are represented as events that are unexpected but, once recognized, become a part of expectations and are therefore of no further consequence. They reflect, therefore, a simple assumed imperfection of knowledge linked to the intrinsic randomness of events, and do not reflect the inevitable evolution of knowledge as we search for solutions to problems (see Georgescu-Roegen, 1971, p. 122).[13]

Finally, and as a direct result, in this world of only exogenous change and unexpected novelties, the possibility of the appearance of new alternative solutions is outside the range of predictable behavior. Thus, by the analysis of the role performed by these phases of the process of learning in economic analysis, we reach the same conclusion as before, namely, that the learning process is hinted at in economic analysis but is, and has to be, left unanalyzed.[14]

What conclusions can be drawn from this way of rendering otiose the process of learning? One is that, as Frank Hahn has pointed out (1984, pp. 4, 122-123), many important economic processes simply cannot be handled. For example, we may think of the result in new classical models of the ineffectiveness of monetary policy. Consider this now as possibly linked to the absence of a process of learning. When there really is learning, different possibilities may be introduced as a direct result of a monetary shock. For example, if, as seems plausible, there is some positive correlation between financial support and search activity in new technologies (a point that Schumpeter, 1934, particularly stressed)[15], then a monetary policy which increases the former increases also the latter (and vice versa, of course, if the correlation turns out to be negative).

The same can be said of a sudden shock on the supply side (e.g. an oil price shock). This may translate into a decrease in real income in the absence of a learning procedure, but it may also mean a correction of the unexpected impulse through a search for new ways of lowering costs.

The possibility of these alternative solutions is well known; nevertheless, they remain unanalysed: they have no theoretical status inside the corpus of the traditional theory of choice. On the other hand, what seems to be implied by the alternative analysis we have advanced is that the process of learning, which is now admitted to exist in the process of choice and of forming expectations, is exactly what creates the possibility of these multiple alternatives being adopted.

This evolutionary learning process cannot be incorporated into the static equilibrium approach but requires new modelling procedures. These are beginning to appear, chiefly in the burgeoning literature on technological change and innovation (see, for example, Nelson and Winter , 1982, but also, as one among several helpful attempts, Dosi, Freeman, Silverberg and Soete, 1988, and references contained therein).[16]

E.   A Different Framework for Economic Choice

How can this different view of learning be translated into economic terms and issue in a different view of choice? Here I shall make some suggestions.

We may represent choice as a process of selecting known alternatives within a given framework (represented by habits, rules of behavior, or maximizing procedures). But we may also think of it as an activity of searching for new alternatives, given a specific problem-solving situation that has to be confronted. The process of search cannot be reduced to one of selecting known alternatives. As the activity of selection is only tentative, it always contains the possibility of disconfirmation through the appearance of a new problem.

The choice set must therefore involve not only the alternatives compatible with given knowledge, but also those latent alternatives which represent the possibility of expanding the domain of choice represented by existing models, preferences, and techniques. They remain undiscovered and unexplored until the presence of an error activates a process of search, which brings them to light.

The notion that a latent alternative might be exploited in the process of making choices is already recognized in economic literature. This happens, for example, when these latent alternatives exist and are known, but cannot be utilized because the cost is too high. A lowering of the opportunity cost of their utilization may permit what was previously ruled out.

But when the learning process is introduced, the range of alternatives may be enlarged in order to include *in addition* either alternatives that exist, but are still unknown, or alternatives that do not exist and must be discovered. Both these cases imply a learning procedure, and represent the choice process not only as a (re)allocation of resources among given alternatives, but also as an effort towards the introduction of new ones. The search for a lower opportunity cost of adopting a new technique, for example, transforms the first case into one of the second category.

Many economic examples that show this shift from thinking in terms of given alternatives toward thinking of new (latent ones) through a process of learning may be suggested. The familiar income effect, for instance, contains the possibility that an increase in income allows not only a greater expenditure on goods, but also a different one. In a different class of income, people learn to consume differently. As Milton Friedman pointed out many years ago, the standard theory of choice depends on a distinction being drawn between taste factors and opportunity factors. But an increase in income seems more often than not to alter both (Wallis and Friedman, 1942, p. 187). This example may be regarded as a case in which latent alternatives exist but are not yet experienced because of a specific budget constraint.

Again, economic phenomena such as consumer's surplus hint at the existence of latent alternatives which exist but cannot be exploited by the competitive producer. If we are in a situation of monopolistic competition, however, learning will consist in part in exploring their existence, and in testing and revising previous choices in order to exploit a new source of profits. At the same time, it is also true that in a situation of perfect competition, there is a strong incentive to undertake exploratory learning procedures bold enough to create a quite new situation. Thus we may see the deliberate abrogation of competitive conditions through the formation of coalitions. These examples show the existence of an enlarged set of alternatives when a learning procedure is operating.[17]

Other suggestions along these lines arise naturally if we abandon the strict analysis of individual choice and adopt a more complex analysis of choice involving interacting agents. Then, we cannot avoid confronting strategies among the agents, as is acknowledged in a game-theoretic approach. In such cases, too, we discover that when learning is introduced, the decision process turns out to involve an enlarged set of alternatives and solutions. For example, in noncooperative games of the prisoners' dilemma type, cooperative behavioral rules may be represented as a latent strategy which remains unadopted until a learning procedure (cf. contracting and recontracting) is introduced (as shown, for example, in Shubik, 1982, pp. 286 ff.). In the absence of learning, as in one-shot games, defection is the dominant strategy. Only an iterated game lets people discover that a better payoff may be linked to cooperation.

What still remains unexplained in this more articulated theory of decision is that the "learned" cooperative solution is not the end of the story. Once cooperation has been learned to be the best strategy, then the same learning renders "defection" a new latent strategy. In other words, individuals may learn new ways of adopting defecting behavior. Think again of a competitive firm. The firm adopts passive or cooperative behavior as long as it maximizes profit subject to the *given* set of constraints. But, in effect, it adopts a defecting behavior whenever it strives for new ways of making profits. A successful search for new markets, products, and techniques shows that a new rule of the game has been found in which defection is possible without the firm being subject to old forms of punishment. In the extreme, we have the practice of predatory product innovation, recognized in U.S. anti-trust law.

These examples all make the simple but important point that a wider range of alternatives is available in a framework that includes a learning procedure. This framework may in fact be seen as an analytical structure within which such alternatives can be systematically explored *without having to be dubbed exceptional.*

It may seem to some, however, that the choice process involving learning enlarges so indefinitely the domain of choice as to render it vacuous and lacking in cognitive explanatory power. A major objection to the standard way of representing choice under uncertainty (principally Simon's critique, 1982) is that the complexity of the environment calls for an increased power of computation on the part of individuals. Before long, the choice set comes to include such a number of variables to control that decision-taking itself is made virtually impossible. The solution suggested by Simon is to restrict the range of alternatives available. Choice, therefore, is said to reflect bounds: we choose subject to acquired, simple behavioral rules (on this point, see Heiner, 1983; Loasby, 1989). By contrast, in the solution I have suggested here, the alternatives available may seem to be uncontrollably increased.

But this is only apparently true. First, in removing the hypothesis of perfect knowledge, we are also freed from assuming the complex abilities that this strong assumption forces upon us. Because learning is considered a procedure of trials and errors, we can introduce a correction mechanism into the choice process which registers and reflects the presence of particular problem-solving situations. We choose in quite specific problem-defined contexts; hence, choice is never limitless. Moreover, the appearance of new alternatives is strictly linked to the existing framework of hypotheses, knowledge, and models available. It is not unbounded, casual, and unexpected as in the old framework. In other words, in the alternative proposed here, we gain in freedom and flexibility, not in complexity.

IV. CONCLUSIONS

I have argued that when learning is introduced into economic choice, choice becomes strictly problem-related and involves an active search for new alternatives. As I have represented the process of learning itself, learning starts when a loss of confidence (stemming from the recognition of a limit) in the existing model(s) activates a process of search for new alternatives and solutions. Several elements play a role here.

There is the specific problem situation, which originates the loss of confidence in the model. Then there is the nature of error, which embodies the specific failures of the model. Finally, there are the latent explorable alternatives suggested by the model and by its competitors. All these elements are fundamental to the search process. Together, they circumscribe and define the new direction of search and the possible solutions.

One result of introducing the process of learning into the choice process is that the given initial conditions of choice are changed endogenously. Another is that the choice set may now include the latent alternatives that the process of search activates and discovers.

In general, economic problems connected with change—change in preferences, innovative technologies, changes in rules of behavior, shifting strategies—find in learning as here reconstructed an analytical framework in which they may be treated endogenously.

NOTES

1. "Technically, I think of economics as studying decision rules that are steady states of some adaptive process, decision rules that are found to work over a range of situations and hence are no longer revised as more experience accumulates" (Lucas, 1987, p. 218).

2. However, if we study the literature on REH more closely, we can see that doubts arise about the stability of the environment, the distribution of information, the degree of reliability in knowledge (whether the process is an actual-true process, whether the parameters are known, as for example in the Bayesian analysis applied to REH (Cyert and De Groot, 1974; Townsend, 1978), but never about how to know this process, whether this knowledge can be reached or not. For a critical analysis of Bayesian procedures, see Binmore (1987, p. 211) and Bianchi (1987).

3. On this problem, Simon (1987, p. 27) says: "if we postulate an objective description of the world as it really is, and if we assume that the decision maker's computational powers are unlimited, then two important consequences follow. First, we do not need to distinguish between the real world and the decision maker's perception of it: he or she perceives the world as it really is. Second, we can predict the choices that will be made by a rational decision maker entirely from our knowledge of the real world and without a knowledge of the decision maker's perception or modes of calculation." But these effective consequences seem to derive from the particular process of knowledge entailed in this theory, rather than from the unrealistic assumption of the agent's unlimited computational powers.

4. In learning experiments, subjects are shown to typically organize cognitive structures, rather than to form associations (cf. Gregg, 1974).

5. What I am describing is a logical paradox. REH attempts to endogenize a problem, the agent's learning procedure, in a theory that cannot handle it. The theory cannot cope with the very problem which it contends is important. On the role of paradoxes and anomalies in the neo-Walrasian analysis see de Marchi (1987) where it is clearly stressed how repeated paradoxes which have arisen in the theory left the core of the theory always unchanged. Here, too, the introduction of the new problem of learning leaves the theory apparently modified but the problem really unanalyzed.

6. In laboratory experiments on the learning of computational sequence, for example, it is the analysis of the mean number of errors made by different groups of subjects which is used to indicate how different sorts of pretraining affect learning and cognitive abilities (Greeno, 1974, p. 270).

7. But see also Kelly and his notion of an inquiring person, one who is attempting to come to grips with the world by an empirical process, who seeks to discern patterns in the complex world (Earl, 1983, p. 119).

8. As we read in Simon and Lea (1974, p. 108): "Problem-solving activity can be described as a search through the space...of knowledge states, until a state is reached that provides the solution to the problem. In general, each node reached contains a little more knowledge than those reached previously and the links connecting the nodes are search and inference processes that add new knowledge to the previous store."

9. See also Laudan (1981, p. 184) who states that most seventeenth and eighteenth century authors "were convinced that an appropriate (i.e., infallible) logic of discovery would automatically authenticate its products"; see also Langlois (1982, p. 76).

10. See Suppe (1974, p. 169) "our discoveries are guided by theory, rather than theories being discoveries due to observation"; see also Agassi (1975) and Berkson and Wettersten (1984).

11. In Popper's own felicitous formulation: "Not only do our theories contol us, but we can control our theories...: there is a kind of *feed-back* here" (1972, p. 240). Because we submit to a theory after deliberation, after critical discussion of alternatives, theories are forms of control "which can eliminate errors without killing the organism; and it makes it possible, ultimately, for our hypotheses to die in our stead" (p. 244).

12. See Bausor (1988 p. 17): "Basic cognitive processes, as well as the other psychological bases for choices, all remain essentially unmoved personal properties."

13. Georgescu-Roegen also distinguishes between risk, which describes situations where the outcome is unknown but there is nothing essentially novel, and uncertainty, which applies to cases where the outcome has never been observed and, hence, may involve novelty (1971, p. 122).

14. Here and elsewhere in this article, I am implicitly assuming that the same learning procedure is shared by the theorist and the economic agent. REH theorists, of course, use this assumption. Nonetheless, it has not been examined very extensively. We need more analyses of how real economic agents and organizations learn. As a useful example see the discussion of learning by organizations in Argyris (1982). See, also, the process conception of rationality developed with reference to philosophy of science in Wible (1984).

15. On the role of money in the process of innovation, interpreted as a sequential process of learning, see the important work on innovative choice of Amendola and Gaffard (1988). Here, the increase in demand for a liquid asset that follows the breaking of a sequence is interpreted as that moment of the search activity in which the agent has lost confidence in the existing model, but has not yet found something new. If and when a new conviction is reached, then the asset(s) are used to enable an innovative choice to be made (pp. 43-46).

16. Attempts to justify in evolutionary terms equilibrium solutions have occasionally been made by neoclassical theorists. An example is Friedman's well known argument that only profit-maximizing firms can be expected to survive. Another is Lucas' argument quoted above (1987, pp. 3-4 and n. 1). But, as Winter points out (1971, p. 244), if there is no more consistency over time in the behavior of individual firms than a random or habitual behavior, then success in any single time period implies nothing about success in a future time period. For details, and certain limitations, in the models of Nelson and Winter, see Bianchi (1990) and a recent article by Moss (1990).

17. That the examples do not represent exceptional behavioral solutions is shown by the presence of economic activities like advertising: its role may be seen as a way either of exploiting the existence of latent but not-adopted alternatives for choice, or of creating new ones.

ACKNOWLEDGMENT

I would like to thank for their helpful comments Ken Binmore, Bob Coats, Neil de Marchi, Tony Smith, Ian Steedman, Malcolm Rutherford, Roy Weintraub, and the participants in the Duke Economic Thought Workshop. The precise suggestions of two anonymous referees have enhanced the argument. This research has been conducted with support from the Italian National Research Center (C.N.R.).

REFERENCES

Amendola, M., and J. Gaffard. 1988. *The Innovative Choice.* London: Basil Blackwell.

Agassi, J. 1975. *Science in Flux.* Dordrecht Holland: D. Reidel.

Argyris, C. 1982. *Reasoning, Learning and Action.* San Francisco: Jossey-Bass.

Attfield, C.L.F., D. Demery, N.W. Duck. 1985. *Rational Expectations in Macroeconomics.* London: Basil Blackwell.

Bateson, G. 1971. "The Logical Categories of Learning and Communication." In *Steps to an Ecology of Mind,* edited by G. Bateson. San Francisco: Chandler.

Bausor, R. 1988. "Human Adaptability and Economic Surprise." Pp. 11-33 in *Psychological Economics. Developments, Tensions, Prospects,* edited by P.E. Earl. Boston: Kluwer Academic Publisher.

Berkson, W., and J. Wettersten. 1984. *Learning from Error.* La Salle: Open Court.

Bianchi, M. 1987. "Conoscenza e cambiamento nei modelli con aspettative." *Note Economiche* 2, 1-22.

—————. 1990. "The Unsatisfactoriness of Satisficing: from Bounded Rationality to Innovative Rationality." *Review of Political Economy* 2(2): 149-167.

Binmore, K. 1987. "Modeling Rational Players" (Parts I and II). *Economics and Philosophy.* 3:179-214.

Boland, L.A. 1986. *Methodology for a New Microeconomics.* London: Allen & Unwin.

Bray, M. 1983. "Convergence to Rational Expectations Equilibrium." Pp. 123-137 in *Individual Forecasting and Aggregate Outcomes,* edited by R. Frydman and E.S. Phelps. Cambridge: Cambridge University Press.

Cyert, R.M., and M.H. De Groot. 1974. "Rational Expectation and Bayesian Analysis." *Journal of Political Economy,* 82(May-June): 521-536.

de Marchi, N. 1987. "Paradoxes and Anomalies." Pp. 796-799 in *The New Palgrave; A Dictionary of Economics* Vol. 3, edited by J. Eatwell, M. Milgate, and P. Newman. London: MacMillan.

Dosi, G., C. Freeman, R. Nelson, G. Silverberg, and L. Soete. (eds). 1988. *Technical Change and Economic Theory* London: F. Pinter.

Earl, P. E. 1983. *The Economic Imagination: Towards a Behavioral Analysis of Choice.* New York: M.E. Sharpe.

Georgescu-Roegen, N. 1971. *The Entropy Law and the Economic Process.* Cambridge MA: Harvard University Press.

Greeno, J.G. 1974. "Processes of Learning and Comprehension." Pp. 17-28 in *Knowledge and Cognition,* edited by L. W. Gregg. New York: Wiley & Sons.

Gregg, L.W. (ed.). 1974. *Knowledge and Cognition.* New York: Wiley & Sons.

Hahn, F. 1984. *Equilibrium and Macroeconomics.* Oxford: Basil Blackwell.

Heiner, R.A. 1983. "The Origin of Predictable Behavior." *American Economic Review* 73(Sept.):560-595.

Langlois, R.N. 1982. "Austrian Economics. Comment on Rizzo." In *Method, Process, and Austrian Economics: Essays in Honor of Ludwig von Mises,* edited by I. Kirzner. Lexington, MA: Lexington Books.

Laudan, L. 1977. *Progress and Its Problems. Toward a Theory of Scientific Growth.* Berkeley: University of California Press.

————. 1981. *Science and Hypothesis. Historical Essays on Scientific Methodology.* Dordrecht, Holland: D. Reidel.

Loasby, B.J. 1989. "Herbert Simon's Human Rationality." Pp. 1-17 In *Research in the History of Economic Thought and Methodology,* Vol. 6, edited by W. Samuels. Greenwich, CT: JAI Press.

Lucas, R.E. Jr., and E.C. Prescott. 1971. "Investment under Uncertainty." *Econometrica.* 39 (September):659-681.

Lucas, R.E. Jr. 1987. "Adaptive Behavior and Economic Theory." Pp. 217-242 in *Rational Choice. The Contrast between Economics and Psychology,* edited by R.M. Hogarth and M.W. Reder. Chicago: University of Chicago Press.

Moss, S. 1990. "Equilibrium, Evolution and Learning." *Journal of Economic Behavior and Organization* 1:97-116.

Nelson, R.R. and S.G. Winter. 1982. *An Evolutionary Theory of Economic Change.* Cambridge MA: Belknap.

Newell, A., and H. A. Simon. 1972. *Human Problem Solving.* Englewood Cliffs, NJ: Prentice-Hall.

Piaget, J. 1967. "The Role of the Concept of Equilibrium in Psychological Explication." in *Six Psychological Studies.* New York: Random House.

Popper, K.R. 1972. "Of Clouds and Clocks." In *Objective Knowledge. An Evolutionary Approach.* Oxford: Clarendon Press.

Rutherford, M. 1984. "Rational Expectations and Keynesian Uncertainty," *Journal of Post Keynesian Economics* 3(Spring):377-387.

————. 1988. "Learning and Decision-Making in Economics and Psychology: A Methodological Perspective." Pp. 35-54 in *Psychological Economics,* edited by P.E. Earl. Boston: Kluwer Academic Publisher.

Sargent, T.J. 1986. *Rational Expectations and Inflation.* New York: Harper & Row.

Schumpeter, J.A. 1934. *The Theory of Capitalistic Development.* Cambridge: Harvard University Press.

Shubik, M. 1982. *Game Theory in the Social Sciences.* Cambridge, MA: MIT Press.

Simon, H.A. 1982. *Models of Bounded Rationality.* Cambridge MA: MIT Press.

————. 1987. "Rationality in Psychology and Economics." Pp. 25-40 in *Rational Choice,* edited by R.M. Hogarth and M.W. Reder. Chicago: University of Chicago Press.

Simon, H.A., and G., Lea. 1974. "Problem Solving and Rule Induction: A Unified View." Pp. 105-128 in *Knowledge and Cognition,* edited by L.W. Gregg. New York: Wiley & Sons.

Suppe, F. 1977. *The Structure of Scientific Theories.* 2nd ed. Urbana, IL: University of Illinois Press.

Townsend, R.M. 1978. "Market Anticipations, Rational Expectations, and Bayesian Analysis." *International Economic Review.* 19(June):481-494.

Unwin, N. 1987. "Beyond Truth: Toward a New Conception of Knowledge and Communication." *Mind* 96(383):299-317.

Wallis, W.A. and M. Friedman. 1942. "The Empirical Derivation of Indifference Functions." Pp. 175-189 in *Studies in Mathematical Economics and Econometrics,* edited by O.Lange, F.McIntyre, Th.O.Yntema. Chicago: University of Chicago Press.

Wible, J.R. 1984. "Towards a Process Conception of Rationality in Economics and Science." *Review of Social Economy* 2:89-104.

Winter, S. G. 1971. "Satisficing, Selection and the Innovating Remnant." *Quarterly Journal of Economics* 85:237-261.

THE "VALUE-ADDED" APPROACH TO THE PROHIBITION OF WORK ON THE SABBATH

Yaffa Machnes Reif

Rabbinic Judaism, known today as Orthodox Judaism, defines itself as a system of laws. The Torah, or Law, includes a civil and criminal code as well as a moral and ethical one, and the idiom of religious texts is basically legalistic. This requires that precise definitions be given even to the terminology of ritual and that principles of rational analysis be adduced. At times, this presents an interesting contrast to the methods of teaching of religions which define themselves primarily as faiths.

These interpretations of the commandments and the details of their observance were transmitted orally for centuries until it was felt necessary to commit them to writing lest they be forgotten as a result of the persecution of the Jewish scholars. Among the impetuses for recording this oral tradition were the destruction of the Temple in 70 C.E. and the persecution by Hadrian in 135 C.E. During the latter, the study of the Torah was forbidden. In 210 C.E. Rabbi Judah Ha-Nasi (The Patriarch) published a compilation of the

Research in the History of Economic Thought and Methodology
Volume 10, pages 59-63.
Copyright © 1992 by JAI Press Inc.
All rights of reproduction in any form reserved.
ISBN: 0-55938-501-4

tradition. Known as the *Mishna,* it became authoritative and the basis for the Talmud and all subsequent Jewish religious doctrine (Encylopedia Judaica). The Mishna, Tractate Avot 1:1, claims its authority as the result of an unbroken line of transmission from Moses on Mount Sinai through the prophets and on to the rabbis who are quoted in the Mishna itself.

The biblical commandment that every seventh day be a day of "rest" is basic to both Judaism and Christianity. It is forbidden to work on the Sabbath. However, the Rabbinic approach has led to a definition of "work" which presages by almost two thousand years a basic concept of modern economics.

The sources which we quote will show that what is forbidden as work on the Sabbath is the creation of significant added value. The formulation in the literature began to take shape even before the Common Era and is based on examples from actual daily life in Palestine. A combination of the general principles and the examples given bring us to the modern economic concept of added value.

The main feature of the Sabbath commandment is the prohibition of work. In the Bible, Exodus 20:9, it is written:

Six days shalt thou labor and do all your work,
but the seventh day is a sabbath unto the Lord thy
God. Thou shalt not do any *work*...

The rabbis of the time sought an exact definition of *work,* since their approach was that of legal scholars, and they exploited another context of the word to do so. Exodus 35:21 refers to the "*work* of the tent of meeting," that is, the various operations and tasks that were done in building the Sanctuary for prayer and sacrifices. This building was dismanteled and reassembled a number of times during the forty years that the Children of Israel wandered in the desert before entering the Promised Land.

The rabbis then used this context to define *work* as any of the operations, tasks, or crafts employed in the building or subsequent dismantlings and reassemblies of the Sanctuary. In the Mishna, Tractate Shabbat 7:2, thirty-nine general categories are listed such as sowing, plowing, reaping (of the plants from which raw materials were derived), weaving, sewing, writing, striking with a hammer, carrying and throwing from one domain to another, and so forth. In Tractate Shabbat 7:2 we find:

The main labors [prohibited on the Sabbath] are forty less one: sowing, ploughing, reaping, binding sheaves, threshing winnowing, cleansing, grinding, sifting, kneading, baking, shearing (the) wool and washing or beating or dyeing it, spinning, weaving, making two loops, weaving two threads, separating two threads, tying a knot or loosening one, sewing two stitches, tearing in order to sew two stitches, hunting a deer and slaughtering it or flaying it or salting it or curing its skin or scraping it or cutting it up, writing two letters, erasing in order to write two letters, building, demolishing, extinguishing, kindling, striking with a hammer, carrying from one domain into another. These are the chief labors [forbidden on the Sabbath]—forty less one.

By studying the list, we find that labors are defined in agriculture, in industry, and even in services. The last labor describes transportation.

The thirty-nine main labors are called "fathers" and they have "offspring," derivative acts. For example, writing is a father and one of its offspring is borrowing, which may lead to writing. (Shabbat 23:1):

A man may borrow from his fellow jars of wine or jars of oil, only provided that he does not say to him, 'Lend me', and likewise a woman of her neighbor loaves of bread. And if he do not trust him, he leaves his cloak with him and settles the account with him after the Sabbath.

The concept of added value in performance is not at all abstract. For each *work*, a set minimum amount is defined. For example, to violate the prohibition against writing one must write two letters of the alphabet. Writing only one letter or parts of two letters is not permitted, but it would not involve any legal or moral penalties.

The basis of the two-letter amount demonstrates clearly the notion of added value. In reassembling the sanctuary, the various parts had to be put together in their original form. To facilitate this, the boards were lettered at the appropriate points, and two *alephs* or two *beths*, and so forth, were matched.[1] Writing just one letter would have been meaningless. Two letters made reassembly possible (Rabbi Yose, Shabbat 12.3).

All labors are characterized by creating a positive added value, and those who perform any such labor for the sole purpose of destruction or spoiling are not guilty of violating the Sabbath. On the other hand, if a destructive act is performed as part of a process of subsequent restoration, then the perpetrator is guilty. The amount for the destructive act is then the same as for a positive one. Thus, erasing two letters does not constitute a violation unless one intends to write something new in its place, in which case the erasing adds value (for more examples, see Eider, 1970.)[1]

The definition of *work* is independent of the effort or of the quantity of inputs used. A person might exert a lot of effort and employ an enormous quantity of production factors, but unless one creates a positive added value, one is not guilty of doing *work*.[2]

The rabbis knew that labors like curing and feeding have significant positive added value but nevertheless ruled that the injunction to save life dominates Sabbath observance (Shabbat 2:5):

If one extinguish the light for fear of idolators, or of robbers, or of melancholia, or to enable a sick person to sleep, he is absolved. But if his intention be to spare the lamp, or to save the oil, or to preserve the wick, he is guilty.

A similar ruling applies to penned animals (Shabbat 24:3):

> ... nor may they place water before bees or before pigeons that are in a dovecote, but they may set it before geese and fowls and before domesticated pigeons.

Their explanation is that bees can find their own water but birds that are kept indoors and cannot find water for themselves should be fed on the Sabbath.

The prohibition of *work* is not given only to the goodwill and conscience of the Jew. Courts punished people who were found working on the Sabbath. The criterion for positive added value thus had to be objective and observable by an outsider. A person may think and plan many activities without any offense being done but is not allowed to give orders to others to work, even if the workers are not Jewish (for whom the Sabbath prohibitions do not apply) (Shabbat 23:3):

> A man may not hire laborers on the Sabbath, nor may a man say to his fellow that he should hire for him laborers.

The order which others may hear is forbidden while personal thoughts by oneself are allowed.

Another example for the objective criterion is the following (Shabbat 13.3):

> Whosoever rends in his anger or for his dead and those who act destructively are not culpable.

Although the destructive activity eases the anger and increases the welfare of the one who does it, according to objective criteria, one has decreased the value of the cloth. Therefore, this action is not defined as *work*. Making a person feel better by a destructive act and contemplation about planning future work are not defined as *work* since outsiders cannot observe any added value.

The Mishna requires that the creation done as some acts of *work* should exist at least until the end of the Sabbath so it allows another objective inspection.

(Shabbat 12:1):
This is the general principle: anyone who performs work and his work is stable on the Sabbath is culpable.

(Shabbat 12:5):
If anyone wrote with liquids, or with fruit juice or in road dust or in writer's sand, or with anything else that does not last, he is not guilty of violating the Sabbath.

(Shabbat 15:2):
Rabbi Judah laid down a general principle: they are not culpable for tying a knot that is not permanent.

These examples show the wish to describe an objective criterion that can be observed by outsiders who can define someone else's *work*. This aspect is also very important in modern economic life. At present, we use the calculation of "added value" to measure the part of a firm in producing the Gross National Product and as a basis to levy a tax. This modern legal approach to the subject of added value also requires a clear definition as observed by an outsider, an accountant or a tax inspector. Examination may take place after production is completed.

As we see, the idea of the added-value approach was found in Jewish legal literature of approximately 1800 years ago. The recording of the theological tradition was done to transmit these precepts to future generations. The investigation of the development of legislation in many communities points to the influence of the legal arrangements described in the *Mishna*. This theological book has been learned daily by generations all over the world and its legal traditions may also be of interest to contemporary economists.

NOTES

1. The Hebrew alphabet also served as a numbering system, as, for example, Roman numerals. Arabic numerals, derived from the Indian number system, came into use much later.

2. A woman who takes a needle with an eye from her house to the public domain or a signet ring is liable for punishment for profaning the Sabbath. But if the needle did not have an eye or the ring had no seal, then she is not liable (Shabbat 6.1, 3). The eye of the needle and the seal of the ring characterize these tools as factors in creating value in contrast to an eyeless needle or a seal-less ring, which can be considered only as jewelry.

REFERENCES

Eider, Shimon D. 1970. *Halachos of Shabbos*. Lakewood, N.J.
Enclyclopaedia Judaica. 1971. Vol. 12, pp. 93-109. Jerusalem, Keter Publishing House.
Mishna Shabath, Order Moed. 1963. Translation by P. Blackman. New York: The Judaica Press.

SOCIALISM AND THE MARKET:

JOHN STRACHEY'S REVOLUTION BY REASON, 1925

Noel Thompson

I

Again and again in the political and economic literature of the 1920s the sentiment was expressed that the Great War had created the possibility of making the world anew. Thus, Sidney Webb, in 1929, wrote that "with all its evils" the war had "broke[n] up the ice pack and thrown the whole world open to new ideas" while, in a similar vein, the Conservative authors of *Industry and Trade,* 1927 wrote that it had "shattered preconceived economic notions, proved possible theoretic impossibilites, removed irremovable barriers, created new and undreamt of situations" (Boothby, Macmillan, and Stanley, 1927, p. 35). The conviction that the world should be remade was no longer seen as the monopoly of utopian dreamers. It had become a general belief, so accepted and so much a part of the climate of opinion that it had almost acquired the status of the commonsensical. Thus, those whose business it had

Research in the History of Economic Thought and Methodology
Volume 10, pages 65-87.
Copyright © 1992 by JAI Press Inc.
All rights of reproduction in any form reserved.
ISBN: 0-55938-501-4

always been to talk and write of the building of a new world acquired a new authority. They had become the realists and those who sought to preserve or reconstruct the antebellum status quo were now the dreamers. In this general sense, socialists and socialism were the beneficiaries of the Great War.

In other and more specific ways,however, the disparate strains which comprised the corpus of British socialist thought drew strength from the war experience. For Fabian socialists, the war provided proof positive that it was through the extension of purposive social control over economic activity that communally beneficial objects could be attained. It was the efficient, scientific administration of economic activity, not the anarchic, self-interested pursuit of gain, which had won the war and which had, therefore, proved itself best able to manage the peace. Further, the war seemed to have confirmed the Fabian prediction of an ineluctable progress towards collectivism in modern industrial societies. Thus, by the war's end the munitions industry, investment, the railways, food distribution and the allocation of labor were to a greater or lesser extent under the control of the state (Peden, 1985, pp. 37-39). The social control of economic activity had indeed been extended and there seemed to be no reason to expect that the trend would be reversed. Works such as Sidney and Beatrice Webb's (1920a) *Constitution for the Socialist Commonwealth of Great Britain* and the second edition of their *Industrial Democracy* (1920b), are testimony to the intellectual self-confidence of Webbian Fabian socialism in the immediate post-war period, while documents such as *Labour and the New Social Order* (1918) bear witness to the profound influence which that stain of socialism had within the ranks of the Labour Party.[1] Beatrice was, of course, exaggerating when in December 1917 she described Sidney as the intellectual leader of the Labour Party, but not overmuch (Pelling, 1968, p. 42).

Other currents of socialist thinking, too, were given fresh impetus by the war. For if the expanded administrative authority wielded by the state was welcomed by some as the harbinger of a rational management of economic activity, others saw it as confirming their view that such an aggregation of power would lay the basis for political authoritarianism. If the state had ordered economic life during the Great War, it had also used coercion to impose that order; if the war had been prosecuted more effectively through the expansion of state power, it had been at the expense of tanks on Glaswegian streets and the general infringement of civil and economic liberties. It is understandable, therefore, that guild socialism, which stressed the need for the decentralisation of power through the autonomy of productive units organised and managed by those who worked in them, should have expanded its influence and enjoyed the popularity which it did after 1918. Certainly there was a prodigious torrent of guild socialist literature emanating from the National Guilds League and writers such as G.D.H. Cole, A.R. Orage, A.J. Penty, S.G. Hobson and others,[2] and guild socialist ideas did, for a time, exert considerable influence within the ranks of the Independent Labour Party (I.L.P.), which actually accepted the guild socialist programme in April, 1922.[3] In addition, there was the practical and, for a time, successful expression of guild socialism through the National Guild of Builders, while the period 1917-1920 saw the acceptance, by several major unions, of the idea that publicly owned industries could and should be jointly managed by representatives of the state and the workers (Glass, 1966, p. 48). However, for all this, the postwar influence of guild socialism was short-lived. Unemployment rose rapidly in the aftermath of the short post-war boom and the trade unions, the means by which many guild socialists hoped to give effect to their ideas, were weakened. Further, with the economic downturn came the collapse of the National Guild of Builders in 1923. In such circumstances the notion of workers' autonomy lost both its attractiveness and its plausibility.[4]

In addition, there were the divisions within guild socialism. On the ideological plane, there was the division between the medievalism of a writer like A.J. Penty[5] with his roots in the works of Carlyle, Ruskin, and Morris (see Glass, 1966, p. 9), and the modernism of G.D.H. Cole, who predicated his vision of a decentralised socialism upon a modern industrial economy. On the strategic plane, too, there were divisions between those who favoured a combative, if necessary, revolutionary approach to the creation of guild socialism and others who saw it as triumphing through the slow permeation of the values of craftsmanship. In this context, the 1920s were to see the movement of many of those guild socialists imbued with revolutionary spirit into the ranks of the British Communist Party, which was founded in 1921.

Also, in the 1920s G.D.H. Cole effectively abandoned guild socialism, which thereby lost its most prolific propagandist. *Guild Socialism Restated* (Cole 1920) represented his last major attempt to give expression to the theory and practice of guild socialism. It also made plain, perhaps even to Cole, the Kafkaesque bureaucratic complexities of a decentralised marketless socialism, where decisions on pricing, output, allocation, distribution, and so forth were supposedly made on the basis of direct and complete knowledge of all the decisions being taken by the guilds and cooperatives and associations of guilds and cooperatives of which the guild socialists' commonwealth was to be composed (see Glass, 1966, pp. 128fff). As such, the work made clear the absence from guild socialism of a practical socialist political economy applicable to the problems confronting the British working class in a modern, complex industrial economy. This absence must be seen as a further factor, and an important one, in guild socialism's rapid demise.

Marxian socialism in Britain also emerged strengthened from the war. The revolution in Russia, hyperinflation, and economic breakdown over much of central and eastern Europe, abortive revolutions in Germany, Hungary, and Austria, all seemed to vindicate the Marxian prediction of capitalism's inevitable and imminent destruction. Further, communism could no longer be dismissed as existing only in the fantasies of socialist ideologues, for it was a reality over a sixth of the globe. It now had, as one commentator has put it, "the test of experience" (Macintyre, 1980, p. 221). In Britain, the flow of Marxist literature became a torrent, fed by the work of a new generation of British Marxist writers—Noah Ablett (1919), Maurice Dobb (1922), Mark Starr (1925), Eden and William Paul, J.T. Walton Newbold—and by the English translations of the works of Russian communists such as Malinowski's (A.A. Bogdanov, 1925) *Short Course of Economic Science* and Bukharin and Preobrahzhensky's (1969) *ABC of Communism* in 1922. However, while the general influence of Marxism within the British Labour Movement in this period should not be discounted, particularly its critique of capitalism, its constructive proposals had little impact.[6] Leaving aside the antipathy of the greater part of the labor movement to notions such as the revolutionary overthrow of capitalism and the dictatorship of the proletariat, a centrally planned economy of the kind which the Marxists proposed had little obvious relevance to the immediate problems which the British working class confronted in the early 1920s.

Like the guild socialists, Marxist writers saw the market as anarchic, wasteful, and, through its commoditization of labor, essentially exploitative. The abandonment of the market was, therefore, a fundamental prerequisite for the construction of a socialist economy. "Production ... would be consciously and systematically organised by society as a whole" (Bogdanov, 1925, p. 383) with state ownership of the means of production, distribution, and exchange providing the basis and power necessary for the scientific ordering of economic life. Replacing the information-disseminating role of the market would be a "gigantic statistical bureau whose decisions would be based upon exact calculations" (Bogdanov, 1925, p. 383); such calculations proceeding on the basis of physical magnitudes or, where valuation was necessary, units of labor time. The general objective was "a new society (which) will be based not on exchange but on a natural self-sufficing economy"; under communism, "production is not for the market but for use... we no longer have *commodities* but only *products* (p. 389)." Thus, as with the guild socialists, the abandonment of the market shackled Marxian communism to a constructive political economy which, leaving aside the problems in a British context of establishing the political preconditions for its implementation, simply contained little of practical relevance either in terms of how to effect the transition from a capitalist to a socialist economy or as regards the particular problem which loomed increasingly large on labour's economic horizon—unemployment.

It was Fabian or Webbian socialism which, therefore, provided the political economy of the British Labour Movement. It was, for example, Fabian economic thinking—critical and constructive—which dominated the economic literature produced by the Labour Party in the 1920s. Yet, the political economy of Fabian socialism, too, had its limitations, limitations which also derived from a determination to banish the market from within the walls of the New Jerusalem. Thus, for the Fabians, raised as many had been on a diet of indigenous positivism, the evolutionary views of T.H. Huxley, and the achievements of natural science, there was, inevitably, something intellectually repugnant about a so-called (market) system where final consequences were the outcome of self-interested, atomistic decision-making on the basis of relative or total ignorance.[8] Such a "system" was viewed as intrinsically "anarchic and unsound" (Shaw, 1962, p. 67). It was characterized throughout by "competitive confusion" with "unco-ordinated centres of management, unaware of each others proceedings and constantly in conflict and confusion" (Shaw, 1896, p. 11; Webb and Webb, 1920, p. 324). What resulted, inevitably, was waste and inefficiency, made all the worse by the contemporary emergence of "rings, corners, syndicates, pools and monopolies" whose interest lay in underproduction (Olivier, 1904, p. 12). This was no way to run a complex industrial economy. Ultimately, the market must be replaced by the rational, social control of economic activity. Thus, it was believed that municipalization, nationalization and the growth of consumer cooperatives would effect a "gradual substitution of organised co-operation for the anarchy of the competitive struggles"; "the organisation of ... public industry" was to be extended to "supplant more and more the individual producer... with production ordered and rational instead of anarchical ... as it is today (Shaw, 1962, p. 192)." This incrementalist strategy, this death of market capitalism by a thousand bureaucratic cuts, might necessitate the continued use of the market en route to an economic life rationally ordered by an enlightened, socially motivated bureaucracy. However, insofar as the market continued to exist, it was very much something to be tolerated rather than embraced and used for socialist purposes.[9]

In contrast to guild and Marxian socialism, this conception of socialism in terms of the piecemeal ordering of economic life by the gradual attenuation of the market, did at least provide an economic strategy which, as the war period had shown, could be practically applied. The Fabian vision of socialism may have been bureaucratic, elitist, uninspiring, and potentially authoritarian but it did at least furnish a set of attainable objectives. It is true that the *inevitability* of this kind of gradualism had been called into question in the immediate post-war period. Thus, with the cessation of hostilities in 1918, controls were lifted and state intervention in the economy considerably reduced (Lowe, 1978), but there was no obvious reason why such retrograde developments could not be reversed and, as works such as E.M.H. Lloyds's *Experiments in State Control* (1920) and *Stabilisation, an economic policy* (1923) showed, a wealth of experience in the public regulation and control of economic activity had already been acquired during the war and could be drawn on in the future.

A more serious problem with a socialist economic strategy, such as that of Fabianism, which had as its essence the incremental destruction of the market, was that it effectively ruled out a range of policy prescriptions which a more positive attitude to the market would have permitted. Specifically, the Fabian conception of the market as the *fons et origo* of the economic ills afflicting the nation inevitably called into question the ultimate efficacy of expansionary monetary and fiscal policies using such a flawed transmission mechanism. Thus, for example, the Fabian emphasis upon 'the anarchic irresponsibility of the private consumer" (Webb and Webb, 1920b, p. 674) the ignorance of the private entrepreneur producing for an uncertain market, the endemic nature of monopoly within contemporary capitalism, and the deleterious allocative, distributive, and disequilibrating consequences of these phenomena,[10] all impled that expansionary monetary and fiscal policies would simply exacerbate poverty, waste, and depression rather than cure them. Such policies were effectively ruled out, therefore, as a means of advancing the socialist cause.

It is true, of course, that in the Minority Report of the Poor Law Commission (Penty, 1909), Beatrice Webb had outlined a contracyclical public expenditure strategy. However, it must be emphasized that this represented an attempt to "regularise" demand and to reduce the level of cyclical disorder which afflicted the contemporary economy. The aim was not to embark on an expansionary monetary or fiscal policy. As the *Report* made clear the objective was not to raise permanently the level of aggregate demand and thence the level of economic activity but to dampen the amplitude of the economic cycle. "We think," stated the authors of the *Report,* "that the government can do a great deal to *regularise* the aggregate demand for labour as between one year and another by a more deliberate arrangement of its orders for work of a capital nature (Penty, 1905-1909, 1909, p. 1195)." This would involve "no artificial stimulus to demand," no addition to aggregate demand over time, but simply a change in the timing of part of 150 million pounds annual expenditure of "national and local authorities" on "works and services" (p. 1196). It is true that the authors of the *Minority Report* believed that such a contracyclical policy would 'actually increase, taking the ten years (of the assumed economic cycle) as a whole, the demand for labour over and above what it would have been' but they (Beatrice Webb among them) were quite adamant that it would not touch the roots of the problems of unemployment and poverty which were, and would remain, "a constant feature of industry and commerce as at *present administered"* (pp. 1198, 1177).

So, in its attitude to the market, Fabian socialist political economy ruled out a whole range of macroeconomic policy options; policy options which, it will be shown in the next section, allowed: first the dovetailing of short-run measures of social amelioration with a major advance toward the ultimate objective of a socialist commonwealth; second, the possibility of national rather than piecemeal planning; and third, escape from an uninspiring and constraining incrementalism.

To summarize. The early 1920s saw the demise of guild socialism while Marxian socialism, in terms of its constructive economic proposals, had little influence and less relevance. It was Fabianism, therefore, with all its analytical and prescriptive limitations, which emerged in this period as the dominant strain of socialist political economy. Yet, in the mid 1920s the hegemony of Fabianism was to be profoundly challenged; by a socialist political economy which in its preparedness to use the market to effect socialist change, in its grasp of and willingness to utilize the market's transformative potentialities to build a New Jerusalem, broke not only with Fabianism but with the previous hundred years of socialist economic writing in Britain. It is with one of the key figures" in this challenge and with one of the major contributions to it, that this paper is concerned. That figure is John Strachey and the work, *Revolution by Reason,* which was written and published in 1925.

II

Evelyn John St. Loe Strachey was the son of John St. Loe Strachey, editor of the *Spectator* and purveyor of an undiluted, laissez-faire liberalism which in its almost complete opposition to state intervention in the economic life of the nation and its virulent antagonism to anything which smacked of socialism, was a positive anachronism even prior to the Great War.[12] The father's great mentor on matters of political economy was Frederic Bastiat, his political heroes were Cobden and Gladstone, and he saw Lloyd George's People's Budget as the "degeneration of Liberalism into Jacobinism" (Morris, 1986, pp. 131-132). Yet, it was through his father and the *Spectator* that Strachey was to meet men such as E.D. Morel and Arthur Ponsonby, liberals who in despair at the sacrifice of liberal values by the Party during the war had gravitated, usually via the Union for Democratic Control, into the Labour Party.[13] Thus, it was under the influence of such men that Strachey, after an initial flirtation with Conservatism at Oxford, joined the Labour Party (1924) and became a socialist.[14] It was shortly after this that *Revolution by Reason* (1925) was written.

It is, of course, misleading to write of John Strachey's *Revolution by Reason.* The work was dedicated "To O.M. who may one day do the things of which we dream" and, as Strachey made clear, his *Revolution by Reason* was very largely the amplification of the ideas contained in a small pamphlet with the same title, written by Oswald Mosley and published some months earlier.[15] There are minor differences between the two works (see Skidelsky, 1975, p. 146); but it would be fair to say that both the short pamphlet and the longer work were a product of the joint thinking of Mosley and Strachey and, indeed, Strachey's *Revolution by Reason* was written and discussed during a holiday which the two had together in Venice in the summer of 1925. Commentators have speculated on the relative intellectual inputs of the two men and come to different conclusions.[16] However, while interesting, this question is a largely unimportant one as far as this paper is concerned. Both Mosley and Strachey had the necessary intellectual equipment and both had read the kind of works which would have allowed them to write *Revolution by Reason*. In any case, as Skidelsky (1975, p. 138) has written with regard to their intellectual relationship, "when two minds meet and sparks fly who can say which one started the blaze."

Let us begin then with Strachey's critique of capitalism and, in particular, his discussion of its macroeconomic deficiencies. The substance of this critique is to be found in chapters 3 and 8 of the work. Chapter 3 provided an unoriginal, lowest-common-denominator, socialist assault upon capitalism, that linked the competitive pressures of the system with the reduction of wages to a subsistence level and that phenomenon to a chronic underconsumption which eventuated in glutted markets, unemployed labor, and underutilized productive capacity. Thus, under capitalism, the "owner" of the means of production "who manages to produce cheapest, will undersell and so gradually exterminate the other producers. But, other things being equal, the cost of labour... will be the determining factor in the price at which they sell their products." Therefore, the "owner" who pays the laborers he hires the lowest amount, short of a wage which makes them physically or mentally insufficient, will tend to undersell and so ruin the "owner" who pays higher wages (pp. 62-63). "With one hand," therefore, wrote Strachey, "the Capitalist system gives us the means to create undreamt of quantities of things we all need but on the other hand it has to withhold from ninety percent of the population the "purchasing power" needed to secure more than the barest minimum of them. And our Captains of Industry wonder why it seems impossible to dispose of their products" (pp. 70-71). The only reason why the system did manage on occasion to function near full capacity was because of the safety valve of exports which allowed "owners" to dispose of products surplus to domestic requirements in noncapitalist markets at profitable prices. However, for Strachey, this safety valve was now rapidly shutting. "Today," he wrote, "this arrangement is rapidly becoming impracticable. The Capitalists' islands in the great unexploited ocean of "Non Capitalism" are becoming ever more numerous and more extensive. Indeed it might be truer today to say that the world was a great Capitalistic, industrial continent in which there were still lakes and seas of unexploited areas." Thus, "The great Capitalist States [were] like shipwrecked mariners on a desert island watching their store of water (markets) slowly decreasing and eyeing each other suspiciously, knowing that sooner or later it must come to a fight to the death for the last drop.... it is this special feature of Capitalism.... this necessity to export owing to an inability to distribute enough purchasing power to provide an effective home market for the goods it produces... which keeps the world in a state of bellicose disorder" (pp. 72-73).[17] Thus, like many previous socialist writers Strachey, linked competition, exploitation, working-class impoverishment, underconsumption and the breakdown of capitalism.

Chapter 8, however, provided a more interesting and more sophisticated explanation of general economic depressions; such phenomena were seen as resulting from an imbalance between the producer and consumer-goods sectors of the economy, an imbalance which derived from a maldistribution of wealth in favor of those, the rich, with a high propensity to save. For Strachey, such a maldistribution of wealth led to high levels of investment, a rapid increase in the output of producer goods which, when absorbed by industry, led to an expansion of the output of final products beyond that for which there was a demand at existing prices. The resulting price deflation in the consumer-goods sector led "owners" to contract productive activity, with the appreciation of the real value of their investible funds encouraging them to hold those funds in more liquid form and, in this way, depression was transmitted to the economy as a whole. In Strachey's words "if it (a nation) saves more than a certain proportion of its income *it will not spend enough money to absorb the goods and services produced by its existing instruments of production without a general fall in prices.* But a general fall in prices acts... as the most effective check to further productive activity. Hence if its proportion of savings is too high it will year by year add to those instruments of production and therefore to its productive capacity, without increasing at all its power of consumption at a given price-level. *Thus it will soon be able to produce much more than it allowed itself to consume"* (pp. 223-224, original emphasis).

However, whether or not we accept Strachey's more or less sophisticated explanation of capitalist depressions, the point to make is that as capitalism's fundamental flaw lay in an endogenously generated chronic tendency to a deficient demand for final products, the way forward necessarily lay in expanding the purchasing power of the masses, that is, those with a high propensity to consume. As he put it in *Revolution by Reason,"* what we need are not new secondary, but new primary goods. Any policy which will lead to an increase of the ratio of spending to saving will produce a higher percentage of primary goods to secondary goods. And this is exactly what is most necessary for our economic well-being... the essential condition for the working of modern industrial production *is the creation and maintenance of a steady and widespread effective demand for goods and services"* (pp. 229-230). So how was this to be done?

For Strachey, it was necessary to increase the purchasing power of those with a high propensity to consume, namely, the working classes. This was to be done by the creation of "a public banking system capable of giving such accommodation to industry as will enable it to increase the purchasing power of the workers" and by the establishment of "an Economic Council" which would ensure the use of such monetary facilities "by forcing up... money wages and other receipts ... of the working-classes' (p. 128) through the imposition of progressively rising minimum wage levels upon productive enterprises (p. 133ff).

Crucial to the success of such a strategy was the expansion of production pari passu with demand, and to achieve, this Strachey recognized it would be necessary that "the increased demand [should] flow into the market steadily and gradually" and that there should also be a comparable sustained increase in the nation's capacity to produce. Here, again, the Economic Council would play a crucial role assuming responsibility for establishing the "total potential production of 'useful' goods and services with existing productive resources" while calculating simultaneously "what real minimum wage at present prices this would make possible for the worker." In addition, the Economic Council would be responsible for the coordination, control, and reorganization of industry where that was necessary to allow it to cope with a substantial increase in working-class purchasing power. Here it could and would use the leverage furnished by a public banking system, which would provide the financial assistance necessary for firms and industries to meet their minimum wage obligations only on condition that capitalist producers "accept[ed] the Council and co-operated logically with it in a general policy of National Planning" (pp. 135-136, 162). Thus, it would promote rationalization, eliminating wasteful duplication, inefficient practices, and obsolescent plant and equipment— telling, for example, "the mine owners and the Railway Companies that they must create national corporations which would provide the community with the essential commodity coal, and the essential service, transport, with the utmost efficiency possible" (p. 145).

The key to this transformative strategy and, indeed, much of its political and social appeal lay in its use of the market. Thus it avoided, as Strachey saw it, the overconcentration of economic power which characterized state socialism and, therefore, any suggestion of the coercive conscription of labor or the imposition of a particular basket of goods and services on the consumer. Planning there would be, but it would be planning in response to the expressed needs of the working classes mediated by the market rather than planning imposed by a state bureaucracy. For Strachey to begin by nationalizing and then planning "the organisation of supply" was "to begin at the wrong end" (p. 149). To do so would involve the creation of "an economic dictatorship under which an all-wise Government provides only those things it thinks its citizens *might* want. We prefer to let those citizens express their real wants by giving them purchasing power" (p. 150). Thus, enhanced purchasing power gave to the working classes, through the medium of the market, real control over the allocation of the nation's resources.

In this context, therefore, planning would be "planning not in the abstract, but to meet demand... There is an essential difference between planning to meet a genuine, spontaneously manifested new demand and planning to give people what the Government thinks they ought to want" (p. 179). The market could be relied upon, therefore, to transmit to producers and the Economic Council the information necessary for a speedy transformation of the British economy; it would be the market which showed how production might best be geared to maximize social welfare rather than to satisfy bourgeois, bureaucratic, or aristocratic whim. Thus a redistribution of purchasing power in favor of the working class would reverse the existing situation where "firms which are engaged in the production of luxuries for the rich are numerous, prosperous and expanding" while "firms...engaged in the production of necessaries for the workers are comparatively few, small and decaying." Working-class purchasing power expressed through the medium of the market would therefore serve as "the instrument...[needed to] effect that vast transformation in industry which we have seen to be so difficult and so necessary, *and yet effect it without any violent upheaval*"; "the increase and transference of purchasing power is all that is needed. The issue of advances to undertakings of a socially useful character would follow quite automatically" (pp. 111, 121, 242, emphasis added).

Finally the market was to play a fundamental role as regards the external consequences of and constraints upon such an expansionary strategy. Thus, Strachey recognized that part of an increase in working-class purchasing power would leak abroad on imports and, *ceteris paribus,* a balance of payments deficit would result. Strachey's solution was, however, to allow the value of sterling to fluctuate in the international currency market until the exchange rate was such as to restore the balance between exports and imports. This "process of the automatic balancing of imports and exports by means of movements of the exchange" was seen by Strachey as operating "rapidly and effectively...Therefore, there can be no considerable danger that our exports and imports should not balance" (p. 199).

A social and economic revolution could therefore be effected and the capitalist character of production fundamentally changed without the wholesale destruction of economic, social, and political institutions and without the suffering and excesses of a violent social upheaval. The Economic Council and the public banking system would play their roles in smoothing the path of this revolution but its *fons et origo* was to be the new economic power of the masses expressed through the market. What Strachey preached, therefore, was not so much a revolution by reason as a revolution by the impersonal forces of a sanitized market. The contrast with previous socialist attitudes to the market could not be more stark.

The consequences of this departure from most previous socialist thinking about the market were profoundly liberating. First, this use of the market allowed Strachey to escape the enervating incrementalism of Fabian political economy. Thus, the channeling of increased purchasing power through a sanitized market would effect an immediate and profound change in the structure, organization and control of economic life and in the economic power wielded by the working class. Second, Strachey's strategy embodied a notion of overall national planning (absent from Fabianism) and furnished a basis for the rational economic calculation of planners which avoided the major problems of planning under marketless socialism where calculation was assumed to proceed in terms of units of labor time or physical magnitudes. So, at one and the same time, Strachey's preparedness to utilize the market rendered his socialist political economy immune from the attack of writers such as Hayek and von Mises and allowed him to avoid those barren theoretical deserts into which the mirage of an operationally effective labor theory of value had tempted previous generations of socialist thinkers. Third, Strachey's theoretical use of a market allowed him to propose a strategy which avoided a limiting emphasis on nationalization and municipalization as *the* means of subjecting economic activity to social control, which characterized Fabianism. Fourth, Strachey's use of the market allowed him to circumvent those criticisms which focussed on the authoritarian consequences of centralized economic decision-making by permitting considerable autonomy to a range of privately owned enterprises. Fifth, the market, as Strachey used it, enabled him to endow the concept of consumer sovereignty with both social purpose and practical macroeconomic significance. Sixth, Strachey's use of the market was the key element in his ability to dovetail short-term, electorally attractive, measures of social amelioration with longer-term socialist objectives relating to the control and restructuring of the economy. Finally, using the idea of fluctuating exchange rates, Strachey was able to confront and discuss the external consequences of his socialist economic strategy in a way which socialist political economy, until that time, had signally failed to do.

Why was Strachey able to make this liberating break with previous traditions of socialist political economy? Here it is of fundamental importance to understand the nature of Strachey's intellectual debts, for Strachey was, and remained throughout his life, a synthetic rather than an original thinker, and in order to understand his intellectual trajectory, it is always important to be clear as to which stars, at any given moment, loomed largest in his ideological firmament.

III

When *Revolution by Reason* has been noticed by commentators, its intellectual roots have been alluded to rather than discussed. In one respect, this is understandable. Strachey himself made clear where his indebtedness lay and quite explicitly acknowledged the influence of Marx and Keynes in chapters 2 and 3 of the work and, indeed, his book may be read as an attempt to marry the critical economic analysis of Marx with the positive policy prescriptions of Keynes' *Tract*. However, the whole story is more complex and a telling of it goes a long way to explaining why Strachey was able to break from the traditions of economic thinking which had characterized British socialism in the nineteenth and early twentieth centuries. Thus, leaving aside, for the moment, the obvious and undoubted impact of Keynes and the possible importance of Marx, there stalks throughout *Revolution* the spirit of Hobson, both in Strachey's discussion of the economic dynamics of imperial expansion and his explanation of economic depressions in terms of a structural imbalance between the producer and consumer-goods sectors of the economy. Further, there is the possible general influence of new liberalism, both as it emanated from the pen of Hobson and from those with whom Strachey was in close contact in the early 1920s. There are also shades of Major Douglas in Strachey's notice of the monetary dimension of underconsumption and in his emphasis upon the need for the money supply to expand *pari passu* with output.

Let us begin, however, with Marx. Strachey himself stated at the end of chapter 3 that he had given "the classical Marxian case against the private ownership of the means of production" (p. 87) and that chapter represents a substantial part of the critical base upon which the prescriptive superstructure of the constructive proposals was erected. Yet, in this chapter, neither the theory of exploitation as he expounds it nor the theory of capitalist crisis derived from it are distinctively Marxian. Thus, the linking of the competitive pressures upon wages and the exploitation of labor with underconsumption and crisis was the lowest common denominator of socialist political economy from the time of Owen and the Smithian socialists onward. In addition, while Strachey makes the odd allusion to class and class struggle, he was quick to suggest that when discussing the "major division of society—it will be better to use...the term "Owner" instead of "Capitalist" and "Labourer" instead of "Worker", as being more conducive to clear thinking than the better-known terms, *around which a certain warmth of emotional association has arisen"* (p. 58). Also, where Marxian terminology such as the "means of production" is deployed, Strachey is careful to put it in inverted commas and, indeed, the work in general is pleasantly free from the kind of jargon which usually deformed the prose style of these British socialists upon whom Marx had had substantial influence. Also, in terms of its policy prescriptions, the work is clearly as un-Marxian as it is un-Fabian in character. There is the preparedness to work with the market, there is the willingness to allow a significant measure of economic power to remain in the hands of the capitalist class and, with respect to economic activity, an acceptance of a plurality of organizational forms. In addition, there is Strachey's antipathy to revolution and revolutionary struggle in the British context and his emphasis on the need for a middle way between revolution and the inevitability of gradualness. Also, there is Strachey's suspicion of the centralization of economic decision-making as regards the allocation of resources and his emphasis upon the notion of consumer sovereignty. Finally, as regards Marx's direct influence upon Strachey, there is Strachey's admission some years later (1931) in a letter to Palme Dutt that at that time he was "attempting to educate himself by acquiring the ground of Marxist theory. For example, I am in the middle of the second volume of *Das Capital*, which I am ashamed to say I have never read before"[18] The "never read before" may, of course, simply apply to volume two but if so, this at least suggests that Strachey was not influenced at first hand by Marx's simple and extended reproduction schema. If Marx was influential, therefore, his influence was of the most undifferentiated kind. There is nothing distinctively Marxist about *Revolution by Reason*.

By contrast, the influence of Keynes was obvious and, on the prescriptive side, decisive. Strachey admitted that the quantity theory of money which he elaborated in chapter 2 of *Revolution* and which provided the theoretical underpinning for his monetary-policy prescriptions, was that "properly" and "succintly stated by Keynes in the *Tract* as $n = p (k + rk')$" (Thomas, 1973, p. 35).

In addition, Strachey's whole understanding of the micro and macroeconomic consequences of falling prices, his rejection of the notion that price deflation was a smoothly acting, immediately operative equilibrating mechanism, and his advocacy of a managed currency were all derived with acknowledgement from Keynes (p. 150). It is true that Strachey also made mention of Hawtrey and in particular Robertson[19] as having influenced his thinking on money but there is no reason to doubt that the influence of Keynes was both profound and paramount. In addition, it was almost certainly from the *Tract* too that he acquired the idea of fluctuating exchange rates as both a necessary adjunct to a managed currency and a means of eliminating the balance of payments problems which might arise from the pursuit of an expansionary strategy.

But what of the possibility that Strachey's thinking on monetary policy was influenced by the social creditism of Major Douglas? Certainly, the economic thinking of Douglas had an impact in I.L.P. circles in the post-war period. His ideas were discussed at I.L.P. conferences in the early 1920s and as late as 1924 such a conference approved "an inquiry into the Douglas system."[20] However, by the time Strachey joined the Labour Party, some time in 1924, the influence of Douglas and social creditism within the Party was on the wane. The Labour Party in 1922 published *Labour and Social Credit,* attacking Douglas' ideas, while in the same year they were also dismissed by J.A. Hobson in an article in the *Socialist Review*. However, it must nonetheless be admitted that social creditism was part and parcel of the intellectual atmosphere which Strachey breathed in the early 1920s. In addition, at least two commentators have suggested that in this period, Strachey was strongly influenced by Douglas. Thus, J.E. King in a recent article (King and Dutton, 1986, p. 261) has referred to Strachey as a disciple of Douglas while J.T. Finlay (1972, p. 154) has gone so far as to state that in the mid-1920s, "Strachey...was all but a Social Creditor, citing as evidence his appearance at a 1926 conference of the Economic Freedom League."[21]

Here, it must be said straightaway that Strachey makes no mention of the Major in *Revolution by Reason*, a work which generously acknowledges the contribution which other writers—R.G. Hawtrey, D.H. Robertson and, most obviously, J.M. Keynes—had made to Strachey's thinking on monetary theory. Second, Strachey made quite clear that monetary reform would not of itself solve the macroeconomic difficulties which confronted capitalism, while Douglas (1920, p. 86) was convinced that "a modified system of credit could transform the world in five years."[22] Third, Strachey's explanation of general economic depression made no reference to Douglas' A + B theorem and was essentially non-monetary and, therefore, fundamentally different from that of Douglas. Finally, Strachey's desire for a nationalized banking system was inconsistent with Douglas' views on financial reform, while Douglas' views on the need to establish "true prices" were alien to the whole ethos of *Revolution by Reason*.[23]

Strachey did accept that the money supply should increase in line with the capacity of the nation to produce,[24] and he would certainly have agreed with Douglas (1920, p. 91) that, "The only sane limit to the issue of credit for use as purchasing-power is the limitation imposed by the ability to deliver the goods for which it forms an effective demand, providing the community agrees to their manufacture." However, while acknowledging the need for monetary policy to be conducted in such a manner, Strachey was quick to point out that "it must not be supposed that Mr. Keynes has overlooked this aspect of the monetary question" (p. 52). Such views, Strachey argued, were implicit in the *Tract on Monetary Reform*. Even on this point, therefore, it would be wrong to credit Douglas with any significant impact upon Strachey's thinking, except in so far as he reinforced ideas already derived from Keynes.

The possible influence of Hobson on Strachey is much more problematic. Hobson's influence upon economic thinking within the I.L.P. in the early 1920s was undoubtedly profound and, in contrast to social creditism, it waxed rather than waned in the period immediately prior to the publication of *Revolution by Reason*. Thus Hobson's macroeconomic critique of capitalism and his policy prescriptions found expression both in the *Socialist Review* and *The New Leader* in the period 1922-1923: his *Economics of Unemployment* was published in 1922, and he made a decisive contribution to the I.L.P. Living Wage Commission, the report of which, *The Living Wage* was published in 1926.[25] H.N. Brailsford, who worked with Hobson on the Living Wage Commission and who acknowledged Hobson's influence in a prefatory note to *Socialism for Today*, may have been another conduit for the Hobsonian influences on Strachey, for Strachey lists Brailsford amongst the friends who helped "with suggestions, corrections and objections." It is, therefore, almost inconceivable that Strachey could have been unaware of

Hobson's economic thinking. It is true that, like Douglas, Hobson was not cited in *Revolution* and, in addition, Strachey concluded his exposition of the causes of general depression under capitalism by describing it as "the classical Marxian case against the private ownership of the means of production." However, the simple, underconsumptionist explanation of depression contained in chapter 3 has little in common with those advanced by either Marx or Hobson but is of a largely undifferentiated kind which could have come from all or none of a variety of sources.[26] This chapter did also contain an explanation for "imperialism" and "war" which is reminiscent of Hobson's *Imperialism* but Strachey again links this explanation to the name of Marx. In addition, it must be said that, in discussing the economic imperatives for imperialism, Strachey places particular emphasis upon the capitalist pursuit of foreign markets to realize the value of products in the absence of domestic outlets, an economic theory of imperialism which has much more in common with Luxemburg than it has with either Hobson or Lenin, who locate the economic dynamic of imperialism in the frenetic capitalist search for more profitable outlets for investible funds than those to be found domestically.

Yet, if chapter 3 of *Revolution* linked unemployment and the general underutilization of resources with a tendency to deficient aggregate demand due to working-class impoverishment, Strachey, in the final chapter of the work, furnishes an explanation of depression which, in its whole emphasis upon the maldistribution of wealth and the sectoral imbalance which results from that, is more nearly Hobsonian. As he expounds his explanation of general economic depression in chapter 8, there is, quite clearly, as with Hobson, no suggestion of deficient *aggregate* demand. Rather, the origins of macroeconomic dysfunction are conceived in terms of an imbalance between the producer and consumer-goods sectors which in turn arises from the maldistribution of wealth (pp. 222-223). What is different about Strachey is that, more overtly than Hobson, he confronts the classical view of the price mechanism's equilibrating function in such circumstances, arguing, courtesy of Keynes, that by altering entrepreneurial behaviour, it is the deflation of prices which causes and prolongs the depression of economic activity. Nevertheless, Hobsonian inflections abound in chapter 8.

However, it is not simply the chapter 8 analysis of the roots of macroeconomic depression which suggests Hobsonian influence but the whole notion that the imbalance between the producer and consumer-goods sectors could be rectified by an expansion of working-class purchasing power. Hobson and Strachey differed, of course, in the manner in which they sought to achieve this. Strachey, courtesy of Keynes, emphasized an expansionary monetary policy while Hobson stressed a redistributive fiscal policy, but the essential object was the same for both. Here, again, there is a strong suggestion of Hobsonian influence.

In this context, it is also interesting to note the respective reactions of Hobson to *Revolution by Reason* and Strachey to *The Living Wage* of Hobson, et al. Hobson (1925) in a *New Leader* review of *Revolution by Reason* titled "Can We Tame and Harness Capitalism?", argued that "it may well seem that the amount and nature of the control involved in these proposals demands an efficiency and honesty of expert officialdom that would be unattainable."[27] But his criticism did not extend to Strachey's analysis of the problem nor to the general, market-mediated, expansionary thrust of his proposals. Strachey's views on the *Living Wage* proposals were expressed at the 1926 I.L.P. Conference where he stated that they were valuable but inadequate, lacking the kind of monetary policy which Strachey saw as a necessary concomitant of the expansion of aggregate demand (Macintyre, 1974, p. 43). However, it is quite clear that Strachey accepted the general analysis of the problems afflicting contemporary capitalism advanced in *The Living Wage* and also the notion that the way forward lay through the expansion of working-class purchasing power.

The balance sheet of likely influences therefore looks like this. The influence of Marxian socialism was of the most general kind. C.H. Douglas *may* have had some impact upon Strachey's thinking on monetary questions. J.A. Hobson, directly or indirectly, almost certainly did have a considerable impact while the influence of Keynes was, undoubtedly, considerable. Leaving aside Douglas, therefore, the decisive intellectual influences upon Strachey would seem to have been those which emanated from "new liberal" thinkers.

Here, too, a more general influence may be noted. For, as mentioned, it was the "new liberals" such as E.D. Morel and Arthur Ponsonby who played a major part in Strachey's decision to join the Labour Party in 1924 (see Macintyre, 1976, n. 34). They, along with others, such as J.A. Hobson, migrated from the Liberal to the Labour Party during and immediately after the war. Their impact upon the Party in the immediate post-war period was considerable and, in the years prior to the publication of *Revolution by Reason,* they helped create a climate of opinion which, in the view of subsequent commentators, was more open to alternatives than the Fabian conception of socialism which had previously and, after 1927, was subsequently to dominate the Party.[28]

In this context, it should also be pointed out that in the early 1920s, Mosley had worked closely with the Liberals. He was also a member of the 1917 Club[29] which, in addition to Ponsonby and Morel, included Hobson as an active member. At this time, as Skidelsky (1975, p. 109) has phrased it, liberal ideas "certainly gripped him intellectually." It is true that the liberalism which gripped him was of a traditional kind based on low tariffs, currency stabilization, and Gladstonian fiscal orthodoxy but while, by the end of 1923, Mosley had certainly rejected the latter two components of the economic philosophy of traditional liberalism, he continued to adhere to free-trade principles. It seems reasonable to suggest that this flirtation with liberalism would have rendered him more amenable to the thinking of someone like Keynes and more generally sympathetic to the virtues of the market. Given the closeness of their intellectual relationship, such sympathies may also have left their mark on Strachey.

One final point may be made in support of reading *Revolution by Reason* as an early contribution to the political economy of liberal, market socialism and that is Strachey's own assessment of the work. Thus Strachey's interpretation, given admittedly from the standpoint of a dogmatic communist in 1934, saw it as "utterly bereft of that indispensable instrument of social analysis, the Marxist and Leninist critique of capitalism; soaked on the contrary in the most specious sophistries of the capitalist economists" (Strachey, 1934, pp. 67-68). Some allowance must be made here, of course, for the ritualistic breast-beating of the convert but it is interesting that Strachey's view has been echoed by a more recent commentator who has described the work as "a brilliant attempt to explore the possibilities of orthodox economic ideas"; (Booth, 1983, p. 37) though it should be stressed that it was an "exploration" with the goal of socialism always very much in mind.

Returning then to the question as to why Strachey broke with previous traditions of socialist economic thinking on the market, it can now be suggested that it was the influence, direct or indirect, of new liberals and the new liberalism which was decisive. It was this influence which freed Strachey from the aversion to the market which characterised Fabian, guild and Marxian socialism, allowing him to discuss its socialist potentialities and so to formulate a liberal-socialist political economy in which the market played a central and prescriptively liberating role. *Revolution by Reason*, therefore, provides a classic example of Liberalism's capacity in this period to transcend the constricting confines of a Liberal Party which was becoming a political irrelevance. It also exemplifies the way in which, in the words of one commentator, the "major ingredients of liberal ideology were preserved, even developed, within the scope of British socialist thought" (Freeden, 1986, p. 209).

However, the post-war challenge of liberal socialism failed, in the sense that it failed to undermine the hegemony of Fabian political economy within the Labour Party. Thus, the 1927 Labour Party Conference at Blackpool effectively rejected the liberal socialist strategy by throwing out the Living Wage proposals. It was, therefore, on the basis of an essentially Fabian economic strategy that Labour fought and won the 1929 election, a strategy whose bankruptcy was clearly manifest by 1931. Yet, from the late 1930s onwards, the advocates of liberal socialism once again sought to win over the Labour Party. It is interesting that, after a period in the wilderness of inter-war Marxism-Leninism, John Strachey should have played a prominent part in this renewed ideological challenge.[30]

NOTES

1. See the assessment of Booth and Pack (1985, p. 8):

In typically Webbian terms *Labour and the New Social Order* proclaimed the end of the capitalist system and its replacement by a new, co-operative, planned equitable, democratic social order.

On the quintessentially Fabian nature of this document, see also R. Miliband (1972, p. 62).

2. G.D.H. Cole in fact wrote eleven books on guild socialism in the period 1913-21. Post-war books by A.J. Penty include *Guilds and the Social Crisis* (1919) and *Guilds, Trade and Agriculture* (1921). For A.R. Orage, see his *Alphabet of Economics* (1917). On the literature of guild socialism generally see Carpenter (1920).

3. For a discussion of the influence of guild socialist ideas   within the Independent Labour Party, see Dowse (1966).

4. After 1922-1923, while guild socialism "still retained a place (in socialist thinking)... greater attention was paid to more immediate measures for dealing with unemployment" (Oldfield, 1976, p. 11).

5. See Penty (1918, p. 46):

To medieval social arrangements we shall return, not only because we shall never be able to regain complete control over the economic forces in society except through the agency of restored guilds but because it is imperative to retain a complete state of society.

6. As Macintyre states (1980, p. 58):

Both in its   literature and its everyday working political practice British Marxism was oppositional, dwelling on the defects of the existing order and seldom pointing to a preferable alternative.

In so far as the alternative was pointed to it was simply not applicable to British circumstances.

7. Bukharin and Preobrahzhensky (1969) also assumed that under fully-fledged communism calculation would proceed in physical terms. Thus they wrote of paying the workers in kind, of 'the direct exchange of commodities between communist enterprises' and of the elimination of money (pp. 390-391). For similar views amongst pre-war Marxists whose work circulated in Britain (Thompson, 1988, pp. 225-242)

8. Hobhouse wrote (1893, p. 53):

[T]he economic well-being of society is the true end of industry, and... this end will ... be reached better by an intelligent organisation of industry, than by the haphazard interaction of unintelligent forces.

9. See Durbin's (1984, p. 32) comment:

Shaw and Webb both imply that socialism will have arrived when the entire market operation is administered through nationalisation, municipalisation and government regulation.

10.   For a fuller discussion of the late nineteenth- and early   twentieth century Fabian socialist critique of the market, see Thompson (1988, pp. 250-258).

11.   Also of importance here is H.N. Brailsford, whose *Socialism for Today*, based on articles which appeared in the *New Leader* during the early months of 1925, was published in October, 1925. Brailsford's critical macroeconomic analysis of capitalism was remarkably similar to that of Strachey, as were the essentials of his economic policies for effecting a transition to socialism. This is hardly surprising, as both Brailsford and Strachey had common sources of inspiration in Hobson and Keynes. In this paper, I argue that, with respect to Strachey, it was these influences which laid the basis for his challenge to the economic strategy of Fabianism; the same could be said for Brailsford. The chief difference between Strachey and Brailsford in 1925, as it was between *Revolution by Reason* and *The Living Wage*, 1926 was that while Strachey saw monetary expansion as the key to providing a living wage and raising aggregate demand, Brailsford emphasised redistribution and saw monetary policy (again the inspiration is Keynes' *Tract*) as one important means of keeping the price level stable.

12.   The best source for the thought of Strachey's father is Morris (1986).

13.   For a study of the migration of disgruntled liberals into the Labour Party during and immediately after the war, see Cline (1963).

14.   S.D. Macintyre (1974, p. 11) wrote of Strachey having been converted to socialism by E.D. Morel. Hugh Thomas (1973, pp. 39-40),emphasised the influence of Arthur Ponsonby, with whose daughter Strachey was friendly immediately prior to joining the Party.

15.   The full title of John Strachey's work was, in fact, *Revolution by Reason: An Outline of the Financial Proposals Submitted to the Labour Movement by Mr. Oswald Mosley*. The full title of Mosley's pamphlet was *Revolution by Reason: An Account of the Birmingham Proposals. Together With an Analysis of the Financial Policy of the Present Government Which Has Led to Their Great Attack Upon Wages*; this pamphlet was based on a speech which Moseley gave to the I.L.P. Summer School in August, 1925.

16.   See, for example, the different opinions expressed by Mosley (1968, p. 185); Macintyre (1974, p. 50); Skidelsky (1975, p. 138); Thomas (1973, pp. 49, 51).

17.   Strachey (1925, pp. 72-73) wrote:

So the whole export plan of competitive Capitalism proves only a palliation of its fatal defect, which is that it can never provide the demand for the goods it produces.

18.   This is quoted from Thomas (1973, p. 113), although it does not discount the possibility of the economic thinking in *Capital* exerting an influence on Strachey through the writing of others.

[W]hat it (a price fall) does…is to set a premium on leaving money idle…This of course acts as the strongest possible deterrent upon production.

20.   For a discussion of the influence of Douglas' ideas on the I.L.P. and also on guild socialism, see Finlay (1972, pp. 120-122 and 202-209).

21.   On Strachey's appearance at this conference see McCarthy (1947, p. 29). Strachey (1925, p. 150) makes particularly favourable mention of D.H. Robertson's *Money*.

22.   Thus for Strachey the major problem resided not in the monetary system but in the distribution of economic ownership. It was this which governed the distribution of economic power.

23.   See, also, Finlay's (1972, p. 206) remark that Mosley and Strachey "were to be very important in moving the I.L.P. in a direction not too different from social credit."

24.   Strachey (1925, pp. 47-48) wrote:

But certain...writers have attempted to go a step further...On a national scale...it is possible to consume, and therefore to produce, only as many commodities as the nation has purchasing power to obtain...Therefore, there can be no increase in the consumption of goods without a corresponding increase in the amount of money in circulation.

25.   On the rapid spread of Hobsonian ideas within the I.L.P. in the early 1920s, see Dowse (1966, pp. 96-98). Hobson also became chairman of the Labour Party Advisory Committee on Trade Policy and Finance (Clarke, 1978, p. 198). In this capacity, he exerted an influence on D.H. Cole which is manifest in economic articles which Cole wrote for the *New Statesman* (see, for example, Cole, 1922, 1923).

26.   A discussion of general underconsumption is to be found in Labour Party literature and within the Labour Party in the immediate post-war period, see Mackay, Forsyth, and Kelly (1966).

27.   To the title of Hobson's (1925) article, Strachey responded that he sought to "abolish not tame" capitalism.

28.   For a discussion of the impact of this exodus upon the Labour Party see Cline (1963). M. Freeden's (1986, p. 210) remark that this was "a remarkable coup of permeation, one that the Webbs—had their eyes been open—would have regarded with ill-conceived envy" hits the nail on the head.

29.   For a discussion of this and the role of the 1917 Club in bringing together liberal and socialist intellectuals, see Allet (1981, p. 39).

30.   See, for example, Strachey's (1940) *A Programme for Progress,* which was described by J. R. Campbell (1940), a member of the British Communist Party as "precious near to...one of those social-democratic utopias like the I.L.P. Living Wage Plan of 1926-29."

REFERENCES

Ablett, N. 1919. *Easy Outlines of Economics.* Oxford.

Allett, J. 1981. *New Liberalism: The Political Economy of J.A. Hobson.* Toronto University Press.

Besant, A. 1889. "Industry Under Socialism." Pp. 150-169 in *Fabian Essays.* London: Allen & Unwin.

Bogdanov, A. (pseud.) (A.A. Molinowski). 1925. *A Short Course of Economic Science,* London.

Booth, A. 1983. "The Labour Party and Economics Between the Wars." *Bulletin of the Society for the Study of Labour History* 47: 31-42.

Booth A., and M. Pack. 1985. *Unemployment, Capital and Economic Policy in Great Britain 1918-39.* London, Blackwell.

Boothby, R., H. Macmillan, and O. Stanley. 1927. *Industry and Trade.* London: Macmillan.

Brailsford, H.N. 1925. *Socialism for Today.* London: New Leader.

Bukharin N., and E. Preobrahzhensky. 1969. *The ABC of Communism.* Harmondsworth, UK: Penguin.

Campbell, J.R. 1940. "Immediate Programme or Social-Democratic Utopia." *Labour Monthly* 22: 361-363.

Carpenter, N. 1920. "The Literature of Guild Socialism." *Quarterly Journal of Economics* 34: 763-75.

Clarke, P. 1978. *Liberals and Social Democrats.* Cambridge: Cambridge University Press.

Cline, C. 1963. *Recruits to Labour: The British Labour Party 1914-31.* New York: Syracuse University Press.

Cole, G.D.H. 1920. *Guild Socialism Restated.* London: Parsons.

_____ 1922. "The Economics of Unemployment." *New Statesman* 10 (December).

_____ 1922. "An Economic Fallacy." *New Statesman* 17 (November).

Dobb, M. 1922. *The Development of Modern Capitalism: An Outline Course For Classes and Study Circles.* London: Labour Research Department.

Douglas, C.H. 1920. *Credit Power and Democracy.* London: Palmes.

Dowse, R.E. 1966. *Left in the Centre: The I.L.P., 1883-1940.* London: Longmans.

Durbin, E. 1984. "Fabian Socialism and Economic Science." Pp. 32-54 in *Fabian Essays in Socialist Thought,* edited by B. Pimlott. London: Heinemann.

Finlay, J. 1972. *Social Credit: The English Origins.* London: McGill.

Freeden, M. 1986. *Liberalism Divided: A study in British Political Thought, 1914-39.* Oxford University Press.

Glass, S.T. 1966. *The Responsible Society: The Ideas of the English Guild Socialists.* London: Longmans.

Hobhouse, L.T. 1893. *The Labour Movement.* London: Fisher Unwin.

Hobson, J.A. 1925. "Can We Tame and Harness Capitalism?" *New Leader,* 5.

King, J. and Dutton, H. "'A private perhaps but not a major...'": the Reception of C.H. Douglas' Social Credit Ideas in Britain, 1919-39." *History of Political Economy* 18: 259-279.

Lowe, R. 1978. "The Erosion of State Intervention in Britain, 1917-24." *Economic History Review* 31: 270-286.

McCarthy, E. 1947. "A History of the Social Credit Movement." Master's thesis, University of Leeds.

Macintyre, S. 1974. "John Strachey: The Development of an English Marxist, 1901-31." Master's thesis, Monash University.

———. 1980. *A Proletarian Science, Marxism in Britain 1917-33.* Cambridge: Cambridge University Press.

Mackay, D.I., D. Forsyth, and D. Kelly. 1966. "The Discussion of Public Works Programmes 1917-35: Some Remarks on the Labour Movement's Contribution." *International Review of Social History, 11:* 8-17.

Miliband, R. 1972. *Parliamentary Socialism: A Study in the Politics of Labour.* London: Merlin.

Morris, A. 1986. "A Study of John St. Loe Strachey's Editorship of the Spectator." Ph.D. dissertation, University of Cambridge.

Mosley, O. 1925. *Revolution by Reason: An Account of the Birmingham Proposals.* London: Blackfriars Press.

———. 1968. *My Life.* London: Nelson.

Oldfield, A. 1976. "The Independent Labour Party and planning, 1920-26." *International Review of Social History* 21:1-29.

Olivier, S. 1904. "Capital and land."' *Fabian Tract* No. 7, 6th ed. London: Fabian Society.

Orage, A. 1917. *Alphabet of Economics.* London: Allen & Unwin.

Peden, G. 1985. *British Economic and Social Policy: Lloyd George to Margaret Thatcher.* Oxford: Allan.

Pelling, H. 1968. *A Short History of the British Labour Party.* London: Macmillan.

Penty, A.J. 1918. *Guilds and the Social Crisis.* London: Allen & Unwin.

———. 1921. *Guilds, Trade and Agriculture.* London: Allen & Unwin.

Shaw, G.E. 1896. "Report on Fabian Policy." *Fabian Tract* No. 70.

———. 1962. "The Economic Basis of Socialism." Pp. 3-29 in *Fabian Essays.* London: Allen & Unwin.

Skidelsky, R. 1975. *Oswald Mosley.* London: Macmillan.

Starr, M. 1925. *A Worker looks at Economics.* London.

Strachey, J. 1925. *Revolution by Reason: AN Outline of the Financial Proposals Submitted to the Labour Movement by Mr. Oswald Mosley.* London: Parsons.

———. 1934. "The Education of a Communist." *Left Review* 1:67-68.

———. 1940. *A Programme for Progress.* London: Gollanez.

Thomas, H. 1973. *John Strachey.* London: Methuen.
Thompson, N. 1988. *The Market and Its Critics: Socialist Political Economy in Nineteenth Century Britain.* London: Routledge.
Webb, S., and B. Webb. 1920. *A Constitution for the Socialist Commonwealth of Great Britain.* London: Longmans.
————— 1920a. *Industrial Democracy.* 2nd ed. London: Longmans.

SYMPOSIUM ON MILTON FRIEDMAN'S METHODOLOGY

AN INTERVIEW WITH MILTON
FRIEDMAN ON METHODOLOGY

J. Daniel Hammond

NOTE

This interview between Milton Friedman and Dan Hammond took place at the Hoover Institution on May 24, 1988. Financial support was provided by the Earhart Foundation.

Hammond: The first paper that I wrote about your work (*Hammond, 1986*) *was an interpretation of the causal structure of your version of the quantity theory of money. In your letter commenting on my paper, you objected strongly to my fundamental premise, that you think of the money supply* (*or changes in it*) *as a cause of the price level and nominal income* (*or changes in their values*). *You wrote: "I have always regarded 'cause' as a very tricky concept. In my technical scientific writings I have to the best of my ability tried to avoid using the word"* (*see appendix*). *In the 1974 Institute of Economic Affairs publication,* Inflation: Causes, Consequences, and Cures *you wrote essentially the same thing: "I myself try to avoid use of the word 'cause', . . . it is a tricky*

Research in the History of Economic Thought and Methodology
Volume 10, pages 91-118.
Copyright © 1992 by JAI Press Inc.
All rights of reproduction in any form reserved.
ISBN: 0-55938-501-4

and unsatisfactory word" (p. 101). *What specifically is the problem you see in framing a discussion of macroeconomics such as the debate between monetarists and Keynesians as a debate over the causes of price level and income changes?*

Friedman: The problem that bothers me about cause is that it almost invariably leads into a problem of infinite regress. There is no such thing as *the* cause of anything. In a way, it's the same problem as the problem that bothers me about people who talk about theory versus facts. As you probably know, I've always thought the best definition I could give of the difference between a theory and a fact is that a fact is a theory that we take for granted for present purposes. But there's no such thing as *a fact*. There's a way of looking at some facts and that's really a theory. But to go back, once you start talking about cause—money is the cause of inflation. Well, then, what caused the money? And there's no stopping. The stopping point has to be based on the purposes of your investigation, on convenience and so on. People are always trying to get to ultimate causes. I think it's a foolish search. And that's fundamentally why I've tried to avoid using the word. That's why when I have used it I've tended to use it as "proximate cause" or something like that. A statement that A is necessary and sufficient for B, might equally be that B is necessary and sufficient for A. It doesn't tell you that one is the cause and one is the effect. And indeed in most such relationships, it can run either way. If you have a necessary and sufficient condition so that A and B always go along with one another, then B is as much a cause of A as A is a cause of B. In order to distinguish between the two by saying which one is exogenous and which one is endogenous you have to bring in some outside information that is not contained in them.

What kind of information is that, the outside information? Isn't that information about causality in some sense?

Yes, it is in some sense, but that's the difficulty. You can't say causality without saying, "in some sense." That's why I prefer, if I can, to use words that indicate in what sense I'm using causality. So I would say, well, I observe that increases in the money supply have always gone along with increases in income. Which came first? I look around and try to see. I want to step one step back in this causal chain and go to the next level. What is it that produced the money supply increase? What is it that produced the change in income, etcetera? Let me give you a very simple example. The case is a beautiful case—it's the case of the 1880s and 1890s and the effect of silver agitation on the price level. We had deflation. Did we have deflation because the money supply was going down relative to output? It's not at all clear.

We had deflation because the agitation for silver made people think we were going to go off the gold standard.

If you're going to talk about causes, independent causes—it would be a more accurate description to say that the cause of that deflation was the agitation for inflation—that is, money was a medium through which that acted. In most cases, when money produces inflation, the reason money increases is because some sovereign is trying to get some more money or because somebody's discovered gold. But this is an interesting case because the reason you have the rate of change in the money supply that you did was that the money supply had to increase less than it otherwise would have in order to produce the deflation that you had to have to enable a capital outflow, which was produced by the fear of people that we were going off the gold standard. We discussed that case at length in *Monetary History* as you probably know.

It's always seemed to me one of the most fascinating cases because it illustrates so many different principles. It also shows what's wrong, in my opinion, with some of the more extreme versions of rational-expectations hypotheses. Here you had a situation in which interest rates were high because everybody expected inflation. What you actually had was deflation. Were those expectations irrational? Not at all. There was a very high probability you would have inflation, given them. So that's the difficulty I think. At any rate, that's getting off the topic.

So on the problem of infinite regress—does that have to be an overwhelming problem, that you stay away from causality because there's no obvious stopping point?

Of course not.

But if you analyze affairs without using causal language, you still have the same problem, don't you—

Yes.

—in deciding how far back you go?

Oh, sure, you have the same problem, but it seems to me—and maybe I'm wrong in this,—maybe it would have been just as simple to use the word cause and to try to make clear what I meant by it. As I mentioned to you, I think in one of my letters, I don't find Mackie's (1974) definition of cause very final (see appendix A). What caused the short circuit he refers to? You're back in the infinite regress problem. You haven't really solved what I think is the basic problem.

No, you haven't, but you have a framework with a number of different factors, each of which contributes to the result.

I understand. It's a very intelligent and thoughtful approach. I found it interesting and different from anything I'd seen, but I don't really think it solves my problem with the word cause.

Now, let me look at the second—

Could I ask you about one other thing here?

Sure.

In your paper, "The Monetary Studies of the National Bureau," (Friedman, 1964), you summarize the results of the studies this way, which sounds to me like you're talking about causes and effects and avoiding the word. You say, "Changes in the quantity of money have important and broadly predictable economic effects. Long period changes in the quantity of money relative to output determine the secular behavior of prices. Substantial expansions in the quantity of money over short periods have been a major proximate source of the accompanying inflation in prices." Would you have any objection to identifying that as a discussion about causes and effects?

If I take your phraseology and say cause in some sense, no. But leaving out the "in some sense," yes, because I still have to ask, why? That is only a statement about proximate causation.

Proximate in the sense of being nearest.

Let me put it differently. It seems to me, it indicates how you go about trying to understand the phenomenon—what you look for at the next step. It's not a stopping point. The problem with the use of the word cause is that I think there's a great tendency for people who use the word cause to think that once they can say that A is the cause of B, they can stop their analysis. Whereas from my point of view, to say that the changes in the quantity of money relative to output determine the long-run price level, that's a correct statement. But it doesn't tell me why the quantity of money went up as it did. And it will be different in different cases. The cause in one case is the discovery of gold in California and Australia; the cause in another case is the need of a sovereign to get more money, etcetera. I'm trying to look for a way in which I can unravel a problem and break it up into its relevant parts, and this tells me where to look for the next stage.

But it's only the beginning?

It's only the beginning. And cause sounds like you're going to close it off.

Well, I've picked up from reading W.C. Mitchell and from reading J.N. Keynes and some others the idea that at the turn of the century there was an association between the term "cause" and the term "final cause"—that when people spoke of the cause of, say, the business cycle, they were thinking in terms of a final cause—you've gotten to the end of that chain.

That's right.

Did that make an impression on you?

Not that I know of.

Do you know how you came to—

No, I haven't the slightest idea. I have to confess, that in reading what all you people write, I get tremendous insight into what I thought. (Laughter) It's wonderful how much better hindsight is than foresight. I may say that, personally, I have never been very introspective in that kind of a way or personally psychoanalytic and I haven't the slightest idea how I came to that view.

Could you tell me a bit about the effect, to the extent that—

Are you talking about the second question?

No, we're still on one here—on a follow-up. I'm interested in your response— any effect that your exchanges between John Culbertson in 1960 and 1961 and with Tobin in 1970 perhaps had on your thought about causality in economics because both of those were—

I don't think it had any effect on causality at all.

They were both about causality.

I know. They both had to do with the question of precedence in time. My feeling is that they pointed out a defect in my exposition, but not in my thought, and that really I had never supposed that precedence in time per se necessarily indicated causation. That is, I was fully aware of the earlier literature of causation versus correlation and spurious trends, etcetera. So it would never have occurred to me to say that because A precedes B, that means that A is the cause of B in the sense in which they were trying to use it. But I could see that they had a valid case for complaint that my language suggested that. So I think it did have an effect on the language I used subsequently. I think the reason I stressed the lags in the case of money, was not as a means of determining cause, but as a means of pointing out why it would be difficult to use knowledge about the relation between money and income as a control device. If they operated simultaneously, you could lean against today's wind, but if there is a lag and especially if the lag is variable—the length of it doesn't matter from this point of view so much—it's the variability of it that's crucial. Then it would be very difficult to use it. That was why I was so much interested in the lags in the money case. By the time I came to that point, I didn't have any question about whether money had an independent influence. As I say, this may all be retrospective nonsense because it's very hard to go back and say exactly what you thought at the time.

That's the impression I've gotten from reading in your work before that. One other question before we move on to two. One of the criticisms that Culbertson made that echoed a criticism by C.R. Noyes (1945) of your dissertation was that you're isolating one factor and ignoring other factors which are important causes, and this makes your results suspect. Did those criticisms have much of an impact?

I don't believe so. I cannot recall that they had any. I can recall definitely that the issue of timing did have an impact, but this I don't recall having any impact. Remember, what they are doing is echoing a standard complaint, and if it had any influence on me it would have come from Mitchell, not from them—much earlier. Mitchell was always talking about the pound of *ceteris paribus*; once you let these dogs out, who knows what happens, etcetera. So any influence it would have had would have been much earlier.

What was your response to Mitchell at the time?

Of course he's right. But you don't draw the conclusion he drew. You draw the conclusion rather that you've got to find a way in which you can determine which of the variables are important, and see what in fact happens to them and what their influence is. See, he tended to regard that as a stopping point. Whereas again, it seemed to me it wasn't a stopping point. It pointed out a very real problem, of which I may say, nobody was more aware than Alfred Marshall. So there wasn't really anything new about that.

You see problems in framing economic issues such as the Keynesian-monetarist debate as disputes about the causal role of money. For the most part you have not used the word "cause" in your writings. Yet you have used it on accasion in your "popular" writings. For example, your 1963 lectures for the (Indian) Council for Economic Education are entitled (Inflation: Causes and Consequences (Friedman, 1963), and chapter nine in Free to Choose *(Friedman and Friedman, 1980) includes a section entitled "The Proximate Cause of Inflation." Does this indicate an essential rift between your "scientific" economics and your "popular" economics?*

It isn't a rift between my scientific economics and my popular economics. It's the fact that I'm addressing a different audience. The circumlocutions that may be appropriate for a scientific audience will lose you your popular audience. And in general, you have a different aim in view when you're writing for a scientific than for a popular audience. For a scientific audience, you are really part of an ongoing process of cumulative knowledge, you hope, in which the other side has built on your work, or will add to it, or will subtract from it, or will test it, and so on. In respect to popular writing, let's say that one is a wholesale activity and the other is a retail activity, and in popular writing you're trying to convey certain ideas to people, and you don't want excessive qualifications to get in the way. I think there are two equal problems in popular writing. One is oversimplification and the other is overcomplexity. You've got to somehow steer between those. I think people who say things that are wrong on the grounds that they can only get a simple idea across, and while this simple idea is wrong fundamentally, it's the right one for this purpose, are doing a great injustice to themselves and to their audience. People can and will understand fairly sophisticated arguments if it's presented simply, in clear language. And I think that the whole trick in popular writing is to try to find the proper balance between them. And I'm sure that explains why I use the word "cause" because it's a much simpler term than to talk about necessary and sufficient, or about determined by, or dependent on, or approximately dependent on. Now proximate cause is obviously an attempt to have my cake and eat it too.

If avoiding the word "cause" in your scientific writings indicates that the analysis is not causal in its structure, what then takes the place of causality in the structure of the theory? Does this not leave you open to the criticism that monetarism or the quantity theory is based on nothing more than correlation between money and the price level or nominal income?

No, I don't think that—I don't know what it means to say that the analysis is not causal in its structure. I just don't understand the language. The whole purpose of an analysis is to try to understand real phenomena in such a way that you can predict what's going to happen. If you want to call it causal—you know, it seems to me that's a purely semantic discussion, and I really find it very hard to get involved in the semantic discussions.

So your avoiding the word cause is really a semantic choice?—

Absolutely, absolutely.

—and indicates nothing beyond that.

Nothing.

Do you recall either Jacob Viner or Frank Knight talking specifically in their theory courses about the meaning of causality or problems with causality in economics?

No. The answer to that is no. I don't recall it.

How about—

Maybe they did— I don't know. I just don't recall it.

Do you recall Wesley Mitchell discussing any kind of philosophical or methodological problems with causality in either his history of thought course or his business cycles course?

I guess I took his business cycles course as well as his history course. I took whatever Wesley Mitchell offered that year. And he surely talked about these issues, but I don't recall anything very definite at this distance in time.

He was concerned with the final cause—with people tracing one—

The problem with causality in respect of Mitchell is that it is all mixed up with the discussion of the role of theory and analysis. And Mitchell was fundamentally antitheoretical. He would never say that. Mitchell was one of the broadest of human beings. He had an extraordinary amount of tolerance for anything. He wasn't going to oppose theory because it was theory. He had a good deal of respect for purely theoretical writing. But fundamentally he was antitheoretical. And somehow or other the discussion of causes gets all mixed up with that. I've been much more interested in the interrelations between theory and empirical work than I have with whether it's causal or not. I must say, frankly, that while I've been skeptical of the word cause, and I've always avoided it, I really haven't given a great deal of thought to the philosophical issues involved in defining cause.

Henry Schultz studied, I believe, under Karl Pearson—

Yes he did.

—the statistician and philosopher, in London. Did you pick up any philosophy from him?

No. Henry Schultz was a good mechanic, but he wasn't really very smart. I remember his talking about Percy Bridgman and operationalism, and so on, and I undoubtedly picked up the words. Henry Schultz had a great deal of influence on me, primarily by recommending me to Hotelling at Columbia. (Laughter) That was unquestionably the major source of influence. Henry Schultz was a fine person. And he is an example of the extent to which perspiration can take the place of inspiration. His book on the *Theory and Measurement of Demand* (Schultz, 1938) is a great book—even the parts I didn't write. (Laughter) I did write parts of it, but not the statistical part. And he had earlier done the statistical work. He took a small problem, statistical demand curves, and he concentrated all his effort on that for years. And the result was a body of knowledge that stands up to this day. It's had a great deal of influence, and deservedly so. As I've gotten older, my opinion of Schultz has gone from one extreme to the other. At the time I was a graduate student, or at the time I was a research assistant, I must say I had close to contempt for him, because he just wasn't very smart. But the more I've observed economics as a discipline, and what people have done, the greater the respect I've had for Schultz. Because he did pick a significant problem. He was willing to learn. I was a brash, abrasive youngster, and when you stop and think of it, it's kind of remarkable that an established professor at the University of

Chicago, Henry Schultz, would have let a brash twenty-one-year-old youngster tell him, "Well, you know that's just plain wrong—the right way to do it is this." I'm not exaggerating. I'm sure I spoke in those terms and in that way. So that he was open to persuasion and open to charges of error. He had no arrogance. None whatsoever. I didn't realize at the time, of course, how rare that is. One of the major flaws of great people, or people who are potentially great, is their unwillingness to have as assistants or associates people who are as good as they are. Henry Schultz did not have that defect at all. He was looking for help wherever he could get it, and he judged help entirely in terms of the contribution it could make to his scientific project. So as I say, as I've gotten older, my opinion of Henry Schultz has gone up. Now, of course you know, his life ended tragically. He was on a vacation in California, driving a car, having just learned to drive six months earlier, and went off the edge of a cliff. And he killed himself and his whole family. That was in about 1937 or 1938 or something like that. To go back to the where we started, so far as Schultz was concerned, what I learned from him, as I say, and you will see it if you look at my Economics 311 and 312 notes, was technique. I was directed to readings, and above all, he recommended to Harold Hotelling that I get a fellowship to Columbia, which Harold Hotelling arranged for me to get, and that was his real contribution. The year after that I came back to Chicago and worked as his research associate, in the course of which, as I say, I worked on his *Theory and Measurement of Demand* (Schultz, 1938) and wrote some of the sections of it, as he acknowledges in the preface. I'm not saying anything out of school. I'm not saying anything he wouldn't have said himself.

Did you read much philosophy?

None.

Any philosophy when you were a graduate student?

None that I recall. Not only that, I don't recall ever having read much philosophy. Certainly, about the only methodology philosophy I've read is Popper. I have read his *Conjectures and Refutations* (Popper, 1963) as well of course, which is not methodology, *The Open Society and Its Enemies* (Popper, 1945). I think these are the two main things of Popper's that I've read. Outside of that, I'm sure I've read bits and pieces of philosophy here and there, but I've never systematically read philosophy.

I noticed that in the New Palgrave, *Alan Walters* (1987) *says that in your 1953 methodology essay you introduced Popper's philsophy of science to economics. Would that be an overstatement, then?*

No. My introduction to Popper did not come from writings. I met him in person in 1947 at the first meting of the Mont Pelerin Society, when Hayek brought a bunch of people together, and I met him at Mont Pelerin. I was very much impressed with him, and I spent a long time talking to him there. I knew about *Logik der Forschung* (Popper, 1935) but it was in German; there was no English translation at that time. I can read a little bit of German, but it's beyond me really, so I never read anything in original German. I didn't read his *Logik der Forschung*, but I knew the basic ideas from my contact with him, and I have no doubt that that contact with him did have a good deal of influence on me.

In that light, it's rather strange that your methodology has been labeled instrumentalism, which is a view that Popper was very critical of.

Much later. Popper has changed as a human being, as well—I don't know about his methodology. I haven't kept up with his methodology. I only know about this attack on instrumentalism from people like you and so on telling me about it. His book on *Conjectures and Refutations* doesn't contain—maybe I'm wrong—but my recollection is it doesn't contain—Does it contain any—

I'm not sure.

I'm not sure either. At any rate, I was very much impressed over the course of the years at how much Popper had changed as a human being, and particularly in the direction of authoritarianism—a certain element of intolerance, which was not present in his earlier years.

Did you meet Hayek at the same time?

No. I had met Hayek earlier than that. Let me see—Hayek wrote *The Road to Serfdom* in 1944. He came to the United States—it was published in the United States in 1945?

I don't recall.

It was published in Britain, I think, in 1944 and the United States in 1945. Aaron Director, who has an office right down here and is my brother-in-law, was responsible for getting the University of Chicago Press to publish *The Road to Serfdom*. He had known Hayek in England, before World War II, when he spent a year in London, mostly with Lionel Robbins and Friedrich Hayek at the London School. So when Hayek came over here, in 1945 or 1946, whenever it was, I met him somehow; I don't really know how. When he called together this meeting at Mont Pelerin, and I was asked to go and did go, that was the first occasion in which I had more than casual contact with him, but I had already read *The Road to Serfdom*, and had already met him.

Hayek is an interesting case from a methodological point of view. Let me go back to something we were saying at lunch, which this brings to mind. I was talking about the fundamental issue of why people hold the views they do. I'm particularly interested from that point of view about the so-called

Austrians, or von Misesians. Because their philosophy which admits no role whatsoever for empirical evidence—it's entirely introspective—leads to an attitude of human intolerance. I think anybody who holds that methodological view either is to begin with, or ultimately becomes, an intolerant human being. And the reason is very simple. If you and I disagree about a proposition, the question is how do we resolve our difference? If we adopt a Misesian methodological point of view, the only way we can resolve our difference is by arguing with one another. I know it from what's inside me, you know it from what's inside you, and so you have to persuade me that I'm, wrong, or I have to persuade you that I'm right. There is no other appeal. And so, ultimately, we have to get to fighting. I'm right, you're wrong; I'm right, you're wrong; I'm right, you're wrong. The virtue of what I take to be the original Popperian methodological view, or of the point of view that I really adopt, which is neither Popperian or von Misesian. What it really is is more Savage-de Finetti. You asked if I read methodology and philosophy; I've read a great deal in the field of statistical methodology and statistical philosophy, and Jimmie Savage was one of my closest personal friends. And as you know, we collaborated extensively. He was one of the few people I knew whom I would unhesitantly classify as a genius. And Jimmie said, and this is a crucial point: "The role of statistics is not to discover truth. The role of statistics is to resolve disagreements among people. It's to bring people closer together."

Go back and look at it in those terms. Suppose you adopt that point of view—the methodological point of view I adopt—and suppose you and I differ, and we come to the point where after arguing with one another we're at an impasse. Well, then we have a recourse. I could say to you, tell me, what evidence would I have to get that would persuade you you were wrong? And you say to me, what evidence would I have to get to persuade you? And then we can go out and look for the evidence. In the way in which Jimmie Savage would describe, that would be to say, you have a set of personal probabilities about events of the world, in which this particular proposition we're arguing is one of them. I have a set of personal probabilities. Those personal probabilities differ. That's why we argue. The role of statistical analysis is to lead us to reconsider our personal probabilities in the hope that our personal probabilities will come closer and closer together. So you start out thinking, in the simplest case, that this coin is a fair coin, and I think it's unduly loaded heads, and so we discuss the experiment which will lead us to discriminate and then we go and toss the coin. And either I say, "You're absolutely right," or vice versa. What we've done is to revise our personal probabilities. Your personal probability was 50 percent—we haven't demonstrated that there's any such thing as "the" probability which is 50 percent. That's what Jimmie means when he says you're not searching for truth. Because if there be a truth, there's no way of knowing when you get it.

The trouble I always have with those people who say, you're not looking for truth. Of course I'm looking for truth. But the question is, how do I know when I get it? And the answer is, I never will. And therefore, no matter how much evidence I get, I never can have one hundred percent confidence that I have the truth. Going back to the von Misesians, that's why I think that their praxeological philosophy leads to intolerance. You'll notice that Mises himself was a highly intolerant person. Ayn Rand was a highly intolerant person. As he's become older, Popper has become an intolerant person. Hayek is a very interesting case, because I think Chicago in particular had a sufficient influence on him so as to move him away and he is not nearly as intolerant as the other von Misesians. Same thing was true of Fritz Machlup, who was another disciple of von Mises, but neither of them were anything like as intolerant as von Mises himself. But this crew of people down at the Mises Institute which is near you—

At Auburn.

They're just as intolerant a bunch as you can find. Now, how does that get us into some of the issues we're talking about here? Very directly. One of the most beautiful little examples of evidence that contradicts a theory is the evidence that I presented in one of my articles on the National Bureau's work on what was wrong with von Mises's cycle theory. I don't know if you remember; it hasn't gotten much attention. But I think it's really a beautiful little methodological example. The von Mises theory of the cycle is that the "cause"—they would use the word cause—the cause of the depression is the prior expansion. That means, it would seem to me, that if you have a big expansion, you are going to have a big depression. You have a little expansion, you'll have a little recession. So I went and I looked at the relationship between the amplitude of a recession and the amplitude of expansions and the amplitude of the succeeding recessions. There's zero correlation. On the other hand, there's a very high correlation between the amplitude of the succeeding expansion. That's utterly inconsistent with the von Mises theory. It must be that what happened during the recession influences the suceeding expansion. It seems to me that that one little bit of evidence is decisive refutation of von Mises. Have the von Misesians in any way stopped saying exactly what they were saying for fifty years? Not a word of it. They keep on repeating the same nonsense. What they call scientific work isn't scientific work at all. Because they regard facts as ways of illustrating theory, not as ways of testing theory. So their scientific work is from my point of view useless. I don't know about their philosophical work.

Going back to something you said at lunch along those same lines—you said that today you believe that ideology is more important in influencing people's views of the facts than you once thought. At this point, would you look back on the origins of the National Bureau of Economic Research—of what they expected to do—to accomplish—as being a little naive in terms of applying the tools of science to settle issues once and for all?

I said to you at lunch two things. I said I had come to question it, but I still took it as an operating hypothesis. Let's see what I mean by those two statements because they bear on exactly what you're saying. Insofar as it is true that the views of facts are determined by ideology, there isn't anything you can do about it. On the other hand, insofar as there is some truth in the opposite relationship or in the fact that people are willing to be persuaded by evidence, then there is something you can do about it. And that is what Mitchell set up the National Bureau to do. It was a worthwhile purpose and it remains a worthwhile purpose. The only difference is, I'm not as optimistic about how far reaching its effects can be. But nonetheless it's the only possible hypothesis, it seems to me, which I can proceed on as a working matter.

In "The Marshallian Demand Curve" (Friedman, 1949) you echo Marshall's description of economic theory as an "engine for the discovery of concrete truth." You compare the Marshallian conception of economic theory with the Walrasian conception of what theory should be and should do. My understanding of your distinction is that Marshallian theory is problem-oriented in the following sense: (1) that it is focused on actual problems from the world of experience; (2) that one begins analysis of a problem well-armed with observed and related facts; (3) that the structure of analysis is dictated by the specific problem one is dealing with; (4) that real-world institutions are accounted for and dealt with; (5) that definitions of terms are problem-specific; and (6) that mathematical considerations do not take a dominant place in the analysis. The Walrasian approach is to be more concerned with generality; to make theory more abstract, and less connected with problems of policy or experience and institutions; to check the theory or otherwise resort to empirical evidence only after the theory has been worked out; and to emphasize logical consistency and mathematical elegance. Do you have a sense of how you first came to make this distinction and how or why you saw it as important?

I don't really have the sense of how I first came to make the distinction or why I said it was important. I haven't thought about the question, and offhand in thinking about it, I really don't know. It's a distinction I made from fairly early on.

You made it early, and I've come to think that it may be one of the keys to your methodology and perhaps—

I suspect that came from Burns. That's my guess, but I really couldn't document it—because he was so imbued with Marshall. You see, he was very much a disciple of Marshall on the one hand, and Wesley Mitchell on the other. And Wesley Mitchell would have impelled in him aversion to the pure abstract

Walrasian, while Marshall would have impelled in him his problem-seeking approach. I suspect that that's where it comes from, but I really can't say. That's just pure rationalization.

Your criticism of Lange's Price Flexibility and Employment *as "taxonomic theorizing" in your 1946 review (Friedman, 1946) bears a certain resemblance to Viner's first publication, "Some Problems in the Logical Method in Political Economy" (Viner, 1917). There he argued that there are three methods of obtaining generalizations for deductive analysis: (1) by complete enumeration of individual propositions; (2) by assumption; and (3) by inductive inference. He argued that the first, which appears similar to what you call taxonomic theorizing, is not a practical manner of reasoning. The second, Viner contended, becomes induction when brought in contact with reality. So, he argued, all reasoning requires induction unless it is "wholly abstract or hypothetical." Do you recall this or other particular methodological writings of Viner's as having an important influence on your own views about methodology?*

To the best of my knowledge, I don't believe I ever read that essay of Viner. I may have, but I don't remember ever reading Viner's essay. I don't think he assigned it in class—I'm pretty sure he didn't. I have no recollection of ever having read it, which doesn't mean I didn't.

Would he have made the Marshallian-Walrasian distinction?

He very well may have, yes. He was very much of a Marshallian, of course. And he very well might have.

You said in the dialogue on the history of law and economics at Chicago (Kitch, 1983) that Jacob Viner began the real tradition of Marshallian (as opposed to Walrasian) analysis at Chicago. Did he use these labels in his economic theory class or did you or someone else coin the label in an interpretation of what Viner taught?

I don't recall his using those labels. So far as the use of the actual labels was concerned, I probably am responsible for coining them in connection with the review that I wrote of Jaffe's translation of Walras's *Elements* (Friedman, 1955). But I wouldn't swear on a stack of Bibles that he didn't use the labels.

Would you say that his 301 course had much of a methodological content?

That depends on what you mean by methodological. It had no explicit methodological content whatsoever. But there was a very strong implicit methodological content, since you came away very clearly with the feeling that you were talking about real problems. Part of the distinction is viewing economics as a branch of mathematics—as a game—as an intellectual game and exercise—as Debreu, Arrow, and so on—and it's a fine thing to do. There's nothing wrong with that. After all, mathematics is a perfectly respectable intellectual activity, and so is mathematization of economics or anything else. The other part of it is viewing it (using Marshall's phrase) as an engine of analysis. And there was no doubt that Viner viewed it as an engine of analysis, and no doubt when you were in his course that you came away with the feeling that economics really had something to say about real problems and real things. In that sense, it had methodological content.

Would you say—

Let me give you a little example, which comes closer in some ways to your interest. Viner's review of a book on the cement industry (Viner, 1925)—I've forgotten whose book it was—in which he made fun of the author who pointed out that all of the cement producers were charging the same price and concluded: "After all, it's an essential feature of a purely competitive equilibrium that all the prices of the same product are the same everywhere." And Viner literally made fun of him, arguing that that was sure evidence that you were not in a purely competitive situation. Well, you can see that that really has a very strong methodological element in it, and really reflects the distinction between these two approaches.

And I suppose Knight's courses would have? Or—

No.

Maybe not.

No. Knight's would not have had any methodological component at all. Knight never was influenced by any facts that he didn't observe casually himself. Knight was very funny that way. He was absolutely persuaded that inequality tended to increase. At least a half a dozen times, we talked him out of it. And a half a dozen times he would come back. He'd be perfectly willing to be talked out of it, and he'd be persuaded that there was a logic both ways, and it didn't have to happen. Next time the subject came up he'd be right back.

You indicated to me in correspondence (March 28, 1986) that your interest in methodology was not sufficient to get involved in the debate that grew out of your 1953 essay. Do you see your work as becoming less methodologically oriented after 1953?

I'm a little uncertain how to answer your question. I don't know what it means to say that the work is more or less methodologically oriented. I have since 1953 not written anything that was explicitly devoted to methodology. My remarks about methodology have always been comments in the course of some other discussion. They've been by-products of something else. On the other hand, so far as my positive work is concerned, it's obviously been affected by my methodological views. In that sense, it's been methodologically oriented.

But if you mean, have I deliberately undertaken work in order to illustrate methodological principles, the answer is no. I've undertaken work to try to find out something, and I believe that there's a certain way of finding out something that is more effective than some other way, and that's the way I tend to go about things. But it hasn't been methodologically oriented in any other sense.

Before 1953—

It wasn't before 1953 either. I don't really remember why I wrote that article, to tell you the truth.

Well, that's what I was going to ask. I find a lot of methodology in your work before 1953, but it's almost always within the context of some economic problem, and I was going to ask, why that introduction to a collection of essays? (1953a)

I really don't know. I really can't answer you. What I don't know is whether the idea of the collection of essays came first, or the essay came first. What happened was that a friend of mine who was running the social science branch of the University of Chicago Press came to me with the idea that I should produce a collection of essays. I was amenable to that, and I think we put together this collection. What I don't know is whether then I said, "Well gee, there ought to be an introduction to this," and so I wrote this as an introduction, or whether I had written the essay earlier, and said, "This is a good place to put it."

You made a comment on Ruggles for the AEA collection (Friedman, 1952) which was very short, but it showed up—

That was some kind of a meeting or something, a conference or something in which I was invited to do that, to comment on Ruggles.

I don't remember what the occasion was—

And of course, I should say, that no doubt one of the things that sharpened my interest in this goes back much earlier, to the period when I was at the National Bureau, and particularly when I was serving as the Secretary or something of the Conference on Income and Wealth. I edited the first three volumes of their series. And I believe that had quite a bit to do with forcing me to clarify my ideas about how one should go about empirical work. Because so much of the national income stuff was pure empiricism of the rawest kind. And I kept revolting at the kind of considerations that the measurers were bringing in, trying to decide various issues, like what value should be attached to government services, and things like that. I think you will find that most of my comments on papers in those first three volumes reflected my approaching them from the theoretical point of view, and being dissatisfied with the purely empirical approach. So I suspect that helped, but then I got diverted, because I first went to Washington during the War, for two years in the Treasury, and then to New York for two years in the Statistical Research Group as a mathematical statistician. So why in the early 1950s I was led to write this essay, I have no idea.

Would it be an apt characterization of your interest or perspective on methodology to say that you are a Marshallian on methodology in the following sense: you think methodology can be important within the context of particular questions about economic theory, but is less useful as an area of inquiry unto itself?

I don't want to make any judgment about what's useful as an area of inquiry. I'll make a judgment about what's useful to me. I decided that I was more interested in doing economics than in writing about how economics should be done. This was partly determined by the fact that I came to the conclusion from the empirical point of view that there was very little correlation between what people said about methodology and the way in which they did economics. And therefore, it must be that straightening anybody out on methodology had very little influence on what he did. So I decided I'd better do methodology, as it were, instead of make methodology, if you want to put it in those terms. But I'm not going to make any judgment about what's useful for other people. The proof of that pudding is in the eating. If somebody finds it useful, it's useful.

But for yourself, this might be an apt characterization of your perspective?

Yes, unquestionably, it was an apt characterization for me. This wasn't the way in which I thought either my interest or my abilities were best directed. On a broader level—if I may bring Alfred Marshall back into it from a wholly different point of view—Alfred Marshall, to begin with, was extraordinarily sensitive to criticism. When somebody—in a footnote in an article in the QJE— made a negative criticism of, not his *Principles*—this was before that, but *The Economics of Industry,* which he wrote with his wife, or which his wife wrote and he signed—I'm not sure which (Marshall and Marshall, 1879), he immediately came back with a three-page answer. And he did this three or four times, and then he suddenly decided that he wasn't going to waste his time answering criticisms, and for the rest of his life he never answered a criticism. On the whole, I think that's the right approach. And I decided early on that, so far as possible, I was going to resist the temptation to respond to criticisms unless it advanced the subject in question. I haven't succeeded in following that perfectly, but I've tried to follow that practice. And since I wasn't doing any more work in the field of methodology, it didn't seem to me I ought to spend any time answering the various comments that came along.

A distinction between theoretic and atheoretic analysis was very much the point in Jacob Viner's 1929 review of F.C. Mills' The Behavior of Prices *and in the 1939 appraisal of the book sponsored by the Social Science Research Council (Bye, 1940]. What do you see (or did you during the 1930s) as the relationship between the early NBER business cycle work of Mills and Mitchell and neoclassical price theory?*

There's no doubt in my mind that I regarded Mills' *Behavior of Prices* (1927) as a horrible example of the way you should do empirical work, and that I thought it was some of the worst of the NBER stuff. The NBER cycle work of Mitchell was not the same as that. That had more meaning and more substance. That was simply because Mitchell was a smarter person than Mills. Mills, if you'll pardon my crude characterization, was not very smart. He was like Schultz. But he picked out the wrong problem, while Schultz was wiser in picking out the problem he picked out.

You said earlier that Mitchell was not a theorist.

He was not.

But in your commemorative paper, you entitled it "Wesley C. Mitchell as an Economic Theorist" (Friedman, 1950) and you didn't make that argument there.

I didn't make that argument there. I really haven't given you the right impression. Mitchell was not a natural theorist. That is, the difference between Mitchell and me is not at all in our abstract ideas of what theory ought to do or what its role is. In that sense, Mitchell was as much of a theorist as I am. The difference between us is that my natural instincts are theoretical and his natural instincts are not. That's what I meant by the statement that Mitchell was not a theorist. I don't mean that he didn't have respect for theory or that he wasn't concerned with theory, but he wasn't a natural theorist. He couldn't make theory. He could do theory, but he couldn't make it. And in that sense—his work was on a different level than Mills' altogether.

NBER-style business cycle analysis has come to be associated largely with your work (and Mrs. Schwartz's). But before that, the association was with Mitchell, Burns, and Mills. T.C. Koopmans treated Burns and Mitchell's Measuring Business Cycles *harshly in his review (Koopmans, 1947). For largely the same reasons, Viner had earlier been very critical of Mills'* The Behavior of Prices *(Viner, 1929). Having had close ties yourself to Burns, Mitchell, and Viner, and having been in close proximity to the Cowles Commission at Chicago, where did your sympathies lie in this debate on the nature and role of theory in business cycle analysis?*

Koopmans was just foolish. There is no doubt whatsoever that in a debate between Koopmans, my sympathies were entirely on the Burns-Mitchell side. I thought that Koopmans' was a very sophomoric attack and had no effective positive content—he didn't tell you where you went from here. And, of course, you realize that I had been involved in very long arguments with the Cowles Commission people when they were in Chicago. And that I was anything but an admirer—anything but a devotee, or a disciple of their belief that the way to understand the working of the world was to construct big econometric models. In fact, I was a major critic of the kind of thing they were doing in Chicago. I introduced the idea of testing their work against naive models, naive hypotheses, and so on. So that I was very unsympathetic to Koopmans from the beginning—before he wrote the article. And certainly I didn't get any more sympathetic as a result of that article.

Would you have said that they were working on either the Walras problem or the Cournot problem? You made that distinction—

They were working on the Walras problem—unquestionably.

In a long footnote in "The Methodology of Positive Economics" (Friedman, 1953b, p. 12-13) you discussed the 1940s Cowles Commission work on making theories testable, out of which grew the idea of the "identification" problem. I read the tone of the footnote to be mildly critical of the Cowles Commission program. Did you think they were on the wrong track?

Oh, sure I thought they were on the wrong track—no question.

There's a body of their work explicitly on causality—by Koopmans and Orcutt and Simon.

I never really got involved in that. I don't even know whether I read most of it. When I said I thought they were on the wrong track, it had nothing to do with that. It had to do with their belief that you set up these big models—I think the comment I wrote at one point (or said—I don't know) in connection with Christ's evaluation of the models really expressed my views at that time.

One concern that was expressed about Wesley Mitchell and the NBER during the 1920s and 1930s was that they were setting out to make economic theory anew. Along this line, what was your impression from your association with Arthur Burns at Rutgers and Mitchell at Columbia?

I really don't know how to answer your question, because that was never a concern I had or thought that they were trying to do. As I say, coming to it with my own background from Chicago, I was very much more of a theorist in a certain sense—I started from theory to a greater extent than they did. But I don't think they were setting out to make economic theory anew. They may have envisioned a different type of theory. I really have no very sensible things to say in answer to that.

It is part of the received history of Chicago economics that Knight's and Viner's concern and ability to make price theory the focal point of the graduate curriculum is a big part of that which set Chicago apart from other schools. In going from Chicago to Columbia as a graduate student in 1934, back to Chicago in 1935, and to Columbia again in 1938, did you find that Chicago during that period really was distinctive (compared to Columbia)?

There's no doubt that Chicago was distinctive, and has been ever since. The real distinction was not making price theory the focal point of the graduate curriculum. That isn't the real distinction at all. The fundamental distinction is treating economics as a serious subject versus treating it as a branch of mathematics, and treating it as a scientific subject as opposed to an aesthetic subject, if I might put it that way. The fundamental difference between Chicago and for example, Harvard, and Columbia to a lesser extent—Columbia at that time was something of an amalgam of Chicago and Harvard. The fundamental difference between Chicago at that time and let's say Harvard, was that at Chicago, economics was a serious subject to be used in discussing real problems, and you could get some knowledge and some answers from it. For Harvard, economics was an intellectual discipline on a par with mathematics, which was fascinating to explore, but you mustn't draw any conclusions from it. It wasn't going to enable you to solve any problems, and I think that's always been a fundamental difference between Chicago and other places. MIT more recently has been a better exemplar than Harvard. And of course, there are no such things as one hundred percent pure cases either at Chicago, or elsewhere.

You stated in your Trinity University Nobel Economists lecture (Friedman, 1986) that you thought the combination of theory at Chicago and institutional detail and empirical work that you found at Columbia was ideal for a budding economist in the mid-1930s. Was the friction between theorists such as Viner and institutionalists such as Mitchell an important part of this fertile experience? Did you get from either of them the impression that you (or anyone) would have to choose one way or the other?

No, I never got the impression I'd have to choose one or the other. I thought I got a great deal out of Viner, and I thought I got a great deal out of Mitchell. I got different things. But, I never felt that there was a—

And Clark?

And Clark. I didn't get a great deal out of Clark, as I said, because he was more or less an amalgam, a mixture of the two. Mo Abramovitz was one of my closest personal friends at that time and since, and I always found it puzzling what Mo got out of Clark, to tell you the truth. But he did—he got a great deal out of him and thought he was a remarkable person. I liked Clark—I'm not in any way running him down. He was an extraordinarily able man. His *Economics of Overhead Cost* is a first-rate book. What was his thing he wrote in the 1930s having to do with planning—Planning Public Works, or something like that [Economics of Planning Public Works, 1935]. I didn't find that at all helpful, so that I never really got a great deal out of Clark from my point of view.

Harold Hotelling, Mitchell, and Henry Schultz were all three heavily involved in statistical work during the 1930s. Are there distinctions to be made in how you would attribute influence on your own development as an economic statistician among these three of your teachers?

There's a very, very big distinction among them. Henry Schultz is distinctive from the other two in the sense that he chose a narrow subject, and he dug very deep on it. And the range of tools he deployed were fairly narrowly limited to multiple regression. He had some interest, I may say, in spectral analysis or periodogram analysis, Fourier series, partly because he had acquired a beautiful machine, a mechanical machine—it was lovely to look at and he displayed it to all visitors but he never used it—which had nice spherical glass balls and so on that rolled across the surface, and if you rolled it over a graph series it would generate the Fourier series that produced it. So Henry Schultz was very clear and very specialized.

Harold Hotelling and Mitchell were wholly different. They were poles apart. There was no relation between them at all. Harold Hotelling was a mathematician. Mitchell was a statistician. It was mathematical statistics that interested Harold Hotelling. But Harold Hotelling had an amazing character of analyzing what looks like a purely abstract unimportant problem, that turned out to be extraordinarily relevant and of great practical importance, although not by using statistical data or anything. Let me give you some examples. His article in the 1930s on "The Economics of Exhaustible Resources" (Hotelling, 1931) is undoubtedly the most important bit of writing that has been done in that area. It has underlain all of the postwar discussion of the oil problem—of the effect of OPEC and so on. If you look at that material, you'll find that the reference most often cited is Harold Hotelling. Why did he undertake it? It was a purely abstract idea, but he somehow had the insight that it was going to be important. He wrote an article on canonical correlation which ultimately turned out to be the foundation of factor analysis. During World War II, when he worked with us at the Statistical Research Group, we had a problem of how you were going to test a Norden bombsight. The Norden bombsight was a famous bombsight that was used for sighting from an airplane, where you would drop a bomb. They were very complicated mechanisms. We, the Statistical Research Group, were very heavily involved in quality control, in judging production lines. That's where sequential analysis was developed. And Hotelling was given the problem of trying to work out a method of quality control for the Norden bombsight. When he finally delivered his report, the last Norden bombsight had been manufactured. It was utterly useless for practical purposes, but it turned out to be the founding document for multivariate analysis later on. So, Hotelling had a really enormous insight in economics and in statistics—his Edgeworth taxation paradox article (Hotelling, 1932), his exhaustible resources piece in economics. His canonical correlation, and his Norden bombsight thing, and a couple of other things he did had the same kind of an impact on the purely statistical side. But, you can see that's a different universe from Mitchell. Mitchell could no more have done any of that than he could have flown to the moon. What Mitchell had was an extraordinary capacity for bringing together a very large mass of material, extracting common elements, and describing what he found in language that was clear, unambiguous, and understandable. Mitchell had a great capacity for clear writing—and speaking—you could listen to an extemporaneous lecture or talk of Mitchell's, and take it down word for word, and you would find that it was perfect. It could be published word for word without a grammatical error, or any infelicity or anything. He was absolutely remarkable in that respect.

Do you think that Knight and Viner had any direct influence on your way of doing empirical work statistically?

No. None whatsoever. Hotelling and Schultz had much more influence on it.

How about Allen Wallis? Was there a difference between the—

No. Allen and I would have agreed almost entirely on everything. Allen—again, he was one of my closest friends at Chicago, and has remained so the rest of my life. I tried to persuade Allen not to become Dean of the School of Business. I still think that if he hadn't gone off into administrative work, he would have made very important contributions to economics and statistics. But, it's clear that his comparative advantage was in administrative work and he's had a remarkably successful career in this field. But from the very beginning, I think Allen and I saw eye to eye. I don't believe there was ever any real difference of opinion.

Would you classify yourself as a Bayesian?

Yes, and no. I don't like to use the word Bayesian. I would rather refer to de Finetti and Savage, and they are regarded as Bayesians. But the crucial thing is not inverse probability. What's crucial is the notion of personal probability. It's really objective probabilities versus personal probabilities as the key element. I would classify myself as personal probability, and I would say that from a methodological point of view, Jimmie Savage has exerted as much of an influence on me as Popper did. And if Jimmie Savage was alive, he would have said the same thing about me I know. We were very good friends, but also we had a great deal of influence one on the other. And the articles we wrote jointly were really joint, though there are some parts of them that were clearly Jimmie's. Surely the purely axiomatic logic, the underpinnings of measuring utility, are all Jimmie's. But I really can't say that there's any part of it that he didn't contribute to or that I didn't contribute to.

You suggest in the 1981 discussion on the history of Law and Economics at Chicago (Kitch, 1983) that Aaron Director was an important influence on your research. George Stigler mentioned in the same discussion that Director insisted on profit-maximization explanations of behavior, as opposed to detailed accounts. If one takes this type of analysis as a hallmark of Chicago economics and of your own, how would you compare Director's influence to that of Knight and Viner?

Your question is really very difficult. Because if you look at what Director did—the fascinating thing about him is that he was one of the students of Knight who I think was in some ways rendered infertile by Knight, repressed by Knight. He came to Chicago as a student of Paul Douglas, and the only real book he wrote was a book he wrote jointly with Paul Douglas before he came under the influence of Knight (Douglas and Director, 1931). Aaron, at the Law School, did not write much himself, but he had a tremendous influence on other people. The most important article John McGee ever wrote was an article on the Standard Oil-Rockefeller case (McGee, 1958). The allegation was that Standard Oil got a monopoly by undercutting its competition with the idea of subsequently being able to raise its price and get it all back. It was unquestionably Aaron who pointed out that that made no logical economic sense, and McGee who went back to zero in on the case and found that it didn't make any empirical sense either. If you look at the introduction to Bob Bork's book on antitrust (Bork, 1978) you will find there that he attributes to Aaron fundamental responsibility for his own change of ideas. If you take the work that's been done on tie-in pricing, it traces back to the influence that Aaron had on the people who did it.

So, where Aaron had his influence, he was different from either Knight or Viner. Knight was a philosopher, as I say, fundamentally. Viner was a marvelous teacher, an excellent technician of theory, and his basic interest was in the history of economic thought. Aaron had a great deal of interest in the history of economic thought also, but he also had a real interest in how to apply the theoretical ideas of the economics of the firm to the individual firms or the individual industries. And, in the course of teaching, particularly in the course of teaching the course at the law school with Ed Levi on anti-trust, the subject matter that he was teaching sort of generated all these interesting examples. How do you explain the fact that IBM would only rent and not sell its machines; it required the people who rented the machine to buy their punchcards from it and not from anybody else. The antitrust cases automatically brought up these puzzles. How do you explain them? We say that these companies are trying to maximize profit. How does this fit in with maximization of profit? And that was the origin of much of Director's influence. If you look at my price theory book, there is in the back a collection of problems which I gave to students. A large fraction of those problems came out of Aaron Director, exactly in that way. And that's the sense in which he was different from either Knight or Viner. He had, as it were, Viner's command of economic theory, and belief in economic theory as a real thing, but he had something that I think neither Knight nor Viner did have, which was this interest in solving these concrete problems—in particular, problems in the area of Industrial Organization. That's what led him to found the whole field of Law and Economics.

Using your terminology, would you refer to him as a Marshallian?

Oh yes.

The same sense that you are?

The same sense, absolutely.

Reder (1982) argues that the key to the dominance of the "Chicago view" at Chicago was in the appointments of yourself, George Stigler, and Allen Wallis to the faculties. He gives the label "Tight Prior Equilibrium" to this "Chicago view." "Tight Prior Equilibrium" is the use of Pareto optimality as a premise of applied work, in conjunction with other assumptions taken as "first approximations": transaction prices are market clearing; information is acquired to the point at which its marginal cost equals its price; and neither monopoly nor government intervention prevents marginal products and resource prices from being equalized across uses. Do you see this identification of the "Chicago view" as essentially the same as the "Marshallian" approach? Are there important differences? Would it matter to you whether one or the other was used to describe your approach?

What Reder is describing is substance rather than methodology, and so I don't regard his identification of the Chicago view as essentially the same as the Marshallian approach at all. But neither do I regard it as in contradiction. I think you're talking about different things. About nonintersecting things as it were. The Marshallian approach has to do with what you're trying to achieve, what your purpose is, what your objective is, and how you go about it. What he calls the "Chicago view" is a set of tentative hypotheses, substantive hypotheses, accepted as starting points for investigation, and I think that's a correct description. But the starting point for an investigation, and the methodological approach to an investigation, are two very different things, and I would say that those two views are complementary, rather than any way contradictory or competitive. And I think that covers that part.

Thank you so much. I certainly appreciate it.

That's all right.

APPENDIX

HOOVER INSTITUTION
ON WAR, REVOLUTION AND PEACE

Stanford, California 94305-2323

June 13, 1985

Mr. J. Daniel Hammond
Department of Economics
Wake Forest University
Winston-Salem, North Carolina 27109

Dear Mr. Hammond:

I appreciate your sending me a copy of your paper on "Monetarist and Anti-monetarist Causality." My feeling after reading it, if I may put it very bluntly, is that I have been stuffed with straw and attacked. I have little quarrel with your substantive conclusions; I have a considerable quarrel with the rhetoric.

I have always regarded "cause" as a very tricky concept. In my technical scientific writings I have to the best of my ability tried to avoid using the word. In the quotation with which you start the paper I do not say at all that money stock is a cause. I believe that you will not be able to find a statement in the *Monetary History* or in other scientific writings of mine in which I make such an assertion. This is clear form your own summary of our comments about the theoretical and empirical elements in respect of inflation.

I must confess that I departed from my determination to avoid using the word "cause" in *Free to Choose* which was intended for a relatively popular audience but even there, in addition to the quotes you give from it, it seems to me it is relevant to note that first I say: "The recognition that substantial inflation is always and everywhere a monetary· phenomenon is only the beginning of an understanding of the cause and cure of inflation"; and then I go on to say which direction you have to go. Moreover, with respect to whether inflation is always and everywhere a monetary phenomenon, on the bottom of page 255 of *Free to Choose* I point out that this is essentially an empirical statement, that "to our knowledge there is no example in history of a substantial inflation that lasted for more than a brief time that was not accompanied by a roughly correspondingly rapid increase in the quantity of money; and no example of a rapid increase in the quantity of money that was not accompanied by a roughly correspondingly substantial inflation." I do not believe that those statements justify your statement on the bottom of page 14: "Milton Friedman's identification of money growth as THE cause of inflation . . ." Even in the less rigorous *Free to Choose* statements I insert weasel words such as "substantial," "rapid," "roughly correspondingly." Clearly, for anybody who is at all sophisticated about the economic relations those qualifications are inserted precisely because I believe that other factors do affect what happens to inflation because the theoretical analysis in terms of the quantity theory that you outlined is really what underlies my analysis.

I have no quarrel with your saying that Kaldor uses the same implicit concept of causation as I do. I believe he is simply factually wrong in his assertions about what happened, but that is a wholly different argument than the one you make here.

In short, you have attributed to me a definition of "cause" as a general definition that to the best of my knowledge I have never stated or published anywhere. With respect to the Mackie definition of "cause," it is a plausible one but I am by no means persuaded that it resolves the ambiguities. The problem is in your simple example if you say the short caused the fire you have to ask what caused the short. This is a process of infinite regress. That is why I have tended to try in my technical writings to avoid using the word "cause." Indeed, even in *Free to Choose* on page 253 the heading of that section is "The Proximate Cause of Inflation."

One final comment. Antonio Martino's statement comes closer to fitting your straw man than any statement of mine you have quoted. But I doubt that you would want to have your paper rely on a quotation from him rather than from me. I personally share your criticism of his statement. It is a careless and superficial statement, and he would be the first to admit it if he were pressed on it.

Sincerely yours,

Milton Friedman
Senior Research Fellow

REFERENCES

Bork, R. 1978. *The Antitrust Paradox: A Policy at War With Itself.* New York: Basic Books.
Burns, A.F. and W.C. Mitchell. 1946. *Measuring Business Cycles.* New York: National Bureau of Economic Research.
Bye, R.T. 1939. *Critiques of Research in the Social Sciences*, II, *An Appraisal of Frederick C. Mills' The Behavior of Prices.* New York: Social Science Research Council.

Clark, J.M. 1923. *Studies in the Economics of Overhead Cost.* Chicago: University of Chicago Press.

_____. 1965[1935]. *Economics of Planning Public Works.* New York: Augustus M. Kelley.

Culbertson, J.M. 1960. "Friedman on the Lab in Effect of Monetary Policy." *Journal of Political Economy* 69 (October): 467-477.

_____. 1961. "The Lag in Effect of Monetary Policy: Reply." *Journal of Political Economy* 69 (October): 467-477.

Douglas, P.H. and A. Director. 1931. *Problem of Unemployment.* New York: Macmillan.

Friedman, M. 1946. "Lange on Price Flexibility and Employment." *American Economic Review* 36 (September): 613-631.

_____. 1949. "The Marshallian Demand Curve." *Journal of Political Economy* 57 (December): 463-495.

_____. 1950. "Wesley C. Mitchell as an Economic Theorist." *Journal of Political Economy* 58 (December): 465-493.

_____. 1952. "Comment." Pp. 455-457 in *A Survey of Contemporary Economics,* vol. 2, edited by B.F. Haley. Chicago: Richard D. Irwin, Inc.

_____. 1953a. *Essays in Positive Economics.* Chicago: University of Chicago Press.

_____. 1953b. "The Methodology of Positive Economics." Pp. 3-43 in *Essays in Positive Economics.* Chicago: University of Chicago Press.

_____. 1955. "Leon Walras and His Economic System." *American Economic Review* 45 (December): 900-909.

_____. 1963. *Inflation: Causes, Consequences, and Cures.* Bombay: Asia Publishing House for the Council for Economic Education.

_____. 1964. "The Monetary Studies of the National Bureau." Pp. 7-25 in *The National Bureau Enters Its 45th Year,* Forty-fourth Annual Report of the National Bureau of Economic Research. New York: National Bureau of Economic Research.

_____. 1974. "Inflation, Taxation, Indexation." Pp. 71-88 in *Inflation: Causes, Consequences, Cures,* IEA Reading no. 14. London: Institute of Economic Affairs.

_____. 1986. "My Evoluation as an Economist." Pp. 77-92 in *Lives of the Laureates,* edited by W. Breit and R.W. Spencer. Cambridge: MIT Press.

Friedman, M. and R.D. Friedman. 1980. *Free to Choose.* New York: Harcourt Brace Jovanovich.

Friedman, M. and A.J. Schwartz. 1963. *A Monetary History of the United States, 1867-1960.* Princeton: Princeton University Press.

Hammond, J. Daniel. 1986. "Monetarist and Antimonetarist Causality." Pp. 109-126 in *Research in the History of Economic Thought and Methodology,* vol. 4, edited by W.J. Samuels. Greenwich, CT: JAI Press.

Hayek, F.A. 1944. *The Road to Serfdom.* Chicago: University of Chicago Press.

Hotelling, H. 1931. "The Economics of Exhaustible Resources." *Journal of Political Economy* 39 (April): 137-175.

_____. 1932. "Edgeworth's Taxation Paradox and the Nature of Demand and Supply Functions." *Journal of Political Economy* 40 (October): 577-616.

Kitch, E.W., ed. 1983. "The Fire of Truth: A Remembrance of Law and Economics at Chicago, 1932-1970." *Journal of Law and Economics* 26 (April): 163-234.

Koopmans, T.C. 1947. "Measurement Without Theory." *Review of Economics and Statistics* 29 (August): 161-172.

Lange, O. 1944. *Price Flexibility and Employment.* Bloomington, IN: Principia Press.

McGee, J.S. 1958. "Predatory Price Cutting: The Standard Oil-(N.J.) Case." *Journal of Law and Economics* (October): 137-169.

Mackie, J.L. 1974. *The Cement of the Universe: A Study of Causation.* London: Oxford University Press.

Marshall, A. and M.P. Marshall. 1879. *Economics of Industry.* London: Macmillan.

Mills, Frederick C. *The Behavior of Prices.* New York: National Bureau of Economic Research.

Noyes, C.R. 1945. "Director's Comment." Pp. 405-410 in M. Friedman and S. Kuznets, *Income from Independent Professional Practice.* New York: National Bureau of Economic Research.

Popper, K. 1935. *Logik der Forschung.* Vienna: Springer..

————. *The Open Society and Its Enemies.* London: Routledge and Kegan Paul.

————. 1963. *Conjectures and Refutations.* New York: Harper and Row.

Reder, M. 1982. "Chicago Economics: Permanence and Change." *Journal of Economic Literature* 20 (March): 1-38.

Schultz, H. 1938. *Theory and Measurement of Demand.* Chicago: University of Chicago Press.

Viner, J. 1917. "Some Problems in the Logical Method in Political Economy." *Journal of Political Economy* 25 (March): 236-260.

————. 1925. "Objective jTests of Competitive Price Applied to the Cement Industry." *Journal of Political Economy* 33 (February): 107-111.

————. 1929. "Review of *The Behavior of Prices.*" *Quarterly Journal of Economics* 43 (February): 337-352.

Walters, A. 1987. "Friedman, Milton." Pp. 422-427 in *The New Palgrave: A Dictionary of Economics*, vol. 2, edited by J. Eatwell, M. Milgate, P. Newman. London: Macmillan.

FRIEDMAN'S PREDICTIVIST INSTRUMENTALISM—A MODIFICATION

Bruce J. Caldwell

In an article titled "A Critique of Friedman's Methodological Instrumentalism" (1980) as well as in my book, *Beyond Positivism* (1982, henceforth *BP*), I argued that Milton Friedman's methodology could be reconstructed as a variant of the philosophical position known as instrumentalism. In this paper, I review the origins of my views in the work of Ernest Nagel. Next, an error in my presentation is corrected and a modification is offered. I argue that Friedman can still be viewed as an instrumentalist, but that his is a predictivist rather than a noncognitivist variant of the doctrine. Where appropriate, I will compare my views with those of the other participants in the symposium.

I. ORIGIN OF MY IDEAS ON INSTRUMENTALISM

My point of departure was "The Cognitive Status of Theories," chapter 6 of Ernest Nagel's magisterial *The Structure of Science* (1961). Nagel argued that

Research in the History of Economic Thought and Methodology
Volume 10, pages 119-128.
ISBN: 0-55938-501-4

both realism and instrumentalism could be presented as reasonable positions, that "opposition between these views is a conflict over preferred modes of speech" (p. 152). This stance appealed to me at the time I was writing, though I suspect that many would not accept it today.

Nagel defines an instrumentalist as one who:

> maintains that theories are primarily logical instruments for organizing our experience and for ordering experimental laws. Although some theories are more effective than others for attaining these ends, theories are not statements, and belong to a different category of linguistic expressions than do statements. For theories function as rules or principles in accordance with which empirical materials are analyzed or inferences drawn, rather than as premises from which factual conclusions are deduced; and they cannot therefore be usefully characterized as either true or false, or even as probably true or probably false. However, those who adopt this position do not always agree in their answers to the question whether physical reality is to be assigned to such theoretical entities as atoms (p. 118).

Nagel contrasts instrumentalism with realism. Realists view theories as literally true or false, even though in practice the best that one may be able to do is to establish them as more or less probable. Realists also believe that the objects ostensibly postulated by theories actually exist.

Nagel also discusses the strengths and limitations of instrumentalism. There are two major strengths. First, instrumentalism accurately describes the way that theories are often actually used by scientists: as instruments for some practical purpose. Second, it avoids numerous difficulties associated with other views. For example, it is not necessary to worry about the literal truth or falsity of theories, which is particularly liberating for theorists. (This point was made by Giedymin, cited in *BP*, p. 52.) Or, as Nagel mentions, theories are often formulated using ideal, limiting concepts (perfect vacuum, perfect competition) which are for the most part not descriptive of anything observable. When viewed as statements, these must be viewed as false. The instrumentalist can easily justify the use of such concepts because they make the theory simpler. "Despite the fact that a theory may employ simplifying concepts, it will in general be preferred to another theory using more 'realistic' notions if the former answers to the purposes of a given inquiry and can be handled more conveniently than the latter" (p. 132).

The limitations are three. First, just because theories are often *used* as instruments does not imply that terms like "true" and "false" cannot be used to characterize them. Next, when theories are used as premises in scientific explanations, they are statements about which it makes sense to ask about truth and falsity. Finally, scientists who claim to be instrumentalists often speak like realists—they talk as if they believe that theoretical entities actually exist, for example.

II. MY INTERPRETATION OF FRIEDMAN
AS AN INSTRUMENTALIST

In *BP*, I mentioned the instrumentalist-realist debate concerning whether theoretical terms make real reference, but I did not follow up on it because no economic methodologist had ever discussed the question of reference in that particular context. Though at the time I was writing (the late 1970s) it seemed clear that realism was becoming increasingly important in the philosophy of science, I could not see its relevance for economics. That is probably why I found Nagel's agnostic treatment of the issue so attractive.

Of all the writings on economic methodology reviewed in *BP*, Friedman's work was the most difficult to interpret because of his paucity of references to philosophers. In an article published in 1973, Stanley Wong argued that Friedman could best be characterized as an instrumentalist. After reading Nagel, it seemed to me that this was, indeed, the best way to interpret the Chicago economist's position. This view was further supported by Larry Boland's (1979) addition to the literature. My contributions in *BP* and in my (1980) *Southern Economic Journal* piece were two. First, I labeled Friedman's position "*methodological instrumentalism*," which was meant to emphasize that Friedman was never interested in the *philosophical* questions which surrounded the instrumentalism-realism debate. (Thus, I agree completely with Dan Hammond's point that Friedman's context was very different from those of his later interpreters.) Next, I offered a critique of Friedman's methodological position.

Fairly soon after the publication of my article and book, it was pointed out to me in correspondence from Boland and Dan Hausman that I had made a mistake in characterizing Friedman as an instrumentalist. As was shown above, instrumentalists believe that theories, because they are instruments, *cannot be usefully characterized as true or false.* Friedman's most noteworthy claim is that the realism of a theory's assumptions should not matter in our assessment of the theory's adequacy, that the ability to predict and simplicity are the only appropriate criteria of theory appraisal. In my discussion of Friedman, I equated "realism" with "truth-value." I then argued that Friedman is an instrumentalist. But this is a mistake. If it is correct to equate realism with truth-value, then Friedman is saying that the assumptions of economic theory *can* be characterized as true or false: *namely, they are **false**.* However, their truth or falsity ("realism") *does not matter, because only predictive adequacy matters.* My error was to equate Friedman's claim that *truth and falsity do not matter* with the instrumentalist claim that theories *are not true or false.*

How important was the error to the rest of my argument? In one sense, it was an egregious mistake, since one of the announced goals of my early work was to clarify the confusion I had found in the methodological literature. But the error did very little damage to my own critique of Friedman. A cursory examination of the arguments in *BP* bears this contention out.

My first move was to point out two standard philosophical arguments against instrumentalism. The first is that explanation should share equal billing with prediction as a goal of science. Logical empiricists had asserted the logical symmetry of explanation and prediction. Their opponents in the 1960s argued that often scientists are able to explain phenomena (like evolution, or the characteristics which suicides might share) without being able to predict them. On the basis of such counterexamples, the symmetry thesis was denied and it was claimed that the goals of science should include both explanation and prediction.

This argument, because it insists that science explains as well as predicts, shares common ground with the one presented by Tony Lawson in his symposium contribution. Lawson's argument is more ambitious, however, since it would seem to leave out the possibility of prediction in any but a closed system. Since the systems studied by most scientists (economists included) are open rather than closed, explanation takes precedence over prediction as the goal of science. Lawson completes his argument by offering a specific realist account of what constitutes an adequate scientific explanation.

The second argument is that theories *can* be usefully characterized as true or false. This second argument *does not* work against Friedman, since he admits that the assumptions of economic theories are true or false. (As noted above, he says that they are mostly false, but that *their falsity does not matter.*) With some modification, though, even this second argument can be made to work against Friedman. Most *philosophers* who believe that theories are true or false also believe that the truth or falsity of a theory's assumptions *does matter*, and matters very much. Indeed, this is one reason why philosophers find Friedman's position so bizarre. (Since his position is not viewed as bizarre by many economists, this leads philosophers to draw the obvious inference about economists-in-general, as well.)

Having presented the philosophical case against instrumentalism, I then made the key observation that any adequate critique of Friedman would have to go beyond the philosophical disputes and deal with his position as it relates to the practice of economics.[1] Two further arguments were then presented. The first was a challenge of Friedman's claim that prediction is the *only* goal of *economic* science. The second was a demonstration that Friedman did not adhere *in his own work* to his strictures concerning simplicity. Neither argument concerned the truth value of statements.

III. FRIEDMAN AS A PREDICTIVIST INSTRUMENTALIST

It may still be true that Friedman is best characterized as an instrumentalist. But it is also clear that the standard categories do not fit him very well. Some new categories will be proposed in an attempt to clarify the situation.

Let us begin by defining two variants of instrumentalism. They differ according to their starting points. *Noncognitive instrumentalism* begins from a descriptive statement about the cognitive status of theories (theories are instruments, and therefore cannot be viewed as true or false). *Predictivist instrumentalism* starts out from a normative statement concerning the proper goal of science (the only goal of science is the development of theories which are good instruments for prediction).[2] An instrumentalist could hold either view, or both together. (It will turn out that Friedman can be read as affirming predictivist instrumentalism but denying noncognitive instrumentalism.) Let us examine each of the forms of instrumentalism more closely to see how they fit in economics.

A. Noncognitive Instrumentalism and Economics

The entire issue of whether noncognitive instrumentalism offers a suitable methodology for economics depends on whether one believes that theories are statements (in which case they can be characterized as true or false) or rules of procedure, inference tickets, or instruments (in which case they cannot be characterized as true or false).

Most economists have never explicitly considered this issue. However, economists sometimes say things which might be construed as supportive of noncognitive instrumentalism. Consider the assertion, "My theory is just an instrument for some purpose; I do not think of it as true or false." One who makes such a claim may well be a conscious advocate of noncognitive instrumentalism. But there are other possibilities. For example, an economist might make the statement in justifying his failure to reject the useful but false theories so commonly encountered in the discipline. Alternatively, one might refer to a theory as an instrument in an attempt to be a careful and modest researcher. After all, it takes considerable cheek to assert that one has a true theory. It seems more modest, and perhaps even more scientific, to claim that one's theory is only an instrument.

Both Dan Hausman (1989) and Uskali Mäki (1989) have argued that among economic methodologists, Fritz Machlup comes closest to endorsing this version of instrumentalism.[3] Machlup referred to theories as "inference tickets" and "rules of procedure" (Machlup, 1955, p. 16), terms which a noncognitive instrumentalist certainly would use. He expropriated these ideas from philosophers in an attempt to walk a middle road between the extremes of (what he called) ultraempiricism and a priorism. But this was only one part of his methodological thought. Machlup also opposed the popular positivism of his day, preferring a subjectivist approach that leaned heavily on the work of such writers as Max Weber and Alfred Schütz. This led him to make some recommendations which are difficult to square with noncognitive instrumentalism: for example, that the assumptions of economic theory be "understandable" (1955, p. 17). Machlup was exposed to a wide variety of methodological views in his days in Vienna. As a result, his own approach was an eclectic and idiosyncratic blend of a number of possibly incompatible positions. As such, the noncognitive instrumentalist model is insufficiently rich to capture the totality of Machlup's methodological views.

B.   Friedman's Predictivist Instrumentalism and Economics

Predictivist instrumentalism states that the *only* goal of science is the development of theories which are good instruments for prediction. Given this end, the best attributes a theory can possess are predictive adequacy and simplicity.

In its pure form, this doctrine is agnostic concerning the key issue facing noncognitive instrumentalists, the cognitive status of theories. For the predictivist instrumentalist, theories may be viewed *either* as statements or as instruments. But in *his* version of predictivist instrumentalism, Friedman is *not* agnostic. For Friedman, theories are statements which can be considered true or false. Thus, Friedman affirms predictivist instrumentalism but denies noncognitive instrumentalism.

One final element must be added to get a full statement of Friedman's methodological position. If theories contain statements which can be true or false, should we seek true theories, or false theories, or does it not matter? Friedman's answer is that the "realism of assumptions" (their truth-value) does not matter.

Friedman's predictivist instrumentalism can therefore be stated as follows:

The only goal of science is the development of theories which are good instruments for prediction. Given this end, the best attributes a theory can possess are predictive adequacy and simplicity. The "realism of assumptions" (their truth-value) does not matter. Indeed, many of the "best" theories in economics have assumptions which are false.

Friedman's predictivist instrumentalism is much better than is noncognitive instrumentalism for describing the views of economists. (Of course, this may be due simply to the influence that Friedman's essay has had on the profession.) Predictivist instrumentalism accomodates the fact that economists often view the discovery of predictively adequate theories as their sole goal. Similarly, when economists use assumptions which are unrealistic, they are more likely to say that the use of unrealistic assumptions does not matter than they are to say that the assumptions are neither true nor false.

The claim that prediction is the *only* goal of science is the most controversial part of this position. If accepted, it would make the search for true, explanatory theories at best incidental to the search for the best predictor. Realist philosophers of science would reject Friedman's position on these grounds.

Within economics, I think that fewer economists would so quickly reject this claim, primarily because Friedman's position has entered the rhetoric of the profession. But our *practice* is not consistent with it. Predictive adequacy is valued highly by economists, but it is not the *only* goal of economics. Friedman's predictivist instrumentalism at best describes only a part of what economists do.

It can be finally noted that, *even if* one were to accept the proposition that prediction is the sole goal of science, this does not imply that the truth and falsity of assumptions does not matter, nor that the simpler theory is the better theory.

Dan Hausman (1989) shows that the former claim need not hold. Say a theory which once predicted well suddenly starts predicting poorly. How might we go about trying to figure out what went wrong? Hausman answers that an efficient way is to inquire about the truth or falsity of some of its assumptions. Thus, *for instrumental reasons* (that is, in order to find the best predictor), we may well be interested in the truth and falsity of assumptions.

Though there are problems with defining simplicity, I argued in *BP* that the simpler theory need not be the one that predicts best. The example is the Phillips Curve. The stationary, "simpler" Phillips Curve does less well at predicting the events of the 1970's than does the more "realistic" Friedman-Phelps apparatus. That Friedman developed this apparatus, and even referred to it in his Nobel address as an example of scientific progress in economics, is one of the sweeter ironies of this tale.

IV. SOME CONCLUDING REMARKS

In conclusion, I will briefly mention some points of contact between my framework and the far richer engine of analysis proposed by Mäki. Because of the complexity and detail of Mäki's system, it may not be apparent that the two frameworks are broadly consistent with one another. But they are. An ontological, referential, representational, and veristic nonrealist is the same thing as a noncognitive instrumentalist: both think that their theories do not refer to or represent anything existing in the world. In describing Friedman's position, I argued that he denied noncognitive instrumentalism. This is equivalent to Mäki's claim that Friedman is a semantical realist in all the dimensions mentioned above. I pointed out that for predictivist instrumentalists like Friedman, predictive adequacy and simplicity are important attributes of a theory. This is equivalent to Mäki's claim that Friedman values certain realistic attributes of neoclassical theory ("is capable of predicting well") as well as certain unrealistic attributes ("is simple").

Our accounts differ in two respects. In my presentation, I equate "realism of assumptions" with "truth-value." Mäki presents a much richer and more general interpretation in which "realisticness" *can* refer to truth-value, but also to other characteristics of representations. Second, I argued that false assumptions do not matter to Friedman (what matters is predictive adequacy), whereas Mäki claims that Friedman views false assumptions *as a virtue*.

For a predictivist instrumentalist who also denies noncognitive instrumentalism (like Friedman does), there are actually *three* alternatives. These can be stated in the form of imperatives:

1. Seek true theories which predict well!
2. Seek false theories which predict well!
3. Seek theories which predict well, their truth or falsity does not matter!

Mäki attributes version number two to Friedman, whereas I attribute version number three to him.

Both interpretations find support in Friedman's text. Interestingly, our disagreement may be due to differences in our respective interpretative frameworks. Most realists think that we *should* seek theories which are true, that is, they endorse imperative number one. As a realist, Mäki's interpretative eye was drawn to those passages in Friedman's essay in which the opposite claim is made. Because I focused on Friedman's predictivist instrumentalism, I was drawn to those passages in which the importance of prediction was emphasized. In addition, in *BP* I always tried to present whatever position was under examination *in its best possible light* before submitting it to criticism. This is relevant because I believe version number two to be a straw man. It implies that we should choose a theory we know to be false over one we believe to be true if both predict well. It also implies that we should seek out false theories to substitute for all theories we believe to be true. Version three thus seems to be the more defensible one.

It must be added that *neither* framework attempts to explain *why* Friedman viewed prediction as so important and "unrealistic assumptions" as inconsequential. Dan Hammond suggests an answer to these questions. Friedman is a Marshallian, a practical, applied economist who wants to solve problems in the real world. But he also recognizes that the tools available to him (and for Friedman, the only tools are those of neoclassical theory) have assumptions which are problematical. Friedman's response is to argue that it is not necessary to worry about these problematical, "unrealistic" assumptions. *Were Friedman to stop here,* his position would be indistinguishable from the Walrasians, who also use theories with false assumptions. This is precisely why prediction is so important for Friedman. **Prediction is his link to the real world.** It is what separates his views from those of Walrasians like Lange and Lerner or, for that matter, Arrow and Debreu. Hammond's great contribution is to get us to step back from the philosophical categories to get a handle on the issues which actually motivated Friedman in his work.

ACKNOWLEDGMENT

I would like to thank Warren Samuels and Dan Hausman for their insightful comments on the paper. Remaining errors are my own.

NOTES

1. Given the disagreement that existed in the philosophy of science, it was crucial to go beyond that discipline in developing criticisms of methodological positions in economics. This point was emphasized early on in *BP*:

> A study of economic methodology from a philosophy of science perspective may help one to clarify, unify, categorize, and explicate debates in the former field. But it will not provide ultimate grounds for arbitrating among well-developed and well-argued alternative positions. (p. 3).

The sorts of additional questions which were asked included: Is this position practicable in economics? Does it accurately portray any current practice? Does its proponent's work reflect its usage? Is it internally consistent? What would be the benefits and costs of its adoption?

2. The term "noncognitive instrumentalism" is borrowed from an article by Sidney Morgenbesser (1969), though I use it in a slightly different way. Dan Hausman alerted me to the importance of Morgenbesser's piece. I discovered, after completing the paper, that Alan Coddington had earlier (1979) used the term "predictionism" to refer to what I have labeled Friedman's predictivism. Coddington makes a number of important points, but unfortunately, the article has gone unappreciated.

3. Actually, Hausman argues that while Machlup is the closest thing we have to a noncognitive instrumentalist in economics, he nonetheless badly misapplied the doctrine. Machlup used it to insulate the "theoretical" claims of neoclassical economics from testing. Logical empiricists had used it to argue that it was possible to still accept theories which had theoretical claims which were untestable.

REFERENCES

Boland, Lawrence. 1979. "A Critique of Friedman's Critics." *Journal of Economic Literature* 17:503-522.

Caldwell, Bruce. 1980. "A Critique of Friedman's Methodological Instrumentalism." *Southern Economic Journal* 47:366-374.

_____. 1982. *Beyond Positivism*. London: Allen and Unwin.

Coddington, Alan. 1979. "Friedman's Contribution to Methodological Controversy." *British Review of Economic Issues* 2:1-13.

Friedman, Milton. 1953. "The Methodology of Positive Economics." Pp. 3-43 in *Essays in Positive Economics*. Chicago: University of Chicago Press.

Hausman, Daniel. 1989. "Economic Methodology in a Nutshell." *Journal of Economic Perspectives* 3:115-127.

Machlup, Fritz. 1955. "The Problem of Verification in Economics." *Southern Economic Journal* 22:1-21.

Mäki, Uskali. 1988. "How To Combine Rhetoric and Realism in the Methodology of Economics."
    Economics and Philosophy 4:89-109.
————. 1989. "On the Problem of Realism in Economics." *Ricerche Economiche* 43: 176-198.
Morgenbesser, Sidney. 1969. "The Realist-Instrumentalist Controversy." Pp. 200-218 in
    Philosophy, Science and Method: Essays in Honor of Ernest Nagel, edited by S.
    Morgenbesser, P. Suppes, and M. White. New York: St. Martin's Press.
Nagel, Ernest. 1961. *The Structure of Science.* New York: Harcourt Brace.
Wong, Stanley. 1973. "The F-Twist and the Methodology of Paul Samuelson." *American
    Economic Review* 62:312-325.

THE PROBLEM OF CONTEXT FOR
FRIEDMAN'S METHODOLOGY

J. Daniel Hammond

I. INTRODUCTION

One facet of the increased specialization in economics over the past half-century is the separation of the community of methodologists from economic theorists. This is not to say that methodological disputes and theoretical disputes no longer become intertwined or that theorists have no interest in methodology or methodologists in theory. But there has been something of a split both in popular perception and in reality. With regard to perceptions, it is necessary to look no further than editorial remarks of referees and editors of mainline (i.e., not history of thought or philosophy of science) economics journals about the market for methodology among their readers. As for the reality, while labeling (as methodology or as theory) seems to often be a crucial factor in these "market surveys," the days when the main texts of theory and of methodology were written by the same individuals are past. The tradition of great theorists/methodologists that stretches from Hume through Mill, Cairnes, Robbins, and Knight, to name a few, seems to have come to an end.

Research in the History of Economic Thought and Methodology
Volume 10, pages 129-147.
Copyright © 1992 by JAI Press Inc.
All rights of reproduction in any form reserved.
ISBN: 0-55938-501-4

Today, there is very little overlap between the people reading papers at the History of Economics Society meetings and those reading papers at the American Economic Association meeting economic theory sessions. Undoubtedly, one part of the dynamic of this separation of methodology from theory is the replacement of philosophy with mathematics as the immediate substratum of economic theory. Methodology, after all, is a philosophical enterprise. Classical economists were moral philosophers. Today's economic theorist is a mathematical economist.

So, philosophy in the classical period and mathematics more recently are part of the context of the economic theory of the periods. They and other parts of the context from which the economics of any period develops are essential to an interpretation of texts and to an understanding of the discipline's evolution. For the making of theory or methodology, it takes little effort to keep the current context in mind, for it cannot be escaped. But, for the historian of methodology (or the historical dimension of methodology), context is more of a problem. For there an ongoing history, and thus an ongoing evolution of context, is being dealt with. It is easy to lose sight of the fact that we read a thirty-year-old text, for example, from a different perspective than that from which it was written. Thus, the message we find in the text and our response to it depend crucially on the context that we as readers bring to it, and this may be quite different from the author's.

This symposium on "Realism, Instrumentalism, and Friedman's Methodology" is about context. Both realism and instrumentalism are important categorical contexts for modern philosophy of science and economic methodology and, as such, they have become parts of the context for the discussion of Milton Friedman's methodology. Whether they were parts of Friedman's context for writing "The Methodology of Positive Economics" (1953b) is another matter. This particular paper uses realism and instrumentalism as means for raising questions about the contexts of the writing and the reading of "The Methodology of Positive Economics." The issue is whether there are important differences in these two contexts. That is, to borrow terms from Leijonhufvud (1968), are there important differences between "Friedman's methodology" and "the methodology of Friedman"? The second section of the paper considers the meaning and implications of realism and instrumentalism in philosophy and in evaluations of Friedman's methodology. This is followed by a survey of the evolution of the context for interpretation and criticism of Friedman's 1953 essay. The fourth part of the paper draws on Friedman's methodological publications other than the 1953 essay and on a recent interview with Friedman (published as part of this symposium) to distinguish Friedman's context from the contexts of his methodologist critics.

II. PHILOSOPHICAL REALISM
AND INSTRUMENTALISM

There are many different varieties of philosophical realism, so any attempt to do justice to them all would be futile. Yet, by examining a few, we can glimpse their variety and commonality. Instrumentalism is more easily circumscribed, for it is generally viewed as one particular type of antirealism. An apt place to begin a survey of philosophical realism and instrumentalism is with Karl Popper.

A. Popper's Realism

Popper treated both realism and instrumentalism in *Realism and the Aim of Science* (1983), which was written over the 1951-1956 period as a postscript to *The Logic of Scientific Discovery* (1959),[1] and in "Three Views Concerning Human Knowledge" (1963b), first published in 1956. Popper took a realist position in opposition to instrumentalism. His argument was a response to logical positivist interpretations of physics. Mach, Bohr, and Schlick viewed physical theory as in Popper's words, "*nothing but an instrument* [emphasis his], for the deduction of predictions of future events (especially measurements) and for other practical applications; and more especially...not...as a genuine conjecture about the structure of the world, or as a genuine attempt to describe certain aspects of our world" (1983, p. 111). In this passage, Popper defines instrumentalism and, by contrast, his brand of realism. The key to Popper's realism is that theories are seen as "genuine conjectures" about the world. They are descriptive statements, which are either true or false. Instruments are neither true or false, only more or less useful. Theories, according to Popper's realist account, are subject to being tested for falsity, although there is no practical possibility for certain verification. Instruments are tested only for their range of applicability; tests of truth-value are inconsistent with their nature. Theories allow us to learn something we did not previously know about the nature of the world, or equivalently to predict that which is unknown. But instruments are not used to produce new knowledge; they enable us only to predict that which is already known.

Popper traced instrumentalism to Berkeley's skeptical "mistake," which was to presume that "to be is to be known" (1963b, p. 117). The "problem of induction" underlay positivist instrumentalism. We can produce knowledge only through our senses, but there is no logic of induction whereby we can verify that knowledge. Therefore, we cannot truly know anything of the nature of the world. According to this view, theories are not used to produce true knowledge (i.e., they do not explain) but are only instrumental to less ambitious ends such as prediction and measurement. Aside from Berkeley, Mach, Bohr, and Schlick, Popper saw J.S. Mill, Poincaré, Wittgenstein, and Duhem as instrumentalists. Some of these were scientist-philosophers while others were strictly philosophers. Popper suggested that instrumentalism is singularly a philosophical notion and that working scientists are realists.

The particularity of Popper's realism can be seen in his opposition to an alternative realist position, essentialism. Essentialists presume that entities have essential natures and that theory describes those essences. Popper did not object to the first presumption, but he did to the second. His realism has a less demanding "stopping rule" for explanation; it does not require description of essences. Popper also objected to the essentialist notion that theory, in describing essences, is indubitable. In Popper's realism, theories always remain less than certain conjectures by virtue of the impossibility of providing exhaustive tests.

B.   Hacking's Realism

A second variety of realism is presented by Ian Hacking in *Representing and Intervening* (1983). For the purpose of differentiating his realism from Popper's, Hacking opens his book with a comparison of Popper and Carnap, who represents the logical positivism to which Popper was opposed. After listing several points of disagreement between the two, Hacking offers eight specific points of agreement to suggest the fundamental sameness in Popper's and Carnap's pre-Kuhnian views of science. These points are:

1.   Natural science as the best example of rational thought;
2.   A sharp distinction between observation and theory;
3.   The cumulative growth of knowledge;
4.   The tight deductive structure of science;
5.   The importance of precision in scientific terminology;
6.   The unity of science,
7.   The context of justification as crucial, and the context of discovery as not important; and
'8.   The timelessness of science.

Against this background, Hacking develops his distinctively post-Kuhnian brand of realism, suitable for science seen as a "motley" enterprise.

Hacking's distinction between realism and antirealism is, on the level of representations, virtually the same as Popper's. Realists claim that the entities, states, and processes described by correct theories do exist. Theories are either true or false and, with varying degrees of success, scientists pursue truth. Antirealists claim that theoretical objects do not exist; they are fictions used to predict or manipulate the world. We should not regard even the most successful theories as true.

However, Hacking's ultimate emphasis is not on the representational character of theory but rather on theory as a means of intervening in the world. Popper, the instrumentalists, and Hacking all see theories as instruments. As antirealists in the representationalist sense, the instrumentalists see them as nothing but instruments. Popper sees them as instruments, but as primarily true or false conjectural representations of the world. And Hacking sees them as true or false claims about the world, but importantly if not primarily as instruments for manipulating the world.

What allows Hacking to focus on the instrumental nature of theory, yet to remain a realist, is his post-Kuhnian context. Thomas Kuhn's *The Structure of Scientific Revolutions* (1962) broke the earlier context of Popper and Carnap in the following ways:

1. There is no sharp distinction between observation and theory;
2. Science is not cumulative;
3. Science does not have a tight deductive structure;
4. Scientific concepts are not particularly precise;
5. There is not a methodological unity between or within sciences;
6. The context of justification cannot be separated from the context of discovery; and
7. Science is in time and is historical.

This Kuhnian view of science, which was not available to Popper, is an essential part of the context for Hacking's realism.

Causality is also central to Hacking's realism:

> Scientific realism is commonly discussed under the heading of representation. Let us now discuss it under the heading of intervention. My conclusion is obvious, even trifling. We shall count as real what we can use to intervene in the world to affect something else, or what the world can use to affect us.... Natural science since the 17th century has been the adventure of the interlocking of representing and intervening (1983, p. 146).

Following this introductory statement, Hacking calls attention to the parts of the scientific enterprise that were overlooked or dismissed as unimportant, if not unscientific, by "theoretical" philosophers such as Popper and Carnap. He argues that in many cases of actual scientific practice, experiment has a useful life apart from testing Popperian theoretical conjectures. Scientists are creators not just of theories but of materials and technologies.

Hacking draws on Dudley Shapere (1982) to argue that scientists' conception of observation is much richer although less tidy than that of representational philosophy of science. Observation as persistent attention to quirks (i.e., being observant) is often as important as reporting what one sees, and what one sees depends as much on technological devices as on one's senses. Like Popper,

Hacking thinks that working scientists come by realism naturally but, unlike Popper, he makes the engineering side of science a vital part of the context for his realist philosophy of science.

In *Representing and Intervening*, Hacking's focus is almost entirely on the physical sciences. The few remarks he makes about social science are less than laudatory. By his standard of scientific success, the "collaboration" of "speculation, calculation, and experiment," Hacking suggests that social science is not as well developed as natural science. "Social scientists don't lack experiment; they don't lack calculation; they don't lack speculation; they lack the collaboration of the three. Nor, I suspect, will they collaborate until they have real theoretical entities about which to speculate—not just postulated 'constructs' and 'concepts', but entities we can use, entities which are part of the deliberate creation of stable new phenomena" (1983, p. 249).

C. Miller's Realism

Richard Miller's *Analyzing Marx* (1984) and *Fact and Method* (1987) offer another post-Kuhnian realism that involves more attention to and more favorable treatment of social science. Like Hacking, Miller tries to make the working scientist's context a key part of his own. His focus is on the nature of explanation and standards of adequacy for explanations. He offers an alternative to the covering-law model and to Bayesian probabilistic accounts that is radically context dependent. By Miller's account, explanation is description of underlying causes sufficient under the actual circumstances to bring about the phenomena in question. An adequate explanation is an adequate description of these causes. But there is no timeless universal standard of adequate description or even of the nature of causality.

> It seems much truer to the facts about causality to take the category as covering a variety of processes, whose title to causal status does not derive from a fit with such a definition. At the core of the family of causes are a variety of processes of making things happen, recognized as such by primordial common sense, processes as diverse as pushing's changing the position of an object, a desire's leading someone to pursue a goal, a blow's causing pain, or pain's making someone cry. As science develops, the repertoire of kinds of causes is revised (1984, p. 285).

While Popper disagreed with essentialists over "stopping rules" for scientific explanation but agreed with them that the rules were universal, Miller sees nothing wrong with the fact that practical stopping rules differ between disciplines, and also within a discipline between problems. This is actually an economic perspective on adequate explanation. The appropriate looseness or tightness of the stopping rule depends on the context of the problem at hand, and the person in the best position to determine that optimum is not the philosopher but the chemist, economist, or medical doctor dealing with the phenomenon. In opposition to Popper, Miller argues that Darwin had a genuine theory of evolution, because he identified the causal mechanism. Unlike Popper, Miller sees the content of the context of justification as theory versus theory rather than theory versus world. "A hypothesis is confirmed if there is a good argument for an account of why the data are as they are that entails the approximate truth of the hypothesis as against the basic falsehood of its rivals" (1984, p. 295).

III. THE INTERPRETIVE CONTEXT FOR FRIEDMAN'S METHODOLOGY

A. Friedman's Instrumentalism

What has come to be called "Friedman's methodology" is based almost entirely on readings of his 1953 essay. For some time now, Friedman's argument there has been characterized as instrumentalism. With various qualifications, this has been the interpretation of Wong, Boland, Blaug, Caldwell, and Mäki. Responding to Samuelson's F-twist critique of Friedman's essay, Wong wrote that neither Friedman nor Samuelson sees theory as "explanatory and informative." Of Friedman's position, he wrote, "That Friedman is an instrumentalist is quite evident" (1973, p. 314). This was "evident" because of Friedman's argument that assumptions should not be tested for veracity. "All methodological prescriptions that Friedman makes are subsidiary to one overriding methodological maxim—that of successful prediction" (1973, p. 314). Wong took his definition of instrumentalism straight from Popper's "Three Views Concerning Human Knowledge" (1963b).

Boland (1979) goes much further than Wong, who simply took the twin maxims of not verifying assumptions and requiring predictive success of theories and noted their compatibility with instrumentalism. Boland makes Friedman out to be a thoroughgoing instrumentalist philosopher of science. He adds that Friedman's concern over the positive-normative distinction, an inductivist concern, is the most important noninstrumentalist element of his methodology.

Frazer and Boland (1983) argue that Friedman is *both* an instrumentalist *and* a Popperian. Hirsch and de Marchi (1984) respond to this rather remarkable claim with the assertion that any agreement between Friedman's methodology and Popper's philosophy is no more than superficial, and that Friedman is a Deweyan instrumentalist rather than a positivist instrumentalist. Wible (1984) gives a similar interpretation.

Blaug (1980) differs from Boland in seeing Friedman's essay as an unsophisticated and inconsistent methodological treatise, but agrees that its primary thesis is the instrumentalist conception that theories are "nothing but instruments for generating predictions" (p. 112), a conception that rules out any role for isolating causal mechanisms connecting events or otherwise explaining behavior.

Caldwell (1980, 1982) compares Friedman's position with logical positivism and logical empiricism. The earlier positivists, the logical positivists, thought explanation was impossible, that statistical correlations from which predictions could be made were all that could be asked of science. The logical empiricists who replaced them allowed an explanatory role for theory. Caldwell finds passages in Friedman's essay compatible with both of these philosophical doctrines and comes to the conclusion that, all in all, Friedman's position is best labeled as methodological instrumentalism. He adds the modifier methodological to point out that Friedman was not writing from the context of philosophy. Caldwell then makes effective use of the differences between philosophy and economics in his critique of Friedman's position from both perspectives.

In his contribution to this symposium, Caldwell (1992) notes that Friedman departed from the instrumentalist conception of theoretical hypotheses as neither true nor false, that is, not statements about the world, but logical rules. His new interpretation is that Friedman views hypotheses as statements and, as such, as either true or false, but thinks the falsity (lack of realism) of statements used as premises in theory does not matter. Caldwell modifies his label for Friedman's methodology accordingly to "predictivist instrumentalism."

Uskali Mäki (1986) argues that there is not enough consistency in Friedman's essay to warrant the application of any philosophical label. There are snatches of three different positions: positivism, pragmatism, and realism. Friedman's emphasis on prediction is the positivist tendency. His suggestions that the makeup of the community of scientists is important for the perception of facts and choice of theories tends toward pragmatism. And his suggestion that theory may be unrealistic only in reference to observable reality, but representative of deeper reality, tends toward realism. Quite unlike Boland, who finds a complete and sophisticated philosophical position outlined in the essay, Mäki finds inconsistency in that positivism and pragmatism are incompatible instrumentalisms, each of which is incompatible with realism.

In his analysis of realism in economics, Mäki (1989, 1992),argues that, with respect to the theory of the firm, Friedman's position in the essay is one of ontological, referential, representational, and veristic realism; yet it remains instrumentalism. Ontological realism means in this case that Friedman believes neoclassical business firms are real entities, that they exist. Referential realism means that neoclassical theory refers to those firms. Representational realism means that the theory has the semantic property of representing the real-world neoclassical firms. And veristic realism means that the representations have the additional semantic property of being either true or false. But since

Friedman thinks that the representations are false ("unrealistic") and that false theories can be used for instrumental purposes (prediction), Mäki concludes that he is a methodological nonrealist or, in Caldwell's terminology, a methodological instrumentalist.

Lawson (1992), like Mäki, finds elements of Friedman's essay that suggest instrumentalism, or idealism, along with indications of realism. He argues that Friedman is a realist about causal mechanisms but is misled by a commitment to actualism. This belief that scientific progress is based on the discovery of constant conjunctions of events leads Friedman to the instrumentalist notion that although causal mechanisms exist and are identifiable, their identification is superfluous.

B. The Context of Interpretation

These interpretations and critiques of Friedman's methodology share context in the rather obvious way that they all compare Friedman's essay with philosophical doctrines. Philosophy, even more than economics or economic methodology, is their context. Wong has eighteen references from philosophy that have nothing directly to do with either economics or economic methodology (out of a total of fifty-two). As noted, he takes his definition of instrumentalism straight from Popper. Another important part of Wong's context is Samuelson's critique of Friedman. Wong takes the role of arbiter in a debate between the two. Boland's paper contains fewer total references (eleven) than Wong's. Ten of these are to Friedman's essay and critiques of it. The eleventh is Robbins' *An Essay on the Nature and Significance of Economic Science* (1935). But even without references to works of philosophy, Boland, to a greater extent than the authors of any of the other critiques we have examined, takes a particular philosophical doctrine as the context for reading Friedman's essay.

Blaug treats Friedman's essay within a context of the history of economic methodology, and he treats that history within the context of philosophy of science. Popper's philosophy is the most prominent part of that context. Caldwell (1980, 1982) also uses the philosophy of science as deep context and economic methodology as immediate context, although he restricts the philosophy and history of methodology to the twentieth century and presents the methodological history as a series of debates. He reveals in his contribution to this symposium (1992) that the most important part of the philosophical background for his initial interpretation of Friedman was Nagel's *The Structure of Science* (1961). The crucial part of the context for Caldwell's modification is Mäki's (1989) analysis of types of realism and realisticness. Philosophy is explicitly the main context for Mäki's 1986 critique of Friedman's essay, although he includes only one reference out of eleven that is a work of philosophy, that being Feyerabend's *Against Method* (1975). Caldwell's two other papers are similar in this respect. They provide a philosophical analysis of realism with minimum reference to other works of philosophy. In an important way, Mäki is building his own philosophical context. The second important part of Mäki 's (1989) context is methodological treatments of the theory of the firm by Kirzner, Machlup, and Simon.

Another important contextual element shared by these critics of Friedman is their preponderance of attention to Friedman's 1953 essay relative to other methodological works of Friedman's.[2] In a sense, this is natural, given the history of the essay since 1953. Though roundly criticized by methodologists, it has been for most of the economics profession the methodological Bible. Leaving aside the question of why general economists and methodologists began to give this one work such attention, or which came first—the general interest or that of methodologists—by the time Wong's critique appeared in 1973, the essay was clearly a very important part of the neoclassical economics literature.

But it is a mystery, given the amount of ink methodologists have spilled over the essay and their uncertainty as to how it should be interpreted, that they have not made more use of Friedman's other works. For the essay was not Friedman's first foray into methodology. Earlier important methodological works include his 1946 review of Lange's *Price Flexibility and Employment,* his 1947 review of Lerner's *The Economics of Control,* "The Marshallian Demand Curve" (1949), and "The 'Welfare' Effects of an Income Tax and an Excise Tax" (1952). All of these were reprinted along with "The Methodology of Positive Economics" in *Essays in Positive Economics* (1953a). As shown by Hammond (1990) these preessay papers provide a view of Friedman's methodology different from his critics' interpretations in numerous ways, the most important of which, for the purposes of this discussion, is that Friedman's context is economics rather than either philosophy or economic methodology. There are also postessay writings of Friedman's that can be used to identify his context, for they have the same theme as the preessay works. The most important of these is his 1955 review of Jaffe's translation of Walras' *Elements* (1954).

Wong, Boland, and Blaug do not cite any other work by Friedman in their critiques. Caldwell (1982) makes limited use of three papers written after the essay: the Nobel lecture (1977b), Friedman and Meiselman (1963), and Friedman's discussion of "The Rediscovery of Money" (1975). Caldwell's modification (1990) makes no use of any other of Friedman's writings. Mäki (1986) notes that Friedman's stress on the role of theory in providing generalizations about observable phenomena, which is evidence for a positivist reading of the essay, was carried over from his 1946 review of Lange's *Price Flexibility and Employment.* He finds support for a pragmatist reading of the essay in Friedman's remarks about the oral tradition at Chicago (1972) and in "The Marshallian Demand Curve" (1949). And he finds support for his conclusion that Friedman is inconsistent (rather than for a realist reading) in Friedman's 1977 critique of Galbraith for his lack of realism (1977a). Mäki (1992) and Lawson (1992) make use only of the essay.

We have seen in these critiques of Friedman's methodology published in the 1970s and 1980s that there has evolved a very particular context for reading the essay. We will now go back in time to the earliest critiques to trace this evolution.

C. Evolution of the Interpretive Context

The earliest commentary on Friedman's essay is in Koopmans' *Three Essays on the State of Economic Science* (1957). Koopmans' contexts for both writing his book and reading Friedman are wholly economic—economic theory and methodology. Thus, he does not bring an explicit philosophical perspective to his critique of Friedman. The impetus for writing his book was to explain for general economists the fundamentals and the methodological rationale for mathematical, or formal, economics. This rationale is to provide a clear separation of reasoning and recognition of facts "for the better protection of both" (1957, p. viii). Reasoning thus proceeds in mathematical economics by what Koopmans calls the postulational method, which is the examination of the postulates of theory for clarity and formal tracing of their implications. Within this endeavor, realisticness is of little concern. But Koopmans suggests that sorting premises out by their realisticness will naturally and properly precede this. As the immediate context for his discussion of Friedman's essay, Koopmans uses Robbins (1935). He argues that despite their obvious differences, Robbins and Friedman fail in the same way, by not allowing the search for premises more realistic than profit maximization, that is, for their scientific conservatism.

The second critique of the essay, by Klappholz and Agassi (1959), marks the introduction of philosophy into the discussion. Agassi was a research student and, later, research assistant to Popper. He worked for Popper during the period when the postscript to *The Logic of Scientific Discovery* was being written. Klappholz and Agassi's paper is a review of books by S. Schoeffler and A. Papandreou, but in the course of it they criticize Robbins and Hutchison along with Friedman. Their point is to bring Popper's *The Logic of Scientific Discovery* to bear on the economic methodology debate. Like Koopmans, they criticize Friedman for scientific conservatism, but in this case the charge is that his methodological rule is more confining than the Popperian "critical approach" requires. Archibald (1959) followed with another, very similar, critique from the Popperian London School of Economics (LSE) perspective in a review of Koopmans. He, too, argues that Friedman comes close to embracing Popper's critical approach, but in the end encourages scientific complacency.

Rotwein (1959) was the first article devoted exclusively to Friedman's essay. Rotwein cites only three other works, but two of these (Hume's *Treatise of Human Nature* and N. Campbell [1952]) are philosophical. Perhaps more importantly, Rotwein gives credit to three colleagues in the history of science and philosophy and suggests that philosopher Haskell Fain could qualify as joint author. So Rotwein's context for his treatment of Friedman is totally philosophical.

There was a session on "Problems of Methodology" at the 1962 AEA meeting with commentary on Friedman by Nagel (1963), Simon (1963), and Samuelson (1963). Fritz Machlup (1963) introduced Nagel as the session's "exogenous" methodologist. The session took place about a year after the publication of his *The Structure of Science* (1961), the fifth and sixth chapters of which served as the basis of Nagel's philosophical evaluation of Friedman's conception of the nature of theory.[3] It was at the 1962 AEA meeting that Nagel first used instrumentalism as a context for reading Friedman. He made the distinction between genuine statements (i.e., representative statements), of which explanatory theory is comprised, and the rules of instrumental theory. In Friedman's essay, Nagel found suggestions of both positions—that economic theory is explanatory and that it is merely instrumental.

True to Machlup's introduction of him as an "endogenous" methodologist, Simon used economics rather than philosophy as his context. This is the meaning of his opening remark that his discussion will be less abstract than Nagel's. He suggested that Friedman's "principle of unreality" should be replaced by a "principle of continuity of approximation," which would allow "unreal" premises if they were *approximately* true. Consistent with his role as discussant rather than author, Simon included no references with his comments.

Nagel's *The Structure of Science* was, of course, not the only important new element of context for discussion of Friedman's essay at the 1962 AEA meeting, for there, also, Samuelson presented the famous F-twist interpretation. Samuelson's critique and alternative to Friedman's methodology, which have been criticized as severely if not as thoroughly as Friedman's essay itself, included much philosophical name-dropping but scant useful reference. In one useful reference, to Rotwein (1959), Samuelson seconded the suggestion that Friedman should embrace positivism. He evaluated his own position as being close to that of Ernst Mach.

By the time of Melitz's 1965 critique of Friedman and Machlup, a two-part context for evaluating Friedman's essay was firmly established. The first part, as we have seen, was philosophy of science, and this included on the one hand, Popper, and on the other, the positivists. The second part was the prior secondary literature relating to the essay. Melitz acknowledged an "inestimable" debt to Carl Hempel and Paul Benecerraf. His references include works by Hempel, Hempel and Oppenheim, Nagel, Carnap, Gaven Alexander, and Felix Kaufman, as well as many of the previous critiques of Friedman. Of course, once the early critics such as Klappholz and Agassi, and Rotwein, used the philosophy of science to evaluate the essay, subsequent references to them reinforced the philosophical context. It is not stretching the truth to suggest that by the mid-1960s, philosophy had supplanted economic methodology in importance as context for treatments of the essay. This created a situation congenial to the entrance into the debate of other philosophers such as Gerald Massey (1965), who used the then-established philosophical context to confirm his credentials, despite his lack of background in economics. Meanwhile, anything apart from the essay that Friedman wrote on methodology was almost completely ignored. Of the critiques we have examined, beginning with Koopmans, Archibald (1959) has one "other" Friedman reference (Friedman and Savage, 1948) and Melitz has one as well (Friedman 1963). The others have no Friedman references other than the essay.

The growing importance of philosophy in interpretations and critiques of Friedman continued from the mid-1960s. De Alessi (1965) used works by Braithwaite, Nagel, Popper, and Carnap in his argument against Friedman's distinction between theory as language and as a body of substantive hypotheses. Bear and Orr (1967) thanked William Bartley, another of Popper's former research assistants, in the acknowledgments of their examination of the "logical and epistemological implications of Friedman's position" (1967, p. 188). Their paper has the now-familiar list of philosophical references plus some new ones such as Kuhn. Following Popper's and Nagel's concerns with the philosophy of instrumentalism, Bear and Orr interpreted Friedman as an instrumentalist. They used Popper primarily to point out the problems with this position.

Rivett's 1970 paper was something of an anomaly, for its context was weighted toward economics and economic methodology rather than philosophy. But De Alessi's second critique (1971), Rosenberg's (1976), and Musgrave's (1981) moved the literature back toward the established philosophical trend. Wong (1973) and Boland (1979) solidified the emerging consensus that Friedman's position is instrumentalism. Wong rejected both Friedman's instrumentalism and Samuelson's descriptivism as incompatible with explanatory and informative theory. He wrote from a distinctively Popperian perspective and included the then-standard long list of philosophy references. As we have seen, Boland defended Friedman's instrumentalism, but without the explicit philosophy references.

IV. FRIEDMAN'S CONTEXT

We have seen that methodologists and philosophers have not, by and large, availed themselves of other work by Friedman that could have helped set the context for their reading of his essay closer to his context for writing it. In his other work on methodology, Friedman coined terms for what he saw as two competing methodological positions—Marshallian and Walrasian. He first used these terms in "The Marshallian Demand Curve" (1949), though he began developing their content earlier in his reviews of Lange and Lerner.[4] The economic (as opposed to philosophical) character of his categories comes through even in the names. So in using categories such as positivist, instrumentalist, realist, Popperian, and so forth, Friedman's methodologist and philosopher critics are not using Friedman's categories. The content of Friedman's categories is sketched in section V of "The Marshallian Demand Curve." The point of difference between the Marshallian and Walrasian approaches is not partial versus general equilibrium. Rather, it concerns the purpose behind theory. For a Marshallian, theory is used to deal directly with concrete problems. It is used as "an engine for the discovery of concrete truth" (1949, p. 490, Marshall's phrase):

> Economic theory, in this view, has two intermingled roles: to provide "systematic and organized methods of reasoning" about economic problems; to provide a body of substantive hypotheses, based on factual evidence, about the "manner of action of causes." In both roles the test of the theory is its value in explaining facts, in predicting the consequences of changes in the economic environment. Abstractness, generality, mathematical elegance—these are all secondary, themselves to be judged by the test of application....
>
> Doubtless, most modern economic theorists would accept these general statements of the objectives of economic theory. But our work belies our professions. Abstractness, generality, and mathematical elegance have in some measure become ends in themselves, criteria by which to judge economic theory. Facts are to be described, not explained. Theory is to be tested by the accuracy of its "assumptions" as photographic descriptions of reality, not by the correctness of the predictions that can be derived from it (1949, pp. 490-491).

It is revealing to examine what, in addition to the reviews of Lange and Lerner, was Friedman's context for writing "The Marshallian Demand Curve." It was primarily price theory rather than methodology. Friedman challenged the interpretation of Marshall found in "Chicago" texts, such as Stigler's, as well as in others, such as Hicks'. Yet he suggested that the genesis of his ideas was in Viner's economic theory course and he cited Knight's "Realism and Relevance in the Theory of Demand" (1944). Textual interpretation of Marshall's *Principles* (1920) and other works makes up a substantial portion of the paper. In his methodological discussion, Friedman cited Marshall's *Principles*, "The Present Position of Economics" (1956a), "Mechanical and Biological Analogies in Economics" (1956b), and letters, along with Triffin's *Monopolistic Competition* (1940) and Lange's *Price Flexibility and Employment* (1944).

Friedman's reference to Triffin's book harks back to his own brief review (1941). In that review, Friedman defended the use of Marshallian industries and supply-and-demand curves. He accepted Triffin's argument that the concept of industry is incompatible with monopolistic competition, but concluded that what should be dispensed with is not the industry but monopolistic competition. Friedman's only references in the review are to sections in Marshall's *Principles*.

His much longer review of Lange includes only one reference, to Pigou's *The Economics of Welfare* (1932). His review of Lerner has references to Knight's *The Economic Organization* (1933), Simons' *Personal Income Taxation* (1938), Burns and Mitchell's *Measuring Business Cycles* (1946), Pareto's *Cours d'Economie Politique* (1897), and Lange and Taylor's *On the Economic Theory of Socialism* (1938). "The 'Welfare' Effects of an Income Tax and an Excise Tax" (1952) is presented explicitly and exclusively as a methodological piece.[5] Yet, all of the references are to works in economic theory. Friedman's review article on Walras (1955) likewise contains references only to works of economics.

V. CONCLUSION

Both the content and citations of these "other" methodological writings of Friedman's from the period preceding and just after "The Methodology of Positive Economics" (1953b) suggest that his context for writing the essay was markedly different from the context that has evolved for interpreting it. Friedman drew methodology more directly out of economic theory than have his interpreters and critics. Neither philosophy nor the standard canons of economic methodology were referential benchmarks for him.

Friedman addressed questions about the background for his work in a recent interview (Hammond, 1992).[6] He indicates that he has never systematically read philosophy. He recalls reading Popper's *Conjectures and Refutations* (1963a) and *The Open Society and Its Enemies* (1945), but not *The Logic of Scientific Discovery* (1959). Friedman claims that Popper's influence on him came through their meeting at Mont Pelerin in 1947.

Friedman suggests that an important methodological influence came from his friend, colleague, and coauthor, L.J. Savage. The key idea that Friedman learned from the statistician Savage is an implication of the interpretation of probabilities as personal rather than objective. The idea is that the role of statistical analysis is to resolve disputes—"to lead us to reconsider our personal probabilities in the hope that our personal probabilities will come closer and closer together" (Hammond, 1992, p. 101).

Friedman's remarks in the interview indicate that he does not have a clear a memory of the origins of the Marshallian-Walrasian distinction. His conjectures, that it emerged from lessons learned from Arthur Burns and Jacob Viner and from his encounters with economic analysis as it was being done by those around him, are consistent with the pattern of citations in his papers that use the distinction. His is an economist's (or perhaps a statistician's) methodology, as opposed to a philosopher's or methodologist's methodology.

The argument that has been developed here is not meant to foreclose evaluation of Friedman's essay from a philosophical perspective or from any other. The point is rather to establish the distinction between the writer's and the reader's context to recover the history of both. We have seen that Friedman's critics' contexts diverged from his own very early in the progression of interpretations and critiques. Thus "Friedman's methodology" took on a persona markedly different from the methodology of the person Milton Friedman.

ACKNOWLEDGMENTS

Thanks are extended to Larry Boland, Bruce Caldwell, Neil de Marchi, John Lodewijks, John Moorhouse, and Warren Samuels for very helpful comments on an earlier draft. Financial support was provided by the Earhart Foundation and the Wake Forest Graduate Council.

NOTES

1. originally published as *Logik der Forschung* in 1934.
2. The exchange between Frazer and Boland (1983) and Hirsch and de Marchi (1984) is a notable exception. They use other methodological writings of Friedman and his nonmethodological work to draw inferences about his methodology. As this paper is being written (1989) Hirsch and de Marchi are at work on a major study of Friedman's methodology making use of a broad selection of his work.
3. Caldwell was to later use the sixth chapter as his context.
4. See Hammond (1990, 1992).
5. See page 25 and note 3.
6. The interview was taped on May 24, 1988, and subsequently edited by Milton Friedman.

REFERENCES

Archibald, G.C. 1959. "The State of Economic Science." *British Journal for the Philosophy of Science* 10 (May): 58-69.
Bear, D.V.T., and D. Orr. 1967. "Logic and Expediency in Economic Theorizing." *Journal of Political Economy* 75 (April): 188-196.
Blaug, M. 1980. *The Methodology of Economics.* Cambridge: Cambridge University Press.
Boland, L.A. 1979. "A Critique of Friedman's Critics." *Journal of Economic Literature* 17 (June): 503-522.
Burns, A.F., and W.C. Mitchell. 1946. *Measuring Business Cycles.* New York: National Bureau of Economic Research.
Caldwell, B.J. 1980. "A Critique of Friedman's Methodological Instrumentalism." *Southern Economic Journal* 47 (October): 366-374.

_____. 1982. *Beyond Positivism: Economic Methodology in the Twentieth Century.* London: Allen & Unwin.

_____. 1992. "Friedman's Predictivist Methodological Instrumentalism—A Modification." In *Research in the History of Economic Thought and Methodology.* Vol. edited by W.J. Samuels. Greenwich, CT: JAI Press.

Campbell, N. 1952. *What is Science?* New York: Dover.

De Allessi, L. 1965. "Economic Theory as a Language." *Quarterly Journal of Economics* 79 (August): 472-477.

_____. 1971. "Reversals of Assumptions and Implications." *Journal of Political Economy* 79 (July): 867-877.

Feyerabend, P.K. 1975. *Against Method: Outline of an Anarchistic Theory of Knowledge.* London: NLB.

Frazer, W.J., Jr., and L.A. Boland. 1983. "An Essay on the Foundations of Friedman's Methodology." *American Economic Review* 73 (March): 129-144.

Friedman, M. 1941. "Review of *Monopolistic Competition and General Equilibrium* by Robert Triffin." *Journal of Farm Economics* 23 (February): 389-390.

_____. 1946. "Lange on Price Flexibility and Employment." *American Economic Review* 36 (September): 613-631.

_____. 1947. "Lerner on the Economics of Control." *Journal of Political Economy* 55 (October): 405-416.

_____. 1949. "The Marshallian Demand Curve." *Journal of Political Economy* 57 (December): 463-495.

_____. 1952. "The 'Welfare' Effects of an Income Tax and an Excise Tax." *Journal of Political Economy* 60 (February): 25-33.

_____. 1953a. *Essays in Positive Economics.* Chicago: University of Chicago Press.

_____. 1953b. "The Methodology of Positive Economics." Pp. 3-43 in *Essays in Positive Economics.* Chicago: University of Chicago Press.

_____. 1955. "Leon Walras and His Economic System." *American Economic Review* 45 (December): 900-909.

_____. 1963. "More on Archibald versus Chicago." *Review of Economic Studies* 30:65-67.

_____. 1972. "Comments on the Critics." *Journal of Political Economy* 80 (September-October): 906-950.

_____. 1975. "Twenty-five Years after the Rediscovery of Money: What Have We Learned? Discussion." *American Economic Review* 65 (May): 176-179.

_____. 1977a. *From Galbraith to Economic Freedom.* London: Instite of Economic Affairs.

_____. 1977b. "Nobel Lecture: Inflation and Unemployment." *Journal of Political Economy* 85 (June): 451-472.

Friedman, M., and D. Meiselman. 1963. "The Relative Stability of Monetary Velocity and the Investment Multiplier in the United States, 1897-1958." Pp. 165-268 in *Stabilization Policies,* edited by the Commission on Money and Credit. Englewood Cliffs, NJ: Prentice-Hall.

Friedman, M., and L.J. Savage. 1948. "The Utility Analysis of Choices Involving Risk." *Journal of Political Economy* 56 (August): 270-304.

Hacking, I. 1983. *Representing and Intervening.* Cambridge: Cambridge University Press.

_____. 1990. "An Interview with Milton Friedman on Methodology." In *Research in the History of Economic Thought and Methodology,* vol. 10, edited by W.J. Samuels. Greenwich, CT: JAI Press.

Hammond, J.D. 1990. "Realism in Friedman's *Essays in Positive Economics.*" In *Perspectives on the History of Economic Thought,* edited by D.E. Moggridge. Upleadon: Edward Elgar.

Hirsch, A., and N. de Marchi. 1984. "Methodology: A Comment on Frazer and Boland, I." *American Economic Review* 74 (September): 782-788.

Hume, D. 1888. *Treatise of Human Nature.* Ed. L.A. Selby-Bigge. Oxford: Oxford University Press.

Klappholz, K., and J. Agassi. 1959. "Methodological Prescriptions in Economics," *Economica* 27 (February): 60-74.

Knight, F.H. 1933. *The Economic Organization.* Chicago: University of Chicago Press.

————. 1944. "Realism and Relevance in the Theory of Demand." *Journal of Political Economy* 52 (December): 289-318.

Koopmans, T.C. 1957. *Three Essays on the State of Economic Science.* New York: McGraw-Hill.

Kuhn, T. 1962. *The Structure of Scientific Revolutions.* Chicago: University of Chicago Press.

Lange, O. 1944. *Price Flexibility and Employment.* Bloomington, IN: Principia Press.

Lange, O., and F.M. Taylor. 1938. *On the Economic Theory of Socialism.* Minneapolis: University of Minnesota Press.

Lawson, T. 1992. "Realism, Closed Systems and Friedman." In *Research in The History of Economic Thought and Methodology,* vol. 10, edited by W.J. Samuels. Greenwich, CT: JAI Press.

Leijonhufvud, A. 1968. *On Keynesian Economics and the Economics of Keynes: A Study in Monetary Theory.* New York: Oxfod University Press.

Lerner, A.P. 1944. *The Economics of Control.* New York: Macmillan.

Machlup, F. 1963. "Problems of Methdology—Introductory Remarks." *American Economic Review* 53(May): 204.

Mäki ,U. 1986. "Rhetoric at the Expense of Coherence: A Reinterpretation of Milton Friedman's Methodology." Pp. 127-143 in *Research in the History of Economic Thought and Methodology,* vol. 4, edited by W.J. Samuels. Greenwich, CT: JAI Press.

————. 1989. "On the Problem of Realism in Economics." *Ricerche Economiche,* 43 (March): 176-188.

————. 1992. "Friedman and Realism." In *Research in The History of Economic Thought and Methodology,* vol. 10, edited by W.J. Samuels. Greenwich, CT: JAI Press.

Marshall, A. 1920. *Principles of Economics.* 8th ed. London: Macmillan.

————. 1956a. "The Present Position of Economics." Pp. 152-174 in *Memorials of Alfred Marshall,* edited by A.C. Pigou. New York: Kelley & Millman.

————. 1956b. "Mechanical and Biological Analogies in Economics." Pp. 312-318 in *Memorials of Alfred Marshall,* edited by A.C. Pigou. New York: Kelley & Millman.

Massey, G.J. 1965. "Professor Samuelson on Theory and Realism: Comment." *American Economic Review* 55 (December): 1155-1164.

Melitz, J. 1965. "Friedman and Machlup on the Significance of Testing Economic Assumptions." *Journal of Political Economy* 73 (February): 37-60.

Miller, R.W. 1984. *Analyzing Marx: Morality, Power and History.* Princeton: Princeton University Press.

————. 1987. *Fact and Method: Explanation, Confirmation and Reality in the Natural and the Social Sciences.* Princeton: Princeton University Press.

Musgrave, A. 1981. "'Unreal Assumptions' in Economic Theory: The F-Twist Untwisted." *Kyklos* 34: 377-387.

Nagel, E. 1961. *The Structure of Science: Problems in the Logic of Scientific Explanation.* London: Routledge & Kegan Paul.

————. 1963. "Assumptions in Economic Theory." *American Economic Review* 53 (May): 211-219.

Pareto, V. 1897. *Cours d'Economie Politique.* Lausanne.

Pigou, A.C. 1932. *The Economics of Welfare.* 4th. ed. London: Macmillan.

Popper, K.R. 1945. *The Open Society and Its Enemies.* London: Routledge and Kegan Paul.

————. 1959. *The Logic of Scientific Discovery.* New York: Basic Books.

————. 1963a. *Conjectures and Refutations.* New York: Harper and Row.

————. 1963b. "Three Views Concerning Human Knowledge." Pp. 97-119 in *Conjectures and Refutations.* London: Routledge and Kegan Paul.

————. 1983. *Realism and the Aim of Science.* Totowa, NJ: Rowman and Littlefield.

Rivett, K. 1970. "'Suggest' or 'Entail'?: The Derivation and Confirmation of Economic Hypotheses." *Australian Economic Papers* 9 (December):127-148.

Robbins, L. 1935. *An Essay on the Nature and Significance of Economic Science.* 2nd. ed. London: Macmillan.

Rosenberg, A. 1976. *Microeconomic Laws: A Philosophical Analysis.* Pittsburgh: University of Pittsburgh Press.

Rotwein, E. 1959. "On 'The Methodology of Positive Economics.'" *Quarterly Journal of Economics* 73 (November): 554-575.

Samuelson, P.A. 1963. "Problems of Methodology—Discussion." *American Economic Review* 53 (May): 231-236.

Shapere, D. 1982. "The Concept of Observation in Science and Philosophy." *Philosophy of Science* 49 (December): 485-525.

Simon, H.A. 1963. Problems of Methodology—"Discussion." *American Economic Review* 53 (May): 224-231.

Simons, H.C. 1938. *Personal Income Taxation.* Chicago: University of Chicago Press.

Triffin, R. 1940. *Monopolistic Competition and General Equilibrium Theory.* Cambridge: Harvard University Press.

Walras, L. 1954. *Elements of Pure Economics or the Theory of Social Wealth.* Trans. by W. Jaffe. Homewood, IL: Irwin.

Wible, J.R. 1984. "The Instrumentalisms of Dewey and Friedman." *Journal of Economic Issues* 18 (December): 1049-1070.

Wong, S. 1973. "The 'F-twist' and the Methodology of Paul Samuelson." *American Economic Review* 63 (June): 312-325.

REALISM, CLOSED SYSTEMS, AND FRIEDMAN

Tony Lawson

I. INTRODUCTION

The search for stable relationships connecting sets of events is, I think, an undeniably pervasive feature of current economic analysis. Yet it represents an activity, I want to argue, that is largely misconceived. In place of approaches that tie economic analysis to formulations based upon constant conjunctions of events, I want to defend a particular version of *realism* that lays the emphasis, instead, upon identifying and understanding enduring generative structures and mechanisms that lie behind and govern the events or social phenomena that we experience.

A critical examination of the constant conjunction of events presupposition, then, and a defense of the realist alternative, is set out below in section II. In section III, the arguments developed in section II are brought to bear upon Friedman's well-known and highly controversial contribution to methodology. Here, I suggest that the debate over how Friedman's essay should be interpreted, though wide-ranging, has failed to draw out the significance of

Research in the History of Economic Thought and Methodology
Volume 10, pages 149-169.
Copyright © 1992 by JAI Press Inc.
All rights of reproduction in any form reserved.
ISBN: 0-55938-501-4

the constant conjunction of events view of theorizing, as an essential presupposition. Once this is effected, I argue in section IV, then major aspects of Friedman's account can be discarded as inadequate for, and indeed largely irrelevant to, any attempt to come to grips with (that is understand, explain, predict, and formulate appropriate policy concerning) the natural and social world in which we live. It also becomes possible to suggest why previous interpreters have failed convincingly to ascribe to Friedman's arguments anything like a coherent position.

II. AN OUTLINE AND DEFENSE OF REALISM

At a very general level, any account of (scientific) realism asserts the existence of the objects of analysis as independent of the analysis in which they feature. The specific version of realism that I want to defend here one that, following Bhaskar (1978), can be appropriately referred to as transcendental realism, as recognises the existence or reality not only of events in, and states of affairs of, the world, and of our experiences of them, but also of the generative structures and causal mechanisms that govern the events that we experience.[1] Most of what is misleadingly termed "applied" economic analysis seems to be concerned with 'modeling' some economic phenomenon of interest. The transcendental realist position that I want to defend is distinguished from most such analysis in that it accepts that the structures and mechanisms posited at the 'modelling' or explanatory stage are, or may be, real, and must be subject to further empirical scrutiny. This involves both assessing the power of accounts of postulated mechanisms to illuminate a range of empirical phenomena as well as checking the reality of the postulated mechanism by identifying, in turn, those further mechanisms that govern the operating of the original mechanism of interest. Thus, and in contrast to much of mainstream economics, the aim is not merely to achieve an "artificial construction," or a "convenient fiction," or some such, but to identify and understand real structures that actually govern some manifest phenomenon.

But, equally significant, transcendental realist analysis is also distinguished from most mainstream approaches to economic modeling in that the existence of constant conjunctions of events is not a necessary condition for the ascription of a significant result or a law. Laws, in other words, are not tied to constant conjunction of events based formulations. Indeed, the primary focus of science, in the realist view, is not the flux of events at all, but to repeat, the generative structures that lie behind and govern it.

A. Closed Systems and the Significance of Experiment

Why accept this transcendental realist account, and why pose it against the *actualist* view that *closed systems*—that is, systems in which constant conjunctions of events occur—are necessary to ascribing some conjecture as a significant theory or a law?

The first point to observe is that in the field of economics, significant invariant event regularities are yet to be observed. Nearly fifty years ago, in the context of a search for such event regularities, Haavelmo (1944) justified his efforts in developing the "probability approach in econometrics" with the observation that "economics, so far, has not led to very accurate and universal laws like those obtaining in the natural sciences" (p. 15). With the passage of time, however, this situation does not seem to have changed significantly. In the main, econometricians appear to be continually puzzling over why it is that presumed identified event regularities, or "estimated relationships" always, "break down" as soon as new observations become available (see Lawson, 1989a).

But, outside astronomy at least, nor is it the case that universal event regularities occur pervasively in the "natural sciences" either. Perhaps it will be objected here that I am neglecting the numerous results obtained in situations of experimental control. Is it not the case that scientists working on laboratory experimentation are frequently reporting results of the form "whenever event X then event Y"? Consequently, is it not the case that a consideration of experimental work serves to undermine the position that I am taking?

To the contrary, as Bhaskar's (1978) highly illuminating analysis of experimental work indicates, far from undermining the above claims (and the transcendental realist case in general), such considerations reinforce them. Bhaskar's contribution is to draw out the significance of two readily available observations. The first is that most of the constant conjunctions of events that constitute significant results in science *only* in fact occur in experimental situations—in general, *closed systems* are not spontaneously occurring. The second observation is that laws supported in experimental activity are frequently successfully applied outside of the experimental situation.

These observations raise certain problems for actualist accounts which tie laws to a constant conjunctions of events. For, if scientific laws, or significant results, only occur in such restricted conditions as experimental set-ups, then this bears the (rather inhibiting) implication that science and its results, far from being universal, are effectively fenced off from most of the goings on in the world. In other words, most of the accepted results of science are not of the form "whenever event X then event Y" after all, but are of the form "whenever event X then event Y, as long as conditions E hold," where conditions E typically amount to a specification of the experimental situation. This also bears the rather counterintuitive implication that any actual regularity of events that a law of *nature* supposedly denotes does not, in fact, generally occur independently of human intervention. But, in addition to such problems and at least as seriously, the constant-conjunctions view of laws leaves the question of what governs events outside of experimental situations not only unanswered, but completely unaddressed. In doing so, it also leaves the observation that experimentally obtained results *are* successfully applied outside experimental situations without any valid explanation.

For the transcendental realist, however, explanatory problems of this sort do not arise. Experimental activity, and the application of experimentally determined knowledge outside of experimental situations, can easily be accommodated through invoking an ontology of generative structures and causal mechanisms that lie behind and govern the flux of events. The fall of an autumn leaf does not typically conform to an event regularity, and precisely because it is governed, in complex ways, by the actions of different juxtaposed and counteracting mechanisms. Not only is the path of the leaf governed by gravitational pull, but also by aerodynamic, thermal, inertial, and other forces. In this realist view, then, experimental activity can be explained as an attempt to intervene in order to isolate a particular mechanism of interest by holding off all other potentially counteracting mechanisms. The aim is to engineer a closed system in which a one-to-one correspondence can obtain between the way a mechanism acts and the events that eventually ensue. In other words, in this transcendental realist view, experimental activity can be rendered intelligible *not* as creating the rare situation in which a law is put into effect but as intervening in order to bring about those special circumstances under which a (nonempirical) law can be empirically identified. The law itself, of course, is always operative—if the triggering conditions hold, the mechanism is activated, whatever else is going on. In this transcendental realist view, for example, a leaf is subject to the pull of gravity even as I hold it in the palm of my hand. Through this sort of reasoning, then, the transcendental realist can also easily accommodate the application of scientific knowledge outside of experimental situations. The context or *milieu* under which any mechanism will be operative is irrelevant to the law's specification. Once activated, the mechanism is operative whatever empirical pattern ensues.[2]

In short, the transcendental realist account of generative structures and causal mechanisms, but not the "actualist" account of laws as necessitating empirical regularities, can render significant aspects of scientific activity—and human capability in general—intelligible. For reasons such as this it seems to me that this specific realist view constitutes the most satisfactory account of both scientific activity, and of what there is generally, that is available. The drawing of this conclusion, of course, does not rule out the possibility that further observed phenomena may eventually be thrown up that the transcendental realist account cannot accommodate, or that a more illuminative, that is explanatorily powerful, account may eventually be forthcoming. But for the time being, at least, it appears to constitute an account that is worth developing.

Most of the discussion so far has referred implicitly to the situation in the "natural" sciences. However, because the transcendental realist view invokes an ontology of generative structures that are operative in both closed *and* open systems alike, it is apparent that it is just as relevant for coming to grips with the economic and social world where only open systems arise. For example— and as the contributions to Labour Market Segmentation Theory in particular (e.g., Wilkinson, 1981) tend to suggest—labor market phenomena are governed by such structures as labor/employer, skilled/unskilled worker, male/female, or immigrant/nonimmigrant relationships, which tend to operate in similar ways in varying contexts. However, because in any given context different selections of mechanisms are juxtaposed against each other in complex ways, empirical invariances typically do not arise (see Lawson, 1989b). The transcendental realist position, then, appears to be at least as relevant to the economic and social realm as any other.

B. Implications

An implication of all this for actually doing economic analysis, clearly, is that the criterion of theory assessment must typically be explanatory and not predictive. It is important to be clear about this. It is not that the goal of explanation is being introduced solely in order to supplement that of prediction. Sometimes this supposition is taken as a step toward the refutation of instrumentalism. Caldwell (1980), for example, draws attention to a widespread postwar rejection by philosophers of science "of the notion that the only goal of science is prediction" (p. 369); he sees this as a decisive rejection of instrumentalism—"if science seeks theories that have explanatory as well as predictive powers, then theories that merely predict well may not be satisfactory, and the view that theories are nothing more than instruments for prediction must be rejected" (p. 369). But instrumentalism in economics is to be rejected not merely because it cannot deliver *all* that is required, for, most of the time at least, it cannot deliver anything at all—including that which it specifically claims to achieve. The criterion of predictive accuracy (or predictive power), is only relevant when there are grounds for supposing a closed system— for supposing a constant conjunction of events prevails. But this is a comparative rarity—not only in economics but, outside astronomy, in most of the natural sciences as well. Consequently, science must be seen as *essentially* explanatory, and typically *non*predictive[3]—and economics more or less exclusively so. In short, in the transcendental realist view the goal of science is to identify and understand significant generative structures that govern the events we experience. By way of such knowledge, it may be possible to explain phenomena of interest, but explanations need not, and in an open system typically will not, entail successful, or even justified, event-prediction.

Now, the above considerations also bear consequences at the level of theoretical critique. Specifically, by drawing attention to the inadequacy of the widespread, if unthinking, presupposition in economics that laws must be tied to closed systems, realism can pave the way for a critical examination of, among other things, mainstream prescriptions, especially as found in particular influential contributions that implicitly rest on this presupposition. Such an exercise represents the object of the remainder of this paper. It is widely observed that Friedman's (1953) essay continues to be the most influential methodological account concerning the nature of economic analysis (see, e.g., Hodgson, 1988). Some sympathetic interpreters, such as Boland (1979), even suggest that Friedman's account is virtually unassailable. I now want to indicate why I take the latter suggestion to be mistaken. In the next section, then, Friedman's implicit adherence to actualism—to the tying of laws to closed systems—is described. The specific problems that arise for Friedman because of the way in which this is done, are drawn out in the section which then follows.

III.   FRIEDMAN AND CLOSED SYSTEMS

My intention here, then, is to indicate the extent to which Friedman's methodological essay takes for granted, if implicitly, that a constant conjunction of events is always to be sought for. The first point to emphasise is (the, of course, widely acknowledged one) that Friedman, throughout his contribution, emphasises predictive accuracy or "predictive power" as the criterion by which theories are to be assessed. This, immediately, if implicitly, reveals a presumption of the general availability of spontaneously occurring or artificially created closed systems. Now, it seems clear that artificially created ones are not possible in economics. Indeed, Friedman quickly rules out the possibility of carrying out controlled experiments in the social sciences (p. 10),[4] suggesting, instead, that we "must rely on evidence cast up by 'experiments' that happen to occur" (p. 10). However, these "experiments" of nature are apparently of a satisfactory form, for Friedman also presumes that "the inability to conduct [controlled] experiments is not a fundamental obstacle to testing hypotheses by the success of their predictions" (p. 10). In otherwords, spontaneously occurring closed systems—those in which a regularity amongst events holds—are apparently presumed to occur.

So where, and how, are these closed systems to be found? Central to Friedman's reasoning on this is the notion of a "class of phenomena" that any "hypothesis is designed to explain" (p. 13). A predictive test of a hypothesis, apparently, is "relevant" only if the deduced facts to be confronted with empirical observation are about this class of phenomena (p. 13). There are two things about this restriction that need emphasising. First, it explicitly rules out the realist activity of checking the reality of any posited generative structures through explaining the conditions, or identifying the mechanisms, that maintain them (see Lawson, 1989b). This relates to Friedman's much-noted comments concerning the irrelevance, for him, of questions of the realism of assumptions in hypothesis testing—or the impossibility of determining whether a hypothesis "works" other than through considering the predictive accuracy of its implications for the class of phenomena the hypothesis in question is explicitly designed to explain. But second, the restriction that any hypothesis be assessed only with respect to a "given class of phenomena" must be recognized as only part of the story. A further, implicit, requirement, that to some extent tends to be masked, is that this relevant "class of phenomena" must, typically, be itself even further severely restricted before it comprises a body of data that is considered appropriate or relevant for testing Friedman's hypotheses. And the point I really want to emphasise—and below substantiate—is that the relevant class of phenomena must not only be further restricted, but must be restricted in *such a way* that a closed system is presumed to be specified. In other words, in limiting the set of phenomena by which a hypothesis can be validly tested, a set of circumstances must first be specified under which a constant conjunction of events is thought to occur. Thus, if I am correct, then Friedman's views on how theories or hypotheses are to be tested, provide a pointer to how or where he believes closed systems spontaneously occur.

A. Closed Systems and Friedman's Examples

It should be revealing, then, to consider, Friedman's illustrative examples of protoscientific hypotheses at this point. Four are provided altogether. Most of the literature that addresses Friedman's contribution has focussed on the first two—which are clearly the two most substantial. Consequently, because these will be the more familiar examples, they will be considered first below. However, Friedman's remaining two examples will also, in due course, be remarked upon.

Friedman's most discussed illustrative examples are stated in the following way:

(i)   Under a wide range of circumstances, bodies that fall in the actual atmosphere behave *as if* they were falling in a vacuum (p. 18).

(ii) [Leaves on a tree] are positioned as if each leaf deliberately sought to maximise the amount of sunlight it receives, given the position of its neighbours, as if it knew the physical laws determining the amount of sunlight that would be received in various positions and could move rapidly or instantaneously from any one position to any other desired and unoccupied position (p. 19).

In considering the valid assessing of these hypotheses, I now want to indicate, Friedman first places a restriction on the class of phenomena that is relevant for this task, and then further restricts this set of phenomena until a closed system is effectively presumed to obtain.

First, in considering the above hypotheses, it seems clear that the phenomena of "bodies falling in the atmosphere," and "leaves on trees" must be relevant to assessing the respective hypotheses. The point is that it is only these "classes of phenomena" that can be used in assessing the respective claims. Thus, the further realist question of what mechanisms govern, for example, the "deliberating" and "seeking" capacities of leaves as posited in the second hypothesis, is expressly ruled out. In short, the reality of any explanation is not at issue:

> Is the hypothesis rendered unacceptable or invalid because, so far as we know, leaves do not "deliberate" or consciously "seek", have not been to school and learned the relevant laws of science or the mathematics required to calculate the "optimum" position, and cannot move from position to position? Clearly, none of these contradictions of the hypothesis is vitally relevant; the phenomena involved are not within the "class of phenomena the hypothesis is designed to explain"; the hypothesis does not assert that leaves do these things but only that their density is the same *as if* they did (p. 20).

The second, less obvious, point is that the relevant classes of phenomena have to be restricted yet further before a valid assessment of either hypothesis can be made. Consider the hypothesis relating to falling bodies. Clearly, the claim that bodies falling in the atmosphere move just as they do in a vacuum (which is puzzling, at first sight, if we think of the fall of leaves or feathers), immediately emphasises the implicit presumption of a closed system. For a vacuum, of course, is a particular, and typically engineered, closed system, or situation in which an event-regularity holds. As Friedman observes, it "is an accepted hypothesis that the acceleration of a body dropped in a vacuum is a constant—g, or approximately 32 feet per second per second on the earth" (p. 16); and that "the distance travelled by a falling body in any specified time is given by the formula $S = 1/2 \ gt^2$, where S is the distance travelled in feet and t is time in seconds" (p. 16). According to the realist account, of course, a vacuum is precisely the idealized experimental situation in which all causal mechanisms other than gravitational forces have been held off, so that the gravitational pull can be identified empirically.

Clearly not all bodies falling in the atmosphere do fall in accordance with the above noted event-regularity or formula. Friedman suggests that the formula, in fact, holds for compact balls dropped from roofs of buildings— or, at least, that it holds closely enough given an acceptable margin of error (p. 16). But the formula clearly does not hold for an autumn leaf, or, as Friedman himself observes, for a feather or for a compact ball dropped from an airplane at an altitude of 30,000 feet. Nor, of course, does it even hold for a compact ball dropped from the roof of a building if a sufficiently strong wind is blowing, and so forth. Is, then, the hypothesis thereby rejected by such observations? Apparently not—it is merely that in these cases the hypothesis does not work (p. 19). Instead, it is such considerations and observations that must be used to further restrict the set of phenomena (within the relevant class of phenomena) before the valid testing of the privileged hypothesis in question can happen. This is the essence of the qualifier "under a wide range of circumstances" that comes with the statement of the hypothesis. The point is to specify *as part of the hypothesis* circumstances under which a closed system is expected to obtain—circumstances in which some event-regularity or empirical formula can be confidently expected to hold:

> The important problem in connection with the hypothesis is to specify the circumstances under which the formula works or, more precisely, the general magnitude of the error in its predictions under various circumstances. Indeed, ...such a specification is not one thing and the hypothesis another. The specification is itself an essential part of the hypothesis, and it is a part that is peculiarly likely to be revised and extended as experience accumulates (p. 18).

As more and more instances of falling bodies are examined, of course, the specified set of circumstances under which the hypothesis invariably holds will, in fact, be found to be further and further restricted—tending, if the realist view is correct, toward the set of circumstances found only in experimental situations when all relevant mechanisms other than gravitational forces have effectively been held at bay. Or, more accurately in this case, the ultimate set of specified circumstances will exclude all relevant mechanisms excepting those, if any, whose effects are so dominated by the earth's gravitational pull that the measured results differ from the vacuum-based formula by less than some prespecified margin of error.

In short, Friedman's falling-bodies hypothesis is taken to be validly testable only when an effective closure is presumed to hold. The same is true of the leaf hypothesis. As Friedman suspects, the latter "constructed hypothesis" is "valid, that is, yields 'sufficiently' accurate predictions about the density of leaves, only for a particular class of circumstances" (p. 20). In short, the hypothesis is valid only when a closed system obtains such that leaves are denser on the sunnier side.[5]

To sum up, then, Friedman's position, as indicated by an examination of his most discussed illustrative examples, amounts to an assertion that the valid assessment (i.e., testing) of any hypothesis be confined to a highly restricted set of phenomena—a presumed and specific constant conjunction of events which the hypothesis is explicitly designed to entail.

B.   Friedman's Remaining Examples

For the sake of completeness, it seems necessary that I briefly indicate that the above conclusions also hold with respect to Friedman's remaining, but less frequently examined, two illustrative hypotheses. In Friedman's own words, these are:

(iii) [An expert billiard player makes] his shots *as if* he knew the complicated mathematical formulas that would give the optimum directions of travel, could estimate accurately by eye the angles, etc., describing the location of the balls, could make lightening calculations from the formulas, and could then make the balls travel in the direction indicated by the formulas (p. 21).

(iv) under a wide range of circumstances individual firms behave *as if* they were seeking rationally to maximise their expected returns (generally if misleadingly called "profits") and had full knowledge of the data needed to succeed in this attempt; *as if*, that is, they knew the relevant cost and demand functions, calculated marginal cost and marginal revenue from all actions open to them, and pushed each line of action to the point at which the relevant marginal cost and marginal revenue were equal (p. 21).

Unfortunately, while such examples are consistent with what I am arguing, their relevance is obscured by erroneous implicit presumptions. The problem is when do billiard players or firms *ever* behave in the manner described or supposed? Certainly Friedman provides no evidence that they ever do. Instead, he suggests, in the case of billiard players, that "unless in some way or other they were capable of reaching essentially the same result, they would not in fact be *expert* billiard players" (p. 21). In the case of surviving firms he similarly asserts that "unless the behaviour of businessmen in some way or other approximated behaviour consistent with maximization of returns, it seems unlikely that they would remain in business for long" (p. 22). Now these last remarks are just wrong—they do not follow logically and do not seem to be born out empirically. An expert billiard player need be no more than a billiard player who is better then most others. Certainly all billiard players, in my experience, do frequently make mistakes. Nor am I aware of evidence to suggest that firms ever act in accordance with the manner supposed. How do we even know that there is not some alternative outcome to the existing one in which even the surviving firms would be better off? Clearly we do not. In short, it is not obvious that there are *any* circumstances under which the postulated event-regularities hold. But these observations should not detract from the essential point to be drawn here. Friedman clearly believes that he has identified situations in which constant conjunctions arise within some class of phenomena of interest, and that the formulation and testing of law-like statements, or hypotheses, is, under the circumstances, appropriate.[6]

In sum, it was noted in section II that most of the accepted results of science are not of the form "*whenever* event X then event Y" *unless* any such statement is implicitly understood as being qualified by a specification of the (typically experimental) conditions under which such an accepted law-statement holds. Friedman's position, then, can be seen as resting on an implicit recognition of this situation. Indeed, it has the merit of attempting to make the necessary qualifications explicit—even if Friedman does fail to realize that it is an idealized experimental situation that has, typically, to be specified. In other words, in his argument for further restricting any relevant class of phenomena by which a hypothesis can be assessed, Friedman can be understood as attempting to specify, always, a presumed closed system in which a constant conjunction of events is thought to hold.

IV. SOME PROBLEMS WITH FRIEDMAN'S POSITION

Not surprisingly, then, I now want to argue that there are some problems that arise within Friedman's account that can be seen as variants of those facing actualist accounts in general, as discussed in section II above. There it was noted that problems exist for the actualist both in rendering experimental activity intelligible and in accommodating the observation that scientific knowledge is in fact applied outside of the experimental situation. Analogous problems to these can now be seen to arise for Friedman, even if he does not address the experimental situation explicitly.

A.   On Rendering the Search for a Closure Intelligible

First, having noted that Friedman's procedure entails the search for a closure as a necessary element of obtaining significant scientific hypotheses, the issue that remains to be examined is the extent to which his approach is coherent. On what grounds does Friedman support this strategy? What presuppositions are revealed? These sorts of questions, of course, bear upon the debate that has occurred as to how Friedman's essay should be interpreted—and specifically on the frequently raised question as to whether or not Friedman's position should be regarded as a form of "predictive instrumentalism." If Friedman's approach is coherent, it should be relatively straightforward to tie down some appropriate label, and if it is not coherent, it may be easy to see why his account has given rise to conflicting interpretations.

Why, then, does Friedman adhere to the actualist view that laws or significant hypotheses necessitate constant conjunctions of events? It could be for one of two reasons. It could be that Friedman subscribes to the view that it is only events and states of affairs (which constitute the objects of experience) that are real— in which case if science, and human capability in general, are to be explicable at all then the constant conjunction view of laws, or of significant results, must follow. Or it could be that Friedman in fact accepts something like the transcendental realist ontology of generative structures and causal mechanisms as defended here, but unnecessarily confuses the issue through unthinkingly adhering to an actualist view of empirical laws. In other words, it may be that

Friedman's ontological presuppositions necessitate the constant conjunction view or it may be that they do not and the constant conjunction view is no more than an ill-thought and unnecessary commitment which merely confuses matters.

Strictly speaking, of course, both are positions of *realism*. The former, positing an ontology restricted to events and states of affairs that we experience, can be identified here as a form of *empirical realism*, while the viewpoint allowing an ontology that also includes generative structures and casual mechanisms I shall continue to refer as transcendental *realism*. The empirical realist may be either an *empiricist* for whom a constant conjunction of events is both necessary and sufficient for science or an *idealist* or *rationalist* for whom the objects of science also include models and hypotheses interpreted as merely artificial constructs, but for whom a constant conjunction of events remains necessary for the ascription of a significant result, if no longer sufficient. Instrumentalism, of course, belongs to the latter idealist camp along with fictionalist, conventionalist and a multitude of other (generally positivist)[7] positions. Thus, strictly speaking, any claimed opposition between instrumentalism and realism-in-general is in many cases a false one. It is only a substantive opposition if the version of realism in question involves something like the commitment to real generative structures along the lines being defended here.[8]

Clearly, Friedman, most of the time, views models and hypotheses as essential to science and so does not belong to the classical empiricist tradition. But is his position most usefully interpreted as idealist (and therefore possibly instrumentalist), or as transcendental realist? Certainly, all the observations noted throughout concerning his implicit attachment to the actualist view of significant hypotheses or laws, coupled with his overriding concern for the criterion of predictive accuracy, are immediately consistent with the idealist point of view. And this idealist interpretation appears to be born out by the way that many commentators have interpreted the following well-known passage:

> Misunderstanding about this apparently straightforward process [of testing the "validity" of a hypothesis] centres on the phrase 'the class of phenomena the hypothesis is designed to explain." The difficulty in the social sciences of getting new evidence for this class of phenomena and of judging its conformity with the implications of the hypothesis makes it tempting to suppose that other, more readily available, evidence is equally relevant to the validity of the hypothesis—to suppose that hypotheses have not only "implications" but also "assumptions" and that the conformity of these "assumptions" to "reality" is a test of the validity of the hypothesis *different from or additional to* the test by implications. This widely held view is fundamentally wrong and productive of much mischief (p. 14).

If this passage is read, as many apparently do read it, as saying that it is impossible to assess any of the assumptions made (to check "the conformity of these 'assumptions' to reality") other than through seeing if the implications of the composite hypothesis are born out, then the idealist [and potentially instrumentalist] tag may be appropriate.

But there are problems with this idealist labelling of Friedman's position, just as there are confusions in reading the above passage in the suggested way. The source and nature of these can be illuminated by first considering the confusions and limitations within the idealist position itself. Consider again Friedman's example of a compact ball falling from the roof of a building. Suppose that one day a wind, perhaps a hurricane, blows strongly enough for the falling ball's behavior to be significantly unlike what it would be if it were falling in a vacuum. What is the idealist to infer here? Is it to be concluded that the circumstances are inappropriate for the hypothesis of "falling as if in a vacuum" to be tested, or is it to be considered that the circumstances *are* appropriate for such a test, and that the hypothesis is in fact rejected? The idealist has no legitimate way of deciding. For, in this account, theories of putative causal mechanisms, such as claims about winds or hurricanes, can be no more than artificial constructs, and only observable events and states of affairs are (or can be known to be) real. In other words, if on the one hand the hypothesis in question can be validly tested only when certain specified circumstances, (including "a hurricane is not blowing") hold, and if on the other hand we can know that the relevant specified circumstances (such as 'a hurricane is not blowing') hold only by observing that the events in question, or specified class of phenomena, conform with our hypothesis, then clearly a chain of circular reasoning is unleashed.

If, then, Friedman's numerous assertions that it is always necessary to specify the circumstances under which a hypothesis is expected to, or does, work, is to be rendered intelligible, while the circularity of reasoning facing the idealist position is to be avoided, it is clearly necessary to invoke something like the transcendental realist ontology of generative structures and causal mechanisms that are productive of, but irreducible to, the manifest phenomena that we experience. In this view, it is acknowledged that the reality of the hurricane can and must be further and independently scrutinized—both in terms of the explanatory power of the hurricane conjecture with respect to a wide range of phenomena, and also through identifying and understanding those mechanisms that govern the hurricane's formation, reproduction, and transformation. In short, the question of whether a hurricane is blowing can and must be assessed independently of the observation of the specific falling bodies under focus. In this way, the problems of the idealist are avoided, while Friedman's numerous assertions about specifying the conditions under which a hypothesis holds can be rendered intelligible, as an attempt to specify the conditions when only one causal mechanism is operative.

Now how does Friedman himself actually confront or contend with these sorts of issues—issues that the idealist seems unable to handle coherently?

Consider his specific comparison of the dropping of a compact ball and a feather from the roof of a building to the ground. He writes:

> [T]he difference in shape of the body can be said to make [air pressure at sea level] significantly different from zero for a feather but not for a compact ball dropped a moderate distance. Such a statement must, however, be sharply distinguished from the very different statement that the theory does not work for a feather because its assumptions are false. The relevant relation runs the other way: the assumptions are false for a feather because the theory does not work. This point needs emphasising, because the entirely valid use of "assumptions" in *specifying* the circumstances for which a theory holds is frequently, and erroneously, interpreted to mean that the assumptions can be used to *determine* the circumstances for which a theory holds, and has, in this way, been an important source of the belief that a theory can be tested by its assumptions (p. 19).

Although relevant here, this statement slightly detracts from the question really at issue. If we are to use "assumptions" in any way to specify the circumstances in which a theory holds, we need to know that, when the "theory does not work," it is certain assumptions that are false rather than the hypothesis as a whole. Indeed we need to know *which* assumptions are false for the feather when the theory does not work. Similarly, of course, we need to know which assumptions are false for the compact ball (and any other object) when the theory does not work—in the above example it may be the assumption that "there is no hurricane blowing" that is false. If we do not specify in this way the particular circumstances in which a hypothesis breaks down, of course, then, in an open world, all hypotheses tied to event-regularities will eventually be contradicted (and consequently all will stay). Certainly, as we have noted throughout, Friedman is clear in his belief that the set of circumstances for which a hypothesis can be expected to hold *can* be specified using knowledge of particular assumptions in this way. In fact, in the example of the falling feather, Friedman seems to suggest that the relevant false assumption has something to do with air pressure given the feather's shape. But by what criteria or reasoning process can this conclusion be reached? We can only make such an assessment if we take claims about air pressure, or aerodynamic forces, and so forth, to be about causal entities actually acting upon the feather's path of fall, whose reality can be further, and independently, scrutinized. This, as we have noted, is precisely what the idealist denies to be possible. Friedman, however, does not so much deny the possibility of establishing the reality of some putative causal mechanism as he argues that it is unnecessary and irrelevant to the task at hand. (The latter part of the claim, of course, being erroneous.) Thus, Friedman certainly seems to accept the reality of air pressure as a causal force (p. 17) and although, as noted above, he argues that the reality of the "mobility" and "deliberating" powers of leaves should not be investigated, he seems implicitly to assume it can be independently established as the following statement about the leaf hypothesis indicates:

> Despite the apparent falsity of the "assumptions" of the hypothesis, it has great plausibility
> because of the conformity of its implications with observation (p. 20).

Returning to the statement noted earlier about testing a hypothesis by "its assumptions" (which has often been given an idealist interpretation), it should be noted that, whatever else Friedman claims, he *does not deny* here that the "conformity of these 'assumptions' to 'reality'" can be independently assessed. He merely suggests that any such apparent conformity cannot constitute "a test of the validity of the hypothesis *different from* or *additional to* the test by implications" (p. 14). Of course, because "validity" here for Friedman is taken explicitly to mean predictive accuracy, the statement is tautologically correct. In other words, because the emphasis is *solely* on the predictive accuracy of the hypothesis with respect to specific phenomena, the reality of the postulated mechanisms is not something considered explicitly at issue. But, to repeat, it is not explicitly denied, thereby, that the reality of the assumptions is independently assessable.

Indeed, in the passage that follows on from the statement just discussed Friedman acknowledges explicitly, if at first sight only conditionally, that the realism of assumptions can be independently assessed:

> In so far as a theory can be said to have "assumptions" at all, and in so far as their "realism"
> can be judged independently of the validity of predictions, the relation between the
> significance of a theory and the "realism" of its "assumptions" is almost the opposite of
> that suggested by the view under criticism. Truly important and significant hypotheses will
> be found to have 'assumptions' that are wildly inaccurate descriptive representations of
> reality, and, in general, the more significant the theory, the more unrealistic the assumptions
> (in this sense). The reason is simple. A hypothesis is important if it "explains" much by
> little, that is, if it abstracts the common and crucial elements from the mass of complex
> and detailed circumstances surrounding the phenomena to be explained and permits valid
> predictions on the basis of them alone. To be important, therefore, a hypothesis must be
> descriptively false in its assumptions; it takes account of, and accounts for, none of the
> many other attendant circumstances, since its very success shows them to be irrelevant for
> the phenomena to be explained.
>
> To put this point less paradoxically, the relevant question to ask about the "assumptions"
> of a theory is not whether they are descriptively "realistic," for they never are, but whether
> they are sufficiently good approximations for the purpose in hand. And this question can
> be answered only by seeing whether the theory works, which means whether it yields
> sufficiently accurate predictions. The two supposedly independently tests thus reduce to
> one test. (p. 15)

Unfortunately, although this passage is illuminating here in that it reveals an explicit commitment to realism, it also opens the door to yet a further confusion. It presumes that an abstraction amounts to a hypothesis that is necessarily descriptively false in its assumptions—and this is apt to mislead. If, say, in attempting to explain why a particular motorist adheres to the highway code (when he or she does), I focus only upon causal factors such as a will to live, politeness, a knowledge of the relevant rules, a knowledge of the consequences of not adhering to the highway code, driving habits, and so forth, and I ignore such factors as the motorist's name, color of eyes, or length of nose, and so forth, I am, of course, making an abstraction. That is, I am leaving out of my analysis some aspects of the concrete entity or structures which I focus upon for my explanation. But the resulting conception is not thereby something that is necessarily descriptively false or a fiction. For the realist, at least, the point of abstraction is to leave out that which is considered inessential to explaining some phenomena, in order to focus on that which is essential or, as Friedman correctly remarks, "crucial." But the intention through abstraction is still to identify something that is real for all that. Certainly the fact that abstraction is always involved in explanation does not, of necessity, license the wholesale (and acknowledged) fictionalizing that is involved with claims about consciously deliberating and instantaneously mobile leaves, and so forth. In short, for the realist, the aim of abstraction is to identify something that is real and essential in order that some phenomenon of interest be explained—and this is entirely possible. (For a further discussion of this, see Lawson, 1989b.)

But these comments on abstraction must not detract from the point mainly at issue here. This is that Friedman's comments reveal an implicit acknowledgment that the reality of "assumptions" can be independently assessed, which suggests that, at base, he is in fact a transcendental realist.[9] Which, of course, we all are. The point is to be clear about what this entails, and specifically to reject, as unnecessary and inhibiting, the widespread, if unthinking, commitment to actualism.

In sum, then, it appears that Friedman is not in fact arguing that it is impossible to identify and understand real causal mechanisms—that the reality of putative generative structures cannot be established. Instead, he is effectively suggesting that economists should not bother with such matters because to do so is unnecessary and not the way in which science proceeds. On this last set of arguments, as we have seen of course, Friedman is just wrong. Just as rendering experimental activity explicable warrants the invocation of something like the realist ontology of causal mechanisms, so too does any attempt to render intelligible Friedman's own methodological descriptions and prescriptions—and it does so whether or not Friedman is explicitly aware of this. All this, of course, bears implications. For, in order to render Friedman intelligible in this way, the specific consequences of adhering to actualism must be abandoned. In particular, explanatory, rather than predictive, power must become the dominant criterion of theory adequacy, while the objective of assessing the reality of posited mechanisms has to be explicitly acknowledged. And, in place of tying hypotheses to patterns of events, law-like statements must be recognised, instead, as designating causal mechanisms which, when activated, are always operative whatever else is going on. Thus, with respect to Friedman's falling bodies hypothesis, the sort of reasoning employed much earlier by J.S. Mill, for example, seems much more to the point:

> Thus if it were stated to be a law of nature, that all heavy bodies fall to the ground, it would probably be said that the resistance of the atmosphere, which prevents a balloon from falling, constitutes the balloon an exception to that pretended law of nature. But the real law is, that all heavy bodies *tend* to fall; and to this there is no exception, not even the sun and moon; for even they, as every astronomer knows, tend towards the earth, with a force exactly equal to that with which the earth tends towards them (Mill, 1844, p. 160).

B. On the Application of Scientific Knowledge—and Making Sense of Economic Policy

Finally, the same sort of conclusions and considerations just noted must be emphasized if we are to make sense of Friedman's apparently overriding motivation to formulate economic policy. As noted in section II, the actualist insistence on tying laws or significant hypotheses to constant conjunctions of events, entails that scientific activity—including the justified application of knowledge and policy formulation—is restricted to the sort of closed systems that are found only in experimental situations, leaving the question of what governs phenomena outside of these situations unaddressed. At the same time, the fact that scientific knowledge is successfully applied outside of such experimental situations remains, for the actualist, inexplicable.

If Friedman's insistence that hypotheses hold only in certain specified circumstances, amounts, as I have argued, to an implicit attempt to specify the sort of closed systems usually found only in experimental situations, then, of course, the same problems of applying his own preferred hypotheses similarly apply. In fact, to the extent that Friedman expects his arguments to bear, ultimately, upon the nonexperimental situation of economics, then, of course, the difficulties involved are even more severe. For, if the actualist is compelled to restrict all legitimate scientific activity to the sort of closed systems usually found only in experimental situations, and if experimental situations do not occur at all in economics, then the conclusion seems inescapably to follow that economics is fenced off from scientific activity altogether. And if there are no closed systems, so that there are no significant hypotheses to be found, then there is not even the possibility of having accepted knowledge to apply outside of closed systems, whether or not such activities could be provided with some rationale. In short, to the extent that the social world is completely open, the actualist appears to possess no basis for establishing knowledge, and no rationale for policy at all.

The solution, of course, is to abandon the actualist presumption of ubiquity constant of spontaneous conjunctions and to take seriously the transcendental realist ontology of generative structures instead. In this way, the search for event regularities in closed systems, and the application of knowledge in open ones, can be rendered intelligible. In this view, the natural and social sciences can be seen to share much in common. They differ to the extent that some of the natural sciences, on occasion, can engineer, through experiment, an artificial closure. But this situation represents the exception rather than the rule. To hold up this exception as a paradigm example to which economics is supposed to conform, is to force economic analysis into the mode of natural science at precisely the point where it is least appropriate to do so. By rejecting actualism and the pretence of engineering or somehow effecting a closed system, economics can proceed in many ways like any other science, albeit without the possibility of achieving a crucial test situation (see Lawson, 1989b). In short, and despite Friedman's many repetitions to the contrary, economics is essentially explanatory and not event-predictive.

V. FINAL COMMENTS AND CONCLUSION

In order to render aspects of successful scientific activity intelligible, it is necessary to abandon the conception of laws, or significant hypotheses, that ties them to closed systems—those in which constant conjunctions of events occur. The same response is required if Friedman's numerous methodological comments and prescriptions are to be rendered at all intelligible. Instead, it is necessary to invoke explicitly something like the realist ontology of generative structures that are productive of, but irreducible to, the manifest phenomena that we experience. In this way, the possibility of invariant laws can be sustained even in an open system—as designating the (generally nonempirical) ways of acting of generative structures independently of any particular pattern of events that may ensue. In this view, the objective of economics is to identify and understand significant structures and mechanisms in order that economic phenomena of interest can be explained.

In criticising Friedman's account, I have argued that, like much current economic analysis in general, it attempts to combine *both* an implicit transcendental realist ontology of generative structures (or something very much like it) *and* an unthinking commitment to the tying of laws to effectively closed systems. The outcome, inevitably, is a significant degree of confusion. Thus, when Friedman presumes that a closed system can be taken as given, the transcendental realist ontology is effectively abandoned. But when Friedman needs to specify the circumstances in which a constant conjunction of events can hold, the transcendental realist ontology, which is clearly warranted, is itself implicitly taken as given.

Given that much current economic analysis appears to accept Friedman's unthinking commitment to the general availability of stable event-relationships, it is perhaps not surprising that many interpreters of Friedman have taken his apparently explicit rejection of various transcendental realist considerations as the most essential aspect of his contribution. This presumably, if confusedly, has licensed the widespread interpretation of Friedman's position as instrumentalist. Perhaps not everyone has gone as far as Boland (1979, p. 503) in claiming that Friedman's "methodological position is both logically sound and unambiguously based on a coherent philosophy of science—Instrumentalism." But a few appear to have gone along with it to a significant extent (e.g., Frazer, 1984). However, I think the arguments above indicate that while, in an open world, instrumentalism is anything but a coherent philosophy of science, Friedman's position, although containing insight, is hardly logically sound and unambiguously grounded. On the contrary, Friedman's position is confused. It contains conflicting elements of realism and antirealism. Although the emphasis may be explicitly, most of the time, on the latter, his implicit commitment to realism, as noted, is always required if his numerous strictures are even to begin to get off the ground.[10]

In the end, however, the question of which way, or how coherently, Friedman's position can be interpreted, is not the most significant issue. It is useful as an illustration of how the commitment to actualism—to the tying of law-like statements to closed systems—can lead to confusion. The point is to reject actualism. If significant features of scientific activity are to be rendered intelligible and economic analysis is to claim any legitimate role in attempts to understand and constructively transform the world in which we live, a transcendental realist account of causation, or something very much like it, needs to be developed in its place.

ACKNOWLEDGMENT

I am grateful to Jo Fedderke for helpful comments on an earlier draft of this paper.

NOTES

1. This particular version of realism, stimulated to a large extent by Bhaskar (1978), has, in recent years, been increasingly adopted and developed in fields outside economics (see, e.g., Chalmers, 1988; Gregory and Urry, 1988; Sayer, 1984). The present contribution owes much to this general literature, and most especially to the contribution of Bhaskar.

2. Although this realist account clearly stands in stark contrast to much of orthodox economics, its basic components, it should be emphasized, are not particularly novel to economics, but can be found in the writings of J.N. Keynes, J.M. Keynes, Marshall, Marx, and J.S. Mill, among others. Thus, J.S. Mill, for example, writes concerning the "method of investigation proper" of "political economy;;'

If indeed every phenomenon was generally the effect of not more than one cause, a knowledge of the law of cause would, unless there was a logical error in our reasoning, enable us confidently to predict all circumstances of the phenomenon . . . Effects [however] are commonly determined by a *concurrence* of causes. If we have overlooked any one cause, we may reason justly from all the others, and only be the further wrong . . . [A person's] error generally consists . . . in making the wrong *kind* of assertion: he predicated an actual resut, when he should only have predicated a *tendency* to that result—a power acting with a certain intensity in that direction. . .

Thus if it were stated to be a law of nature, that all heavy bodies fall to the ground, it would probably be said that the resistance of the atmosphere, which prevents a balloon from falling, constitutes the balloon an exception to that pretended law of nature. But the real law is, that all heavy bodies *tend* to fall; and to this there is no exception, not even the sun and moon; for even they, as every astronomer knows, tend towards the earth, with a force, exactly equal to that with which the earth tends towards them (Mill, 1844, p. 160).

3.   Of course, this is not to claim that the prediction of the way that a mechanism will act is ruled out. Thus, it may often be possible to form some legitimate view, or justifiably "predict", the direction of change to the level of events. If, for example, a policy of tax-cutting is introduced, it will usually, of course, be possible to predict the immediate impact of this policy on say, consumer spending—that is, the induced direction of change in consumer spending can be rationally anticipated. However, because of the complex combination of juxtaposed counteracting mechanisms, the actual level of consumer spending will typically not be predictable. Of course, if further countervailing mechanisms are simultaneously *initiated* (or even induced) the actual empirically "observable"—direction of change itself may also be unpredictable.

4.   In what follows, all references to Friedman's writing, unless explicitly indicated otherwise, are to Friedman (1953).

5.   If, for example, the sunnier side of a tree is trimmed, and the remaining leaves fail to "move rapidly or instantaneously" to any unoccupied sunnier spot, then tree trimming presumably represents the sort of circumstances in which the hypothesis does not hold, and in which its valid testing, and so forth, is thought to be inhibited.

6.   Put differently, Friedman presumes that a set of phenomena has, in each case, been restricted in such a way that a single posited (set of) generative structure(s) is sufficient for its prediction. Indeed, at one point Friedman explicitly acknowledges: "It is frequently convenient to present . . . a hypothesis by stating that the phenomena it is desired to predict behave in the world of observation *as if* they occurred in a hypothetical and highly simplified world containing only the forces that the hypothesis asserts to be important" (p. 40).

7.   For a useful discussion of positivism in economics, see Caldwell (1982).

8.   For interesting discussions of different forms and facets of realism, see the contributions of Mäki (e.g., 1988).

9.   This conclusion also follows easily from a consideration of a wider range of Friedman's publications. For a useful contribution addressing this point, see Hammond (1988).

10.   The fact that Friedman, eventually, explicitly accepted the tag of instrumentalist does not affect the argument here at all. A consequence of the view being defended here is that when Friedman, like any other economist or scientist, is practising science, he is implicitly acting on realism. But it is not necessary, in order for this to be so, that Friedman is consciously aware that this is the case. Nor does it follow that this is the only philosophy that Friedman may be acting upon at any moment in putting together his total contribution. Indeed, it is precisely because this is so that the sort of confusions noted in Friedman's work can arise. In short, and despite suggestions by some (for example, Boland, 1984) to the contrary, it is quite legitimate for philosophical reflection to bear critically on *any* aspect of the enterprise, *including* Friedman's own conception of what he is doing.

REFERENCES

Boland, L.A. 1979 "A Critique of Friedman's Critics." *Journal of Economic Literature* XVII: 503-522.

————. 1984. "Methodology: Reply." *American Economic Review* 74(4):795, 797.

Bhaskar, R. 1978. *A Realist Theory of Science*. Sussex. UK: The Harvester Press.

Caldwell, B.J. 1980. "A Critique of Friedman's Methodological Instrumentalism." *Southern Economic Journal* 47:366-374.

————. 1982. *Beyond Positivism: Economic Methodology in the Twentieth Century*. London: Allen & Unwin.

Chalmers, A. 1988. "Is Bhaskar's Realism Realistic?" *Radical Philosophy* 49:18, 23.

Frazer, W.J. 1984. "Methodology: Reply." *American Economic Review* 74(4):793-794.

Friedman, M. 1953. *Essays in Positive Economics*. Chicago: University of Chicago Press.

Gregory, D. and J. Urry. 1985. *Social Relations and Spacial Structures*. London: Macmillan.

Haavelmo, T. 1944. "The Probability Approach in Econometrics." *Econometrica* 12 (Supplement):1-118.

Hammond, J.D. 1988. "Realism in Friedman's *Essays in Positive Economics*." Paper presented at the 1988 History of Political Economy conference, in Toronto.

Hodgson, G. 1988. *Economics and Institutions: A Manifesto for a Modern Institutional Economics*. Philadelphia: University of Pennsylvania Press.

Lawson, T. 1989a. "Realism and Instrumentalism in the Development of Economics." *Oxford Economic Papers* 41(1):236-258.

————. 1989b. "Abstraction, Tendencies and Stylised Facts: A Realist Approach to Economic Analysis." *Cambridge Journal of Economics* 13(1, March):59-78.

Mäki, U. 1988. "How to Combine Rhetoric and Realism in the Methodology of Economics." Economics and Philosophy 4(1):89, 109.

Mill, J.S. 1844. *Essays on Some Unsettled Questions of Political Economy*. London: J.W. Parker.

Sayer, A. 1984. "Method in Social Science: A Realist Approach." London: Hutchinson.

Wilkinson, F.S., (ed.). 1981. "Dynamics of Labour Market Segmentation." San Diego: Academic Press.

FRIEDMAN AND REALISM

Uskali Mäki

I. THE SPELL OF FRIEDMAN'S ESSAY

Milton Friedman's "The Methodology of Positive Economics" is a peculiar piece of scholarly achievement. A quarter of a century after its publication, it continues to hold the attention of economists as well as specialists in the methodology of economics, probably more so than any other text on the topic. Many economists find Friedman's message appealing, whereas most methodologists are critical of it. In any case, both critics and defenders seem to be under the spell of the essay. They find it necessary to return to the essay over and over again, either as an authoritative point of reference in support of their own ideas or as an object of critical (or, more often today, of neutral interpretive) analysis.

This situation raises a problem: why is this so? How should we explain the long-standing popularity and the continuously dominant role of Friedman's essay? In trying to answer this question, I think the following features of the essay should be kept in mind.

First, the essay is plagued with obscurity. The essay lacks coherence and often puts its points ambiguously. This both gives room and brings about a

Research in the History of Economic Thought and Methodology
Volume 10, pages 171-195.
Copyright © 1992 by JAI Press Inc.
All rights of reproduction in any form reserved.
ISBN: 0-55938-501-4

need for interpretation.[1] Different interpretations fit different background commitments and serve different interests. Philosophically sophisticated readers may easily find Friedman's obscurity intolerable and a sufficient reason for refraining from detailed scrutiny. For reasons based on two other features of the essay, however, I do not find this a welcome attitude.

Second, the essay is blessed with a considerable degree of persuasiveness. Although it does not provide a well-formulated methodological theory, the message and some of the formulations have strong intuitive appeal among practicing economists for reasons that, as a by-product, I hope to make understandable in the present paper. Sometimes this persuasiveness is based on obscurity, but this is not always the case.

The third relevant feature of the essay is its richness. It touches several extremely important and difficult methodological problems within economics and elsewhere. It is seminal in that it offers topics for further investigation. I dare say that, as yet, this richness has not been exhausted by commentators. In the present paper, I will utilize this feature by taking Friedman's essay not only as an object of interpretation but also as a source of inspiration for clarifying and developing my own thoughts about the character of economic theories.

From the point of view of our tasks in the present paper, the most important set of obscurities is related to the term "realism" in Friedman as well as in the subsequent discussion, written or oral, by economists and methodologists. The central thesis of Friedman's essay is formulated as being about the "realism of assumptions" to the effect that this "realism" is irrelevant to the acceptance of an economic theory. I will show that, in this usage, the term "realism" is multiply ambiguous.

In earlier works (e.g., Mäki 1988) I began to analyze and apply the notion of realism with a view to eliminating the ambiguity surrounding it. In a later paper (Mäki 1989a) I pursued this project further by introducing a distinction between "realism" and "realisticness." In the present essay I will develop and apply those ideas in the context of Friedman's methodological proclamations with the purpose of clarifying what Friedman can be interpreted as having said and my own thoughts about economics as well. I begin with specifications of some of the relevant meanings of "realism," especially those concerned with ontological and semantic matters. I will then point out some of the meanings of "realisticness" and "unrealisticness" related to economists' discourse about their theories. These specifications should help explain why "realism" (designating a collection of ontological and semantic doctrines) and "realisticness" (designating a collection of attributes predicable of representations) should be kept distinct. In the rest of the paper, I will show how these various notions can be used for interpreting, criticizing, and defending the obscure message of Friedman's essay.

The most popular label recently attached to Friedman's view has been "instrumentalism," which has been taken to denote a conception opposite to "realism" (Wong, 1973; Boland, 1979; Caldwell, 1980). While I agree with this practice with reservations, it seems to me that grounds for this labeling have not been sufficiently well analyzed. In particular, the nature of Friedman's instrumentalism has not been completely understood. A central thesis of this paper is that *Friedman can be read so as to make him endorse several kinds of realism and that their range is dependent on how ("un)realisticness" is interpreted.* It will be argued that this insight has to underly any allegation of Friedman being an instrumentalist. In the process, new light will be shed on the ambiguities and internal inconsistencies that plague Friedman's essay.

I take it for granted that Friedman has not provided what might be regarded as a sophisticated and detailed metatheoretical account of economics. Therefore, projecting his conception on the basis of his explicit pronouncements requires a considerable degree of interpretation. I should warn the reader that no final and complete interpretation of his authentic views is attempted here. The perspective is that of a philosophically informed reader of *the text* of "The Methodology of Positive Economics," and the question is this: What could we take some of the formulations in the essay to mean? The question is *not:* What did *the person* Milton Friedman mean? This is an important remark that should not be obscured by the fact that I will often formulate my suggestions with Milton Friedman as the subject of certain metatheoretical beliefs.

II. REALISMS

The senses of the term "realism" to be introduced in what follows[2] are typically "philosophical" in that they are suggested specifications of some of the uses of the term that are current in philosophers' discourse on ontological and semantic questions. This implies that I do not take as my point of departure those senses of realism that are constituent of economists' everyday usage of the term. In spite of this, my suggestions have been designed so as to be of relevance in analyzing questions related to the peculiarities of economics.[3]

The meaning of "realism" is sometimes restricted to its purely ontological sense; then it is understood as having the form of the statement, "*X* exists," or, "*X* is real," or, "There are *X*s."[4] *X* may designate, at the most general level, the world; or, less generally, particulars or universals (or both), essences or appearances (or both), possible worlds or only the actual world, and so forth; or it may designate observable events, physical entities, mental powers, social structures, and so forth; or, more particularly, genes, inflation, cities, and so forth; or, at the most particular level, the genes of Milton Friedman, the inflation rate of Chile last year, Chicago, and so forth.

Let us say that the above statements and others similar to them exemplify *ontological realism.* The *X* or *X*s that are said to be real are looked upon "from the point of view of reality." If the Xs are objects postulated in theories, then statements concerning their existence are concurrently statements about the semantic properties of those theories; they say that those theories or their individual components *refer* to something that exists independently of them. If we claim that there are genes, inflation rates, and cities, this amounts to saying that genetic theories, macroeconomic theories such as monetarist theory, and some urban theories factually refer to elements in their extensions. To say so, or more generally, to say that linguistic expressions may, should, or do refer to entities in the real world is to subscribe to what may be called *referential realism* with respect to those expressions.

Reference to specific real things "picks them out" from among all the constituents of the world, but does not yet characterize those things. This is accomplished by representations. Theories, statements, and terms may *represent* entities in the real world in that they attribute properties to those entities, that is, tell us what they are like, how they behave, evolve, and so forth. To claim that theories, sentences, and terms may, should, or do have this semantic property is to advance the thesis of what might be called *representational realism.*[5] Furthermore, linguistic representations consisting of statements may be claimed to be *true or false* partly by virtue of what their referents are like, that is, by virtue of the way the world is. In other words, truth and falsity are among the possible semantic properties of theories and statements. Let us call this thesis *veristic realism.* Referential, representational, and veristic realism together comprise what may be called *semantic realism.*

The above versions of realism can be connected to other specifications. Consider, for example, the relation between science and common sense, where common sense is related to the cognitive and conceptual capacities of lay persons, in contrast to specialists in the relevant scientific discipline. Are the (often observable) objects of linguistic representations typical of commonsense frameworks (such as green cucumbers and fat prime ministers) real? What about the (often unobservable) objects of scientific theories (such as black holes and structures of social power)? Are commonsense representations true, or can they be? What about scientific representations? Let us say that the *minimal* version of *commonsense realism* amounts to realism about commonsense objects and representations. The *radical* version adds to this nonrealism about scientific objects and representations. The *minimal* variety of *scientific realism* consists of realism about scientific objects and representations. The *radical* version includes, in addition, nonrealism about common sense. These definitions imply that the minimal versions of commonsense realism and scientific realism are mutually compatible, whereas the radical versions are not. (see Mäki 1984). To be reckoned with is the *essentialist* form of scientific realism; it says that scientific theories may have essences as their real objects and that they may be true about those essences.

Another additional specification is that of *descriptive* versus *normative* attitudes toward realism in the above senses. For instance, descriptive commonsense ontological realism about properties might say that colors exist, while the statement that certain physical theories should be true (or false) about the structure of matter exemplifies normative scientific veristic realism. Let us finally say that *methodological* (or *axiological*) *realism* is a subspecies of normative veristic realism which states that truth about the real world should be pursued.

III. REALISTICNESS AND UNREALISTICNESS

The categories of realism characterized above are not those of an economist who makes judgements about what is often called the "realism of assumptions" made in economic theories. But the economist, in the context of the issue related to assumptions, also uses the term "realism." This is also the case in Friedman's essay. This terminological practice is misleading. In order to help avoid unnecessary confusion, I have suggested (in Mäki 1989a) that we adopt, beside "realism," the term "realisticness," and that we should keep them separate.

While "realism" is a name for members in a set of philosophical doctrines, "*realisticness*" characterizes features of representations. In the context of economics, realisticness is an attribute (or a set of attributes) of economic theories and their constituent statements. Thus, we may say, "The assumptions of theory T are unrealistic." We should not talk about the realism of assumptions and theories, but rather about their realisticness. There are several senses in which a representation can be said to be realistic or unrealistic. Some of these, cultivated (implicitly at least) by economists as well, can be briefly mentioned.

There are semantic senses of "realisticness" and "unrealisticness" which are dichotomous in that a representation either is or is not realistic in those senses. A representation can be said to be *referentially realistic* if it refers to reality, and *referentially unrealistic* if it fails to refer to items in the real world. A representation is *representationally realistic* if it represents real features of real things, and *representationally unrealistic* if it fails to do so. A representation is *veristically realistic* if it is true of the real things that it refers to, and *veristically unrealistic* if it is a false representation of its real referent.

Each of these semantic senses can be connected to various specifications concerning the character of the actual or potential referent of the representation in question. If the presumed referent is observable, assessments about *observational realisticness* can be formulated. For instance, the theory of cardinal utility may be regarded as observationally unrealistic, because it is not a representation of directly observable realities. If the referent is part of the unobservable essence of the object under study, we may form opinions about what may be called *essential realisticness*. For example, the theory of surplus value is often claimed by Marxist economists to provide a true (i.e., veristically realistic) representation of the essence of capital.

As can easily be seen, the semantic senses of "realisticness" are directly related to forms of semantic realism. If a representation is referentially realistic, one should be a (descriptive) referential realist about it (but not so if the representation is referentially unrealistic). If it is representationally realistic, it is rational to adopt (descriptive) representational realism in regard to it (while representational nonrealism is required if it is representationally unrealistic). In the case of the veristic versions, the situation is not similarly symmetrical. By definition, if a representation is veristically *either* realistic *or* unrealistic, veristic realism is a correct attitude towards it in *both* cases. Furthermore, commonsense realism is an appropriate view of observationally realistic representations, while scientific-essentialist realism fits representations that are essentially realistic.

There is no doubt that veristically unrealistic representations abound in scientific theories. This observation does not lead us very far if we do not realize that a representation may be false in many ways, that is, that claims of falsehood in representations are in need of qualifications. Statements like

(1)   The earth is at the center of the solar system.
(2)   The surface of the earth is covered with vodka.
(3)   The mass of the earth is greater than that of Jupiter.

are false in a different way than statements like

(4)   The earth is a mass point.
(5)   The earth has a spherical shape.
(6)   The surface of the earth is completely covered with water.
(7)   Half of the surface of the earth is covered with water.
(8)   The mass of the earth is 6×10^{27} grams.

Let us say that statements such as (1)-(3) are *hopeless falsehoods*. In intuitive terms, their "distance" from the truth is so great that it is hopeless to engage in only minor revisions in order to attain the truth; instead, they have to be replaced by completely different statements. ("Minor" and "completely different" may be taken to denote notions that are relative in respect to context and purpose.)

Statements (4) to (8) differ from each other in character, but none of them is a hopeless falsehood (relative to typical contexts in which such statements occur). Statement (4) is an *idealization* in that it involves so called limit concepts. A limit concept is designated by a variable with the value 0 or $|\infty|$. In (4), the spatial dimensions of the earth are claimed to be zero, which does not correspond to the way the world is. Statement (5) can be called a *simplification.* The shape of the earth in fact is not quite that of a round ball, but rather that of a hackly ellipsoid flattened at the poles; (5) simplifies the shape by ignoring, for example, topographical details such as mountains and valleys. As to statements (6) and (7), both of them are false, since in fact some 71 percent of the surface of the earth is covered by water. To name these kinds of veristic unrealisticness, (6) may be called an *exaggeration,* while (7) is an *understatement.* Idealizations are extreme exaggerations or understatements. Finally, let us call statement (8) an *approximation.* An approximate estimate of the mass of the earth is reported, but the precisely correct value is not given (a closer approximation would be 5.976×10^{27} grams).

Representations of the kinds (1)-(8) are unrealistic in that what they state is false about their referents. They fail to satisfy the requirement of "nothing but the truth." Representations may be unrealistic also in the sense that they fail to provide "the whole truth," that is, they fail to mention all features of their referents, or the range of their referents is restricted. Let us say that such representations are *isolations*: they isolate objects and some of their properties from the rest of all objects and properties. The less a representation is based on isolations, the more realistic it is in being more *comprehensive* or *encompassing* (i.e., in covering a wider range of elements or details in a given situation). It is especially important to understand that isolation does not imply falsehood: an isolating representation may be true about the isolated aspects of the world.

Isolation is related to some idealizations and simplifications in the following way. If a statement represents an object in terms of a limit concept to the effect that one of the properties of the object is represented by a metric variable with the value 0, then the other features of the object under consideration have in practice been isolated from this very property. This is the case with the spatial dimensions of the earth in statement (4). Furthermore, sometimes when a statement involves simplification, this brings about isolation from those elements or features of the object that it in fact has and that are responsible for its more complicated nature. This happens to mountains and valleys in statement (5).

We have not yet covered all meanings of the term "(un)realisticness" relevant to discussions on economic theories. Some of its senses are clearly pragmatic. We may say that a representation is realistic if it has been tested and if the belief related to it is regarded as well *confirmed* by the test, and unrealistic if the belief is regarded as *disconfirmed.* Another pragmatic sense is related to plausibility. A representation is realistic if it is found *plausible,* and unrealistic if it is found *implausible.* Yet a third, and a most typical, pragmatic sense is in question when we say that a representation is realistic if it is *practically relevant or useful,* and unrealistic if it is *practically irrelevant or useless.*

Unlike referential, representational, and veristic realisticness, many other senses of realisticness and unrealisticness are not dichotomous in that they allow for differences of degree. Thus, we may say that a representation is more or less realistic (or unrealistic) in being *more or less* simplifying, exaggerating, isolating, approximating, confirmed, plausible, or practically useful than some other representation.

Both realisticness and unrealisticness are properties of representations. Technically, they can be treated as predicates attributable to representations. In its dichotomous meanings, the predicate "is realistic" is given a disjunctive definition by stating, "is realistic" $=_{df}$ "refers to reality" v ... v "represents observables" v ... v "is true" v ... (where "v" should be understood in the inclusive sense of "or"). Similarly with "is unrealistic." For those meanings which permit differences of degree, we have to formulate the definition as follows: "is (more or less) realistic" $=_{df}$ "is (more or less) complex' v ... v "is (more or less) comprehensive" v ... v "is (more or less) plausible" v "is (more or less) practically relevant."

Some of the senses of realisticness and unrealisticness are related hierarchically in that questions concerning some of them can be raised only provided questions of some others have been settled in certain ways. For instance, we cannot make claims about the truth or falsity of economic theories if we do not presuppose that those theories are realistic in referring to and representing really existing elements and features in the economy. To give another example, claims about the idealizing or exaggerating character of a statement in economic theory are possible only if the statement is regarded as strictly false.

As I said earlier, in some of their senses, "realisticness" and "realism" are connected. For instance, if we say, "The neoclassical theory of the firm is about real firms" (i.e., is referentially and representationally *realistic* in this sense), we are descriptive referential and representational *realists* about the theory; if we say, "Economic theory should be true" (i.e., should be veristically *realistic*), we subscribe to methodological (or axiological) *realism* about economic theorizing. But it is important to see that there are other meanings of the terms that have no analytical link with each other. Thus, if we say, for example, "The assumption of rational expectations is well confirmed in the case of financial markets" (i.e., is realistic in one sense), or "Neoclassical theory of the firm leaves out of consideration the role of management" (i.e., is unrealistic in another sense), or, "The assumption of the existence of perfect futures markets in the theory of general equilibrium is implausible" (i.e., is unrealistic in a third sense), we do not, without additional premises, make points directly related to realism, nonrealism, or antirealism.

In the opening section, I claimed that the term "realism" as used by Friedman and other participants in the assumptions controversy is multiply ambiguous. In the light of the above distinctions, it is now possible to specify the contents of this claim. First, realism and realisticness have not been kept separate; there are written texts where the author uses "realism" both as a label for a philosophical doctrine and also in the context of the "realism of assumptions" issue as a substitute for "realisticness." Second, the various sorts of (un)realisticness (and, often, of realism) have been treated unanalyzed, often as if (un)realisticness constituted a homogenous property. The statement, "Theory *T* is (un)realistic," so often encountered in discussions about economic theories, is hopelessly ambiguous.

To be sure, Friedman's methodological statements and arguments involve a number of different kinds of realisticness and unrealisticness. It is important for an exegetical analyst to understand that Friedman himself does not seem to be aware of the differences. He treats the various kinds as if they amounted to the same thing. In consequence, he gives the impression that an argument concerning one kind (related to a selected example given by him) as such counts as an argument concerning other kinds as well. In what follows, I will identify some of the kinds of realisticness and unrealisticness that can be found in Friedman. I will also examine which of these types have implications concerning realism and nonrealism.

IV. REALISM AND UNQUALIFIED FALSEHOOD

Let us begin the analysis of Friedman's proclaimed views with unqualified falsity as the meaning of "unrealisticness." This specification is very much in line with Friedman's own formulations and also prevalent in much of the subsequent discussion, for instance in Boland (1979). Surprising, perhaps, in the light of earlier commentaries on the character of Friedman's methodology, it will immediately turn out that he can be interpreted as an advocate of several versions of realism. In particular, I argue that there is no difficulty in interpreting Friedman as an ontological and semantic realist.

This can be shown by beginning with a demonstration which shows that Friedman is a veristic realist about (at least much of) neoclassical theory: he can be read as thinking that the assumptions of this theory have a truth value— namely, that of false—and that being unrealistic in this sense is a good thing. As a descriptive point, he says that businessmen "do not actually and literally" behave as they are assumed to behave in neoclassical theory (Friedman, 1953, p. 22). Furthermore, he says that the creation of the theory of monopolistic competition was originally motivated by "supposedly directly perceived discrepancies between the 'assumptions' [of the theory of perfect competition] and the 'real world'" (p. 31). From a normative viewpoint, Friedman (p. 14) states that "[t]o be important, therefore, a hypothesis must be descriptively false in its assumptions," and "[t]ruly important and significant hypotheses will be found to have 'assumptions' that are wildly inaccurate descriptive representations of reality." (The notion of descriptive falsehood is ambiguous, as I will point out in a later section.) Thus, it seems that, for Friedman, the basic statements of economic theory are veristically unrealistic in having falsity as one of their (desired) semantic properties. This means that he is a veristic realist.

This in turn implies (as the last quotation shows directly) that Friedman thinks the assumptions are representationally realistic. Consequently, he is also a representational realist about neoclassical theory. Assumptions of neoclassical economic theory are semantically fully fledged statements in Friedman's implicit semantics. Finally, claiming that the entities the theory represents exist in reality implies that Friedman thinks that the theory is referentially realistic. Thus, he is a referential realist about neoclassical theory and an ontological realist about (at least many of) its objects, such as business firms. In sum, Friedman thinks that neoclassical theory refers to and represents objects which really exist (i.e., it is realistic) and gives a false representation of them (i.e., it is unrealistic).

V. INSTRUMENTALISM AND THE FRIEDMANIAN MIXTURE

Although, starting from unqualified falsehood as the specification of "unrealisticness," Friedman can be considered an ontological, referential, representational, and veristic realist, I still think that it is correct to characterize him as an instrumentalist as well. But his is not an instrumentalism for which "theories are not true or false, but only instruments" (Caldwell, 1980, p. 368; see Caldwell, 1992, for correction). This latter notion of instrumentalism seems to have been borrowed from philosophers of physics and applied as such to issues of economic methodology. Physical theories contain terms that denote unobservable entities such as photons, quarks, electromagnetic fields, curved space-time, and so forth. Some physicists and philosophers with phenomenalist inclinations have regarded these unobservables or theoretical entities as pure fictions with no real existence beyond the thoughts of theoreticians. This view implies the opinion that theoretical sentences containing such expressions are not genuine statements about reality, that is, statements that refer to, represent, and are true or false with respect to aspects of the real world. These denials of ontological and semantic realism can be dubbed *ontological instrumentalism* and *semantic instrumentalism,* respectively. They give rise to the denial of methodological realism: since theoretical sentences in physics do not and cannot have a truth value, true theories should not be pursued. Instead of appraising theories in terms of their semantic properties, they are to be weighed as to their pragmatic properties such as usefulness, acceptability, fruitfulness, applicability, convenience, and so forth. Recommending the pursuit of these pragmatic virtues instead of truth can be called *methodological* (or *axiological*) *instrumentalism*. Thus, it is possible to base methodological instrumentalism about physics on ontological and semantic instrumentalism about physical theories.

As we have seen, Friedman cannot easily be seen as one who subscribes to ontological and semantic instrumentalism; on the contrary, he seems to be a realist about ontological and semantic matters. However, at the same time, he is a methodological instrumentalist. Neoclassical theory, or its fundamental constituents, is, in Friedman's mind, false about the real world, and this is nothing to complain about. Truth in economic theory—as opposed to the veracity of economic predictions—is not something to be sought. This last principle is methodological nonrealism, or, as Bruce Caldwell (1980) aptly puts it, methodological instrumentalism. Friedman's essay is partly a plea for the use of a false theory for instrumental purposes. The whole point of the peculiar Friedmanian variety of economic instrumentalism is that it is a mixture of ontological and semantic realism, on the one hand, and methodological instrumentalism, on the other. Let us call this the *Friedmanian mixture*.

This mixture of realist and instrumentalist ingredients may reveal some reasons for the intuitive appeal that Friedman's views seem to enjoy among economists. Neoclassical economics does not postulate unobservables of the kind found in physical theories. The presumed fundamental constituents of economic reality are entities like business firms, households, labor inputs, consumer goods, money, prices, taxes, and so forth. Hardly any economist has doubts about their real existence. They are part of our everyday experience and, in a sense, observable. Electrons and black holes are different in this respect. Consequently, it is possible to be a referential (commonsense) realist about economic theories, even if one happened to prefer referential (scientific) nonrealism to realism about physical theories (thus committing oneself to radical commonsense realism).

The key to understanding the difference between the situations in economics and physics in this regard seems to be the following. From a radical commonsense realist point of view, the existence of many fundamental entities of economic theories does not look dubious, whereas the existence of many physical entities does look suspect. The difference appears on the level of reference: it is relatively easier to accept economic theories as factually referential than is the case with physical theories. No change in this respect has to occur in physics when we move from reference to representation; the properties attributed to postulated entities by theoretical representations are often as dubious as those entities themselves to the eye of a radical commonsense realist. The situation is different in economics. Here, entities referred to and believed to exist on the basis of everyday experience, have been attributed properties (such as rational maximization, perfect information, homogeneity, or perfect divisibility) that are not quite those that they are believed to possess, this belief again being based on ordinary observation. Thus, many theoretical representations are believed to be false about the properties of entities that are believed to be real. In spite of this, those representations are regarded by many as useful and acceptable. Hence the appeal of the Friedmanian mixture of ontological and semantic realism and methodological instrumentalism.

Let us take an example. Business firms are obvious instances of the set of ordinary objects which are generally believed to exist and possess certain properties on the basis of commonsense experience. Traditional neoclassical microeconomics depicts business firms as rational and fully informed calculators and profit maximizers without an internal structure, connected to each other by the external ties of price signals under competitive conditions. Firms are assumed to have only one goal, that of maximum profits. Furthermore, they do not try to attain this goal by means of strategic maneuvers, but rather by reacting passively to external stimuli which consist of given changes in cost and demand conditions. Now it seems obvious that one can never observe a firm like this. It looks like a nonobservable theoretical entity, which would seem to suggest that the relevant issue of realism here is one of scientific realism. But this is probably not the way an ordinary economist views the question. I suppose she or he takes it as read that the "assumptions" made are "unrealistic" about real, observable business firms. The relevant issue is faced within the confines of commonsense realism, and it can be settled by adopting the Friedmanian mixture (or, alternatively, by rejecting the traditional neoclassical model in the name of axiological realism).

VI. BELIEF AND ACCEPTANCE

I will next provide a reformulation of the Friedmanian mixture in epistemological terms. For this purpose I propose to make a distinction between acceptance and belief. A theory is *accepted* if it is adopted, held, used, applied, and so forth. A theory is *believed* if it is regarded as being a true account of its objects. It is instructive in this context to consider what Bas van Fraassen (1980, p. 8) takes as "the correct statement of scientific realism": "Science aims to give us, in its theories, a literally true story of what the world is like; and *acceptance of a scientific theory involves the belief that it is true"* (italics partly deleted). Here, scientific realism is defined as a doctrine which binds acceptance and belief intimately together. In my view, this is not (even part of) "the correct statement" of what scientific realism amounts to; it is far too strong to be acceptable as a common characteristic shared by all versions of scientific realism about all acceptable scientific theories.

I would now like to formulate the Friedmanian mixture in the following terms. Economic theories should be accepted as good predictors (but not believed to be true) and rejected as bad predictors (but not believed to be false). Nothing follows from acceptance of a theory about its truth and about the existence of its objects. Beliefs about these questions (i.e., the truth value of a theory and the existence of its objects) are formed on grounds independent of accepting or rejecting a given economic theory. This is possible provided that the objects of economic theory are regarded as commonsense objects, that is, objects that are accessible to us by means of our everyday experience and commonsense frameworks. It would, indeed, seem natural to think of business firms, households, and goods as such ordinary objects. We appear to have information about the existence and properties of these entities independently of what any particular economic theory says about them. It is this information that permits Friedman and others to make the judgement, from a commonsense realist point of view, that the assumptions of neoclassical theory are unrealistic in being false about real firms, households, and goods. Neoclassical theory is not to be believed. But it is to be accepted because of its instrumental virtues.

In contrast to van Fraassen's characterization of scientific realism, I am inclined to regard myself as a scientific realist and also to endorse the statement that acceptance and belief do not always have to go together. For many purposes, belief should perhaps always imply acceptance, but not vice versa. We may accept theories without believing in their truth. Different theories or models may be accepted on different grounds. There may be economic theories that are best suited for the purposes of providing heuristic frameworks for creative modeling, and they might be accepted as fruitful frameworks but not believed. There may be other theories that should be accepted as good systematizers of empirical data, as good predictors and retrodictors, but perhaps they (or at least some of them) should not be believed either. A methodological realist, however, insists on pursuing, among other things, economic theories that can be both accepted and believed, that is, believed to provide a true and explanatory account of the nature of (aspects of) the economy, and accepted on this basis. A realist also insists on pursuing explanations for the instrumental success of nonbelieved theories in terms of theories that are believed.

VII. IDEALIZATION, ISOLATION, AND FALSEHOOD

We have thus far based our discussion on unqualified falsehood as the specification of "unrealisticness" defended by Friedman. In this section, I show that there are other senses of the concept of unrealisticness which are implied in Friedman's examples and general statements, such as a statement's being idealizing, exaggerating, and isolating or noncomprehensive. It is unfortunate (even if perhaps rhetorically functional) that Friedman does not keep these senses separate. This omission leads him and anyone else guilty of the same omission to the Friedmanian mixture. In the following two sections, I show how the avoidance of this omission could help Friedman adopt a more comprehensive realism.

On a general level, the confusion of various senses of unrealisticness is brought out by Friedman's use of the expressions "descriptively false," "descriptively unrealistic," and "descriptively inaccurate" (pp. 14-15). They seem to mean at least false (denial of "nothing-but-the-truth") and isolating (denial of "the whole truth"). There is no doubt that economic theories involve both kinds of unrealisticness.

A most revealing example of confusing these two kinds of unrealisticness with each other can be found on pages 31-32 of Friedman's essay. On page 31, he discusses "the recent criticisms of the maximization-of-returns hypothesis on the grounds that businessmen do not and indeed cannot behave as the theory 'assumes' they do." On the next page, Friedman outlines "a completely 'realistic' theory of the wheat market" that would have to mention the color of the traders' and farmers' eyes and hair, their antecedents and education, the physical and chemical characteristics of the soil on which the wheat was grown, the weather prevailing during the growing season, and so forth (1953, p. 32). Such a "theory" would pursue "the whole truth" (without, of course, ever achieving it; for example, such a "theory" would have to tell the story of the detailed career of the genetic ancestors of each farmer, trader, and seed of wheat during the process of cosmological and biological evolution over billions of years). Of course, any theory has to be unrealistic in being more general and in leaving out such details. The rhetorical aim of outlining such a comprehensive "theory" seems to be to ridicule the critics of neoclassical theory, especially of the maximization assumption which is mentioned both immediately before and after the paragraph concerning the comprehensive "theory." What Friedman certainly manages to do with the example of "a completely realistic theory of the wheat market" is to convince the reader that any theory has to isolate certain factors from others, that is, that no theory can be completely comprehensive. However, unrealisticness in this sense does not, as such, imply anything in regard to truth ("nothing but the truth"). We can still raise the question whether the statements concerning the included factors are true or false—for instance, whether wheat-market agents are in fact maximizers.

Perhaps the confusion becomes more understandable if we are reminded that the sense in which the maximization assumption is unrealistic is not so easily analyzable. To make it a bit easier, let us first take a look at one of Friedman's examples, that of Galileo's law of falling bodies. The law states that $s = 1/2 \ gt^2$, and it is based on several assumptions two of which may be formulated for later comments as follows.

(9)   Air pressure $= 0$.

(10)   The strength of all forces other than gravitation $= 0$.

These assumptions are idealizations. They serve to isolate the impact of gravitation from other possible factors. They are "unrealistic" in that assumption (10) is always false, while (9) is mostly false but may sometimes be true. Friedman's favorite assumption is (9), but as will be seen, it is not quite like the maximization assumption to the defense of which he primarily dedicates himself.

Let us now scrutinize the maximization assumption more closely. Friedman would formulate it as follows:

(11)   Producers and traders pursue maximum expected returns.

Friedman seems to have taken seriously the simple critical point made by some contemporaries, such as Hall and Hitch (1939), to the effect that, in fact, business firms are not maximizers in the sense of engaging in the required marginal calculations and adjustments. Hence Friedman's admission, referred to above in section IV, that the maximization assumption is veristically unrealistic. Unfortunately, he does not analyze the unrealisticness of assumption (11) further. It seems that he just agrees to attribute unqualified untruth to it (which then leads to the Friedmanian mixture).

Let us try to go a little further than Friedman in this regard. To begin, statement (11) can be regarded as one with motives (instead of manifest behavior) as its object. Furthermore, it might be taken to involve isolation: it implicitly isolates the motive of the maximization of expected returns from all other possible motives (such as immediate altruism, satisficing, maximization of sales or market share or personal utility, and so forth) in order to make it possible to examine its impact on market phenomena in the absence of other motives. Construed as an isolation, (11) is unrealistic in denying "the whole truth." A possible reformulation of this aspect of (11) is to say that it involves the idea that the other motives are assumed to have zero strength; in this case, the isolation would be based on an idealization. This idealization is most likely veristically unrealistic, but it is important to see that it does not have the maximization motive as its object.[6]

However, this is not the whole story regarding (11). The assumption also involves the idea that agents do have maximum returns as their goal. Construed as carrying this message, (11) would appear as veristically unrealistic in that it involves an exaggeration. It seems to be a false exaggeration because, many would argue, in reality agents are content with less than maximum returns (instead of pursuing maximum profits, firms may act with an eye on mark-up profits, as Hall and Hitch (1939) argued; or, instead of being maximizers, they may be satisficers, as Herbert Simon has argued). This aspect of (11) would then violate "nothing but the truth."

We have here two perspectives on the character of unrealisticness in (11). On the one hand, the assumption is an isolation that denies "the whole truth"; on the other, it denies "nothing but the truth." I have suggested that Friedman has difficulties in keeping isolation and untruth separate because he finds commonsense realism appealing. The maximization assumption is a good example to illustrate this point. It might be the case that the assumption *appears* as a false exaggeration *because* it isolates the maximization motive from other motives. It might be that agents appear as satisficers (or, in general, something less ambitious than maximizers) because in observed behavior those other motives (and informational restrictions, or what have you) are manifested mixed with a striving for maximum returns. Since a commonsense realist is unable to make a serious distinction between the way the world is and the way the world appears in observation, he is also unable to see the difference between isolation and falsehood.

As part of Friedman's rhetorical tactics, he gives the impression that an argument for (9) can, as such, act as an argument for (11), that is, that a defense of the vacuum assumption serves also as a defense of the maximization assumption. This is based on the presumption that the analogy between these assumptions is sufficiently close. This presumption is problematic, however. Let us pay attention to some of the differences between the two assumptions.

Assumption (9) is an idealization which is usually false, but may sometimes be true. If it happens to be true, it has been made true. That is, the isolation effected by the idealization can be made to materialize under laboratory conditions. Assumption (10) is likewise an idealization by means of which an isolation is brought about. Strictly speaking, it is always false, since it is impossible to remove the impact of the gravitational force of the moon, the sun, and other planets and stars on the falling body under consideration, even though the gravitation of the earth can be materially isolated from the impact of winds and rain and many other factors.

In any case, the economic analogue of assumptions (9) and (10) in our example would be something like:

(12)   All other motives except the maximization motive have zero strength.

This is an idealization that helps isolate the maximization motive from other motives. It should be understood that nothing follows from the truth or untruth of (12) in regard to the respective attributes of (11).

On the other hand, the analogue of the maximization assumption in Galileo's law is not the vacuum assumption but instead something like:

(13)   The gravitational field of the earth pulls physical objects.

It is the gravitation of the earth that is being isolated by means of (9) and (10). The truth or falsity of (9) and (10) does not imply anything about the truth or falsity of (13). Statement (13) may be true even though (9) and (10) are false, and even if they are so far away from the truth that Galileo's law provides severely incorrect predictions.

I have tried to show that Friedman attempts to defend an assumption that he believes (or that he believes other economists believe) is a falsehood by supposing that it is similar in crucial respects to isolations. In doing this, he ignores important differences between various kinds of unrealisticness. Obviously basing his assessments on the tenets of commonsense realism, Friedman seems to think that if an economic representation does not in all respects correspond to the way the economy appears to commonsense experience, then the representation is unrealistic simply in the sense of being false. This leads him to the Friedmanian mixture. I will next show how the mixture could be avoided.

VIII. ESSENTIALIST REALISM

Because Friedman's position on many issues is extremely ambiguous, many will be able to find their favorite methodology in Friedman's essay by suitable interpretation. I will deal with my favorite variant of his methodology in the present and next sections. I will show that rejection of radical commonsense realism and reckoning with the distinctions between various kinds of unrealisticness would enable Friedman and others to adopt a more comprehensive combination of realisms, including axiological realism.

There is a possible interpretation that casts Friedman as a realist about essences in the economy and about theories of those essences. Support for this interpretation is provided by the following statement:

> A fundamental hypothesis of science is that appearances are deceptive and that there is a way of looking at or interpreting or organizing the evidence that will reveal superficially disconnected and diverse phenomena to be manifestations of a more fundamental and relatively simple structure" (Friedman, 1953, p. 33).

The maxim of theory formation based on this principle prescribes that we should "abstract essential features of complex reality" (Friedman, 1953, p. 7). By "abstraction," I suppose Friedman means here what we have called isolation and simplification. It can be understood as a method for pursuing truth about the "essential features" or the "fundamental structure" of the economy. If this interpretation is accepted, then we can hereby interpret Friedman as an advocate of methodological or axiological realism.

Starting from these principles, Friedman could—though he does not— argue, for example, that the neoclassical theory of the competitive firm is a "descriptively false" representation of the appearances of real business firms (i.e., is observationally unrealistic), but that it is also a true representation of the essence or "the fundamental structure" of firms (i.e., is essentially realistic)—which is a good thing (see Mäki 1986a, pp. 136-137). This would make Friedman a referential, representational, veristic, *and methodological* (scientific/essentialist) realist. It is important to see that, without essentialism, methodological realism cannot be sustained. Rejection of radical commonsense realism would enable Friedman and others to replace the Friedmanian mixture with a more comprehensive realism.

Proceeding from these ideas, Friedman could have argued that, within the domain of economics, maximizing constitutes the essence of economic behavior, and the maximization assumption isolates this essence from other motives and conditions and is true about it. Similarly, he could have argued that, within the domain of the theory of the firm, the neoclassical perfect competitor constitutes the essence of business firms, hence the theory is and should be true. In fact he compared marginalist maximizing to agents' observable behavior and neoclassical perfect competitors to empirically observable firms and had to admit that there is a lack of correspondence, that is, that the theory is false. But he also had to argue that there is nothing wrong with this, because he liked the theory. In other words, he accepted the theory without believing it.

The passage quoted above on "a fundamental hypothesis of science" contains an idea that can be interpreted as a commitment to *ontological unification* as a goal of scientific theorizing, a very natural commitment to an essentialist realist. Friedman says that, superficially considered, phenomena appear to be "disconnected and diverse," hence, there seems to be no real underlying connection between them. Friedman also seems to suggest that by constructing a theoretical representation that would truthfully describe a "more fundamental" structure we would be able to reveal those apparently independent phenomena as being "manifestations" thereof. In other words, we would *theoretically redescribe* those phenomena as manifestations or appearances of a single common deep structure. This would eliminate the diversity and bring about ontological unification among the phenomena.

To use our earlier examples, ontological unification by means of theoretical redescriptions could be brought about by using explanatory principles of the following kind.

(14)   The downward motion of physical objects is a manifestation of the pull of the earth's gravitational field.

(15)   The behavior of prices in the consumer goods market is a manifestation of economic agents' striving for maximum returns.

The employment of principle (14) and its like enables scientists to argue that not only is gravity causally responsible for the behavior of falling apples and the trajectories of cannon balls, but it is also the force that keeps the moon at her orbit, generates waterfalls, and so forth. All these and many other phenomena can be accounted for as manifestations of a single "more fundamental structure" by redescribing them as such. Similarly, principle (15) and others like it (replacing "prices in the consumer goods market" with descriptions of other phenomena) can be used to make a case for ontological unification within the domain of economics. The behavior of the prices and quantities of tomatoes, computer software, natural gas, bank loans, crimes, economists, and numerous other phenomena can be redescribed as manifestations of agents' maximizing action. These uses of (14) and (15) do not exclude the possibility that the actual behavior of physical bodies and economic prices is being influenced by other factors besides gravitation and maximization. The point is that it is part of the essence of their behavior that they are manifestations of gravitation and maximization.

The idea of ontological unification effected by theoretical redescription can be incorporated into an essentialist notion of scientific explanation (for details, see Mäki, 1990). This notion can be used to replace predictive success as the criterion of theoretical excellence by explanatory success that is irreducible to predictive achievements. It can be argued that this would be especially welcome in a discipline which studies phenomena that occur in open systems. Of course, this line of reasoning would lead to insights that are very far from Friedman's declared predictivism.

IX. "AS IF"

It is often maintained, almost as if it were a self-evident truth, that by formulating an economic theory in terms of an "as if," Friedman commits himself to instrumentalism. I will next show that even the "as if" formulation of economic theory is, in some cases at least, amenable to a realist interpretation.[7] Let us take a closer look at the following passage:

> One confusion that has been particularly rife and has done much damage is confusion about the role of "assumptions" in economic analysis. A meaningful scientific hypothesis or theory typically asserts that certain forces are, and other forces are not, important in understanding a particular class of phenomena. It is frequently convenient to present such a hypothesis by stating that the phenomena it is desired to predict behave in the world of observation as if they occurred in a hypothetical and highly simplified world containing only the forces that the hypothesis asserts to be important" (Friedman, 1953, p. 40).

Isolation, "as-if-ness," and realism seem to be mixed up in this passage. To make this understandable I suggest that the "as-if" formulation can be used to express at least two different ideas. It is one thing to say that:

(a)   phenomena behave as if the isolated conditions under which only those real
      forces that are mentioned in the theory are in fact acting were realized,

and quite another to say that:

(b)   phenomena behave as if those forces were real.

While (a) is a realist formulation, (b) tends to invite an instrumentalist interpretation. It seems evident that in the quotation above, Friedman is saying (a), namely that phenomena behave as if they occurred in a closed system where only some forces exist and act. In economics, such a closed system is artificially created by a theoretician by theoretical isolation, that is, by *Gedankenexperiment*, by intellectually modifying the situation under consideration so that those forces that are regarded as essential or important by the theoretician are isolated from the rest and their effects are then studied in isolation.[8] In his general statement about isolating forces, Friedman is carrying the flag of essentialist realism.

However, in discussing concrete examples, Friedman seems to take stance (b). In the example about predicting the shots of an expert billiard player, he suggests a hypothesis which assumes that the player bases his shots on some ideal estimating and calculating procedures. "It seems not at all unreasonable that excellent predictions would be yielded by the hypothesis that the billiard player made his shots *as if* he knew the complicated mathematical formulas that would give the optimum directions of travel, could estimate accurately by eye the angles, etc., describing the location of the balls, could make lightning calculations from the formulas, and could then make the balls travel in the direction indicated by the formulas." However, Friedman continues, "our confidence in this hypothesis is not based on the belief that billiard players, even expert ones, can or do go through the process described" (p. 21).

Another example is Friedman's "hypothesis that the leaves [on a tree] are positioned as if each leaf deliberately sought to maximize the amount of sunlight it receives," and so forth. (p. 19). However, he adds, "so far as we know, leaves do not 'deliberate' or consciously 'seek,'" and so forth (p. 20). An economic example that is also revealing in this respect is Friedman's ontological indifference toward the real nature of a firm in applying the theory: "there is no inconsistency in regarding the same firm as if it were a perfect competitor for one problem, and a monopolist for another" (p. 36).

The statements given in these quotations on billiard players, leaves, and firms sound very instrumentalistic, but even they might be interpreted, albeit implausibly perhaps, as being compatible with realism. They could be so interpreted only on the condition that they are related to *hypotheses* in the sense of as yet unestablished statements. When we hypothesize, we take it to be *possible* that the phenomena examined are governed by some hidden forces, mechanisms, or actions. The behavior of a billiard player might in fact be a result of the kind of process described; the behavior of leaves on a tree might be an outcome of their striving for maximum sunlight, and so forth; the behavior of a firm might be a manifestation of its being a monopolist. It is another thing to regard it as established (in the light of whatever is taken as relevant evidence) that exactly those forces are causally responsible for the phenomena to be explained. In the former case, phenomena are regarded as behaving *as if* the hypothetized mechanism had generated them (conjectured hypothesis), whereas in the latter case the mechanism (perhaps together with some other forces) is justifiably believed *in fact* to generate the phenomena and their behavior (established hypothesis).

Let me make this point clear. We have two ways of interpreting stance (b) above. (i) It may be taken as concerning the ontological and epistemic status of a statement as such, regardless of the strength of evidential support at hand. This is a clear-cut instrumentalist or fictionalist way. (ii) It may be understood as being concerned with our attitudes towards the believability of a hypothesis in the light of the available evidence for it. The "as-if" formulation here only reflects our cautiousness with respect to the ontological commitments apparently implied in the hypothesis, not an impossibility or permanent absence of such commitments (which is the case in (i)). What first appears as possible may become established later on. This way is compatible with realism.

However, it seems that often when Friedman talks about "hypotheses," he does not mean hypotheses in sense (ii). For him, they are not conjectures waiting for (even fallible) establishment as true or false. They are just more or less useful tools for attaining some pragmatic aims, fictions with no hope of ever being established as true, that is, statements in sense (i). In sum, the three quotations on billiard players, leaves of a tree, and business firms seem to abhor a realist interpretation, while the first one on forces in general clearly invites a realist understanding.

We have seen that unrealistic assumptions (such as isolations, idealizations, and simplifications) may serve the pursuit of truth in economics, provided this is understood in an essentialist realist fashion. I have also tried to show that this possibility cannot be recognized and utilized if radical commonsense realism is not rejected and if attention is not drawn to differences between kinds of unrealisticness. Neither of these conditions is satisfied consistently by Friedman himself.

X. CONCLUDING REMARKS

1.   I have tried to show that Friedman's relation to realism (or, better, the relation of the text of Friedman's essay to realism) depends on how

unrealisticness is understood. First, if unrealisticness is taken simply as unqualified falsehood, then the view that appears in the essay includes ontological and semantic (commonsense) realism accompanied by axiological instrumentalism. This is the Friedmanian mixture. Second, if falsehood and isolation are kept distinct and if unrealisticness is understood as isolation based on idealization, simplification, and so forth, then it becomes possible to adopt axiological (essentialist) realism as well in the interpretation of the essay. This is Friedmanian essentialism.[9]

2.   The interpretation provided here has not paid attention to all possible varieties of realisticness and unrealisticness, such as the pragmatic notions of "intuitive plausibility" (Friedman, 1953, p. 26) and of assumptions being "sufficiently good approximations for the purpose at hand" (p. 15), and others. Let it be noted that the relation of these notions to varieties of realism is often even more complicated than of those that have been dealt with in the foregoing.

3.   In regard to the controversial issue of the coherence of Friedman's methodological views, the following can be said. First, within the bounds of commonsense realism, the Friedmanian mixture seems coherent. Second, essentialist scientific realism with truth as a positive value cannot so easily be made compatible with what is said within the radical commonsense realist framework. The Friedmanian mixture and Friedmanian essentialism are mutually inconsistent. Third, the charges for incoherence made in my earlier article (Mäki, 1986a) seem to remain valid. For instance, Friedman's essay yields an unsettled conception of the epistemology of justification, one that hovers between "falsificationist positivism" and "pragmatist conventionalism." In sum, I maintain that no such single thing as "Friedman's methodology" is given in the essay, notwithstanding the recurring reference to this fiction by commentators.

4.   It would seem that the Friedmanian mixture is found persuasive by many economists. This is partly due to ambiguities in the essay; ambiguity, however, has its costs. On the one hand, Friedman's ambiguity concerning the meaning of varieties of "realisticness" and "unrealisticness" is a smart (but not necessarily conscious) rhetorical device, but on the other, it blocks the way to a coherent formulation of a more comprehensive realism. Since (un)realisticness can be attributed to representations in general, nothing prevents us from talking about (realist, nonrealist, or antirealist) metatheories as being realistic or unrealistic. Friedman's less than well-formulated metatheory is "realistic" at least in the sense that many economists find it plausible.

5.   I have approached Friedman's methodology as an innocent reader of his classic essay on methodology. I have not been interested in Friedman's methodology in the context of his theoretical beliefs and research work as an economist. Instead, my focus has been on the possible interpretations of the message of the essay. While it is clear that any attempt to give an account of

Friedman-the-scholar-with-a-working-methodology has to be wider in scope, the present approach can be justified as follows. It is an obvious fact that "The Methodology of Positive Economics" remains the methodological text most widely read by economists with different backgrounds, interests, and purposes. Many of these readers come with such backgrounds and purposes that they are not primarily interested in Friedman the scholar. Instead, they relate what they read to the theories and research practices advocated by them personally, by those with whom they agree, and by those with whom they disagree, often with the purpose of justifying one set of beliefs and practices while criticizing another. I am inclined to contend that this is and has been the main function of Friedman's essay in the field of economics. Unfortunately, given the obscurity of the essay, its reception and use has remained extremely unanalytical. One aim of the present paper has been to help remedy this situation.

ACKNOWLEDGMENT

I wish to thank Daniel Hammond, Martti Kuokkanen, Ikka Niiniluoto, and Warren Samuels for comments on an earlier draft.

NOTES

1. There are those who think that Friedman has provided a coherent methodology of economics in the essay; see, for example, Boland (1979). For a contrary view, see Mäki (1986a), in which it is suggested that Friedman's essay contains ingredients of three mutually inconsistent philosophies of science, namely positivism, pragmatist conventionalism, and essentialist realism.

2. Sections 2 to 6 borrow materials from Mäki (1989).

3. While I think the list of realisms to follow covers many of the species that are relevant in regard to the traditional issues within economics, the list is far from comprehensive; it omits some of the meanings of the term that are related, for example, to the theories of universals, perception, and scientific progress.

4. Of course, the expressions "exists" and "is real" are themselves ambiguous and in need of further analysis in a more detailed scrutiny of kinds of realism. I will here abstain from this task, however, since the textual evidence that can be found in Friedman's published work provides little foundation for specified interpretations in this regard.

5. Not to be confused with "representative" or "representational" realism in the theory of perception.

6. For a detailed discussion of the rationales and kinds of isolation and of the role of idealizations in the method of isolation, see Mäki (1992).

7. The bulk of this section is drawn from Mäki (1980).

8. For another attempt to analyze Friedman's position in terms of the notion of a closed system, see Lawson (1992).

9. Daniel Hammond (1989) writes that his reading of Friedman's *Essays in Positive Economics* suggests that Friedman is a realist instead of an instrumentalist. Unfortunately, "realism" in Hammond's idea of Friedman being an advocate of "Marshallian realism" remains unclear. It

seems almost as if espousing *realisticness* anywhere and in any of its forms makes one a *realist* in Hammond's opinion. As I have argued, we have to be careful with these connections. I do share Hammond's view that for Friedman, "there is a reality independent of the economist's mind and theory" (p. 5), that is, that Friedman is an ontological realist. However, I have difficulties in understanding what it means to say that in Friedman's opinion "theory aims for this reality (for truth)" (p. 5). In support of this claim Hammond refers to Friedman's appealing to Marshall's famous phrase to the effect that economic theory is an "engine for the discovery of concrete truth" (p. 6). This suggestion remains less than completely convincing as the notions of "theory aiming for reality" and "concrete truth" are left unanalyzed. On the usual positivistic version of *instrumentalism*, the aim of scientific theory is to provide *true* predictions about observable phenomena. This involves a kind of commonsense realism, but not the idea of a theory preferably being true, that is, not axiological realism in regard to theory. If "aiming for concrete truth" is supposed to mean something other than this to Friedman, it should be explicated. One possibility is, of course, that "concrete truth" is akin to "the whole truth," provided by encompassing descriptions of the economy, with few isolating assumptions. Indeed, Hammond's discussion sometimes gives this impression—for instance, in his comments on Friedman's criticism of Lerner (p. 14). However, recommending the pursuit of encompassing descriptions does not yet make one an axiological or methodological realist. In my own essentialist reconstruction of passages in Friedman's essay, an economic theory based on strongly isolating assumptions may be true of the isolated aspects of the economy; thus, veristic and axiological realism does not presuppose the idea of encompassing theories.

REFERENCES

Boland, Lawrence. 1979. "A Critique of Friedman's Critics." *Journal of Economic Literature* 17:503-522.

Caldwell, Bruce. 1980. "A Critique of Friedman's Methodological Instrumentalism." *Southern Economic Journal*, 47:366-374.

Caldwell, Bruce. 1992. "Friedman's Predictivist Methodological Instrumentalism—A Modification." *Research in the History of Economic Thought and Methodology*, Vol. 10, edited by W.J. Samuels. Greenwich, CT: JAI Press.

van Fraassen, Bas. 1980. *The Scientific Image*. Oxford: Oxford University Press.

Friedman, Milton. 1953. *Essays in Positive Economics*. Chicago: Chicago University Press.

Hammond, Daniel. 1989. "Realism in Friedman's *Essays in Positive Economics.*" In *Perspectives on the History of Economic Thought*, edited by D.E. Moggridge. Edward Elgar.

Hall, R.J. and C.J. Hitch. 1939. "Price Theory and Business Behaviour." *Oxford Economic Papers*, 2:12-45.

Lawson, Tony. 1992. "Realism, Closed Systems and Friedman." *Research in the History of Economic Thought and Methodology*, Vol. 10, edited by W.J. Samuels. Greenwich, CT: JAI Press.

Mäki, Uskali. 1980. "Inconsistencies in Milton Friedman's Methodology for Economics." Discussion Paper No. 147, University of Helsinki, Department of Economics.

————. 1984. "Wissenschaftliche Realismus: Kontroversen und Konvergenzen." In *Realismus und Dialektik*, edited by H.-J. Sandkühler und J. Manninen. Köln: Pahl-Rugenstein.

————. 1986a. "Rhetoric at the Expense of Coherence: A Reinterpretation of Milton Friedman's Methodology." Pp. 127-143 in *Research in the History of Economic Thought and Methodology*, Vol. 4, edited by W.J. Samuels. Greenwich, CT: JAI Press.

————. 1988a. "How to Combine Rhetoric and Realism in the Methodology of Economics." *Economics and Philosophy* 4(April):89-109.

————. 1989a. "On the Problem of Realism in Economics." *Ricerche Economiche* 43.

_____. 1990. "Scientific Realism and Austrian Explanation." *Review of Political Economy* 2: 310-344.

_____. 1992. "On the Method of Isolation in Economics." Pp. 317-351 in *Idealization IV: Intelligibility in Science*, edited by G.D. Dilworth. Amsterdam: Rodopi.

Wong, Stanley. 1973. "The 'F-Twist' and the methodology of Paul Samuelson." *American Economic Review*, 63:312-325.

REVIEW ESSAYS

MULTIPLE REVIEWS OF HUTCHISON'S *BEFORE ADAM SMITH*

I. Robert F. Hébert
II. S. Todd Lowry
III. Michael Perelman
IV. Margaret Schabas

Before Adam Smith: The Emergence of Political Economy, 1662-1776.
by Terence Hutison.
Oxford: Basil Blackwell, 1988.

MASTERING THE HISTORICAL JIGSAW

This is an important book, one that makes a major contribution to our understanding of the nature and scope of economic thought before Adam Smith and, at the same time, tempers the kind of unmitigated hero-worship usually reserved for Smith as *the* founder of political economy. Ever since Richard Jones in 1847 (1964) made the first serious but largely unsuccessful attempt to classify the heterodox content of British economics before Smith, a handful of scholars have tried to tame the abstruse topic. Most have met with little more success than the original attempt by Jones and, over time, the importance of the entire era has receded within the history of economic

Research in the History of Economic Thought and Methodology
Volume 10, pages 199-223.
Copyright © 1992 by JAI Press Inc.
All rights of reproduction in any form reserved.
ISBN: 0-55938-501-4

thought. Its hopelessness is perhaps nowhere better typified than by Mark Blaug's reference to the period as "pre-Adamite."

One major exception to the string of unsuccessful efforts to bring order and meaning out of apparent chaos was E. A. J. Johnson's (1937) classic, *Predecessors of Adam Smith,* written more than a half-century ago. Now Hutchison has given us a second major exception, one that surpasses Johnson's classic in several important respects. In *Before Adam Smith,* Hutchison masterfully and comprehensively sketches the economics of the roughly one hundred years prior to 1776, beginning with the performance of Sir William Petty in 1662 and concluding with the publication of *The Wealth of Nations.* Like Johnson before him, but on a grander scale, Hutchison has ferreted out the elusive strands that connect the economic writings of the period. He gives us more than a capable and comprehensive survey of the period, however. He also gives us perceptive and meaningful insights, evaluations, and interpretations, not only of the preclassical period but of the classical period as well. As a bonus, the exposition is clear and uncomplicated throughout.

Written half a century after Johnson's classic work on the British predecessors of Smith, Hutchison's present book nevertheless invites certain comparisons with that earlier work. For the problem that Hutchison confronts today was set forth in a straightforward manner by Johnson long ago:

> I have long felt...,that British economic literature before Adam Smith has often been misunderstood because many critics have been at too great pains to classify all pre-Smithian writers as mercantilists or free-traders. Either word is hard to define, although unless there is complete agreement as to their meanings, they can scarcely be used as critical categories. There is, I believe, a much more forthright way in which to deal with the voluminous literature of early English economic thought: *the emphasis ought to be placed on a developing fabric of ideas, and each important new intellectual strand influencing the composition of this fabric should be signalized.* In view of the great number of economic writers before Adam Smith, and in view of their widely differing interests, training, and prejudices, this is no easy task. An initial attempt can be made, however, by the careful selection of a limited number of writers whose points of view are representative of a group of economic pamphleteers. By explaining quite completely the corpus of their respective economic ideas, and by linking these segments together, the growth of a fabric of ideas may be outlined with a minimum of unwarranted generalization (Johnson, 1937, p. vii, emphasis supplied).

Hutchison starts his present work from the same premise and uses the same modus operandi. Reaffirming the frequent misunderstanding and underappreciation of pre-Smithian economics, Hutchison sifts through the writings of the past to find identifiable strands of thought that can be woven into a reasonably tight-knit intellectual fabric. His detailed investigations into the economic ideas of the century before Smith continually question the appropriateness of the term mercantilism as a blanket description of the writers of the period. Authors usually labelled mercantilist are, with few exceptions, revealed here as so many minor bricklayers who each placed one or more bricks on the slowly rising edifice of economic liberalism. It is this gradual path to economic liberalism (i.e., acceptance of the principle of market order) that comprises the theme of Hutchison's book, rather than any division between the micro and macro orientation of writers before and/or after Smith.

Beyond this point, however, the parallels begin to fade, and on the whole, Hutchison turns in a stronger performance which will eventually eclipse Johnson's earlier work, for it is at once more comprehensive in its scope, more insightful in its interpretation of evidence, and more bold in its exposition. Johnson's timely and well-executed task limited itself to a singularly British tradition represented by ten writers: John Hales, Gerard de Malynes, Edward Misselden, Thomas Mun, William Petty, Nehemiah Grew, Charles King, David Hume, Malachy Postlethwayt, and James Steuart. (An even smaller list of six writers, all British, comprised the subject of a similar study by William Letwin in 1963). Hutchison paints with a wider brush and gives us a more panoramic view. His broad scholarship ranges over four cultures and eight nations: England, Ireland, Scotland, Germany, Austria, France, Italy, and North America. The number of writers that come within his purview is too large to enumerate fully in this limited space. Suffice it to say that except for Hales and Grew, all of the writers surveyed by Johnson receive detailed treatment by Hutchison. In addition, the ideas of Davenant, Locke, Child, Barbon, North, Pufendorf, Boisguilbert, Mandeville, Gervaise, Franklin, Cantillon, Montesquieu, Forbonnais, Tucker, Justi, Sonnenfels, Galiani, Beccaria, Verri, Quesnay, Turgot, and Condillac, to name only some of the most recognizable names, splash across the canvas that Hutchison fills with colorful aperçus.

Both Johnson (then) and Hutchison (now) approached the same intellectual landscape as an artist does a scene he wishes to paint, yet each produced a different kind of picture. The differences may have been spawned in part by the gulf of time. But a difference in technique can also be observed. Each author chose to anchor his respective study in *The Wealth of Nations*. Smith's crowning achievement in economics dominates this landscape, but like all good paintings, it requires an appropriate background to attain its full effect. Johnson's study paints a rather flat background which places Smith in bold relief, but does not in any way alter our *perception* of the dominant subject. On Johnson's canvas, *The Wealth of Nations* remains the epitome of English classical economics, the blueprint for all subsequent progress in the subject. By contrast, Hutchison's study paints a background of such subtle and powerful depth and perspective that it *changes* our perception of the dominant subject. On Hutchison's canvas, we see *The Wealth of Nations* in a new light. That great work emerges as a more balanced construction, one that contains flaws as well as strengths. Whereas Johnson accepted the strengths of Smith's architecture and glossed over its flaws, Hutchison exposes the flaws in order that we may see economics for what it truly is: a progressive but somewhat erratic discipline that has to a certain extent been retracing its steps for the last century or so. In the world of art, the contrast is best illustrated by juxtaposing Giotto's *Madonna and Child in Majesty* with Dürer's *Adoration of the Magi*. Giotto's technique freezes the major subject on a flat plane, emphasizing its importance by sheer size, not by orthographic projection; whereas Dürer's style reveals such a thorough study of perspective, and conveys such a strong feeling for landscape, that *the* major subject is not immediately obvious. As a consequence of Dürer's rendition, our very perception of that which is focal is altered. By analogy, Hutchison's work is to the history of pre-Smithian economics what Dürer's art was to late 13th and early 14th century Florentine art. Johnson's book became a classic because it was a careful, if limited, survey of a difficult subject. Hutchison's book is destined to become a greater classic because it forces us to reappraise a dominant figure and a major era in the history of economics.

The main outlines of Hutchison's argument can be set forth simply—at the cost, however, of the richness of detail so carefully presented by the author of the work under review. Hutchison ties the emergence of important ideas in economic theory to controversial policy issues—not in the manner of a relativist who is forced to deny progress in the history of ideas, but rather in the mode of an architect who uses policy issues as a useful frame for categorizing ideas. On this basis, he divides the period between 1662 and 1776 into four discrete intervals. The stage is set for the unfolding hundred-year drama by a brief review of the century *before* Petty, which was marked by four distinct streams of economic thought: (1) the later Scholastics of the Salamanca School, who rejected cost-based theories of value; (2) various writers concerned with the rise of prices throughout Europe; (3) Italian contributions on different branches of economics; and (4) pamphleteers, primarily English, who wrote on controversial problems of economic policy. It was during this era that Monchrétien introduced the phrase "political economy," although he did not contribute much to the development of the subject. A survey of the economic literature of this early period fails to turn up much support for the cost-of-production theory of value that later came to dominate English classical economics after Smith.

The first of the four significant intervals of preclassical economics lasted from 1662 to about 1700. The earliest, and greatest, performance of the period was Sir William Petty's. Petty contributed to economic theory, policy, and method, but there is only limited justification for attributing a cost-of-production theory of value to him. This period includes early statistical studies in England by Graunt, Halley, King, Davenant, and Fleetwood, plus the performances of Locke, Child, Barbon, North, and Martyn. It also takes in Colbert's influence in France, and the emergence of the natural-law philosophy of Grotius and Pufendorf in Germany.

The second interval, from 1700 to 1746, witnessed important stirrings of individualism, based in part on the natural-law philosophy that emerged in the previous interval, and a certain preoccupation with monetary questions, particularly the controversial issue of a self-adjusting mechanism in international trade. The peak performance in this period was turned in by Cantillon, with important anticipations by Boisguilbert. Contributions by Mandeville, Gervais, Vanderlint, Law, Franklin, Berkeley, and Carl round out the picture.

The next two intervals comprise what Hutchison calls "the thirty-year boom" in the development of economics. During the first phase of this boom (1746-1756), the roots of political economy were sowed in Scotland by Gershom Carmichael and Francis Hutcheson; cameralism was advanced in Germany by Justi and Sonnenfels; and subjective utility theory flowered in Italy, thanks to Montanari and Galiani. Propelling this intellectual boom were four more-or-less simultaneous developments: enhancement of the international transmission of ideas by a spurt of translations of books on commerce and trade; the establishment, first in France, of a number of semi-specialist journals devoted to economic topics; an increase in personal contacts between leading writers on commerce and political economy; and the creation of several academic chairs in the teaching of economics throughout Europe. During the second phase of the thirty-year boom (1756-1776), French writers rose to a position of pre-eminence, led, of course, by Quesnay and the physiocrats, but also making headway through the efforts of Turgot and Condillac. Italian economic literature also reached new heights at this time, especially in the writings of Beccaria and Verri. In Scotland, philosophical interest in political economy was spurred by Adam Ferguson and John Millar, but it was Sir James Steuart who attempted a comprehensive, systematic treatise on the subject.

In a nutshell, the ideas of at least one hundred different writers on economics, perhaps many more, confronted Adam Smith, in unconnected fashion, when he began to write his great work on political economy. These ideas must have appeared to Smith as so many separate pieces of a jigsaw puzzle that begged to be fitted together. It is testimony to Smith's superior powers of organization and systematization that he was up to the task of completing the puzzle, an accomplishment perhaps without equal in the history of economics. While extolling this achievement, Hutchison nevertheless opens our eyes to the flaws in Smith's performance.

Hutchison concludes his study with two assertions. The first is neither surprising nor controversial. It is that Smith's crowning achievement in economics was to emphatically, systematically, and persuasively establish the principle of the self-adjusting market, a feat that capped a tradition which had been developing, piece by piece, since the time of Petty. By the time Hutchison makes this statement, the evidence to support it has already been impressively piled up through the previous twenty chapters. The second conclusion is a bit less expected, even though the evidence to support it has by this time become equally compelling. It is that Smith set economics back at least one hundred years by rejecting two important elements of his intellectual heritage: (1) the subjective theory of value (which became the focal point of the neoclassical revolt), and (2) the existence of uncertainty, error, and ignorance—features of life that undermine (at least potentially) the macroeconomic notion of a fully self-adjusting economy as regards employment, saving, investment, and money. As a consequence of these "revolutionary" turns in doctrine, English classical economics embarked on a long detour. Hutchison speaks clearly and forcefully to this point in his concluding pages:

> The historical-institutional method and critique, the neoclassical-Jevonian revolt, the Keynesian 'revolution', the expectational Keynesian neo-Austrian protest, make up a considerable part of the history of political economy and economics over the last 100 years or so, since the decline and fall of English classical orthodoxy around 1870. All of these four ideas, theories, or lines of thought, had been initiated, or significantly developed, before 1776, and had been largely excluded from, or diminished in the English classical corpus of doctrines. One has, therefore, to go back to the seventeenth and eighteenth centuries, before English classical orthodoxy came to dominate, if one wishes to follow the history of several of the most significant theories, ideas, and issues, which have been debated and developed in the twentieth century (1988 p. 381).

Is there a more eloquent or persuasive justification for studying the history of economic thought? Hutchison has given us cause once again to question the adequacy of the term "mercantilism" to categorize pre-Smithian economic thought. More importantly, he has demonstrated convincingly that none of us is immune to historical myopia.

Robert F. Hébert

REFERENCES

Johnson, E. A. J. 1937. *Predecessors of Adam Smith: The Growth of British Economic Thought.* New York: Prentice-Hall.
Jones, Richard. 1964. "Essay on Primitive Political Economy." In *Literary Remains,* edited by W. Whewell. New York: Augustus M. Kelley.
Letwin, William. 1963. *The Origins of Scientific Economics. London: Methuen.*

A DETERMINED MARCH

When authors follow high standards of systematic scholarship, their work is necessarily a contribution to the academic corpus. This is particularly true when the subject matter seems to be a hodge-podge of disparate writings loosely lumped together by practical or philosophical concerns over political, commercial, or monetary problems. In this sense, Hutchison's determined march through the early English and French literature, from Petty to Adam Smith—digressing slightly to pick up some German and Italian writers of the period—provides a solid foundation for understanding later economic ideas. He even gives considerable attention to the American, Benjamin Franklin. The survey also serves as a splendid entrée for researchers beginning the study of a particular individual or period. In other words, this book provides a solid formation for both thematic and specific studies of European economic writing from Petty to Smith, the persona associated with the two dates cited in the title.

The generalized evaluation in the preceding paragraph would be taken for granted in picking up the work of an eminent historian of economic ideas such as T.W. Hutchison. Reviewers must, therefore, direct their attention to an examination of the way the author places his subject matter in the broader setting of intellectual and economic history and to the specific thematic analyses developed in this systematic survey of contributors and schools in the field of endeavor we have come to call political economy.

One of the virtues of good scholarship is that we can find grist for our own individual mills set out on the work table to be synthesized into our own lines of thematic interest. The Smith scholar can find references that indicate the origins of many famous formulations traditionally attributed to the citation-averse Scot. For example, concern over not jostling or tripping opponents in the race by Graunt (p. 44), and a discussion of the reluctance of states to release burdensome colonies by Tucker (p. 237), crop up in these writings.

Those interested in more ancient influences can recognize Aristotelian formulations in tripartite distinctions between necessaries, amenities, and luxuries, and in the habitual reference to exchanges between corn and wine when discussing barter and isolated exchange. Such references are conspicuous in the writings of Beccaria, Condillac, and Turgot. These debts to antiquity are not recognized by Hutchison nor usually by others, but the historical reality that nations such as France, in the seventeenth and eighteenth centuries, exported wine and were, at the least, self-sufficient in grain, should have made historians of thought wonder. Hutchison discusses the Aristotelian influence on natural law and utility-scarcity theory (p. 100, and p. 390 n. 5) in which he quotes Odd Langholm's comment on the more direct influence on Scholastic Aristotelians on the Italian tradition rather than emphasizing the Grotius-Pufendorf line of influence on Hutchison and Smith. What is missing, however, is the awareness of the significant ongoing contribution from the classics to the educational tradition of the Renaissance and the Enlightenment. The Aristotelian material, for example, was not all read secondhand any more than were Plato, Xenophon, and Cicero. These remarks, of course, stand as examples of extraneous thematic extrapolations that can be fueled by the detailed exposition which characterizes Hutchison's book.

Let us turn, then, to the explicit thematic motifs followed by Hutchison and evaluate their contributions to a more coherent and intelligible picture of this significant gestation period in the development of modern political economy and its influence on subsequent thought. On these two counts, there is little or no pertinent synthesis on the first, and a basically anachronistic appraisal on the second.

Previous studies have addressed the period covered by Hutchison as part of a broader Mercantilist Period. Heckscher (1937) treats the literature as part of a tradition characterized by policy writings provided for governments. Beer (1967) considers the writings of this period, and earlier as expressions of emerging nation-statehood with the treatment of problems from a nationalistic perspective. Schumpter (1954) tried to concentrate on the growth of relevant analytic perspectives while Spiegel (1983) and Pibram (1983), among other historians of thought, have brought out the methodological diversity of the period. Hutchison basically treats the authors of the seventeenth and eighteenth centuries as a diverse assortment of nearly random speculators on political economy. To varying degrees, the specific economic milieux of these authors are set forth, Petty as an administrator in Ireland, and Boisguilbert responding to the depressed conditions attributed to Colbertism. The influence of Baconian thought is also recognized in the exposition of the statistical work begun in England in the latter part of the seventeenth century. However, as a thematic overview tying the selected period 1662-1776 together, we really have only one dominant theme. This is the general demonstration that practically all the significant ideas developed after 1776 had been anticipated or generally indicated during this period of nascence. The conspicuous minor theme is that the subsequent century of "classical orthodoxy" from 1776 to around 1870 was a digression from the continuum of progress in economic thought. Four major lines of thought emerged from this pre-Smithian period:

> "1. The historical method of the Scottish school . . . .
> 2. The utility and scarcity approach to value and price theory of the natural-law school
>   . . . .
> 3. The theories of money, employment, and 'macro-economics', developed in varying directions . . . .
> 4. The emphasis on uncertainty, ignorance and erroneous expectations, as initiated by Boisguilbert . . . ." (p. 376).

Hutchison's overview is clearly indicated by his summary comment, "In fact . . . . since the decline and fall of English classical orthodoxy around 1870, the history of economic thought has . . . [with qualifications] consisted of challenges . . . [to aspects] of English classical political economy for having excluded or rejected these four—and other—fundamental lines of thought" (p. 376).

Aside from the anachronistic hazards of evaluating the past primarily in terms of what is preeminent in the present, this formulation cries out for some explanation of why these rejected ideas allegedly emerged in the seventeenth and eighteenth centuries, why they were so effectively swept aside by "English classical orthodoxy," and why that orthodoxy "fell' around 1870. The defense can be made that the second and third of these questions is beyond the scope of a study which chooses 1776 as a cut-off point. Our question regarding the genesis of these ideas in the seventeenth and eighteenth centuries, however, is a valid concern of the intellectual historian in the context of this book.

In regard to the first in the group of ideas listed above, that is, the role of historical analysis, we should not forget that Thucydides is generally recognized as the father of scientific or analytic history and his currency in the seventeenth century is validated by the fact that none less than Thomas Hobbes contributed an English translation of Thucydides's *The History of the Peloponessian War*. Also, a much more penetrating and provocative background on the development of the Scottish Enlightenment can be found in MacIntyre's recent book, *Whose Justice? Which Rationality?* (1988)

On the second issue of utility and scarcity in the analysis of value and price, not only is there a rich scholastic component to this tradition, but utility analysis is fairly clear in classical Greek thought and in the Roman Law tradition. Odd Langholm's *Price and Value in the Aristotelian Tradition* (1979) is relevant to this material as Hutchison acknowledges in a note in his introduction. Going back even farther, we should consider Proagoras's famous adage, "Man is the measure of all things," that combined with the Aristotelian adaptation of parts of atomist subjective individualism. These ideas joined to contribute to a continuous tradition of subjective analysis based upon the participating individual. The Mosel scholar, Averroës, passed on this perspective at a methodological level into Scholastic controversy where the Averroists, or nominalists, made subjective perception a primary basis for philosophical analysis. This pertains directly to the scarcity concept in that no amount of any substance, no matter how small, can be construed as *scarce* unless it has been identified or names as being desirable in terms of some subjective measure. In addition, Grice-Hutchinson's (1978) work on Spanish thought which extends to the School of Salamanca, reaching into the seventeenth century, should not have been given such casual mention in the introductory chapter.

The problem lies with the arbitrary beginning of the formal study with Petty's work in 1662. We must remember that Petty received his formal intellectual impetus at the hands of a set of Jesuit schoolmasters on the coast of France. The overlap between late Scholastic rigor and Enlightenment reflection cannot be brushed aside so lightly. We should not fall victim to modern pedagogic requirements for memorizable definitions and classifications, thereby losing our grasp of intellectual continuity.

At a broader level, the ubiquity with which individualist and utility perspectives were being expressed in the popular literature of the late sixteenth and early seventeenth centuries is of considerable importance to the historian of formal theory. In a recent book subtitled *An Intellectual History of Consciousness and the Idea of Order in Renaissance England,* by Stephen L. Colins (1989), it is fairly clearly demonstrated that the intellectual milieu of the literate population had assimilated a subjectivist perspective.

The third significant facet of this period, as Hutchison sees it, is the emergence of discussions that have macroeconomic overtones. This would be expected in a setting where the nation-state was emerging as the reference base for economic activity and political power. However, the discussion of the public concern over monetary policy, public prosperity, and foreign trade was not limited to the seventeenth and eighteenth centuries. Earlier political and economic writings were usually couched in terms of advice to rulers and were known as "mirror for princes" literature, or wisdom literature. The biographical motif was also used, in which deeds of great men were recounted for the guidance of the young and ambitious. Cantillon, for example, commented on Plutarch's account of the ancient Spartan king, Lycurgus, who introduced fiat money for the specific purpose of excluding luxury imports and promoting domestic manufactures. Xenophon's well-known tract, *Ways and Means for Increasing the Revenues of the City of Athens,* was one of the more famous advice pieces from antiquity and was considered a pertinent enough part of the political arithmetic tradition to be appended to the publication in 1698 of Davenant's work on trade and to the 1752 edition of Sir William Petty's *Political Arithmetick.* The point should be made that advice to an absolute sovereign concerning the most efficient way to manage his realm blurs the personal-efficiency concerns of microeconomics into the broader national concerns of macroeconomics. Erasmus's instructional volume directed to the young Charles V of Spain in the early sixteenth century, *The Education of a Christian Prince,* is considered a political tract, but it touches on taxation and public expenditures along with much moralizing on the royal burder of setting a public example and the choosing of effective personnel. As McNally (1988) has noted, albeit not in this context, authors such as Quesnay and Turgot, seeking to influence national economic policy in mid-eighteenth century France, were dealing with concentrated sovereign authority and their work can be characterized as advice to an absolute sovereign authority. It is, therefore, appropriate to raise the question as to when primarily political literature giving advice on running the kingdom becomes political economy.

Finally, Hutchison's emphasis upon the significance of Boisguilbert's treatment of "ignorance, uncertainty and erroneous expectations" in the economic process suggests that this was an innovation of the early eighteenth century. Gerard de Malynes reported in 1622 that the ancient tradition of the Law-Merchant was to refuse to enforce exchanges made between merchants where one lacked experience in the trade, was taken advantage of because of need, or was the victim of unreasonable persuasion (Malynes, 1981, p. 67). He also contended that merchant sellers generally overvalued their goods by 20 percent and buyers underestimated values by 20 percent. Experienced brokers were best relied upon for rational pricing (Malynes, 1981, p. 143). In addition, he pointed out in 1623 that the public interest is not protected by the merchants' profit motive because not only is their benefit not necessarily coterminous with the public interest, but they often, through ignorance, make deals that damage the public interest, but they often, through ignorance, make deals that damage the public interest without benefiting themselves, and even damage their own interests through ignorance (Malynes, 1967, pp. 56, 45). These discussions by Malynes reflect the Roman Law tradition that justice coincides with rational behavior but that optimum rationality is best divined by a trained specialist, ideally, a jurisconsult and not the average man on the street. If we go back another step, we may cite the recent paper by André Lapidus delivered a the 1989 History of Economics Society meetings on risk and uncertainty in Scholastic analysis. (Lapidus, forthcoming).

The point is that the rise to prominence of an economic perspective or analytic method is an important subject for historical understanding but there are generally antecedents from which much innovative thought can be traced. The ultimate interest of the historian of thought is in the explanation of how and why ideas and concepts change, develop, and surface at different times and under different conditions.

In general, Hutchison's book marks the end of the need for books of this genre. Comprehensive surveys of the history of economic thought such as Schumpeter (1956), Spiegel (1983), and Pribram (1983) cannot cover specific periods in such great detail. Hutchison has done the definitive survey on the last half of the seventeenth century and the first three quarters of the eighteenth. Actually, he purports to cover about one hundred and fourteen years in a little under five hundred pages. This book will stand for basic pedagogical purposes and more detail is not in order since the original sources are increasingly available to researchers. However, even at the pedagogic level, the emergence of shorter works that rely on an analytic theme to present a coherent picture of the period can be expected to complete strongly for primary attention. The most conspicuous case in point is David McNally's (1988) *Political Economy and the Rise of Capitalism: A Reinterpretation.* This book traces the emergence of modern political economy from Montchrétien at the beginning of the seventeenth century through Adam Smith. It convincingly demonstrates a focus on agrarian capitalism as the source of surplus for economic growth. In other words, instead of looking back at this period from the point of view of Ricardian or Marshallian economics, he has attempted to formulate a picture of the interaction between economic theory and the primary economic realities of the period. The result is a book that attempts to understand the economic theory of the period rather than to recount it. This results in a much more manageable pedagogic unit with broader insights. While Hutchison's book will take its place on the reference shelf as a valuable source for checking out the details of a particular writer's ideas, interest and discussion can be expressed increasingly to be directed toward books such as McNally's.

S. Todd Lowry

REFERENCES

Beer. 1967. *Early English Economic Thought.* London: Augustus Kelly Reprint.

Collins, Stephen L. 1989. *From Divine Cosmos to Sovereign State: An Intellectual History of Consciousness and the Idea of Order in Renaissance England.* New York and Oxford: Oxford University Press.

Grice-Hutchison, Marjorie. 1978. *Early Economic Thought in Spain.* London: George Allen & Unwin.

Heckscher, Eli F. 1935. *Mercantilism.* Trans. by M. Shapiro. 2 Vols. London: George Allen & Unwin.

Lapidus, André Forthcoming. "Information and Risk in the Medieval Doctrine of Usury: An Exploration in Thirteenth Century Heart and Hand." In *Perspectives in the History of Economic Thought,* edited by New York: Edward Elgar.

Langholm, Odd. 1979. *Price and Value in the Aristotelian Tradition: A Study in Scholastic Sources.* Bergen, Oslo, TromsØ: Universitetsforlaget.

MacIntyre, Alasdair. 1988. *Whose Justice? Which Rationality?* Notre Dame, IN: Notre Dame Press.

McNally, David. 1988. *Political Economy and the Rise of Capitalism: A Reinterpretation.* Berkeley: University of California Press.

Malnyes, Gerard de. 1981. *The Ancient Law-Merchant.* London: Facsimile Edition and Abindon, Oxon: Professional Books.

————. 1967. *The Center of the Circle of Commerce.* london: Augustus M. Kelly Reprint.

Pribram, Karl. 1983. *A History of Economic RTeasoning.* Baltimore and London: The Johns Hopkins University Press.

Schumpeter, J.A. 1954. New York: Oxford University Press.

Spiegel, Henry William. 1983. *The Growth of Economic Thought.* Rev. ed. Durham, NC: Duke University Press.

AN INTELLECTUAL BOOT CAMP

Introduction

Rarely does a reviewer have the opportunity to treat a book that attempts to fill such a large gap in the literature. Despite the enormous outpouring of books on the history of post-Smithian political economy, no one had previously offered a comprehensive history of pre-Smithian political economy. Why has this earlier period not inspired a general history, while so many authors have been drawn to the post-Smithian period?

Adler proposed that we develop particular areas of expertise by forgoing some interests to economize on time. Within this framework, stars can emerge, even when they do not differ in talent. According to Adler:

> [T]he phenomenon of stars exists where consumption requires knowledge.... As an example, consider listening to music. Appreciation increases with knowledge. But how does one know about music? By listening to it, *and by discussing it with other persons who know about it*.... [We are] better off patronizing the same artist as others do.... Stardom is a market device to economizes on learning (Adler, 1985, p. 208).

Without asserting that no significant variations exist in the talents of early political economists, I believe that a similar process is at work in the study of classical political economy. We have mostly agreed upon a fairly well-established canon. Most histories of the period studiously analyze Smith, Ricardo, and Marx, along with a small handful of supposedly secondary figures. Other equally deserving, early political economists escape notice altogether.

Historians of the period are drawn to study the same select group of political economists that their predecessors did. A tradition gradually builds up around these sacred texts. The reader of these works is brought into a multidimensional dialogue that includes the authors under study, their times, and the collective experience of earlier generations of readers of these texts. By working and reworking this core, successive generations find new levels of meaning, some of which probably eluded even the political economists that wrote them. These works acquire a cumulative force—albeit highly symbolic—that calls new generations to confront them once again. This process builds up the stature of the "founders" of political economy, thereby confirming their status as "stars."

The erection of a solid structure of scholarly paraphernalia facilitates analysis. It provides a map of the territory so that a history of classical political economy can navigate along a relatively common set of guidelines, regardless of the perspective that one brings to the period. For the pre-Smithian period, no comparable guidelines exit.

Hutchison deserves credit for taking on the whole of the pre-Smithian political economy. His challenge is even more daunting. The post-Smithian story is usually confined to England (mostly London) and Scotland, with a brief mention of Paris. The pre-Smithian period requires an account of contributions from outlying continental regions (Italy, Spain, Austria, and Germany) that hardly exist in histories of the later period.

History of Political Economy as History

Hutchison would do well to consider a passage from Hume that he cites:

> [History was] not only a valuable part of knowledge, but opens the door to many other parts, and affords materials to most of the sciences...we should be for ever children in understanding, were it not for this invention, which extends our experience to all past ages, and to the most distant nations; making them contribute as much to our improvement in wisdom, as if they had actually lain under observation [Hume, 1741, pp. 566-567].

Disregarding the fact that Hume was commending the study of history to women, I understand him to say that history represents a laboratory in which we can learn to appreciate the unusual. It opens our minds up to possibilities that are hidden from those who are wholly immersed in conventional ways of thought.

History is not merely an intellectual boot camp to prepare us for real-world intellectual combat. History, when written in the fashion that Hume described, is a constant source of wonder and fascination. Think about the freshness in Heilbroner's *Worldly Philosophers* (1967) or Routh's *The Origin of Economic Ideas* (1977). Never mind that neither work represents a breakthrough in scholarship. The fact that a wide audience can find the history of political economy interesting should not be lost on us.

Admittedly, excitement and scholarship are difficult to combine. I remember the feeling of excitement on first reading what seemed to be James Steuart's novel vision of the world. Later, as I became more immersed in subject, I found that many other writers held much the same views as Steuart. My reading of his works became more detached.

Hutchison, too, writes in a detached manner that conveys little evidence of any joy on the part of the author. If draining the excitement out of a period when Western society was first coming to grips with a modern economy is the price we must pay for scholarship, it is a high price.

Hutchison further limits the interest in his work by judging the writers by how close they came to neo-classical economics. In this sense, he reads his subject with the same spirit that Sir T. Munroe alleged the Glasgow merchants brought to the Wealth of Nations, when he wrote:

> I remember about the time of the appearance of *The Wealth of Nations,* that the Glasgow merchants were as proud of the work as if they had written it themselves; and some of them said that it was no wonder that Adam Smith had written such a book, as he had the advantage of their society, in which the same doctrines were circulated with the punch every day [p. 400].

This practice of mining the literature for antecedents of neoclassical economics makes Hutchison's work similar to Schumpeter's, but, with a few exceptions, the book under review lacks the delight that Schumpeter took in deflating the importance of the superstars of economic thought, especially Smith, and elevating the less renowned members of what he called the "troops."

Where Hutchison treats relatively unknown figures, especially those from the European continent, his presentation is considerably more lively than are his discussions of the better-known British writers. His presentation of Galliani's claim to eminence is worthy of Schumpeter himself.

History of Political Economy as Ideology

Unfortunately, the history of political economy less often used as a window that opens up to different perceptions of the world than as a mirror that is used to confirm our present opinions. In Hutchison's words,

> Historians of ideas often get involved in what seem virtually irreconcilable conflicts of
> interpretation partly ... because their interest in some much-admired figure is fuelled mainly
> by a desire to enlist him as a distinguished ancestor of their particular viewpoint (p. 125).

For example, almost everybody finds in reading Ricardo, and only to a slightly lesser extent Smith, confirmation of their own views. Supply-siders and Marxists alike find support for their theories in Ricardo. Both Keynes and Schumpeter vigorously denounced him in an attempt to diminish the stature of those who disagreed with their own ideas.

Most contemporary economists have less emotional stakes in the period that Hutchison studies because they have paid less attention to it. Perhaps for this reason, Hutchison, who has taken relatively harsh stances against leftish ideas in the past, often seems on the surface to be neither strident nor dogmatic. He generally avoids contentious rhetoric, but his ideological preferences still do play an important role.

Hutchison's ideology does erupt through the smooth surface, especially in his discussion of Physiocracy. He cannot resist inserting parenthetical expressions of his opinions on contemporary subjects. For example, in discussing the failure of Colbert's system, he charges that the contemporary socialist systems have failed, writing, "In this century also, a number of highly centralized, authoritarian regimes have attempted to raise the level of economic development by concentrating on the planned expansion of industry" (p. 90). Such remarks do little to enlighten us either about Colbert's time nor the modern social failures, whether socialist- or market-oriented. Hutchison derides reformers, who are charged with naiveté (pp. 135, 138-139). His pretence of objectivity collapses altogether when he denounces the "Colbertist-Stalinist" development policies that were in force when Physiocracy appeared (p. 295). Although he commends the technical virtuosity of the Physiocratic school, he censures their doctrinaire advocacy and only grudgingly grants that they were "perhaps rather less dictatorially directed than the Marxians" (p. 285).

Hutchison alludes to Hayek's notion that Smith and his Scottish colleagues, along with Mandeville and Tucker, were properly deemed to be true individualists, while the French Cartesian tradition, under which the Physiocratic school fell, was nothing more than false individualism (Hayek 1948, ch. 1). The sin of the Physiocrats, in Hayek's eyes, was their belief in "abstract individualism and innate ideas" (Hayek, p. 12n; quoting Bryson, 1945, p. 106). The Physiocrats advocated liberal ideas only because they conformed to their supposedly rational analysis of society. They should have understood that human rationality precludes the discovery of a proper plan for society. One can do no better than to allow each individual to arrange his or her affairs without any outside intervention.

Hayek feared that the belief that it is possible to know through reason what is best for society, even if the resulting policies are agreeable to laissez faire, ultimately lends support to socialist ideas. Neither Hayek nor Hutchison mention that recourse to the natural law may have been a Physiocratic ruse to protect themselves from any unwelcome political fallout from their advocacy of unpopular ideas.

Hutchison's immersion in modern-day political controversies colors all of his discussion of Physiocracy. When the Physiocrats manage to influence the French government to free the grain trade just before a series of bad harvests, we hear about the fanatical Physiocrats, who launch their policies regardless of the institutional framework in which they occur. When true individualists advocate similar policies, they are only motivated by concern for freedom.

Why would Boisguilbert not come in for reprimands similar to those dished out to the Physiocrats? Certainly, his single-minded advocacy of a just price for agriculture would qualify him as a crank. His recommended policy was quite similar to those of the Physiocrats. Moreover, he advocated his just price at a time when its adoption would have proven to be every bit as cataclysmic.

In Hutchison's hands, Boisguilbert is a champion of freedom; the Physiocrats, precursors of modern totalitarianism, despite their energetic struggle against Colbertist-Stalinist policies. The heroes of the Physiocratic experience were Galliani and Turgot, despite the latter's close association with the Physiocrats. Galliani is not doctrinaire. His theory of value is subjective. He draws upon the sophisticated mathematical analysis of Daniel Bernoulli. Unfortunately, we do not get a clear picture of Galliani's alternative to Physiocratic policies, except that Galliani feared excessively rapid policy changes. We learn much about Galliani's value theory, but little about how it related to his economic vision.

The Physiocrats are presented as a group of mad men, hell-bent on imposing their ideas on society. For some members of the school, predominately Mirabeau, Hutchison's portrait is not altogether inappropriate. For the most part, their major failing is merely an unattractive, intellectual arrogance that is not unknown among later economists. How, then, if the Physiocrats were as bad as Hutchison makes them out to be, would a person of Turgot's stature associate himself with the school? Was Turgot wrong to have written of Galliani:

> Neither do I particularly like to see him always so prudent, so much the enemy of enthusiasm, so much in agreement with... all the men who are comfortable in the present and perfectly happy to let the world go as it will, because it goes well for them, and who... having their bed well made do not want anyone to disturb it? (p. 321)

Had Hutchison written history the way that Hume said it should be written, he would have done a real service, opening our eyes to alternative visions; instead, his history merely serves to reinforce prejudices about those who have tried to improve society. Admittedly, many social experiments have gone awry. We do not need to read early political economy to learn this lesson.

Hutchison's Anti-Marxist Project

Hutchison defines his ideological project on the very first page of his book, taking issue with Marx for crediting William Petty as the father of political economy and emphasizing Petty's analysis of the surplus. This assertion is grounded in Hutchison's ideological aim of rehabilitating the literature on utility, value, uncertainty and expectations (pp. 3-4). Toward this end, he consistently selects citations in which an author ruminates on these subjects.

Hutchison attempts to undermine the credibility of Ronald Meek's *Studies in the Labor Theory of Value* (1973). Hutchison asserts:

> Searching for some kind of pedigree for the labour theory of value before the *Wealth of Nations,* Marxian historians have not been able to find very much. There were *obiter dicta*— as Ronald Meek described them—from the great William Petty, which were repeated, but not developed, by Franklin and one or two comparatively little-known pamphleteers. The labour theory of value was mainly a product of the English classical period (p. 381).

Although Meek's book plays an important role in this work, Hutchison does not even mention it until late in the last chapter. C.B. Macpherson's (1962) classic analysis of Locke and the labor theory of value does not appear at all. Hutchison takes pains to explain away any prominent economist's association with the labor theory of value and to expound upon that same author's utility-based theory at length.

Hutchison takes pleasure in demonstrating that the mercantalists were not so mercantilist, since they used utility-based theory. He makes much of the point that Petty used the labor theory of value in his exercises in applied economics and not to further his theoretical investigations. When Joseph Harris makes an exceptionally clear assertion of the labor theory of value, Hutchison introduces it by interjecting, "He started with the debatable statement" (p. 243). Such commentary is not worthy of a scholar of Hutchison's stature.

Hutchison knows full well that Marx never claimed that neither Petty nor anyone else ever supported a pure labor theory of value. Marx was convinced that the nature of value theory remained hidden prior to his own work. These early economists were not interested in a theory of value. They were grappling with the idea that profits depended on access to a tractable labor force. More often than not, when discussing utility, they were actually groping for an appropriate structuring of incentives that would lead workers to accept their condition as workers.

In this sense, the distinction between utility- and labor-based discussions of political economy are irrelevant. Both were concerned with regulating labor.

Those who appealed to utility were pointing to the carrot. Those who cast their argument in terms of labor were recommending that the stick be used for something other than holding carrots.

I believe that Marx was struck by the fact that early political economists were led to employ the labor theory of value quite naturally when trying to come to grips with the problems that they faced. Only in this sense did people such as Petty lend confirmation to Marx's labor theory of value.

Distortions and Obfuscation

Hutchison frequently associates utility based value theory with a preference for freedom and liberty. In order to lend credibility to this association, he goes out of his way to highlight the laissez faire views of the figures whom he applauds. Just as surely, he avoids mention of inconvenient facts that might detract from his ideological venture. For example, John Locke is portrayed as a friend of liberty. In this spirit Hutchison treats us to a long discussion of Locke's advocacy of market forces as the proper regulator of interest rates. Thereafter, we find two brief paragraphs describing some of Locke's illiberal ideas (p. 72). The authoritarian constitution that Locke wrote for South Carolina with its strong defense of slavery passes unnoticed. Hutchison informs us that Mercier was the administrator of Martinique, but the reader learns nothing of that person's views on slavery. In fact, we hear nothing about slavery at all in this book except that Josiah Tucker, a solitary figure in this regard, opposed it.

Perhaps most symptomatic of Hutchison's neglect of the authoritarian side of the political economists of the time is the absence of any mention of Edgar Furniss (1965), except for one brief reference to his discussion of the backward bending supply curve. What about all the repressive and authoritarian measures that Furniss discussed?

More generally, Hutchison is willing to describe the personal interests of economists, but not much of their class interests. We learn that Petty wrote with an eye to obtaining high office (p. 29), while his proposals to transport large numbers of Scottish or Irish people as slaves (p. 38) is dismissed as bizarre without being given any weight in the discussion.

Hutchison gives only a brief mention of Mandeville's insistence that the poor be kept ignorant, despite the fact that Mandeville devoted an entire work to the need to prevent poor children from being taught to read the Bible. Almost an entire page (pp. 123-124) is used to reprint an extract following Hutchison's judgment that "No one before him, and few since, have stated so effectively the fundamental case for the free market economy" (p. 121).

Following this citation, Hutchison deliberately misinterprets Marx, exclaiming that the reader can see why Marx was moved to assert that Mandeville is "infinitely bolder and more honest than the philistine apologist of bourgeois society" (p. 24; quoting Marx, 1963, p. 376). The unsuspecting reader might be led to believe that Marx was responding to Mandeville's rhapsody about money. The actual context of Marx's statement was Mandeville's idea, which Hutchison himself ridicules, that thieves promote aggregate demand by creating a need for locksmiths.

Assuming that Hutchison did intend to create an alternative to Meek's (1973) interpretation of the period, let me make a comparison. Like Hutchison, Meek attempted to redirect the study of political economy. Like Hutchison, he was politically motivated, but their styles were entirely different. I do not recall finding snide comments or ad hominem remarks in Meek's work. He left it for others to draw their own conclusions. Meek titled his book in such a way that he left no doubt that he was intending to highlight a certain kind of theory, although he took the trouble to discuss subjective theories from time to time. I wish that Hutchison had followed the same course, since he has an excellent command of the literature and something to teach us regardless of our politics.

Hutchison's ideological mission seems to have dictated his selection of subjects. Because of his interest in highlighting alternatives to the labor theory of value in the sphere of technical economics, he overlooks some people who may deserve a place in a comprehensive history. Vauban and Defoe are relegated to a single endnote each. Jonathan Swift is absent altogether.

Concluding Remarks

Hutchison deserves to be commended for attempting to produce a comprehensive history. This book does contains a wealth of information. Its treatment of the relatively unknown continental literature, especially that from outside of France, is useful. It is also a worthwhile compendium of alternatives to the labor theory of value. Nonetheless, the book leaves much to be desired. Hutchison diminished its value by his willingness to tailor it to suit his ideological mission. A reader who wants a balanced picture of the subject will be sorely disappointed.

Michael Perelman

REFERENCES

Adler, Moshe. 1985. "Stardom and Talent." *American Economic Review* 75(1, March):208-212.

Bryson, Gladys. 1945. *Man and Society: The Scottish Enquiry of the Eighteenth Century.* Princeton: Princeton University Press.

Furniss, Edgar. 1965. *The Position of Labor in a System of Nationalism.* New York: Augustus M. Kelley.

Hayek, Friedrich A. 1948. *Individualism and Economic Order.* Chicago: University of Chicago Press.

Heilbroner, Robert L. 1967. *The Worldly Philosophers*. 3d ed. New York: Simon and Schuster.
Hume, David. 1739-1740. *A Treatise of Human Nature*. 2d ed. Edited by L.A. Selby-Bigge. Oxford
    at the Clarendon Press.
Hume, David. 1964. "On the Study of History." Pp. 561-568 in *Essays: Moral, Political, and
    Literary*, edited by T.H. Green and T.H. Grose. Aalen: Scientia Verlag.
Marx, Karl. 1963. *Theories of Surplus Value*. Moscow: Progress Publishers.
Macpherson, C.B. 1962. *The Political Theory of Possessive Individualism: Hobbes to Locke*.
    London: Oxford University Press.
Meek, Ronald. 1973. *Studies in the Labour Theory of Value*. New York: Monthly Review Press.
Routh, Guy. 1977. *The Origin of Economic Ideas*. New York: Random House. Schumpeter,
    Joseph. 1954. *History of Economic Analysis*. New York: Oxford University Press.

WHAT WE CALL HISTORY

Such a substantial study in the history of economic thought must have been
a long time in the making. Simply to acquire the requisite languages and read
the primary sources of the pre-Smithean literature is the labor of a lifetime.
Quite appropriately, Terence Hutchison's erudite study of European economic
thought, from Sir William Petty to Adam Smith, builds on a distinguished
career as historian and philosopher of economics that began over fifty years
ago. Hutchison's book is impressive in the way Joseph Alois Schumpeter's
History of Economic Analysis is impressive, for its sheer command over so
many different thinkers and texts. His prose also flows with a tasteful rhythm
and achieves considerable clarity and precision.

This is, without a doubt, a book that every serious scholar of the history
of economics will wish to have on his or her shelf. It is a book to be read
from front to cover, and then to be consulted from time to time, in search
of brief accounts on the contributions of, for example, George Berkeley, Ernst
Ludwig Carl, or Josiah Tucker. Another valuable resource is the chapter-by-
chapter bibliography, which is appropriately divided into primary and
secondary sources. Hutchison's book also includes a four-column chronology,
mapping the leading texts in political economy (one column for English works,
the other for works in Latin, French, German or Italian) to the birth or death
dates of the leading writers as well as to major events in European and
American history. As a reference guide, there appear to be very few misprints
or erroneous names or dates (an exception is the date given for Ricardo's death
in the chronological map). Compared to many recent books in the field, it is
very tastefully produced, with an attractive typeface, quality paper, and
unusually good binding. Basil Blackwell is to be commended.

That said, I find the book somewhat troubling, not so much on account
of the efforts of the author, which must be praised, but because it reaffirms
the still insecure state of the history of economics. Here we find a leading scholar
in the field, who ought to feel considerable liberty in surveying the past, being
overly defensive. Hutchison seems obliged throughout the book to convince

his reader, over four hundred pages worth, that there were valuable insights on economic practices before 1776.

Surely, by this point, there should be no need for such apologies or demonstrations. The myth of Adam Smith as the founder of economics was dispensed with long ago, at least among those who are sympathetically disposed to history in the first place. For those who are not, 1776 might as well be 1976. But for anyone interested in turning back to the *Wealth of Nations* and reading the appropriate secondary literature, there is ample evidence to the effect that, as the Newton of the moral world, Smith stood on the shoulders of giants. It is necessary only to point to Aristotle, Locke, or Hume to convince the sceptic. Recent reprints of Thomas Mun's *England's Treasure by Forraign Trade* or Bernard Mandeville's *The Fable of the Bees,* as well Joyce Appelby's (1978) prize-winning study, *Economic Thought and Ideology in Seventeenth-Century England,* also attest to a growing appreciation of the richness of the early modern period in the history of economics.

Certainly, much work remains to be done. We have, for example, Karen Vaughn's (1980) study of John Locke's economic thought and Eugene Rotwein's (1970) introduction to David Hume's essays on economics, but there is ample room for new and different monographs. Studies of the Physiocrats are more plentiful, though the focus tends toward their analytical contributions and policy recommendations rather than the broader institutional context. Hopefully, with time, we will have more works like Appelby's that give equal attention to content and context and that are sensitive to the fact that economic problems in the past were addressed with different forums and objectives in mind.

Hutchison acknowledges these monographs. But he is still trapped by the textbook mentality. For example, he shows a compulsive tendency to include every known contributor or relevant writer, however cursory his treatment. It would be hoped that such remarks at the end of a chapter as, "Finally a brief mention should be made of Thomas Hobbes" (p. 24) would have passed away with Schumpeter. Hobbes, whose views on human nature and justice loomed so large in the conceptual genesis of Locke or Smith, should either be treated fully, or not at all. A few throwaway lines, as we find here, are aggrevating. They suggest, to me at least, that the book tries to fill a gap that ought never to have existed in the first place.

The other maladies that beset the textbook mould are "precursoritis" and "anachronistitis." Hutchison has a propensity for both. Pierre Nicole, for example, is said to have "proceeded to anticipate precisely Adam Smith's famous observation" (p. 101) on the role of self-interest in the commercial sphere. It is cupidity, not charity, that leads a man to build a house for another. But Nicole died in 1695, long before Smith robbed the butcher, the brewer, or the baker of their benevolence. How could he have anticipated Smith, as Hutchison literally claims? Is not the point, rather, that Smith's views on human nature did not appear in a vacuum? As Albert O. Hirschman's *The Passions and the Interests* (1977) has shown, the gradual countenancing of self-interest and commercial gains arose out of much deeper, more widespread strands in the history of ideas, from Machiavelli to Montesquieu. Alas, Hutchison makes no reference to this very important study, nor does he counteract the view that Nicole simply fell from the sky.

Anachronisms also abound. David Hume, for example, is said to have used the concept of diminishing utility (p. 202), though the quote used to prove the point uses no such term. Hume speaks of happiness, which is surely not equivalent to the concept of utility as we understand it today. Anne Robert Jacques Turgot is reputed to have taken major steps towards both marginal productivity analysis and the Walrasian notion of a numeraire (pp. 312, 317), though again there exist no such words in the references used to support these claims. In a similar vein, the author notes that Francis Hutcheson's use of the word rarity is of "some significance" (p. 195) because of its subsequent use by the two Walras, without establishing a direct link between these writers, let alone acknowledging the possible transmutations a word might undergo on the journey from English to French.

Black holes notwithstanding, time seems to flow in one direction. Certainly, for the historian without alternative geometries readily at hand, it would be imprudent to warp the fabric of space and time. Rather than bestow credit on a Hume or a Turgot for having anticipated an idea that we associate with a later thinker, we either need to challenge and revise the record, or cease to impose our contemporary analysis on the works of the past.

To his credit, Hutchison makes only modest claims for his study. "Our primary aim," he writes, "is to provide a useful chronological account rather than to argue for any particular (or general) interpretation" (p. 8). The author explicitly sets out to present the material chronologically, by way of contrast to Schumpeter's thematic organization and by way of contrast to the many existing studies of the classical economists which, in his view, obscure the chronology "behind the dense undergrowth of often highly speculative, and sometimes tendentious, interpretations, re-interpretations, and misinterpretations" (p. 8).

Hutchison is right to note that the history of economic thought has often been written in order to grind certain ideological axes. He is also right about Schumpeter as a source book. It is hard to follow when one simply wishes to retrieve the thread that linked the Physiocrats to Smith, for instance. But the full solution does not lie in the approach taken here. To amass numerous details on the life and work of the leading contributors and point to affinities and recurrent concepts, is the preliminary step in any historical investigation. But that should be just the point of departure. I would rather take Schumpeter's outrageous provocations any day of the week than the cautious assessments put forth by Hutchison.

As the subtitle to the book suggests, Hutchison's main thesis is that political economy emerged in the mid-seventeenth century, with the work of Petty and his immediate successors, in the sense that they tackled the full spectrum of the eternal questions and answers of political economy. These include the debate over inductive and deductive methods, the emphasis on supply or demand in explanations of value and prices, the role of money in the economy, the capacity of the economy to run on its own accord, and the potential for economic growth. More specifically, Hutchison describes the emergence of the notions of economic harmony, equilibrating tendencies, and freedom of trade in the first half of the eighteenth century with the work of Boisguilbert, Mandeville, Gervaise, Vanderlint, Carl, and Cantillon. Here and there, Hutchison astutely notes that the answers provided then as now fail to get to the bottom of things.

The period under review is primarily characterized by a lack of consensus, at least in comparison to that found with the classical economists. But this may be due to the specific characteristics of higher learning at the time—its lack of overt nationalism, for example. The very range, both geographical and temporal, of the preclassical group suggests to me that deeper forces were at work. Little attempt is made to point to broader developments in the history of science or in the European economy itself. Given that political economy flourished in different parts of Europe at different times, the obvious question to pose is why. Hutchison points to numerous schools of thought that effloresced here and there, but falls short of providing any explanation. Similarly, questions such as why Daniel Bernoulli's insights on expected utility were ignored for over a century and a half (p. 179), or why Quesnay emphasized the existence of natural laws in the economy but Smith did not (p. 62), call out for explanation. Hutchison is like the naturalist who describes the flora and fauna of a region without reference to the evolutionary or geological history that gave rise to such a landscape in the first place.

Hutchison makes a cursory reference to the work of Peter Gay, the eminent historian of the Enlightenment, but much more is called for. Had he incorporated some of the more recent work by, for example, Keith Michael Baker (1975), then a context might have been provided for the material he unleashes. In his treatment of the subjects of political arithmetic and demography, Hutchison neglects altogether the recent scholarship on the subject by Theodore Porter (1986), and Lorraine J. Daston (1988). Obviously, it is not possiuble to look at everything. But even a token gesture in the direction of recent historical research on the period would have greatly enhanced the appeal of the work.

There are also some studies in the sociology of science which attempt to make sense of why science shifted its center of activity over time. Joseph Ben-David (1984), for example, speculates that these movements may stem partly in reaction to the availability of oppportunities for effective political change.

Bright young men are drawn into the natural sciences when there is little prospect for political advancement; a contentious claim, to be sure, but one highly suggestive for a subject like political economy.

Hutchison acknowledges on the opening pages that a single man does not a tradition make. Yet, he fails to explain why Adam Smith stands out on the historical landscape, and even implies that Smith was able to propel himself without help. As he asserts in the closing pages of the book, "Adam Smith, rightly or wrongly, was almost entirely responsible for the rise to dogmatic orthodoxy of the classical, macro-economic model" (p. 378). This is all the more remarkable because, as Hutchison notes, Smith attempted to bury all of the accumulated wisdom on the utility theory of value that he ought to have gleaned in Pufendorf and Galiani. Given the post-Kuhnian literature on the sociology of science, particularly the issue of consensus formation, one would have hoped for a more weighty treatment.

Hutchison is to be commended, however, for sparing us one more treatment of Smith's theory of value. Rather, he promotes Smith as a moral philosopher of considerable breadth. When it comes to analysis per se, Hutchison does not share Schumpeter's harsh condemnations. But he does, nonetheless, convey the impression that Smith might have benefited by a greater appreciation for the work of his predecessors. Certainly, the confusion on the subject of use-value was, in Hutchison's eyes, an unfortunate wrong turn. Again, the notion of blaming Smith for what now seem to be erroneous trains of thought is a peculiar one. It is somewhat like blaming Newton for his adherence to absolute space and time, rather than recognizing that there is a virtue in wading into the more difficult regions of metaphysics and confronting the many conceptual problems head on.

Hutchison's general adherence to Schumpeter's historiographical prescripts, of great men, the vitality of texts, and visions is prominent throughout. More seriously, he is still in the grip of the wrong-headed belief that there exists a "scientific economist" such as Turgot, but a mere propagandist such as Thomas Mun. To be sure, Mun's work took a different form than Turgot's or Smith's. But to depreciate the quite remarkable theoretical insights in his *Discourse* to the point of being "almost completely inchoate and inexplicit" (p. 7) is to impose current forms of expression on works of the past. Mun may not have set the highest standards of rigor, but he certainly made one of the most interesting contributions in the entire history of thought, by explicitly recognizing the existence of economic forces that no legal statute could subvert.

Historians of the natural sciences are usually surprised to learn that there are dozens upon dozens of textbooks on the history of economic thought. While many historians of science came to the subject with an initial degree or two in the sciences, they took Thomas Kuhn's (1970) criticisms to heart. Textbooks are more like travel brochures of a foreign country than the actual trip abroad. Hutchison's book was not written as a textbook, but his reluctance to offer interpretations and his strict adherence to chronology essentially makes it just that. While I do not wish to suggest that we do away with textbooks—they serve a purpose, to be sure—I only hope that scholars in the history of economic thought, particularly those with such a vast command of the subject as Terence Hutchison, will cease adding to the stockpile and get down to the real toil and trouble that we call history.

Margaret Schabas

REFERENCES

Appleby, Joyce Oldham. 1978. *Economic Thought and Ideology in Seventeenth-Century England.* Princeton: Princeton University Press.

Baker, Keith Michael. 1975. *Condorcet: From Natural Philosophy to Social Mathematics.* Chicago: University of Chicago Press.

Ben-David, Joseph. 1986. *The Scientist's Role in Society.* Chicago: University of Chicago Press.

Daston, Lorraine J. 1988. *Classical Probability in the Enlightenment.* Princeton: Princeton University Press.

Hirschman, Albert O. 1977. *The Passions and the Interests: Political Arguments for Capitalism before Its Triumph.* Princeton: Princeton University Press.

Kuhn, Thomas S. 1970. *The Structure of Scientific Revolutions.* 2nd ed. Chicago: University of Chicago Press.

Porter, Theodore M. 1985. *The Rise of Statistical Thinking: 1820-1900.* Princeton: Princeton University Press.

Rotwein, Euguene, ed. 1970. *David Hume: Writings on Economics.* Madison: University of Wisconsin Press.

Vaughn, Karen Iversen. 1980. *John Locke: Economist and Social Scientist.* Chicago: University of Chicago Press.

ASIMAKOPULOS'S *INVESTMENT, EMPLOYMENT, AND INCOME DISTRIBUTION*

Nina Shapiro

Investment, Employment, and Income Distribution
By A. Asimakopulos.
Boulder, CO: Westview Press, 1988.

I. INTRODUCTION

While Keynes considered the ideas "laboriously" expressed in his *General Theory* to be both "simple" and "obvious" (Keynes, 1973a, p. xxiii), they have appeared as neither to his readers. This has been especially the case with regard to the saving and investment propositions. These have seemed "paradoxical," and to some so unsound as to be even "dangerous" (Leijonhufvud, 1981). The determination of savings by investment, and the related notion of the independence of investment finance from "real" conditions (thrift and

Research in the History of Economic Thought and Methodology
Volume 10, pages 225-234.
Copyright © 1992 by JAI Press Inc.
All rights of reproduction in any form reserved.
ISBN: 0-55938-501-4

equilibriium results are the central focus of the *General Theory,* which is concerned above all else with establishing the possibility of an "involuntary unemployment equilibrium."[4]

Although the equilibrating role of output changes is an essential part of Keynes's "message," it is not, as Patinkin thinks, all of the message. The *General Theory* is also about the "unreliability" of the factors which govern investment. Because the results of investment occur in the distant and unpredictable future, the expectations which determine it are subjective and volatile. Their subjectivity explains why investment is "normally" less than the savings desired at full employment, while their volatility makes investment the determinant of output and employment, for "it is usual ... to regard as the *causa causans* that factor which is most prone to sudden and wide fluctuations" (Keynes, 1973b, p. 121). The variability of investment and the insufficiency of its level are an integral part of the analysis.

Keynes's message thus includes the output adjustment of saving and investment that Patinkin emphasizes and the uncertainty and indeterminancy of economic events that Shackle stresses. The message is about equilibrium relations and positions, but the equilibrium it is about is not the "timeless" one of the Walrasian tradition, but the shifting one of the Marshallian. Keynes's analysis is Marshall's minus the Marshallian long run.[5]

III.   FINANCE, INVESTMENT, AND SAVING

For investment to be the "*causa causans* of the system" it must be independent of the other determinant of output and employment, the "propensity to save." If saving constrained investment, it could not fluctuate "widely." Since it could not exceed the available savings, and these are equal to the investment that generated them, investment could not rise above the level it had just reached. Today's investment could be less than yesterday's investment (today's available savings), and it could also be less than the savings desired at full employment. Investment declines and unemployment equilibriums could occur, but investment increases could not, even in the presence of excess capacity and involuntarily unemployed labor.

Whereas the variability of investment depends on its independence from saving, its independence from saving depends on how it is financed. When it is financed in the way assumed by Keynes and Kalecki, its financing "employs no savings" (Keynes, 1973b, p. 219). The finance for investment is supplied by the banks, not by savers, and its availability in both the short and long runs is determined by bank policies and requlations. The public's liquidity preferences can choke off an investment expansion (if the banks let them), but its intertemporal consumption preferences cannot.

Bank loans finance investment increases and the monetary savings generated by the increases "fund" them, repay the loans which financed them, or purchase the securities which were floated for the loans' repayment. If the banks are willing to extend their indebtedness, become more "illiquid," the finance for an investment increase will be forthcoming. And if the savings generated by the increase are not hoarded, so will the revenue needed for its funding. The revenues of investors will increase by the amount of the investment increase, the debt contracted for the purposes of the increase will be liquidated, and the funds tied up in its financing will be released. The finance which banks "organize and manage" is a "revolving fund" that returns to its lenders when it is "expended" (Keynes, 1973b, p. 219).[6]

While investment would be free to fluctuate with long-run expectations if the finance for it was a "revolving fund," this finance, according to Asimakopulos, is not as "circular" as Keynes and Kalecki assumed. The release of the funds which finance an investment increase requires more than their expenditure. It requires a rise in savings equal to the increase in investment, and this will not happen with the funds' expenditure. Keynes and Kalecki thought that it would because they confused the "definitional" equality between saving and investment, the one between actual saving and investment, with the "equilibrium" equality, the one between desired saving and planned investment.[7]

Unlike the "definitional" equality between saving and investment, the "equilibrium" one does not hold at all times, and it is the equilibrium one that has to be satisfied if the investment increase is to be funded. The savings which fund investment are, for Asimakopulos, not the savings the public receives, but the savings it wants to keep, and these desired savings do not rise by the amount of the investment increase until its "full multiplier effects are completed." Until this time, the increase in savings will be insufficient for the funding of the investment increase and thus for the retirement of the debt which financed it. The banks' liquidity position will be restored only when the new short-period equilibrium is achieved.

If the funding of the investment increase is attempted before its multiplier effects are completed, entrepreneurs will find that they cannot fund it at the price expected. The demand for funds (supply of securities) will exceed the supply (demand for securities), which will push up the interest rate and thus bring down investment. Investment will fall back to its former level, and if the adverse effect of its increase on the interest rate had been anticipated, it would not have risen at all. Contrary to what Keynes thought, the capital market *can* "become congested through shortage of saving" (Keynes, 1973b, p. 222).

Asimakopulos's argument for a savings constraint on investment finance is illustrated with two examples. In the first, the planned investment, I, has risen by an amount greater than the actual, A, because "unexpectedly high sales" have resulted in a greater than expected inventory reduction. Since the actual saving, S, is equal to the actual investment, and the rise in A falls short of the rise in I, the increase in S is less than the increase in I. The debt which financed the increase in I thus exceeds the increase in S (by the amount of the unanticipated inventory change) and the savings increase cannot retire the debt even if all of the increase is directed to the debt's repayment.

That the increase in savings can be less than the increase in planned investment is not as surprising as Asimakopulos thinks. Indeed, it would be surprising if savings rose by the amount of the planned investment increase, given that planned investment no more generates savings than does planned ("exante") saving. Neither the revenues of firms nor the income of their employees is affected by an increase in the planned investment. As Keynes emphasized, the investment planned has to be "effected" (the expenditure executed) for it to raise sales proceeds and thus the income and savings of households and firms.

The investment that produces savings is not the planned investment but the "actual," and the "equilibrium" equality between saving and investment holds only because the "definitional" equality does. The equality between the actual saving and investment is "not a mere truism" (Keynes, 1973b, p. 281). It expresses an important fact about the "entrepreneurial" economy, that its income is generated by expenditure. Saving is necessarily equal to investment because the income saved comes from the sales proceeds of entrepreneurs:

> Income is created by the value in excess of user cost which the producer obtains for the output he has sold; but the whole of this output must obviously have been sold either to a consumer or to another entrepreneur; and each entrepreneur's current investment is equal to the excess of the equipment which he has purchased from other entrepreneurs over his own user cost. Hence, in the the aggregate the excess of income over consumption, which we call saving, cannot differ from the addition to capital equipment which we call investment (Keynes, 1973a, p. 64).

While the increase in savings can certainly be less than the planned investment increase, the "saving shortage" that occurs when it is less does not "congest the capital market." The "shortage" equals the value of the unanticipated inventory reduction (the difference between I and A), and this equals the "unexpected" sales increase that produced the inventory reduction. Firms have less inventories than they expected, but they also have more cash, and the cash they have "unexpectedly" received is sufficient to fund that part of the increase in I that cannot be funded with the savings increase. Indeed, insofar as the unanticipated "liquidity increase" is an increase in firms' bank deposits, it reduces their debt to the banks (or alternatively raises the banks' debt to them) by the amount of the "saving shortage." In this case, the expansion increases the firms' debt to the banks by the same amount as it increases savings so that the banks' liquidity position can be restored with the actual savings generated by the actual increase in investment.

Of course, the fact that the savings increase can retire the debt created by the expansion does not mean that the increase will retire it. Those that receive the savings may not want to spend them on the debt's repayment or on the firms' securities. This is the case in Asimakopulos's second saving constraint example, where the actual investment increase equals the planned one but not all of the savings generated by the expansion are "desired." Some are "disequilibrium" savings which "individuals intend to use as soon as possible for consumption." Here the savings increase cannot fund the investment expansion because consumption has not yet risen to its new equilibrium level, that is, the "full multiplier effect" of the increase in I "has not been achieved."

Contrary to what Asimakopulos thinks, the expenditure of the "disequilibrium" savings does not make them unavailable to the firms who need them for debt repayments. Instead of eliminating the savings, their expenditure simply transfers their ownership from the consumers who spent them to the firms whose products the savings purchased. Firms' profits will go up by the amount in which the household saving falls. As emphasized in Terzi's comment (1986-1987) on Asimakopulos's argument, household saving affects not the volume of savings but their distribution between consumers (workers and rentiers) and producers (entrepreneurs).[8]

When the "disequilibrium" savings are added to the "equilibrium" ones the firms have already received (from their profits or securities sales), their funds will be sufficient for the retirement of the debt which financed their expansion. The finance "circle" which initiated the expansion will close, unless the firms do not "want" all of the savings either. Instead of keeping them all, the firms might do what the firms in Asimakopulos's first saving shortage example did: spend a part of the savings on inventory replenishment. This, according to Asimakopulos, is the most likely occurence, given that consumption-goods inventories have been drawn down and the expansion (multiplier) is still in progress (working).[9]

If firms do expand consumption-goods production, they will need more funds than their sales bring in. This need for additional funds has, however, nothing to do with the level of savings (actual or desired). Additional funds are needed in this case for the same reason they were needed in the case of the investment expansion: to finance an increase in the aggregate level of production. As Keynes emphasized, no output expansion, whether it be an increase in capital-goods production, in consumption-goods production, or in both, can be financed with the proceeds from production. Being equal to the output's value (the consumption and investment), the proceeds can finance an output production no greater than the current one, and this is the case regardless of the proceeds' distribution between saving and consumption and how much of the saving is "desired." It is not savings, but "cash," which finances production, "bridges the gap" between the expenditure on its inputs and revenue from its products, and the money needed for its expansion comes from the same "pool of funds" as the money needed for other purposes: the "dishoardings" of the public and credit expansions of banks.[10]

The funds needed for the consumer goods expansion will depend on its size, and its size will depend on the saving propensity if the expansion is "induced" by the investment increase. The higher is the saving propensity, the lower will be the value of the multiplier and thus the output generated by a rise in investment. But while the funds needed for the output expansion depend on the saving propensity, the funds *available* for its financing do not. Nor would a rise in the saving propensity release savings for the funding of investment. All it would do is reduce the size of the output expansion.

At no time during the expansion will a change in the saving propensity affect the savings increase. This will equal, in both "equilibrium and disequilibrium," the rise in investment. The saving propensity may affect the demand for funds, through its effect on the "desired" output expansion (Keynes's "finance" demand) or its effect on the actual output and employment (transactions demand). But it has no effect whatsoever on the funds supplied.[11]

IV. INVESTMENT FUNDING

The requisites of investment's long-term financing depend on the conditions of its short-term financing. If its short-term financing is effected through the expansion of bank deposits, then its long-term financing can be effected with the money savings it generates. Since in this case cash is loaned to investors, cash, and only cash, is needed for the retirement of their debt. Its retirement becomes possible as soon as the money holdings of the public rise by the amount of the cash advanced. If, however, investment was financed short term with "real" rather than monetary funds, if what was advanced to investors was not cash but output accumulations, then they could not retire their debt until the output holdings of the public rose by the amount of the output borrowed. Here the funding of an investment increase would require a rise in desired saving equal to the increase and the saving propensity would constrain investment at all levels of output and employment.

Assume an economy in which all contracts are denominated in real terms, either because there is no money to effect exchange (all goods are bought with goods) or because the only money available is a produced commodity (e.g., gold). Such an economy would have the features of Keynes's "real wage" economy (Keynes, 1979), for factor contracts would be made and paid in the "output in specie" of the factor's production. We could thus think of it as his real-wage economy or, alternatively, as Ricardo's "corn economy" or Walras's "real exchange" (money numeraire) one (which also of course have its defining property).

In our real-wage economy, production would be "financed" with the output saved from previous productions. Those who owned the saved output (the "capitalists") could invest it themselves (advance it to the workers) or loan it out to others who wanted to do so (the "entrepreneurs"). Individuals could invest more output than they had saved, but the community as a whole could not. There would be output (corn or gold) "banks" but no money banks, and since the borrowings of individuals would be confined to the outputs of others, the aggregate of their investment in any "day" could not exceed the saving of "yesterday."

Yesterday's output in conjunction with the saving propensities of the economy's members determine the funds available for investment. The supply of funds is the supply of savings, and while the funds supplied depend on their "classical" determinant, thrift, the funds demanded depend on "productivity." Because the marginal product of the output invested is the profit from the investment, its productivity determines the extent to which it is "desired." In the real-wage economy, the output from production is both its finance and its objective. Goods are purchasing power, the interest on capital, and the incentive for investment.

The output advanced to production will be returned to its owners if: (1) the marginal product of the investment is greater than or equal to the loaned output, and (2) the saving desired out of the product is as great as the saving which financed its production. Only saving can "release" the funds tied up in production; consumption ("spending") merely uses them up. Current saving is as necessary to the "funding" of investment as past saving was to its financing. The conditions under which saving constrains investment finance are those in which the saving *is* the finance.

Just as the labor market operates differently depending on whether the contracts are made in terms of money or goods, so too does the capital market. When the loans contracted are output loans, when the assets supplied and demanded in the market are real ones, a savings shortage can congest it. When, however, the loans are monetary and the assets supplied and demanded are financial, the "market can become congested through shortage of cash," but "it can never become congested through shortage of saving" (Keynes, 1973b, p. 222).[12]

V. KEYNES'S MESSAGE

Investment can be greater than the desired saving for the same reason that it can be less: it takes place in a monetary economy. If "real" money, generalized purchasing power, and the institutions which create it (banks) did not exist, individuals could neither "postpone" their spending nor spend more than they made. Instead of "expenditure creating its own income" (Keynes, 1979, p. 81), supply would create its own demand, and the theory of production and employment could "be worked out" on the basis of "real exchanges" (Keynes, 1973a, p. 20).

The fact that the economy cannot be conceptualized in abstraction from its monetary relations and ends was demonstrated by Keynes. Until this part of his message is grasped, his ideas will seem paradoxical and will not revolutionize economic thinking. There will be no Keynesian revolution.

NOTES

1. The first controversy over these ideas was the 1937/1938 *Economic Journal* debate on the loanable funds interpretation of Keynes's interest rate theory (advanced by Hicks, Hawtrey, Ohlin, and Robertson). Keynes's contributions to the debate are reprinted in volume XIV of his collected writings (Keynes, 1973b), along with his correspondence with the other contributors on the issues and his 1939 *Economic Journal* discussion of his position, "The Process of Capital Formation."

2. The review was originally published in the *Canadian Journal of Economics* and the article on Keynes and Sraffa appeared in an 1985 issue of *Political Economy: Studies in the Surplus Approach*.

3. For Asimakopulos's critique of Robinson's conception of the short run, see his introduction to the collection and the essay on Robinson's contribution, "Joan Robinson and Economic Theory."

4. Thus, Kalecki did not anticipate Keynes's theory of employment, for the focus of his academic writings prior to the *General Theory's* publication was not the short period equilibrium level of output, but its cyclical fluctuations. This position on Kalecki's relation to Keynes, which concurs with Patinkin's but is contrary to Robinson's, is presented in the review of Patinkin's book and in the introductory essay on the similarities and differences between Keynes, Kalecki, and Robinson.

5. This Marshallian view of Keynes is also expressed in the discussion of the effective demand concept, in the chapter titled "Keynes's Theory of Effective Demand Revisited." Here Keynes's formulation of the concept is criticised for its inconsistency with the "Marshallian microfoundations" of his analysis, and a formulation consistent with these microfoundations is developed.

6. As Asimakopulos notes, this view of finance appears in Kalecki's writings before it appears in Keynes's. Kalecki's "circle of finance" notion foreshadows Keynes's "revolving fund" one so that Kalecki did "anticipate" what Keynes came to regard as an essential aspect of his theory, the independence of finance from saving (see Asimakopulos, 1988, pp. 175-176).

7. The same criticism of Keynes is advanced in Leijonhufvud (1981).

8. Also see Terzi (1986/1987) where the effect of household saving on investment finance is examined through an investigation of the flow of funds between households, banks, and firms.

9. The firms might also add some of the savings to their idle balances and if this increase in their liquidity demand (or anyone else's) is not offset by a money supply expansion, the rise in the interest rate could reduce investment. This liquidity constraint on investment has, however, nothing do to with the adequacy, or otherwise, of savings and thus is not relevant to Asimakopulos's saving shortage argument (which assumes, in fact, a constant liquidity preference). See Kregel's response (1985) to Asimakopulos (1986) and Kregel's (1986) and Davidson's (1986) contributions to the *Journal of Post Keynesian Economics*'s symposium on finance and saving. Included in the symposium is Asimakopulos's most recent article on the issue ("Finance, Liquidity, Saving, and Investment").

10. This is repeatedly emphasized by Keynes in the controversy over the loanable funds interpretation of his liquidity preference interest theory. See the finance articles in Keynes (1973b).

11. The case of a saving-propensity rise reducing the demand for funds and "relieving capital market congestion" through the cutting of demand rather than the increasing of supply is discussed

by Keynes in his 1938 reply to Robertson, "Mr. Keynes 'Finance'" (Keynes, 1973b). Also see his December, 1937 letter to Robertson (Keynes, 1973b, pp. 223-226).

12. The economic importance of the terms in which contracts are made is emphasized in Davidson's work (see, in particular, Davidson, 1978).

REFERENCES

Davidson, Paul. 1978. "Why Money Matters: Lessons from a Half-century of Monetary Theory." *Journal of Post Keynesian Economics* 1(1, Fall): 46-70.

_____. 1986. "Finance, Funding, Saving, and Investment." *Journal of Post Keynesian Economics* 9[1, Fall]: 101-110.

Keynes, John Maynard. 1973a. *The General Theory of Employment, Interest and Money,* Volume 7 of *Collected Writings.* London: Macmillan.

_____. 1973b. *The General Theory and After-Part II: Defense and Development,* Volume 14 of Collected Writings. London: Macmillan.

_____. 1979. "The Distinction between a Co-operative Economy and an Entrepreneur Economy." In *The General Theory and After-A Supplement,* Volume 29 of *Collected Writings.* London: Macmillan.

Kregel, J.A. 1984/1985. "Constraints on Output and Employment." *Journal of Post Keynesian Economics* 7(2, Winter): 139-153.

_____. "A Note on Finance." *Journal of Post Keynesian Economics.* 9[1, Fall]: 91-100.

Patinkin, Don. 1982. *Anticipations of the General Theory? And Other Essays on Keynes.* Chicago: University of Chicago Press.

Terzi, Andrea. 1986. "Finance, Investment and Saving: A Comment on Asimakopoulos." *Cambridge Journal of Economics, 10*[1, Maarch]: 77-80.

_____. 1986-1987. "Independence of Finance." *Journal of Post Keynesian Economics* 9[2, Winter]: 188-197.

HILLARD'S *J. M. KEYNES*
IN RETROSPECT

D. E. Moggridge

J.M. Keynes in Retrospect
Edited by John Hilliard.
Aldershot: Edward Elgar, 1988. Pp. viii + 229.

1988 was a vintage year for the Keynes publishing industry. In part, this reflected the usual flow of normal scholarship, including a boomlet in interest in Keynes's method, but it also reflected, with the usual lags between presentation and publication, many 1986 celebrations of the fiftieth anniversary of the publication of *The General Theory of Employment, Interest and Money*. It was to commemorate the latter, as well as the fortieth anniversary of Keynes's death, that the School of Economic Studies of the University of Leeds held a series of lectures, seminars, and workshops during 1986. The purpose of the exercise, according to Hilliard, was "to contribute towards a reassessment of the Keynesian legacy from the perspective of the post-war generation." An incidental effect of the ten resulting essays for this volume is to demonstrate

Research in the History of Economic Thought and Methodology
Volume 10, pages 235-239.
Copyright © 1992 by JAI Press Inc.
All rights of reproduction in any form reserved.
ISBN: 0-55938-501-4

the catholicity of interests and the overall quality of the members of the School of Economic Studies—in part a tribute to the influence and work of one of the contributors, Professor A.J. Brown.

The essays divide themselves into three groups. First, there are what might be called strictly historical essays: Arthur Brown's "A Worm's Eye View of the Keynesian Revolution" and Michael Collins' "Did Keynes Have the Answer to Unemployment in the 1930s?" Second, there are a series of "doctrine historical" essays on Keynes and his ideas: Bill Gerrard's "Keynesian Economics: The Road to Nowhere," Hugo Radice's "Keynes and the Policy of Practical Protectionism," and Michael Hudson's "Keynes, Hayek and the Monetary Economy." To this class might be added the post-Keynesian, neo-Ricardian musings on Keynes and his (or the profession's) failures to properly present (or understand) his message by the editor, John Brothwell, and John Weeks. Finally, there are two essays on more contemporary themes: Rodney Crosley's "Inflation, Unemployment and the Keynesian Wage Theorem" and Michael Surrey's "The Great Recession, 1974-84: Is a 'Keynesist' Approach Plausible?" Although readers will find meat and profit in all the essays in the collection, for purposes of review I will concentrate on the more historical and history of thought items in the collection.

Arthur Brown's essay, which had already entered the footnotes of the literature before publication in Warren Young's *Interpreting Mr Keynes* (1987), is a classic of its kind. Unlike, for example, many of the *Recollections of Eminent Economists* published in the *Banca Notionale del Lavoro Quarterly Review* and collected together and republished by Macmillan (Kregel, 1988), it is not intended to explain how the author came to do what he did or how his early work did or did not lead to his later eminence. Instead, it is a straightforward memoir of Oxford economics around the time of the publication of the *General Theory*. In some ways, its nearest parallel is Austin Robinson's memoir of the Cambridge Faculty in the early 1930s published a decade ago in Patinkin and Lieth's *Keynes, Cambridge and the General Theory* (1978), although Brown's essay has the advantage of being a perspective from lower down the totem pole. It makes clear that for economists entering the profession in the 1930s, Keynes was only a part of the story, albeit an important one, which, according to Brown, included "an empirically quantifiable multiplier, systematic and quantifiable cycle theories, a theory of the short-run equilibrium level of activity and the first steps towards dynamising it." This mixture of theory and quantification proved immensely stimulating, especially in a Britain which at that time had three preeminent international centres of economic research (and the graduate students to go with them), at least two of which were extremely open to Continental influences, which, thanks to contemporary European upheavals, came in personal as well as published form. The resulting stimulus and strong interactions, particularly among the graduate students and younger dons, show clearly in the pages of Brown's memoir as they do in others. So too does the fact that, at least until *after* the end of the 1930s, at least in Oxford, even with the presence of such disciples as James Meade and Roy Harrod, Keynes made little impact on the undergraduate curriculum in economics. As in America, that was to come later.

Michael Collins looks at another aspect of the 1930s—one which has recently spawned a minor growth industry among economic historians—the reappraisal of Keynes's policy advice. His critical survey of the literature in this area, which covers several areas of both economic history and the history of ideas, shows some discrimination, although one wishes on occasion that he did less to survey the literature than to direct it back to considering the real historical options of the period. Thus it may be of some hypothetical interest to know whether a programme of Keynes-style deficit-financed public works could by itself have brought unemployment in 1932 down to the target level suggested by Keynes in 1929, but it does not really bear on the historical question of the viability of those proposals in 1929. Similarly, the exposition of Treasury thinking and the changes therein in response to Keynes's influence is weakened, as is much of the literature he discusses, by a failure to clearly specify the starting point of the discussion and to pay attention not only to what poeple said but also to what they did—a point that most historians of the period seem to ignore when they pass by the dramatic reorganisation of the economic policymaking machinery of British government that followed the 1944 *Employment Policy* White Paper.

Hugo Radice's "Keynes and the Policy of Practical Protectionism"— "practical protectionism" meaning "whatever practical measures may be required to pursue effectively the primary objective of securing full employment in the national (British) economy" (p. 154)—is motivated by contemporary 1980s British policy preoccupations. Yet, leaving his last section dealing with the 1980s to one side, there remains an examination of Keynes's views in "National Self-Sufficiency" (1933), the *General Theory* (1936) and his contributions to three policy debates of his lifetime—the return to gold in 1925, tariffs in 1930-1931 and Bretton Woods. The resulting "mining" of the Collected Writings to support the view that elements of "practical protectionism" were a consistent part of Keynes's appraoch to economic policy is quite successful, although, for this reader, the missing of the explicit link in Keynes's thought between the exchange-rate regime (in this case, the adjustable peg) and controls on capital movements weakens the discussion of his later views and the discussion of the evolution of his views over the International Monetary Fund (IMF) does not really try to cope with many of the details or with his famous posthumous article "The Balance of Payments of the United States" with its famous attack on "ago-old poisons" and "modernist stuff gone wrong and turned sour and silly" (Keynes 1980, p. 445). If it had, it would have been much more successful, and its applications to the 1980s at the end might have been much more moderate and convincing.

Michael Hudson's "Keynes, Hayek and the Monetary Economy" is an
exercise designed to show that both Keynes's and Hayek's approaches to
economic theory rested on the perception that the inadequacy of traditional
theory lay in its lack of appreciation of the fundamental difference a monetary
economy made to theory. He is not concerned with the different ways that
they embodied this perception in their own theories nor with the success or
lack of sucess of those theories. Rather, he is concerned to show that it was
this common perception that was at work in both Keynes's and Hayek's cases.
In Keynes's case, this involves Hudson in an exercise in the history of
nineteenth-century economic thought to show how Say's Law became
embedded in long-term classical theorising and how destructive a shift in
emphasis to the short run à la Keynes of the *Tract* or *Treatise* proved to be.
In Hayek's case, the emphasis is on contemporary continental business-cycle
theorising. The result is a suggestive discussion of how both external and
internal influences combined to determine the interwar research agendas of
two influential economists.

Bill Gerrard's "Keynesian Economics: The Road to Nowhere" is a history
of what he calls "mainstream Keynesianism" and its "search for the 'missing
link' that reconciles the existence of involuntary unemployment with the
market-theoretic appoach" of classical theory. He takes us through the first
phase of Keynesianism, which runs from the IS-LM model of Hicks through
the neoclassical synthesis to the "Keynes-*versus*-the-classics" debate; the second
phase of "disequilibrium Keynesianism" stimulated by Patinkin and, later,
Clower; and the more recent phase three dominated by both competitive and
informational imperfections which he argues "offers an end to the search for
the microfoundations of Keynesian macroeconomics." He argues that all three
phases have provided valuable extensions of traditional theory by providing
a clearer understanding of the implications of systemic imperfections, but asks
the inevitable question of whether mainstream Keynesian economics had
uncovered Keynes's ultimate meaning—"a mythical Holy Grail, much sought
after but never found" (p. 148)? His answer is "possibly not," if only because
he suggests that market-theoretic interpretations of Keynes are imposing a
frame of reference which, of necessity, denies that he broke away from
traditional theory. Yet, as far as this paper is concerned, there are no hints
of what the alternative "Keynes method" is or was. That presumably will be
the subject of another paper. However, the suggestion is that without an
understanding of Keynes's method, mainstream Keynesian theory and policy
have become a "road to nowhere," where theory and policy prescriptions retreat
from Keynes's claims and suggestions into the old, orthodox citadel.

It is, of course, but a short step from Bill Gerrard's paper to the neo-
Keynesian and neo-Ricardian musings of the editor, John Brothwell, and John
Weeks. These accept that the Keynesian revolution in its mainstream guise led
nowhere or, as the editor puts it, "the *General Theory* after fifty years could

be consigned without conscience to the history of economic thought as the work of a minor post- Malthusian" (p. 3). They argue, in varying ways, that by concentrating on Keynes's forms of argument, where he was unable to escape his orthodox past, rather than on his fundamental underlying ideas, the professional mainstream was misled. They are, as is usual in these cases, better at pointing out the deficiencies of the mainstream case than at constructively showing what their alternative is. For their audiences, as well as for this reader, it seems that after several decades of negative comment and criticism, it was surely time to provide at least an operational glimpse of the alternative that is, or was, supposed to be available rather than merely exhort their successors to do so.

For all the laments for the revolution that either led nowhere or never was, it is still remarkable that not only at Leeds, fifty years after the publication of the *General Theory,* there were numerous retrospective reconsiderations and celebrations. This suggests that, although Keynes qua Keynes and his *General Theory* as a book published in February 1936 are now, rightly, the property of historians of economics, his influence still pervades contemporary economics in various important ways. Given that the half-life of the contemporary journal article is just six years, that is testimony enough to Keynes's achievement.

REFERENCES

Keynes, J.M. 1980. "The Balance of Payments of the United States." Pp. 427-446 in *The Collected Writings of John Maynard Keynes,* Vol. XXVII, *Activities 1940-1946: Shaping the Post-War World—Employment and Commodities,* edited by D.E. Moggridge. London: Macmillan.

Kregel, J.(ed.). 1988. *Recollections of Eminent Economists.* London: Macmillan.

Young, Warren F. 1987. *Interpreting Mr Keynes: The IS-LM Enigma.* Cambridge, UK: Polity Press.

HOLLIS'S *THE CUNNING OF REASON*

Geoffrey M. Hodgson

The Cunning of Reason
By Martin Hollis.
Cambridge: Cambridge University Press, 1987, pp. 222, index.

I

This book is one philosopher's survey of the foundations of neoclassical economic theory. Martin Hollis examines the model of rationality which underpins most of formal economics today and finds it wanting. The limitations are as follows: first, preferences are taken as exogenous; second, the individual is taken as an isolated and elemental unit; third, choices are reduced to "now" and there is no unfolding of real time; fourth, there are no institutions, at least in the elementary model, and these either have to be taken as given or in some way explained; and fifth, technology is known, given, and unchanging, thus excluding investment decisions which push out the technological frontiers to unforeseen regions.

Research in the History of Economic Thought and Methodology
Volume 10, pages 241-244.
Copyright © 1992 by JAI Press Inc.
All rights of reproduction in any form reserved.
ISBN: 0-55938-501-4

Hollis does not deny the value of this "atifice." Indeed, he treats it with great respect, both for the formal sophistication of those practitioners which have adopted it, and for the elegant but powerful simplification of the complexity of decision making in economic life.

Thus, there is not a direct confrontation with "rational economic man"; rather, the terrain is carefully excavated, closely examining the philosophical underpinnings as they are revealed. The first area to bear this scrutiny is the field of human interaction, where there are multiple agents and social institutions.

Treading territory that has become familiar in the 1980s, Hollis examines the emergence of norms in this context. The discourse then moves on to the matter of unintended consequences of social interactions, concluding that these can be "compatible with individualism."

Without using the term, the argument treads around the Hobbesian idea of malfeasance, concluding that the model of social interaction in *The Leviathan*—adopted implicitly by many economists—is deficient largely because it excludes the dimension of trust. This is a worthy conclusion, heralded by the synopsis on the cover of the paperback edition, but worthy of much greater philosophical discussion than is given here. Indeed, several recent and older works on the topic of importance are ignored. Perhaps most crucial is the neglect of Emile Durkheim's (1984) critique of contractual reductionism in *The Division of Labour in Society*, as well as others such as Alan Fox's (1974) brilliant portrayal of trust in industrial relations in his *Beyond Contract* and Richard Titmuss' classic case study of *The Gift Relationship* (1971).

The chapter on rational expectations rediscovers G.B. Richardson's (1959) coordination problem, but without acknowledging or recognizing it as such, but usefully concludes that important informational considerations are at stake. This prepares the reader for the next chapter, which is mainly devoted to the work of Herbert Simon on "satisficing." Again, this is a little disappointing, partly because it does not come to grips with the distinction between limited information and limited computational capacity to cope with an analyze information (even if it were available). Arguably, this distinction is crucial to an understanding of Simon's work.

Still later, we enter a discussion of the "realism" of the postulates of rationality. Here, the author raises Milton Friedman's famous article of 1953, and Samuelson's replies. But the important modern discussion of Friedman's alleged instrumentalism and related matters, by economic methodologists such as Lawrence Boland (1981) and Bruce Caldwell (1980, 1983) is simply touched obliquely in a footnote, without developing the issues.

Neither does Hollis really counter one of the central features of Friedman's argument, repeated with eloquence by Fritz Machlup amongst others. This is the idea that the deliberative and calculating aspect of rationality is unimportant; firms are supposed to maximize profits because profit-maximizing firms are the ones that have survived. In my *Economics and Institutions* (1988), I have proposed that this argument does not stand up to critical examination, partly because it is a misapplication of the evolutionary metaphor. The views of Hollis on this issue would have been of interest.

Although the book is written in a clear style which undergraduate students will find useful, the limited number of references and expositions in the text makes it less suitable for student reading. The work presents itself as an isolated discourse written upon a tabula rasa, where in fact it owes a great deal to the authors mentioned in its somewhat patchy bibliography, and many others to boot.

An example is the discussion of unintended consequences; there is no attempt to relate this to the explorations of Marxists, Keynesians, and Austrians on that theme, nor to those that seem to exclude it, such as the behavioralists. Being of relatively modest aims and limited originality—this is not intended as a criticism—the utility of the work would be much increased if it offered some greater guidance through this literature.

However, credit should be given for the intelligence and clarity which pervades this work. It is not without insights and should interest economists in the philosophical underpinnings of what they do.

II

This book is not a comprehensive examination of rationality. There are many issues, such as recent discussions of multiple preferences (Elster, 1986), or of the "paradox of voting" (Margolis, 1982), which receive scant attention. What is of greater concern is the perspective that itself underlies this exploration into rational-choice modeling.

In several passages, the book comes close to, but never reaches, the point of challenging some even more fundamental assumptions its subject. Thus, in one particular discussion, we might raise the question that acting on trust is not acting "for good reason" at all. By taking things on trust, we may not be simply weighing up the costs and benefits of reciprocity; it may be that we are not acting as rational calculators at all. If trust is meaningful, it should exclude a calculus of expected gains or losses.

Likewise, in discussing the formation and maintenance of social norms, or even Simon's notion of satisficing, we may be led to examine the nature and origin of the "decision" rules themselves. In fact, they may not be the result of full calculation or deliberation but of habit or routine: that is, of repetitive behavior that is done simply because it is done, and by chance or intrinsic virtue has survived.

In short, we may be led to challenge what has been called "the rationalist conception of action": the idea that all action is regulated by rational calculation. In trimming our rationalist conceit, we may then find a place for levels of action other than those that are motivated by full, conscious calculation or reasoning.

In this manner, institutional economists such as Thorstein Veblen, and modern writers such as Nelson and Winter (1982) and Anthony Giddens (1984) have emphasized the importance of habits and routines. The latter provide a kind of transmission belt for information which is truly uncodifiable but forms the basis of much social and economic action.

The problem, therefore, is not simply to dwell on the nature of reason but on its limits. Hollis inclines to the classical view of human beings as essentially autonomous and free. To some extent, this may be true, but it cannot be wholly so. The continuity provided by habit and routine is necessary to deal with the complexity of everyday life; excessive and impossible demands would be placed upon reason if every action were a matter of rational calculation.

This perspective involves a radical departure from the dominant views on rationality in both economics and philosophy, Nevertheless, with its economic and sociological antecedents, it is worth considering. Perhaps it is time to challenge more directly the model of rational choice which pervades economics and has spread to other social sciences. Perhaps, even, it is worthy not of awe but of serious concern for the formalistic paralysis that it has created in its wake. Perhaps we may end up with the conclusion that Hollis has been not only too charitable to orthodox economics, but to much of philosophy as well.

REFERENCES

Boland, L. 1981. "On the Futility of Criticizing the Neoclassical Maximization Hypothesis." *American Economic Review* 71:1031-1036.

Caldwell, B.J. 1980. "A Critique of Friedman's Methodological Instrumentalism." *Southern Economic Journal* 47:366-374.

————. 1983. "The Neoclassical Maximization Hypothesis: Comment." *American Economic Review* 73:824-827.

Durkheim, E. 1984. *The Division of Labour in Society*. London: Macmillan.

Elster, J., (ed.). 1986. *The Multiple Self*. Cambridge: Cambridge University Press.

Friedman, M. 1953. "The Methodology of Positive Economics." In M. Friedman, Essays in Positive Economics, edited by M. Friedman. Chicago: University of Chicago Press.

Giddens, A. 1984. *The Constitution of Society: Outline of the Theory of Structration*. Cambridge, UK: Polity Press.

Hodgson, G.M. 1988. *Economics and Institutions: A Manifesto for a Modern Institutional Economics*. Philadelpha: University of Pennsylvania Press.

Margolis, J. 1982. *Selfishness, Altruism and Rationality*. Cambridge: Cambridge University Press.

Nelson, R.R., and S.G. Winter. 1982. *An Evolutionary Theory of Economic Change*. Cambridge: Harvard University Press.

Richardson, G.B. 1959. "Equilibrium, Expectations and Information." *Economic Journal* 69:223-237.

Titmuss, R.M. 1971. *The Gift Relationship: From Human Blood to Social Policy*. London: George Allena and Unwin.

KLAMER, McCLOSKEY, AND SOLOW'S *THE CONSEQUENCES OF ECONOMIC RHETORIC*

Jerry Evensky

The Consequences of Economic Rhetoric
Edited by Arjo Klamer, Donald McCloskey, and Robert Solow.
Cambridge: Cambridge University Press, 1988.

I. INTRODUCTION

Language is the medium within which a community's perspective and standards are defined. It is also the medium through which individuals process and store experience and ideas. Thus, language serves as the medium of exchange between a community's perspectives and standards and an individual's experience and ideas. To the degree that a community determines the language available to an individual, the community acts on the individual. But to the degree that an individual can independently act on language or can borrow

---

Research in the History of Economic Thought and Methodology
Volume 10, pages 245-257.
Copyright © 1992 by JAI Press Inc.
All rights of reproduction in any form reserved.
ISBN: 0-55938-501-4

language from other communities, the individual can act on the community. Since both these actions, community on individual and individual on community, occur simultaneously, the nature of communities and individuals are simultaneously determined.

The Consequences of Economic Rhetoric is the product of a 1986 conference at Wellesley College on the rhetoric of economics. The volume is a fascinating work at two levels. The essays themselves are almost all well-written and thoughtful expressions of individual perspectives on the consequences of economic rhetoric. The sum of the essays, the conversation, reflects the simultaneous determination of community and individual described above. We see in these pages the way in which community shapes an individual's ideas, the way in which an individual can act on language to move a community, and the difficulty of communication among individuals from different communities that speak different languages. In this paper, the essays are reviewed and then the conversation is analyzed.

II. A REVIEW OF THE ESSAYS

The conference was organized by and the volume is edited by Arjo Klamer, Donald McCloskey, and Robert Solow. Given their close identification with the subject and the privileged positions their works occupy in the volume, Klamer and McCloskey seem to be the prime movers behind the project. The volume begins with Klamer and McCloskey issuing a call to all interested scholars, economists in particular, to join in a "new conversation" (p. 3) about the rhetoric of economics. This is the Klamer/McCloskey (hereafter KM) agenda. Such a conversation seems worthy of our attention. Certainly we (economists) can learn something about what we do by examining our rhetoric. The conversation of the economic community, more than any other social science, is dominated by mathematical language. Where did we learn to speak like that? Why did we adopt that language? Our "master metaphor" (p. 14) is the rational-choice model. Again, where did it come from and why do we use it? Being self-conscious about our own conversation can be interesting, enlightening, and may even stimulate fruitful reconstruction of our rhetoric.

Good, good, good, say Klamer and McCloskey. That's the spirit! But that's not the best part. Our conversation about conversation has even more profound implications. Consider: "[A]ll conversations are rhetorical" (p. 13). "Rhetoric is not ornament added on after the substance has been written" (p. 10). There is no capital-T Truth. There are little-t truths, but they are all relative to our conversation. for they are true by definition (e.g., it is 50 degrees out)—they are rhetorical. Rhetoric is all.

Anyone who claims to have discovered the path to Truth is either a fool, a liar, or owns the path and intends to charge you for access if you are foolish enough to follow it. Our new conversation liberates us from that quackery or thievery. There is no path to Truth, no position from which we can see into the mind of God. There is only conversation. Thus, the only way to understand why some beliefs are accepted as warrantable and others are not is to examine rhetoric in order to determine why some arguments succeed and others fail.

The standards? Of course, we will have standards. They will not be imposed on us by some self-appointed priests of Truth. They will emerge from our conversation about conversation. The standard will be: What persuades us? Together, we will decide.

Join us. We offer a better way. Where the old conversations divide us, ours unites us. Where the old conversation is a monologue dictated at us, ours is a dialogue. "A rhetoric of economics examines all the arguments, and encourages admirable goodness in argument all round" (p. 18).

Klamer and McCloskey are calling for a revision of community standards within neoclassical economics. Out with the old (modernist) methodological standards; in with the new standards that will emerge from and evolve with the new conversation. On its face, it appears to be an open invitation to a conversation in which all points of view enter on an equal footing. But that is not the case.

McCloskey has already decided for us that the rhetoric of the Good Old Chicago school is the best way to talk economics. Thus, behind the nominal KM agenda of open and honest conversation lies a hidden agenda: the preservation of the ascendancy of the Chicago community by replacing its shaky epistemological foundation (the modernism McCloskey himself denigrates) with an antiepistemological, rhetorical justification: it must be right because it dominates the conversation. As we will see, exposing this hidden agenda is the point at which Philip Mirowski attacks the KM agenda. Mirowski's is not, however, the most fundamental attack on the KM agenda. That comes from Stanley Fish.

Fish is a member of the community of literary theorists from which Klamer and McCloskey borrow the language on rhetoric. According to Fish, Klamer and McCloskey's entire argument rests on a misappropriation on the language of literary criticism. They have bastardized his community's standards in order to suit their own agenda. It does not work, and the result is a disingenuous argument. Rejecting one priesthood, modernist positivism, they establish another, an "idolized" view of a rhetorical approach (p. 22). Arguing that all conversation reflects the relative positions of the participants, they locate a metaposition that allows us to collectively escape from our individual relativism. Not so, says Fish. There is no escape. To be skeptical of your tacit beliefs, you must escape your relative position. But this contradicts the relativist conception of location. One may intuitively know that one is ideological, but one can not be it and escape it simultaneously. Absent such an escape, the KM agenda lacks any operational value.

In this debate between Fish and KM, we hear echoes of a debate between Joseph Schumpeter and Maurice Dobb. Schumpeter, Dobb, KM, and Fish, all accept "the doctrine of the ubiquity of ideological bias" (Schumpeter, 1954, p. 37). Fish says it "comes with the territory, the territory of being not a machine but a situated human being" (p. 29). For Dobb and for Fish, there is no escape. For Schumpeter and for KM, there is a collective escape. KM finds an escape through the metaconversation; Schumpeter finds it in the development of a neutral "box of tools" (1954, p. 41).

This Schumpeterian faith in a neutral tool kit emerges as the primary theme in the essay by Robert Solow entitled "Comments from Inside Economics." Solow's reaction to the KM agenda is not surprising given his leadership position in the established neoclassical community. In effect, he argues: Don't fix what isn't broken. "Some methods of persuasion [specifically the mathematical and formal statistical techniques that his community holds as the standard of good argument] are more worthy than others. That is what I fear the analogy to conversation tends to bury" (p. 33).

Echoing Schumpeter's view, Solow asserts that, while much of the conversation may be tainted, there are some elements of language, some tools in our rhetorical toolbox, that we can trust for their neutrality. In advocating the abandonment of our current neoclassical rhetorical standards, he says, Klamer and McCloskey "are in grave danger of Going Too Far" (p. 32).

Solow's concern about the KM agenda is that unlike our old trusty tools, the "practice of rhetorical analysis" is not neutral. It can "easily be biased with respect to substance" (p. 35). In his view, we ignore this distinction between rhetoric in general and our neutral tools in particular at our peril. Of course, the strength of Solow's criticism rests on the sturdiness of this distinction.

Solow follows Schumpeter's route to escape from relativism. Unfortunately for both men, Dobb makes a strong case that this route is no escape. It is a dead end. Dobb's (1973) case rests on two points. First, any neutral tool is sterile. If one could get down to a truly neutral "corpus," it would be so devoid of substantive social content as to be uninteresting as social theory (Dobb, 1973, p. 11). Second, any subset of tools has a nonneutral influence on the model one builds. The very choice of tools, be they neutral or not, has nonneutral consequences since different tools lead to different sites and forms of construction (pp. 6-7).

Robert Heilbroner joins the conversation about conversation with his essay on "Rhetoric and Ideology." His concern is that in focusing on the rhetoric of conversation, our attention is deflected from its content. Better we should spend our time examining the questions we ask, because it is at that first stage that ideology enters the conversation. Focusing on the rhetoric of our answers can obscure the ideology embodied in our questions.

Stephen Resnick and Richard Wolff represent the Marxian community at this conversation about conversation. As with politics, rhetorical analysis makes for strange bedfellows, for Resnick and Wolff are fellow travelers along the KM program's antifoundationalist path. Or at least they travel a parallel route.

Resnick and Wolff point out that "there are...significant differences, since our position emerges from the Marxian tradition while theirs does not" (p. 47). For example, coming from a different community, they use a different language to converse about conversation. They speak of "overdetermination" (theories "are not ... determined by facts or by acts of reason," they are overdetermined by the fact that everything—"climate, diet, cultural fashions"— matters [p. 48]) and "constitutivity" (Everything is simultaneous, so any "entry point" is artificial.) (pp. 48, 52-54). With these concepts, they construct the argument that no theory starts from a privileged position since all entry points are artificial; and all theories are "stories built around particular emphasis on aspects of society deemed worthy of theoretical attention" (p. 53), because no theory can encompass everything.

As stories with artificial premises, theories are clearly not about Truth. Thus, the objective of theory cannot be Truth. It is victory. Or, in KM terms, it is persuasion. And which theory, according to Resnick and Wolff, should be victorious? The one with the broadest entry point and the most desirable consequences. Which theory might that be? Surprise: It is Marxist theory.

Resnick and Wolff's argument seems as disingenuous as its neoclassical counterpart, the KM program. As with Klamer and McCloskey, it seems that Resnick and Wolff are primarily interested in using the rhetorical argument to establish a metaposition from which they can claim priority for their own community's belief system. Resnick and Wolff claim that a broad point of entry, class, makes Marxist theory less reductionist than neoclassical theory. They fail to recognize that a broad point is an oxymoron. Once you are reductionist, whether Marxist or neoclassical, you are reductionist. Furthermore, Resnick and Wolff set up consequence as a criterion when they explicitly note that theory cannot predict. The result is an internal contradiction. One must choose among theories ex ante based on the criterion of consequence, and yet no theory can predict.

A.W. Coats rejects the grandiose claims of these rhetorical campaigns. Instead, he recommends "a more direct and conventional sociological approach" (p. 65) to understand how scientific communities' systems of belief are established and evolve. Coats does not reject the conversation about conversation. In fact he applauds it as "promising, even exciting" (p. 64). What he does reject is the KM campaign's adamant assignment of "privileged status to discourse" (p. 79). If our discourse is limited to an analysis of our rhetoric, we are participants in a conversation about conversation "virtually without reference to what is 'out there' in the world" (p. 66). Such a conversation is not only unscientific, it is anti-scientific in its rejection of "the collective quest for 'reliable' intersubjective knowledge that has created the broader scientific community..." (p. 66).

Refusing to be drawn into McCloskey's self-serving representation of the choices: It is me or muddle-headed modernism; Coats describes the strength of the sociology-of-knowledge approach and provides examples of its value. Its strength lies in its recognition that all conceptions of reality are community constructions and thus inevitably relative. At the same time, it does not trivialize such conceptions as "either arbitrary or lax... [or] static" (p. 68).

Coats demonstrates the value of such an approach by reflecting the light it can shed on historical periods, such as Alfred "Marshall's remarkable influence on British economics in the half century or so following his inaugural" (p. 75), and on issues, such as the perpetually troubling overlap and interdependence between the "internal and external sociology of economics" (p. 70).

This internal/external tension in the sociology of economics is the point of departure for Robert Clower's essay on "The Ideas of Economics." Clower suggests that one source of this tension is the divergence between appearance and reality. The lay audience does not recognize the distinction, but the good scientist does. As a result, says Clower, the scientist is constantly engaged in writing stories that "seem unnatural, artificial, and offensive to common sense" (p. 87).

Is this bad? Clower's response is: No, this comes with the territory when one joins the scientific community. But what about the layperson's desire for relevance, for policy prescriptions? Clower's response is: He'll just have to be patient. We are doing the best we can. "Economics has, I think, a great future as a science that produces results" (p. 98).

The heart of Clower's article is a description of the scientific process built around community story building. Scientists "search for 'order in nature'...[by] choosing a set of facts and weaving them into a story..." (p. 89). Since nature is seldom "gracious" enough to make connections simple, scientists use assumptions to think away "extraneous complications" (p. 90). Ergo, the divergence between theory and reality.

Clower credits Galileo with establishing this scientific approach. He notes that "this kind of community enterprise could not long be sustained unless all scholars engaged in it subscribed to certain common ground rules governing the arrangement, analysis, communication of ideas among themselves" (p. 90). This emphasis on community echoes a theme that we have heard in the work of all the contributors reviewed thus far.

What sets Clower apart is his belief that a given community's story, in particular neoclassical theory, is moving in the correct direction and will "produce results" when "factual knowledge" is "available in sufficient detail" (p. 97). This suggests that facts drive theory. But Clower himself acknowledges that "what we are able to see by looking at 'the facts' depends in an essential way on what we expect to see before we look at them" (p. 93). So it seems that we never really "see" facts with an unbiased eye. Furthermore, given his own description of scientists as selecting "from an infinity of possible facts" (p. 87), it is hard to imagine how facts can provide a basis for any community's claim to a privileged position with respect to knowledge.

Christina Bicchieri closes the volume's conversation on the conversation about conversation (parts I and II) with an essay that poses a basic question about the scientific conversation: "Should a scientist abstain from metaphor?" Her answer is no. Not only should scientists use metaphor, they must if science is to be a dynamic enterprise. She sees the question itself as based on a false dichotomy: language is either literal or figurative. In her view, this "separation is too narrow and ultimately impairs our understanding of science." For Bicchieri, literal and figurative are "two poles of a continuum..." (p. 101).

In fact, a given metaphor can move along that continuum. It may enter the discourse as a figurative, heuristic device. If, however, it becomes "entrenched" (p. 105) in the theory; that is to say, if it takes on a cognitive function as a "number of features" of the theory come to "depend upon it" (p. 105), then the metaphor has moved toward the literal end of the continuum. It is this opportunity to play with metaphor, sloughing off some and entrenching others, that gives a scientific community the "capability of opening new problems and indicating research avenues." (p. 112). Clearly, a negative answer to the question she poses in her title would constrain the capacity of a scientific community to grow.

Two themes emerge from this conversation on the conversation about conversation. One has to do with continuity, the other with change. There is a consensus that community is the locus of control with respect to standards. According to K.M., communities impose a discipline on their conversation— "The discipline is: If you don't use it [our standards], out you go"— (p. 14). And yet, as Coats points out, while a scientific community may value "order, continuity, authority and control," no such community is static (p. 68). Communities evolve, they are revolutionized; they come and go. How much language matters in this course of events is the issue of the debate. What is not at issue is that language does matter. As Bicchieri makes clear, acting on language is an fundamental tool in moving a community (as Ricardo did), in revolutionizing a community (as Keynes did), or in forming a community (as Marx did).

Parts III and IV of this volume explore, respectively, the internal and external sociology of economics from the perspective of language. This is an important application of what we learn in the first two parts. Philip Mirowski opens part III of the volume with an analysis of the relationship between neoclassical theory and McCloskey's agenda. His analysis is a sociological one that uses language as its entry point.

Mirowski traces the origins of neoclassical rhetoric back to the Cartesian idea "that the conviction of certainty arose from introspective knowledge, mathematical expression, and the reduction of all epiphenomena of the world to a few simple rules of motion" (p. 119). This view was embodied in the mathematical metaphor of 19th century classical physics and that metaphor was then adopted by neoclassical theory "lock, stock, and barrel" (p. 130). Unfortunately for neoclassical theory, it adopted a "progressively discredited conception of science" (p. 122) as the metaphor around which to build its model.

This cognitive dissonance, scientific true believers worshipping a model constructed around a discredited scientific metaphor, required resolution. How could the metaphor and the model both be saved? Out of Chicago via Iowa comes McCloskey with a novel argument: the "Cartesian model of economic man can be justified with an anti-Cartesian paradigm" (p. 122). It is all so simple: We begin by rejecting the notion that the metaphor has any literal content (a leap from one side of Bicchieri's dichotomy to the other). This insulates it from any notion of its connection to a reality. Then we turn to the metaphor to save itself. Why do we like it? Because it is the winner in the market, and in the absence of any direct access to Truth, we must go with the winner.

Mirowski offers us an excellent analysis of how the neoclassical community formed and how McCloskey has attempted to act on the language of science in order to preserve that (his own) community. Mirowski rejects McCloskey's effort on several counts. First, he considers McCloskey's market test a neoclassical example of realpolitik: The party controls the market; lo and behold, most people buy the party product; the party obviously has the best product. Mirowski also rejects McCloskey's agnosticism with respect to reality. Mirowski makes the case that rhetorical technique cannot be imposed on a subject but, rather, must interact with the subject. Thus, the subject must have an existence independent of the rhetoric. For example, Mirowski writes that since "mathematics appears to 'resist' the original drive to unify the subject matter,... [this fosters] the impression that it exists independent of the objectives and choices of the researcher" (p. 128).

Another example of how an economic community evolved as individuals acted on its language is presented in E. Roy Weintraub's essay "On the Brittleness of the Orange Equilibrium." He traces the evolution of the meaning of the word equilibrium "in a sequence of papers published between 1939 and 1954" (p. 146). Following this concept from Hicks through Samuelson to Arrow and Debreu, Weintraub demonstrates that "the meaning of the word is dependent on the players of the game and the rules they decide to play by at a particular moment in the history of economic thought" (p. 154). His analysis provides an excellent example of a theme that emerges in the volume: Language may act as a constraint on the thinking of a scientific community, but by acting on language one can move such a community.

Frank Denton does with the concept of "significance" in statistical hypothesis testing as Weintraub does with "equilibrium." Denton traces the history of statistical hypothesis testing, provides an excellent overview of the logic of the approach, and examines the problems that emerge as community-based standards of significance are determined. In particular, he offers a thoughtful critique of "information filtering" (p. 174). Such filtering occurs because there is a community bias for results that reject the null hypothesis. As Denton points out, this bias affects journal acceptances and creates an information feedback that affects the behavior of the individual researcher. Here again, we find the interaction among community standards, language, and individual behavior to be strong.

In the opinion of Nancy Folbre and Heidi Hartmann, nowhere is this relationship stronger than with respect to the gender bias of economic theory. Folbre and Hartmann bring the perspective of the feminist community to the conversation. They argue that this perspective is ignored by "[m]ost economists [who] seem persuaded that gender inequalities lie beyond the purview of economic analysis" (p. 184). This presumption is at the heart of both neoclassical and Marxist theory, embedded there by entrenched metaphors. In neoclassical theory, it is the metaphor of rational economic man. In Marxist theory, it is the metaphor of class. Pick your poison, the result is the same: Women are invisible, subsumed within the common interest of their neoclassical household or their Marxist class. The male-dominated economics communities do not see that there is another dimension to human society beyond household or class: gender. Thus, there is no way they can conceptualize the possibility that differences in choice can be explained along that third dimension, as well as along the first two.

Folbre and Hartmann believe that this is no oversight. They argue "[t]hat economic self-interest has influenced the way economists think about the concept of self-interest" (p. 185). It is a rent-seeking argument, and it works: Clearly, if the models subsume the voice of a well-defined group, then that group (women) has no voice. One less voice makes it easier for those not silenced (men) to be heard. To be heard is to have power. To have power is to enjoy a larger piece of the pie. Thus, men enjoy a rent based on their control of, and exclusion of gender from, the language of economic models.

Part IV of the volume includes papers on the relationship of communities within economics to those outside, or the external sociology of economics. Craufurd Goodwin's essay provides an excellent introduction to the issue by setting the sociological scene. According to Goodwin, economists face three audiences: "colleagues and clients... [and] a lay audience" (p. 209). Each audience requires a different "rhetorical posture": "scholar, practitioner, and interpreter or alternatively as (1) philosopher, (2) priest, and (3) hired gun" (p. 209). Goodwin identifies the different metaphors that seem to be associated with each posture (e.g., physics (à la Mirowski) for internal consumption and biology or warfare for external consumption), and notes the difficulty and opportunity that comes with this complex sociology. The difficulty is fairly obvious. Speaking in several languages requires translation, and things can get lost or obscured in translation. The opportunity Goodwin points to is an excellent example of the creative potential language embodies. He argues that stepping outside their own community and speaking with a lay audience offers economists a place where they "can let their minds soar and where they may visualize problems in ways that, at the moment, their profession prohibits" (p. 219).

In his essay on "The Rhetoric of Economics as Viewed by a Student of Politics," Robert Keohane makes a plea to economists to seize the opportunity Goodwin identifies. Keohane is a member of the political science community who describes himself as "sympathetic to the use of rational choice axioms" (p. 241). He wants to work with economists in applying these axioms. But his experience is that economists do not want to converse, they want to "preach" (p. 240). To make matters worse, they preach a very narrow version of the rational-choice model, one built not only on the axiom of rational choice, but also on the axiom that "there is no accounting for tastes" (p. 242). Keohane's plea to economists is: Liberate yourselves. Open up the mind of your community and speak with us as equals. Don't preach *at* us. We, political scientists as well as sociologists and anthropologists, believe "societies select" tastes (p. 243). Speak with each other as you wish, but when you speak with us, do not discount our views.

James K. Galbraith also offers advice to economists on how to approach an external audience, in particular, a political audience. Based on his experience as executive director of the Joint Economic Committee, he provides a fascinating insight into the culture of the Congressional community, and advice on how an economist must adapt his language if he is to succeed in speaking to that community persuasively.

David Warsh, a journalist with the Boston Globe, closes part IV with a review of "Some Rhetoric that Failed." He cites and examines two cases: "the saga of yellow rain" (p. 255) and supply-side economics. The moral of the story seems to be that rhetoric alone will not carry a story. He claims that in both cases, science was victorious over rhetoric.

At this point in the volume, the invited participants have had their say. In the final two chapters, Klamer and then McCloskey reflect on what they learned from the conversation about conversation at the conference.

The conference seems to have moved Klamer. He spends eight pages giving his impression of what went on at the conference and then, under the subtitle "Further Negotiation," he writes: "While writing this interpretation I have become painfully aware of shortcomings in 'rhetoric' and 'conversation' as metaphors for what we do.... It occurred to me that the interactions during the conference resembled a negotiation .... It seems to me now that 'negotiation' is a better metaphor than 'rhetoric' or 'conversation'... Negotiations can result in some kind of compromise; they can also break down" (p. 273).

He closes his essay with "A Manifesto" in which he writes: "I have come to recognize that those of us who are eager to advance the new conversation may overlook the contributions of conventional methodology. The investigation of the logic of economic theories is important and we may not need to deny the realism of scientific objects" (p. 277).

A retreat? No. It sounds more like an entreaty to negotiate. Klamer seems to be saying: OK, I hear you—and some of what you say makes sense. Let us keep talking. Let us negotiate. The alternative is a breakdown in the conversation. Let us not let that happen.

Finally, we receive "The Last Word" from McCloskey. It is predictable. The last word, the first word, and all of McCloskey's words in between are constructed with the same set of metaphors, making the same argument. It goes something like this: My approach offers us all a better place to stand. Why is it better? Because it is not modernism. Because it is "thick and rich and nourishing" (p. 283). These folks who disagree with me are typical of "economists with an interest in philosophical methodology" (291). They do not understand because they are invested in their position and cannot or will not look beyond it. "The working stiffs among economists [would] nod their heads and say, 'why sure, of course.'" (p. 291), if I could just get them to listen. For now I wage my battle alone. If Klamer wants to negotiate, that is his business. Mine is the "principled" (p. 285) position. I do not believe good can compromise with evil, and maintain itself.

So the volume ends as it begins, with McCloskey standing in his presumed privileged position looking down on those who do not have his vision and cannot see that his place is closer to, albeit not in, the mind of God.

III.   CONCLUSION: AN ANALYSIS OF THE CONVERSATION AND ITS LESSONS

Now that everyone has had his or her say, we can say some things about the conversation as a whole. Several things seem clear: Language is the medium thorough which community perspectives and standards are defined. An individual's membership in a given community is reflected in the language he uses. Communities evolve and/or are formed as individuals act on language.

If everything is relative; if, as Fish makes the case, there is no metaposition either methodological or rhetorical that establishes the priority of one argument over another, where do we find our standards? I believe the answer lies in a concept Coats introduces to the conversation: "intersubjective knowledge" (p. 66). If the ideas that emerge from a given scientific community's perspective and standards fit in well with those of other communities working in related areas, if such *independent* communities develop complementary ideas: that is impressive. It does not imply Truth. But it does establish a basis for warrantable belief.

Such a standard also seems to have "cash value." Currently, each independent social-science community seeks Truth through an ever more sophisticated reading and rendering of their respective bibles. In place of this modern scholasticism, the standard of intersubjective knowledge would encourage, indeed it would require, successful conversation (i.e., talking and *listening*) across community boundaries. This would be so because no community could establish the credibility of its ideas independently. For example, it would require neoclassical economists to set aside their dreams of imperial conquest.[1] Instead, they would have to converse with their fellow social scientists, like Keohane, as equals. Similarly, it would behoove the neoclassical and Marxist communities to take each other and the feminist community more seriously. If they would listen, they might surprise themselves and discover some common ground.

Intersubjective knowledge seems to be a good candidate for a standard of warrantable belief, but it is not perfect. Its flaw lies in its practical application. To meet the theoretical standard, the intersection of ideas must be among *independent* communities. The communities involved must arrive at the common ground by honest intellectual triangulation, not by collusion for mutual benefit. The encouraging thing about the standard is that collusion among autonomous groups makes for a very unstable coalition. Thus, while the standard may be imitated, such imitation will probably not have much staying power.

Klamer, McCloskey, and Solow are to be complemented for convening a conversation that included representatives from so many different communities. If we can establish an incentive structure that encourages participants in such a conversation to actually listen to one another, the conversation might lead us to some common ground.

The standard of intersubjective knowledge does not provide an escape from relativism. It does, however, create an incentive to listen to one another. As such, it offers a possible escape from the parochialism that currently pervades the social sciences.

NOTE

1. Jack Hirschleifer writes in a 1985 *American Economic Review* article that "[w]hat gives economics its imperialist invasive power is that our [(the neoclassical community's)] analytical categories ... are *truly* [emphasis added] universal in applicability" (p. 53). Echoes of Schumpeter and Solow.

REFERENCES

Dobb, Maurice. 1973. *Theories of Value and Distribution Since Adam Smith: Ideology and Economic Theory.* Cambridge: Cambridge University Press.

Hirshleifer, Jack. 1985. "The Expanding Domain of Economics." *American Economic Review.* 75(6, December): 53-68.

Schumpeter, Joseph Alois. 1954. *History of Economic Analysis.* Edited by Elizabeth Schumpeter. New York: Oxford University Press.

LOASBY'S *THE MIND AND METHOD OF THE ECONOMIST*

Evelyn L. Forget

The Mind and Method of the Economist.
By Brian J. Loasby.
Aldershot, Hants: Edward Elgar, 1989.

> There are those with burning convictions in the virtues of "small" models and in the absolute need for "full" models; in the uselessness of mathematics in economics and in its absolute necessity; in the need to postulate "market clearing" and in the meaninglessness of this postulate; in rational expectations models and in the madness of such models; in the absolute need for historical and institutional elements and in a purely analytical approach; in short run analysis and in long run analysis; in the uselessness of all theorising and in the uselessness of econometrics and fact collection; in short, in almost anything that has ever been tried. In fact all these "certainties" and all the "schools" which they spawn are a sure sign of our ignorance.... [I]t is obvious to me that we do not possess much certain knowledge about the economic world and that our best chance of gaining more is to try in all sorts of directions and by all sorts of means. (Hahn, 1984, 7-8)

The twelve essays included in *The Mind and Method of The Economist* investigate "the variety of perceptions and analyses of economic issues, and

Research in the History of Economic Thought and Methodology
Volume 10, pages 259-264.
Copyright © 1992 by JAI Press Inc.
All rights of reproduction in any form reserved.
ISBN: 0-55938-501-4

the evolution of ways of dealing with them" (p. vi). But the author of *Choice, Complexity and Ignorance* (1976) has, as we might have expected, attempted to do a great deal more than his modest claim suggests. By emphasizing particular aspects of theories generally regarded as non-Walrasian, Loasby has articulated part of the tradition behind current attempts to develop an analysis of the process of equilibration.

Over the past century, economic science has become increasingly identified with neo-Walrasian general equilibrium analysis; we have a rigorous tradition which examines the characteristics of equilibrium under alternative market structures, contract possibilities, and information sets. As Hahn has acknowledged, "GE is strong on equilibrium and very weak on how it comes about. It is a fair generalisation to say that the theory has proved so far less helpful in studying processes whether of decisions or of information or of organisation" (Hahn, 1984, p. 140). The economists who have asked, instead, how equilibrium might be achieved, have not succeeded in constructing a single and coherent theoretical edifice capable of either competing with, or supplementing, elegant, rigorous, and general neo-Walrasian models.

One of the explanations for this apparent failure is the shared belief (perhaps the only shared belief) that any general theory must be too general to be useful:

> There is no one spot sufficiently firm to allow us to apply sufficient leverage on all our problems. There are several spots each of which will serve very well for more modest ambitions (p. 208).

But this emphasis on "partial" models, which allows a richness of institutional detail not present in a general theory, comes at a cost. To date, there has been no shared tradition upon which to build; so many theorists, with so many similar (but not identical) insights, start from scratch. The result has been a collection of disparate attempts to come to grips with the problem of equilibration, each focusing on how it differs from Arrow-Debreu models, rather than on how it relates to other analyses of equilibration processes. Loasby's book is a much-needed attempt to build a unifying tradition; it emphasizes "connecting principles" and recognizes the need to "search for consensus over the widest possible field" (pp. 197-198):

> A unified framework facilitates the process of scientific discovery by increasing the efficiency of the communication system. It does so by constraining thought; this is essential, but dangerous. (p. 199).

The trade-off is a delicate one; Loasby believes "there are enough 'connecting principles', to use Adam Smith's phrase, to support a reasonably coherent, though imperfectly specified, system of thought which allows for shifts between [research programmes]" (p. 208).

The author claims that "declining confidence in the adequacy of neoclassical economic analysis has provided an opportunity for advocates of other approaches to compete in the intellectual market" (155), and this collection draws together complementary themes which have emerged from the work of a heterogeneous collection of twentieth-century economists. All of the essays in this volume are critical of the fundamental role played by rational choice in an economic theory that systematically considers neither the limitations of human knowledge, nor the role played by evolving organizations and markets in generating and modifying knowledge. Rational economic agents often face problems of discovery and creation, where the notion of constrained choice from a completely specified set of alternatives is meaningless. Economic agents, argues Loasby, behave as scientists rather than optimizers, seeking new knowledge and creating new problems which will, in turn, shape any equilibrium toward which the system may be tending, along with the institutional framework which characterizes it.

The analogy Loasby draws between economic agents operating in the marketplace, and scientists working within research organizations and universities explains the otherwise puzzling inclusion of the first three papers in this volume. "George Shackle's history of Economic Theory" is a sympathetic treatment of Shackle's attempt, in *The Years of High Theory* (1983), to unravel the development of economic theory between 1926 and 1939. By 1914, Shackle argued, a Great Theory had emerged, in which self-interest operating in the context of a complete set of markets ensured that prices and outputs could be understoood as a general equilibrium between "the subjective factors of human wants and the objective constraints of resources and technology" (p. 6). The simplicity of the synthesis was, however, soon undermined by Keynesian economics and analyses of imperfect competition. But the real value of Shackle's work, according to Loasby, is its potential for creating "a general theory of knowledge which seems capable of very wide application: in particular it can help us to interpret economic processes" (p. 14)—the theme that preoccupies Loasby throughout this volume.

"On Scientific Method" is an exposition of the growth of scientific knowledge from the perspectives of Popper, Kuhn, and Lakatos. "Public Science and Public Knowledge" considers the creation of abstract theory as a competitive social process. Both essays build upon the analogy between the creation of economic theory and the growth of market knowledge, and Loasby emphasizes the common absence of an "assured means of eliminating error" (p. 44). These methodological chapters set the stage for what may be regarded as the heart of the book.

Any analysis of the process of equilibration, in which agents learn about the economy in an uncertain environment, must begin with Marshall. "Knowledge and Organization: Marshall's Theory of Economic Progress and Coordination" quite correctly asserts that "the twin themes [of Book IV of the

Principles] are the effects of the growth of knowledge on organization and costs of production, and the effects of the organization of production on the growth of knowledge.... [I]t is the manufacturer supplying the general market who is supposed to be represented by the perfectly competitive firm of later theory, and, in that theory, it is certainly no part of his business—still less the business of his senior managers—to be introducing either novel products or novel methods. But, for Marshall, that is precisely what he is expected to do. Marshallian competition is a Hayekian discovery process" (pp. 54-55). Moreover, Loasby correctly locates the origin of Marshall's analysis of competition as a disequilibrium adjustment process in classical theory (p. 48). Marshall's competitive analysis is firmly based upon an institutional network; the outcome depends upon the characteristics of a particular market. It is hardly surprising that when Marshall then turns to equilibrium modeling in Book V, his analysis lacks the elegance and simplicity we have come to associate with Walrasian models. Whether he considers temporary, short-run, or long-run equilibrium, Marshall considers the process of equilibration and includes a warning about the limitations of static equilibrium analysis in a world of time and uncertainty, when new and unanticipated products and methods are generated by the economic process itself (Marshall, 1961, pp. 460-461). This theme is further developed in "The Working of a Competitive Economy: G. B. Richardson's post-Marshallian Analysis," where Loasby argues that Richardson's too-long neglected work is the true progeny of Marshall's *Principles*.

In "Joan Robinson's 'Wrong Turning,'" Loasby suggests that *The Economics of Imperfect Competition* (1969) abandonned Marshall's competitive analysis. He asserts that "economists were so impressed with the power of the equilibrium method that they began to enquire whether Marshall had made the best use of it" (p. 69). Concluding that he had not, the response was to reformulate Marshall's analysis as a theory of perfect competition. The stage was then set for Sraffa's demonstration that long-run equilibrium was incompatible with increasing returns (Sraffa, 1926; cf. Negishi, 1985, p. 45), and Robinson's subsequent development of the analysis of imperfect competition.

These three chapters suggest a number of "connecting principles"—themes which may prove valuable in the construction of an equilibration analysis. The considerations which Loasby emphasizes include:

1. The recognition that historical, as distinct from logical, time is fundamental to disequilibrium analysis. Loasby takes this statement beyond its usual rhetorical role by clarifying his meaning: "an economy known to be subject to exogenous shocks is an economy for which the list of future states, and therefore the list of contingent commodities, cannot be completed" (p. 100). That is, an analysis in time is an analysis which takes fundamental uncertainty

(as opposed to selective ignorance) seriously. It is also an analysis in which institutions develop and change, and information arrives and is (often imperfectly) processed (Hahn, 1984, pp. 138-139).

2. Such an analysis requires a consideration of non-perfect competition. Competition must be regarded as a process during which economic agents learn something about their evolving markets, and their actual and potential competitors. Atomistic competition is inadequate; firms recognize their interdependence, even in markets with large numbers, and know that their behavior will have consequences. Perfect competition imposes knowledge requirements which are both too stringent and too lenient to be useful in a disequilibrium analysis: agents are assumed to have perfect knowledge of all price offers anywhere in the system so that the unique price vector which will clear the market can be calculated and treated as axiomatic, and yet they are assumed to expect the present set of prices and commodities to persist indefinitely, despite considerable evidence (and effort) to the contrary.

3. Pervasive ignorance and satisficing behavior should not be regarded as market imperfections, but the norm.

4. Market imperfections, in general, are not impediments to equilibrium as much as they are fundamental requirements for the economy to function at all. Market connections and implicit collusion may help to coordinate activities in a stochastic economy in which the future is unknown. Similarly, imperfect credit markets ensure that those firms which have guessed correctly in the past are given the best opportunity to react to current opportunities. While undermining optimality, this is one method by which "reasonable" allocation decisions can be made in an uncertain world.

5. Since behavior must be based upon expectations formed without the possibility of perfect knowledge, information requirements may be reduced by the existence of institutions which allow the actions of other people to be tolerably well predicted most of the time. "Economies are stabilized by their institutions, in the widest sense of that word: by the recognizable sets of decision premises which are embodied in the roles and conventions of the social (including of course the industrial) system" (p. 149).

The next five chapters consider the potential of various schools of thought to contribute to the analysis of equilibration. Managerial theories, developed by Baumol, Williamson, and Marris, are dismissed as a "diversion." While they redefine the objective function of managers, all these theories are still designed as full-information rational-decision models, and therefore have little to offer an analysis based upon "sensible" (as opposed to optimal) behaviour in a situation of imperfect information. "Frank Hahn's 'Struggle of Escape'" is a critical, yet sympathetic, analysis of the intellectual maturation of a preeminent general-equilibrium theorist, who has come increasingly to recognize the limitations of the Walrasian analysis he has done so much to develop. Loasby avoids the too-easy identification of Hahn with all that is sterile in modern economic theory, and yet he (unlike Hahn) remains unconvinced that an analysis of equilibration can be constructed upon a neo-Walrasian foundation. The greatest intellectual virtue of "Herbert Simon's human rationality" is found, according to Loasby, in its lack of generality. While fundamentally interested in processes, Simon does not absolutely reject equilibrium analysis because he regards every model as an incomplete representation of the phenomenon to be investigated (p. 142). Finally, various brands of Austrian economics associated with Hayek, Kirzner, Lachman, O'Driscoll, and Rizzo are evaluated: "the prime inherent virtue of Austrian economics, with its emphasis on subjective assessments and incompletable knowledge, is that it is intellectually an open system. Not everyone likes open systems.... The inherent tendency of neoclassical economics, by contrast, is to force closure, and reach determinateness, or at least the near-determinateness of stationary distributions. The reward is an immensely superior technical apparatus to anything the Austrians have produced" (pp. 166-167).

The Mind and Method of the Economist is not an elegant book. It is a useful book which attempts to draw out the coherent elements in a body of work which is more apparently diverse than uniform. Its goal is similar to Negishi's Economic Theories in a Non-Walrasian Tradition (1985), which aimed "to study economic theories of the past that are not directly related to this Walrasian mainstream, so that we can develop boldly new economic theories that are heretical to the currently prevailing theory" (Negishi, 1985, p. 1). As such, it should encourage communication and help to create the scholarly networks which make theoretical development more efficient. (There is, however, a certain irony in the fact that Loasby does not refer to Negishi.) And it is an optimistic book, concluding that a nonequilibrium research program—despite its lack of rigor—shows promise. Most of all, it is a reliable book, based upon a sensible analysis. Is there a higher accolade?

REFERENCES

Hahn, F. 1984. Equilibrium and Macroeconomics. Oxford: Basil Blackwell.
Loasby, B.J. 1976. Choice, Complexity and Ignorance. Cambridge:. Cambridge University Press.
Marshall, A. 1961. Principles of Economics. 9th (variorum) edn., 2 vols. London: Macmillan.
Negishi, T. 1985. Economic theories in a non-Walrasian tradition. Cambridge: Cambridge University Press.
Robertson, D. H. 1930. "Symposium on Increasing Returns and the Representative Firm. The Trees of the Forest," Economic Journal 60: 80-92.
Robinson, J. V. 1969. The Economics of Imperfect Competition. 2nd. ed. London: Macmillan.
Shackle, G. L. S. 1983. The Years of High Theory: Invention and Tradition in Economic Thought 1926-1939. Cambridge: Cambridge University Press.
Sraffa, P. 1926. "The Laws of Return under Competitive Conditions," Economic Journal 36: 535-550.

NEW BOOKS RECEIVED

Abbott, Andrew. *The System of Professions: An Essay on the Division of Expert Labor.* Chicago: University of Chicago Press, 1988. Pp. xvi, 435. $19.95. paper.

Adas, Michael. *Machines as the Measure of Man: Science, Technology, and Ideologies of Western Dominance.* New York: Cambridge University Press, 1989. Pp. xiv, 430. $29.95.

Altman, Andrew. *Critical Legal Studies: A Liberal Critique.* Princeton: Princeton University Press, 1990. Pp. ix, 206. $26.50.

Babe, Robert E. *Telecommunications in Canada.* Toronto: University of Toronto Press, 1990. Pp. xv, 363. $50.00, cloth: $24.95, paper.

Balzer, Wolfgang, and Bert Hamminga, eds. *Philosophy of Economics.* Boston: Kluwer Academic Publishers, 1989. Pp. 270. $69.00.

Barber, Bernard. *Social Studies of Science.* New Brunswick: Transaction. 1990. Pp. viii, 278. $34.95.

Barreto, Humberto. *The Entrepreneur in Microeconomic Theory: Disappearance and Explanation.* New York: Routledge, Chapman & Hall, 1989. Pp. xii, 156. $35.00.

Barry, Norman P. *An Introduction to Modern Political Theory.* 2nd ed. New York: St. Martin's Press, 1989. Pp. xviii, 309. $39.95, cloth; $14.95, paper.

Bartlett, Randall. *Economics and Power: An Inquiry into Human Relations and Markets.* New York: Cambridge University Press, 1989. Pp. xi, 209. $32.50.

Research in the History of Economic Thought and Methodology
Volume 10, pages 265-272.
Copyright © 1992 by JAI Press Inc.
All rights of reproduction in any form reserved.
ISBN: 0-55938-501-4

Barnard, Georges. *Principia Economica*. Boston: Kluwer Academic Publishers, 1989. Pp. xix, 313. $89.00.

Best, Joel, ed. *Images of Issues: Typifying Contemporary Social Problems*. New York: Aldine de Gruyter, 1989. Pp. xxii, 257.

Biven, W. Carl. *Who Killed John Maynard Keynes?* Homewood: Irwin, 1989. Pp. x, 212. Paper.

Blalock, Hubert M., Jr. *Power and Conflict: Toward a General Theory*. Newbury Park: Sage, 1989. Pp. x. 266. $35.00, cloth; $16.95, paper.

Blumer, Herbert. *Industrialization as an Agent of Social Change: A Critical Analysis*. David R. Maines and Thomas J. Morrione, eds. New York: Aline de Gruyter, 1990. Pp. xxiv, 171. $37.95, cloth; $17.95, paper.

Boland, Lawrence A. *The Methodology of Economic Model Building*. New York: Routledge, 1989. Pp. 194. $45.00.

Bosanquet, Nick. *After the New Right*. Brookfield, VT: Gower-Dartmouth, 1989. Pp. 211. $14.95, paper.

Boudon, Raymond, and Francois Bourricaud. *A Critical Dictionary of Sociology*. Peter Hamilton, trans. Chicago: University of Chicago Press. 1989. Pp. xiii, 438. $49.95.

Boulding, Kenneth E. *Three Faces of Power*. Newbury Park: Sage, 1989. Pp. 259. $28.00.

Bourgin, Frank. *The Great Challenge: The Myth of Laissez Faire in the Early Republic*. New York: Harper & Row, 1989. Pp. xxiv, 246. $8.95, paper.

Briggs, John C. *Francis Bacon and the Rhetoric of Nature*. Cambridge: Harvard University Press, 1989. Pp. xvi, 285.

Buck, James R. *Economic Risk Decisions in Engineering and Management*. Ames: Iowa State University Press, 1989. Pp. xii, 456. $44.95.

Burk, Robert F. *The Corporate State and the Broker State: The Du Ponts and American National Politics, 1925-1940*. Cambridge: Harvard University Press, 1990. Pp. xi, 359.

Clary, Marjorie, and Keith Lehrer, eds. *Knowledge and Skepticism*. Boulder: Westview Press, 1989. Pp. xviii, 186. $38.50, cloth; $15.95, paper.

Clegg, Stewart R. *Frameworks of Power*. Newbury Park: Sage, 1989. Pp. xix, 297. $49.95, cloth; $18.95, paper.

Colander, David, and A.W. Coats, eds. *The Spread of Economic Ideas*. New York: Cambridge University Press, 1989. Pp. xvi, 262.

Collins, Stephen L. *From Divine Cosmos to Sovereign State: An Intellectual History of Consciousness and the Idea of Order in Renaissance England*. New York: Oxford University Press, 1989. Pp. ix, 235. $39.95.

Commons, John R. *Institutional Economics: Its Place in Political Economy*. New introduction by Malcom Rutherford. 2 vls. Brunswick: Transaction Books, 1990. Pp. xxxix, 1-648; 649-921.

Conley, John M., and William M. O'Barr. *Rules Versus Relationships: The Ethnography of Legal Discourse.* Chicago: University of Chicago Press, 1990. Pp. xiv, 222. $14.95, paper.

Darnell, Adrian C., and J. Lynne Evans. *The Limits of Econometrics.* Aldershot: Edward Elgar, 1990. Pp. xvi, 173. $44.95.

Das, Dilip K. *International Trade Policy.* New York: St. Martin's Press, 1990. Pp. xiv, 149. $30.95.

Das, Mitra, and Shirley Kolack. *Technology, Values and Society.* New York: Peter Lang, 1989. Pp. 169. $33.95.

Desai, Meghhad, ed. *Lenin's Economic Writings.* Atlantic Highlands: Humanities Press, 1989. Pp. 363. $49.95.

Deutscher, Patrick. *R.G. Hawtrey and the Development of Macroeconomics.* Ann Arbor: University of Michigan Press. 1990. Pp. x. 285. $37.50.

Dickson, David. *The New Science of Politics.* Chicago: University of Chicago Press, 1988. Pp. xii, 404. $14.95, paper.

Ekelund, Robert B., Jr., and Robert F. Hebert. *A History of Economic Theory and Method.* 3rd ed. New York: McGraw-Hill, 1990. Pp. xv, 688.

Elster, Jon. *The Cement of Society: A Study of Social Order.* New York: Cambridge University Press, 1989. Pp. viii, 311.

Elster, Jon. *Nuts and Bolts for the Social Sciences.* New York: Cambridge University Press, 1989. Pp. viii, 184.

Elster, Jon. *Solomonic Judgements: Studies in the Limitations of Rationality.* New York: Cambridge University Press, 1989. Pp. ix, 232.

Evensky, Jerry. *Economic Ideas and Issues: A Systematic Approach to Critical Thinking.* Englewood Cliffs: Prentice-Hall, 1990. Pp. xxii, 360.

Fine, Ben. *Marx's Capital.* 3rd ed. London: Macmillan: Atlantic Highlands: Humanities Press, 1989. Pp. xii, 104. $36.50, cloth; $12.50, paper.

Fink, Carole. *Marc Bloch: A Life in History.* New York: Cambridge University Press, 1989. Pp. xix, 371.

Fish, Stanley. *Doing What Comes Naturally.* Durham: Duke University Press, 1989. Pp. x, 613. $35.00.

Fuller, Steve. *Social Epistemology.* Bloomington: Indiana University Press, 1989. Pp. xv, 316. $27.50.

Gascoigne, John. *Cambridge in the Age of the Enlightenment.* New York: Cambridge University Press, 1989. Pp. xii, 358.

Glass, J.C., and W. Johnson. *Economics: Progression, Stagnation or Degeneration?* Ames: Iowa State University Press, 1989. Pp. vii, 200. $24.95.

Goldman, Lawrence, ed. *The Blind Victorian: Henry Fawcett and British Liberalism.* New York: Cambridge University Press, 1989. Pp. xv, 199.

Gorz, Andre. *Critique of Economic Reason.* New York: Routledge, Chapman & Hall, 1989. London: Verso, 1989. Pp. 250. $50.00, cloth; $17.95, paper.

Greenaway, David, and John R. Presley, eds. *Pioneers of Modern Economics in Britain.* Vol. 2, New York: St. Martin's Press, 1989. Pp. xvi, 215. $39.95.

Gutting, Gary. *Michel Foucault's Archaeology of Scientific Reason.* New York: Cambridge University Press, 1989. Pp. xiii, 306. Paper.

Heap, Shawn Hargreaves. *Rationality in Economics.* New York: Basil Blackwell, 1989. Pp. ix, 238. $49.95.

Heilbroner, Robert L. *The Making of Economic Society.* 8th ed. Englewood Cliffs, NJ: Prentice-Hall, 1989. Pp. xv, 256. Paper.

Hennings, Klaus, and Samuels, Warren J., eds. *Neoclassical Economic Theory, 1870-1930.* Boston: Kluwer Academic Publications, 1990. Pp. x, 290.

Henry, John F. *The Making of Neoclassical Economics.* Boston: Unwin Hyman, 1990. Pp. xxi, 261.

Hickman, Larry A. *John Dewey's Pragmatic Technology.* Bloomington: Indiana University Press, 1990. Pp. xv, 234. $29.95.

Hirsch, Abraham, and Neil deMarchi. *Milton Friedman: Economics in Theory and Practice.* Ann Arbor: University of Michigan Press, 1990. Pp. viii, 325. $34.50.

Hittinger, Russell. *A Critique of the New Natural Law Theory.* Notre Dame: University of Notre Dame Press, 1989. Pp. 232. $26.95, cloth; $12.95, paper.

Hogarth, Robin M., ed. *Insights in Decision Making.* Chicago: University of Chicago Press, 1990. Pp. xiv, 356. $24.95, paper.

Holcombe, Robert J., and Bryan S. Turner. *Max Weber on Economy and Society.* New York: Routledge, 1989. Pp. vii, 211. $37.50.

Hsaio-tung, Fei. *Rural Development in China.* Chicago: University of Chicago Press, 1989. Pp. xii, 240. $24.95. cloth; $10.95, paper.

Hunt, E.K., and Howard J. Sherman. *Economics: An Introduction to Traditional and Radical Views.* 6th ed. New York: Harper and Row, 1990.

Hunt, Diana. *Economic Theories of Development: An Analysis of Competing Paradigms.* Savage, MD: Barnes & Noble, 1989. Pp. 363.

Johnston, David. *The Rhetoric of Leviathan.* Princeton: Princeton University Press, 1989. Pp. xx, 234. $12.95, paper.

Jones, Norman. *God and the Moneylenders.* Cambridge, MA: Basil Blackwell, 1989. Pp. viii, 217. $49.95.

Jones, Peter, ed. *Philosophy and Science in the Scottish Enlightenment.* Edinbuirgh: John Donald, 1988. Pp. vii, 230.

Kadish, Alon. *Historians, Economics, and Economic History.* New York: Routledge, 1989. Pp. xii, 303. $65.00.

Kasler, Dirk. *Max Weber: An Introduction to his Life and Work.* Chicago: University of Chicago Press, 1988. Pp. xiii, 287. $14.95, paper.

Katz, Bernard S., ed. *Nobel Laureates in Economic Sciences: A Biographical Dictionary.* New York: Garland, 1989. Pp. xvii, 339. $75.00.

Kellner, Hans. *Language and Historical Representations: Getting the Story Crooked.* Madison: University of Wisconsin Press, 1989. Pp. x, 286. $45.00.

Kirzner, Israel M. *Discovery, Capitalism, and Distributive Justice.* New York: Basil Blackwell, 1989. Pp. x, 179.

Kitcher, Philip, and Wesley C. Salmon, eds. *Scientific Explanation.* Minneapolis: University of Minnesota Press, 1989. Pp. xiv, 528. $35.00.

Klamer, Arjo, and David Colander. *The Making of an Economist.* Boulder: Westview Press, 1990. Pp. xvii, 216. $48.00, cloth; $16.95, paper.

Krieger, Leonard. *Time's Reason: Philosophies of History Old and New.* Chicago: University of Chicago Press, 1989. Pp. xii, 202. $32.50.

Krieger, Martin H. *Marginalism and Discontinuity: Tools for the Crafts of Knowledge and Decision.* New York: Russell Sage, 1989. Pp. xxiii, 182. $25.00.

Lallier, Adalbert G. *The Economics of Marx's Grundrisse: An Annotated Summary.* New York: St. Martin's Press, 1989. Pp. xxii, 265. $49.95.

Lieberman, David. *The Province of Legislation Determined: Legal Theory in Eighteenth-Century Britain.* New York: Cambridge University Press, 1989. Pp. xiii, 312.

Loasby, Brian J. *The Mind and Method of the Economist.* Aldershott: Edward Elgar, 1989. Pp. xv, 227. $42.75.

Longino, Helen E. *Science as Social Knowledge.* Princeton: Princeton University Press, 1990. Pp. xi, 262. $35.00, cloth; $13.95, paper.

Luce, R. Duncan, Neil J. Smelser, and Dean R. Gerstein, eds. *Leading Edges in Social and Behavioral Science.* New York: Russell Sage, 1989. Pp. viii, 705. $59.95.

Lutz, Mark A., ed. *Social Economics: Retrospect and Prospect.* Boston: Kluwer, 1990. Pp. xi, 442.

Mansbridge, Jane J., ed. *Beyond Self-Interest.* Chicago: University of Chicago Pres, 1990. Pp. xiii, 402. $55.00, cloth; $15.95, paper.

Mason, Roger S. *Robert Giffen and the Giffen Paradox.* Totowa: Barnes and Noble, 1989. Pp. xi, 153.

Milgate, Murray, and Charyl B. Welch, eds. *Critical Issues in Social Thought.* New York: Academic Press, 1989. Pp. viii, 244. $27.50.

Mirowski, Philip. *More Heat than Light: Economics as Social Physics, Physics as Nature's Economics.* New York: Cambridge University Pres, 1989. Pp. xii, 450.

Morishima, Michio. *Ricardo's Economics.* New York: Cambridge Univesity Pres, 1989. Pp. xii, 254.

Morris, Peter. *Power: A Philosophical Analysis.* New York: St. Martin's Press, 1987. Pp. ix, 266. $35.00.

Neusner, Jacob. *The Economics of the Mishnah*. Chicago: University of Chicago Press, 1990. Pp. svi, 183. $45.00, cloth; $14.95, paper.

Niehans, Jurg. *A History of Economic Theory: Classic Contributions, 1720-1980*. Baltimore: Johns Hopkins University Press, 1990. Pp. x, 578. $59.95.

O'Brien, D.P. *Lionel Robbins*. New York: St. Martin's Press, 1988. Pp. xii, 244. $45.00.

O'Donnell, R.M. *Keynes: Philosophy, Economics, and Politics*. New York: St. Martin's Press, 1989. Pp. xii, 417. $49.95, cloth.

O'Farrel, Clare. *Foucault: Historian or Philosopher?* New York: St. Martin's Press, 1989. Pp. xii, 188. $39.95.

Peacock, Alan, and Hans Willgerodt, eds. *German Neo-Liberals and the Social Market Economy*. New York: St. Martin's Press, 1989. Pp. xviii, 242. $55.00.

Powell, Michael J. *From Patrician to Professional Elite: The Transformation of the New York City Bar Association*. New York: Russell Sage, 1988. Pp. xxvi, 269.

Rauch, Seymour. *Legalized Stealing: The American Way of Life*. New York: Peter Lang, 1989. Pp. 334, $43.00.

Redman, Deborah A. *Economic Methodology: A Bibliography with Reference to Works in the Philosophy of Science, 1860-1968*. Westport, CT: Greenwood Pres, 1989. Pp. svi, 285. $45.00.

Reid, John Phillip. *The Concept of Liberty in the Age of the American Revolution*. Chicago: University of Chicago Pres, 1988. Pp. viii, 224. $25.95.

Reid, John Phillip. *The Concept of Representation in the Age of the American Revolution*. Chicago: University of Chicago Press, 1988. Pp. viii, 251. $32.00.

Reisman, David. *The Political Economy of James Buchanan*, College Station: Texas A&M University Press, 1990. Pp. vi, 204. $39.50.

Rescher, Nicholas. *Moral Absolutes*. New York: Peter Lang, 1989. Pp. x, 115. $29.00.

Rostow, W.W. *History, Policy, and Economic Theory*. Boulder, CO: Westview Press, 1990. Pp. xii, 385. $59.95.

Rounder, Leroy S., ed. *On Freedom*. Notre Dame: University of Notre Dame Press, 1989. Pp. xv, 200. $42.95.

Routh, Gay. *The Origin of Economic Ideas*. 2nd ed. Dobbs Ferry, NY: Sheridan House, 1989. Pp. xii, 360. $39.50, cloth; $19.95, paper.

Roy, Subroto. *Philosophy of Economics: On the Scope of Reason in Economic Inquiry*. New York: Routledge, 1989. Pp.l ix, 236. $37.50.

Russell, James W. *Modes of Production in World History*. New York: Routledge, 1989. Pp. xi, 218. $55.00.

Salmon, Wesley C. *Four Decades of Scientific Explanation*. Minneapolis:

University of Minnesota Press, 1989. Pp. xiv, 234. $14.95, paper.

Samuels, Warren J., ed. *Fundamentals of the Economic Role of Government.* Westport, CT: Greenwood Press, 1989. Pp. xiii, 259.

Samuels, Warren J., ed. *Economics as Discourse: An Analysis of the Language of Economists.* Boston: Kluwer Academic Publishers, 1990. Pp. ix, 258.

Sebastiani, Mario. *Kalecki's Relevance Today.* New York: St. Martin's Press, 1989. Pp. xvi, 366. $55.00.

Seligman, Ben. *Main Currents in Modern Economics.* Introduction by E. Ray Canterbery. New Brunswick: Transaction Publishers, 1990. Paper.

Shand, Alexander H. *Free Market Morality: The Political Economy of the Austrian School.* New York: Routledge, Chapman & Hall, 1990. Pp. x, 228. $55.00, cloth; $16.95, paper.

Sichel, Werner, ed. *The State of Economic Science: Views of Six Nobel Laureates.* Kalamazoo, MI: W.E. Upjohn Institute for Employment Research, 1989. Pp. 114. Paper.

Smith, Tony. *The Logic of Marx's CAPITAL: Replies to Hegelian Criticisms.* Albany: State University of New York Press, 1990. Pp. xii, 271. $17.95, paper.

Staley, Charles E. *A History of Economic Thought.* Cambridge: Basil Blackwell, 1989. Pp. vi, 273.

Starr, June, and Jane F. Collier, eds. *History and Power in the Study of the Law: New Directions in Legal Anthropology.* Ithaca, NY: Cornell University Press, 1989. Pp. x, 377. $42.50, cloth; $14.95, paper.

Steedman, Ian. *From Exploitation to Altruism.* Boulder, CO: Westview Press, 1989. Pp. ix, 249. $47.50.

Stivers, Robert L., ed. *Reformed Faith and Economics.* Latham: University Press of America, 1989. Pp. svii, 244. $29.50, cloth; $14.75, paper.

Swedberg, Richard. *Economics and Sociology.* Princeton: Princeton University Press, 1990. Pp. viii, 361. $50.00. cloth; $12.95, paper.

Taylor, Stanley. *Conceptions of Institutions and the Theory of Knowledge.* 2nd ed. New Brunswick, NJ: Transaction Books, 1989. Pp. vii, 23. $19.95, paper.

Thompson, Noel. *The Market and Its Critics: Socialist Political Economy in Nineteenth Century Britain.* New York: Routledge, 1988. Pp. 306. $57.50.

Tinder, Glenn. *The Political Meaning of Christianity.* Baton Rouge: Louisiana State University Press, 1989. Pp. xi, 257. $29.95.

Waligorski, Conrad P. *The Political Theory of Conservative Economists.* Lawrence: University Press of Kansas, 1990. Pp. ix, 260. $29.95.

White, James Boyd. *Justice as Translation: An Essay in Cultural and Legal Criticism.* Chicago: University of Chicago Press, 1990. Pp. xviii, 313. $29.95.

Wiseman, Jack. *Cost, Choice and Political Economy.* Brokfield: Edward Elgar, 1989. Pp. ix, 294. $49.95.

Wolfson, Murray, and Vincent Buranelli. *In the Long Run We Are All Dead.* end 3d. New York: St. Martin's Press. 1990. Pp. viii, 184. Paper.

Woods, J.E. *The Production of Commodities: An Introduction to Sraffa.* Pp. xii, 345. $49.95.

Wuthnow, Robert. *Communities of Discourse: Ideology and Social Structure in the Reformation, the Enlightenment, and European Socialism.* Cambridge: Harvard Univesity Press, 1989. Pp. xi, 739.

Yamaguchi, Kaoru. *Beyond Walras, Keynes and Marx: Synthesis in Economic Theory Toward a New Social Design.* New York: Peter Lang, 1968. Pp. 346. $43.50.

Research in the History of Economic Thought and Methodology

Edited by **Warren J. Samuels**, *Department of Economics, Michigan State University*

REVIEW: "Methodology and the history of economic thought, two distinct but interrelated economic fields, are currently enjoying a boom , and the volumes under review afford convincing evidence of the intellectual interest and high quality of contemporary work in these areas."

- Kyklos

Volume 7, 1990, 294 pp.
ISBN 0-89232-040-3
$73.25

CONTENTS: Editorial Board. Acknowledgements. Induction, Deduction and the Role of Mathematics: The Whewell Group vs. The Ricardian Economists, *James P. Henderson.* The Single Price Theorem, *Daniel R. Fusfeld.* The Rhetoric of "Government Intervention:" A Suggestion, *Timothy W. Kelsey.* Rorty's Contribution to McCloskey's Understanding of Conversation as the Methodology of Economics, *John B. Davis.* A "Growth of Knowledge" Explanation of the Responses to Chamberlin's Theory of Monopolistic Competition, *Guy Ahonen.* Voluntary Exchange and Economic Claims, *Timothy J. Brennan.* SYMPOSIUM ON THE METHODOLOGY OF RATIONAL EXPECTATIONS. Rational Expectations in the Light of Modern Psychology, *Malcolm Rutherford.* Implicit Contracts, Rational Expectations, and Theories of Knowledge, *James R. Wible.* Rationality, Expectations, and Relevance in Economic Analysis: Implications of the Methodological Gyratopms of Monetary Theory, *Will E. Mason.* Grunberg and Modigliani, Public Predictions and the New Classical Macroeconomics, *D. Wade Hands.* Poster's Foucault, Marxism and History and Barnes's About Science: Review Essay, *Jack L. Amariglio.* White's When Words Lose Their Meaning: Review Essay, *Arjo Klamer.* Johnson's Research Methodology for Economists: Philosophy and Practive: Reivew Essays, *Bruce J. Caldwell and Lewis E. Hill, Texas Tech University.* Woo's What's Wrong with Formalization in Economics? An Epistemological Critique: Review Essays, *Bruce J. Caldwell, Don Lavoie, Philip E. Mirowski, and Larry Samuelson.*

JAI PRESS

Volume 8, 1990, 288 pp. $73.25
ISBN 1-55938-233-3

Archival Supplement 2, 1991, 255 pp. $73.25
ISBN 1-55938-245-7

Volume 9, 1992, 300 pp. $73.25
ISBN 1-55938-428-X

CONTENTS. Editorial Board. Acknowledgments. Astronomy,
Astrology, and Business Cycles: Hyde Clarke's Contribution,
James P. Henderson. Dr. Kondratieff and Mr. Hyde Clarke, *R.D.
Collison Black.* Hyde Clarke's Publications: Papers Presented
at Meetings of Scientific Societies and Other Notes and
Letters of Interest, *James P. Henderson.* Uses of the term
"Natural" in Adam Smith's *Wealth of Nations, Edward Puro.*
Frank H. Knight on the Conflict of Values in Economic Life,
Ross B. Emmett. Ever Since Adam Smith: The Mythical
History of Individual Rationality in Economic Analysis, *Mary
K. Farmer.* Keynes' Critique of Wage Cutting as Antidepres-
sionary Strategy, *John E. Elliott.* Fernandez Florez's *Las Siete
Columnas:* Mandeville Revisited, *Susan Pozo* and *Warren J.
Samuels.* REVIEW ESSAYS. Macintyre's *Whose Justice?
Which Rationality:* A Review Essay, *Alasdair MacIntrye.*
Professor Vaggi and the Physiocrats: New Explorations in
the Classical Theory of Value and Distribution: A Review
Essay, *Peter Groenewegen.* Islamic Economics: A Utopian-
Scholastic-Neoclassical-Keynesian Synthesis: A Review
Essay, *Sohrah Behdad.* Why Bother With the History of
Economics? A Review Essay, *Keith Tribe.* Hollander's
Classical Economics: A Review Essay, *Salim Rashid, University
of Illinois.* Epstein's *A History of Econometrics:* A Review Essay,
Christopher L. Gilbert. Understanding The Popperian Legacy
in Economics: A Review Essay, *Lawrence A. Boland.* Smithian
Excavations: A Review of Maurice Brown's *Adam Smith's
Economics, Rajani Kanth.* New Books Received.

Archival Supplement 3, 1992, 204 pp. $73.25
ISBN 1-55938-503-3

CONTENTS: Edwin R.A. Seligman's Lectures on the History
of Economics: Introduction, *Warren Samuels.* Outline of
Lectures. Readings. Notes From Edwin R.A. Seligman's
Lectures on the History of Economics, *P.S. Allen.*

Volume 11, In preparation, Spring 1993
ISBN 1-55938-502-2   Approx. $73.25

Edited by **Warren J. Samuels,** and **Jeff Biddle,**
Department of Economics, Michigan State University

CONTENTS: Editorial Board. Acknowledgments. Why Did
Malthus Oppose Birth Control?, *Geoffrey Gilbert.* Rational
Expectations, Rational Belief, and Keynes' General Theory,
Wiliam Darity, Jr., and Bobbie L. Horn. Economic Theory in
Industrial Policy: Lessons from U.S.v. AT&T, *Timothy J.*

JAI PRESS INC.
55 Old Post Road - No. 2
P.O. Box 1678
Greenwich, Connecticut 06836-1678
Tel: 203-661-7602